Airco

The Aircraft Manufacturing Company

Other Titles in the Crowood Aviation Series

Aichi D3A1/2 Val	Peter C. Smith
Aeroplanes of the Royal Aircraft Factory	Paul Hare
Avro Lancaster	Ken Delve
BAC One-Eleven	Malcolm L. Hill
Bell P-39 Airacobra	Robert F. Dorr with Jerry C. Scutts
Boeing 747	Martin W. Bowman
Boeing 757 and 767	Thomas Becher
Boeing B-17 Flying Fortress	Martin W. Bowman
Boeing B-52 Stratofortress	Peter E. Davies and Tony Thornborough
Consolidated B-24 Liberator	Martin W. Bowman
Curtiss SB2C Helldiver	Peter C. Smith
De Havilland Mosquito	Martin W. Bowman
McDonnell Douglas A-4 Skyhawk	Brad Elward
Douglas AD Skyraider	Peter C. Smith
English Electric Canberra	Barry Jones
English Electric Lightning	Martin W. Bowman
Fairchild Republic A-10 Thunderbolt II	Peter C. Smith
Gloster Meteor	Barry Jones
Hawker Hunter	Barry Jones
Hawker Hurricane	Peter Jacobs
Junkers Ju 87 Stuka	Peter C. Smith
Lockheed C-130 Hercules	Martin W. Bowman
Lockheed F-104 Starfighter	Martin W. Bowman
Luftwaffe – A Pictorial History	Eric Mombeek
Messerschmitt Bf 110	Ron Mackay
Messerschmitt Me 262	David Baker
North American F-86 Sabre	Duncan Curtis
North American T-6	Peter C. Smith
Panavia Tornado	Andy Evans
Short Sunderland	Ken Delve
Sopwith Aircraft	Mick Davis
V-Bombers	Barry Jones
Vickers VC10	Lance Cole
Vickers-Armstrongs Wellington	Ken Delve
World War One in the Air – A Pictorial History	Ken Delve

AIRCO

The Aircraft Manufacturing Company

Mick Davis

The Crowood Press

First published in 2001 by
The Crowood Press Ltd
Ramsbury, Marlborough
Wiltshire SN8 2HR

**British Library Cataloguing-in-Publication
Data**
A catalogue record for this book is available
from the British Library.

ISBN 1 86126 393 7

Edited, designed and produced
by Focus Publishing, The Courtyard, 26
London Road, Sevenoaks, Kent TN13 1AP

Printed and bound in Great Britain by
Bookcraft, Bath

Contents

Glossary   6

1. HOLT THOMAS, DE HAVILLAND AND THE AIRCRAFT
   MANUFACTURING COMPANY   7
2. FARMANS, BLIMPS AND FLYING BOATS   15
3. THE D.H.1 AND THE D.H.1A – THE COMPETITOR TO THE F.E.2B   27
4. THE D.H.2 – THE FIRST TRUE BRITISH FIGHTER   32
5. THE D.H.4 – THE FIRST EFFECTIVE DAY-BOMBER   48
6. THE D.H.5 – AIR FIGHTING AND GROUND ATTACK WORK   75
7. THE D.H.6 – SIMPLICITY FOR MASS PRODUCTION   86
8. THE D.H.9 – THAT MACHINE OR NOTHING   100
9. THE D.H.9A – FROM BOMBER TO EMPIRE POLICEMAN   133
10. THE AMERICAN CONNECTION – THE LIBERTY PLANE
    AND THE USD-9A   160
11. THE D.H.3, D.H.10 AND D.H.11 – TWIN-ENGINED BOMBERS   170

Appendix I   Manufacturers   179
Appendix II   Serial List – Contracted Airframes   180
Index   186

Glossary

AA	Anti Aircraft (fire)
AAP	Aircraft Acceptance Park
AD	Aircraft Depot
AFC	Air Force Cross
AM1	Air Mechanic First Class
AM2	Air Mechanic Second Class
ARD	Aircraft Repair Depot
ASD	Aeroplane Supply Depot
BEF	British Expeditionary Force
CFS	Central Flying School
DFC	Distinguished Flying Cross
DSC	Distinguished Service Order
ECD	Experimental Construction Depot
ES	Experimental Station
Flt	Flight
Flt Comm	Flight Commander
Flt Lt	Flight Lieutenant
FS	Fighting School
FSL	Flight Sub Lieutenant
FTS	Flying training School
HD	Home Defence
IDE	Instrument Design Establishment
IWM	Imperial War Museum
Lt	Lieutenant
2Lt	Second Lieutenant

MAEE	Marine Aircraft Experimental Establishment
MC	Military Cross
MOS	Marine Observers School
N	Naval (eg 5N Squadron)
NEAFIS	North Eastern Area Flying Instructors' School
NTS	Night Training Squadron
NWAFIS	North Western Area Flying Instructors' School
PC	Protective Cellulose
POW	Prisoner of War
RAF	Royal Aircraft Factory (pre 1 April 1918)
RAF	Royal Air Force (post 1 April 1918)
RFC	Royal Flying Corps
RNAS	Royal Naval Air Service
RS	Reserve Squadron
SAF	School of Aerial Fighting
SAFG	School of Aerial Flighting and Gunnery
SAG	School of Aerial Gunnery
SAGF	School of Aerial Gunnery and Fighting
SNBD	School of (Aerial) Navigation and Bomb Dropping
Sqn	Squadron
TDS	Training Depot Depot
TS	Training Squadron
USAS	United States Air Services
USMC	United States Marine Corps
USN	United States Navy
VC	Victoria Cross
WEE	Wireless Experimental Establishment

CHAPTER ONE

Holt Thomas, de Havilland and the Aircraft Manufacturing Company

When, during the 1950s, the British aviation industry was in its heyday, most of the companies manufacturing its amazing products had been in existence since the Great War, or earlier. Avro, Vickers, Handley-Page and Armstrong-Whitworth had all supplied the infant British air services with machines that helped to win that first aerial conflict. Two other companies, probably the greatest, did not come into existence until after the Great War, although they could trace their origins to that era: these were Hawker and de Havilland. The Hawker companies rose from the ashes of Sopwith, the subject of an earlier book in this series. Similarly, the de Havilland concern emerged from the Aircraft Manufacturing Company, the brainchild of one of British aviation's great visionaries, George Holt Thomas.

George Holt Thomas

George Holt Thomas was unlike Sopwith, Roe and Handley-Page in that he was not an aviator; he was also considerably older than those other 'greats'. He was born at Brixton Hill, London, on 31 March 1869, and was the seventh son of the newspaper proprietor George Luson Thomas. After a private education and three years at Oxford, the son joined his father's business at the age of thirty. By that time he was married to Gertrude, née Oliver, of Newcastle-on-Tyne. He assumed managerial control of the weekly *Graphic* and daily *Daily Graphic* newspapers, and introduced the *Bystander* and the *Empire Illustrated* magazines. He relinquished that direct control in 1906, but continued to influence editorial content from behind the scenes.

It was during a visit to France, in 1906, that Holt Thomas met Henri Farman, that great aviation pioneer, and this aroused his interest in powered flight. Sustained flight was then still constrained by the lack of suitable engines, but Farman began making successful short flights the following year and Holt Thomas followed his career with interest. The Farman brothers, Henri and Maurice, were English by birth but lived in France, and were awarded the French aviation brevets Nos 5 and 6 respectively. Henri occasionally called himself 'Henry', using the anglicized version of his name.

George Holt Thomas realized the military potential of the aeroplane and began a private campaign, via the family newspaper business, for the formation of a military air service. He also emulated the lead given by the national *Daily Mail* (through which Lord Northcliffe had offered a prize of £10,000 for the first London-Manchester flight) in offering £1,000 for the first powered flight of one mile to be made in Britain.

Holt Thomas took great interest in Louis Bleriot's first cross-Channel flight that was achieved on 25 July 1909, watching the preparations from both sides of the Channel. He was also at Rheims the following month, observing the aviation meeting that took place, and making the acquaintance of Louis Paulhan. Holt Thomas appreciated that the success of Paulhan's Voisin was largely due to its Gnome rotary engine.

Inspired by the Rheims meeting, Holt Thomas proceeded to organize a similar event in Britain. The location was at Squire's Gate, Blackpool, and it was staged in conjunction with that town's civic corporation. The pilot was Hubert Latham, who succeeded in producing a spectacular display, despite adverse wind conditions. Holt Thomas' enthusiasm was not satisfied with this provincial show, however, and he realized that his advocacy of the aeroplane would reach a wider audience if a similar display could be organized for the capital. He had assumed the role of Paulhan's agent in England, and set about finding a suitable site near London. A.V. Roe had used the Brooklands motor-racing track from 1907-08 for his early experimental flights, but he had fallen out with that course's management and been forced to move elsewhere. Holt Thomas's persuasiveness with Mr Locke King, Brooklands' proprietor, and Major Lindsay Lloyd, its new manager, led to part of the farmland within the racing circuit being cleared and levelled in preparation for a display by Paulhan in his Farman biplane. The display lasted several days at the end of October 1909, with a flight of 96 miles

George Holt Thomas, the founder of the Aircraft Manufacturing Company.
via B. Gray

(154km) eventually being achieved on 1 November. The vast audience, most of whom had avoided paying by watching the events from outside the circuit, convinced the Brooklands authorities of the financial possibilities of aviation, and as a result they decided that the area inside the racing circuit should be cleared and developed into an aerodrome. This was done by the following spring, with the exception of the famous sewage farm; and thus the creation of that cradle of that early aviation can be attributed, in no small part, to Holt Thomas.

The other pre-war centre for aviation was Hendon, and its development can also be traced back to Holt Thomas. After the Brooklands exhibition, Paulhan had wintered in America, where he gave further demonstration flights. Upon his return, he was contacted by Holt Thomas, who suggested that he attempt the London-Manchester flight in order to gain the, as yet, unclaimed *Daily Mail* prize. Paulhan agreed, and his rival, Claude Grahame-White, indicated his intent to compete for the same. Holt Thomas

looked for a suitable field for take-off, and selected one at Hendon that was being used for aviation experiments by a firm of electrical engineers. Grahame-White elected to start from a field at Wormwood Scrubbs. Paulhan gained the *Daily Mail* prize that April. Grahame-White inspected Paulhan's starting place and acquired the field, along with others adjoining it, and developed the site into what became known as the London Aerodrome.

In July 1911 Holt Thomas, in collaboration with other newspaper owners, promoted a 'Circuit of Europe' competition. The course was approximately 1,000 miles (1,609km) long and ran from Paris-Liege-Utrecht-Brussels-London-Paris, and Lieutenant Conneau of the French navy was the winner. This did not dismay Holt Thomas: what did was the fact that the majority of spectators at Hendon, for the London stage of the course, were French – the British public seemed indifferent to aviation, even though James Valentine was a competitor.

In April 1909 and as part of his continuing campaign in support of the aeroplane, Holt Thomas had highlighted the fact that the British government lagged behind its European rivals in budgets for military aviation: in that year Germany had spent the equivalent of £400,000 and France £47,000, whereas Britain had expended just £5,000. In September 1910 he went to France to view military manoeuvres, and observed with interest the successful use of aeroplanes in the reconnaissance role that was regarded as the preserve of the cavalry. In that same month he attended British army manoeuvres on Salisbury Plain, during the course of which a Bristol Boxkite was flown by Captain Bertram Dickson of the British & Colonial Aeroplane Co – most notably it achieved some success in spotting from the air. Another Boxkite was present, as was a Farman biplane.

Despite the early promise shown by Dickson's efforts, and the attention drawn to them by Holt Thomas, the government was still of the opinion that the

Geoffrey de Havilland seen seated in his second machine that was later bought by Farnborough upon the designer's employment at the Army Balloon Factory; it became known as the F.E.1. JMB/GSL

That second machine in flight, showing the chord-wise extension of its ailerons and forward rudder. JMB/GSL

development of aviation was best left to private individuals. By 1911, however, that opinion was less entrenched, and on 28 February they authorized the formation of an Air Battalion of the Royal Engineers, a step that paved the way for the creation of the Royal Flying Corps.

The Beginnings of the Company

In 1911 Holt Thomas turned his attention to the manufacture of aeroplanes and aero-engines. He created the Aeroplane Supply Company, and acquired the use of premises at Merton in south-west London. He renewed his acquaintance with Henri Farman, and took up the sole British rights for the manufacture of Farman machines from Aeroplanes Henri et Maurice Farman of Billancourt. He also acquired the rights to manufacture Gnome and Le Rhone rotary engines. Holt Thomas had also realized the potential of the airship as a military weapon, being greatly impressed by the large dirigibles produced by Zeppelin in Germany. There was little chance of a British manufacturer acquiring the rights to produce the German design under licence, but Holt

Thomas tried. His lack of success forced him to look to France, and he obtained the rights to copy the Astra Torres design. For this purpose he set up a parallel company, Airships Ltd, which was also based at Merton. The unfortunate demise of Horatio Barber's Aeronautical Syndicate allowed the Aeroplane Supply Company to take over its vacant premises at Hendon in April 1912 and to acquire by auction some of its stock of aviation material.

George Holt Thomas had his firm registered on 6 June 1912 as the Aircraft Manufacturing Company Ltd (AMC). It combined the Aeroplane Supply Company and Airships Ltd, and had a stated capital of £14,700 in 14,000 preferred ordinary shares of £1, and 14,000 deferred ordinary shares of 1s each. Its stated aims were to carry out the business of manufacturers of, and dealer in, aeroplanes, airships and flying machines and to acquire the business carried on by G.H. Thomas of St Stephens House, Westminster and Hendon, as the Aircraft Supply Co. The first directors were G.H. Thomas (managing director) and A.F. Thomas. Registration was by Soames, Edwards and Jones of Lennox House, Norfolk Street, The Strand WC. The use of the abbreviated name 'Airco' dated

from this time, and developed into common usage during the Great War.

The military had woken up to the potential of aircraft, and this had led to the formation of the Royal Flying Corps on 13 April 1912, the new formation subsuming the Air Battalion exactly one calendar month later. That realization of the aeroplane's potential had been made apparent as early as October 1911, when the government announced its intention to hold a competition to find the most suitable machine for both military and naval use. Specifications for competing machines, which had to be of private manufacture, were released later, and these pointed to a plane that could provide a good reconnaissance platform, and could operate away from fixed aerodromes. The competition was known as the 'Military Trials', and was set for the summer of 1912; thirty-two machines were entered, their manufacturers probably valuing the financial potential of service orders above the limited prize money. The Aircraft Manufacturing Co. took advantage of its position as British agent for Farman designs to enter a 1912 Maurice Farman 70hp biplane in the trials. That aeroplane, undoubtedly of French manufacture, was an early form of the Se.7 that became known to the RFC as the 'Longhorn'.

THE NEW ARMY BIPLANE

NOICS.

De Havilland's F.E.1 was reconstructed to become the F.E.2, with a narrower cut-out in the trailing edge of its upper centre-section, and a nacelle added around the pilot's seat, the engine and the fuel tank. The forward elevator was dispensed with. JMB/GSL

Its pilot was Pierre Verrier, and although it performed well in some of the required tests, it showed shortcomings in others. It did, however, undertake *all* the tests in the trials, unlike some of the competitors, and this led to the award of a £100 'consolation' prize. As it turned out, the design was to have a greater longevity than all other official entries – indeed, only the RAF B.E.2, barred from official entry because it was of government design, lasted longer.

The Maurice Farman biplane and the Henri Farman F.20 were the 'bread and butter' of the Aircraft Manufacturing Co. in the heady days leading up to the Great War. It would appear that, at first, machines were simply erected and tested at Hendon after being shipped from France, but production slowly got into its stride, orders coming in from military, naval and civilian customers. Holt Thomas had realized that progress could be made in the production of indigenous machines, and to that end sought the services of a designer: in this, it was fortunate indeed that he had become acquainted with, and had developed a rapport with, Geoffrey de Havilland during visits to the Royal Aircraft Factory at Farnborough.

Geoffrey De Havilland

Geoffrey de Havilland was an undoubted genius and, like many of his famous aviation contemporaries, had developed an early interest in all things mechanical. His indulgence in engines, motor cars and motor cycles was fostered by his elder brother Ivon, and made financially possible by the affluence of his maternal grandfather, Jason Saunders, a businessman and one-time mayor of Oxford. Born on 27 July 1882, he was the second of three sons in a family of five; his father was Charles de Havilland, a curate whose vocation led to work at Nuneaton and then Crux Easton in Hampshire.

In 1900, the eighteen-year-old Geoffrey de Havilland began studies at the Crystal Palace Engineering School. A student apprenticeship in engineering with Willans and Robinson of Rugby was followed in 1905 by employment as a draughtsman with the Wolseley Tool & Motor Car Company of Birmingham.

De Havilland's interest in flying had erupted in 1908, although he had yet to see an aeroplane. He had resigned his post with Wolseley's after a year, having become disillusioned with the monotony of his employment, and being convinced

of his ability to be more creative. He fostered the idea of building his own aeroplane, and his grandfather advanced him £1,000, in lieu of any inheritance, to develop the project. It was obvious to de Havilland that he could not build his aeroplane alone, and so he renewed an acquaintance with Frank Hearle, a marine engineer by training, who had similar interests. Hearle agreed to join him in the venture, in return for the princely wage of 35s a week.

A drawing office was rented from another friend, and workshops found in Fulham. The engine drawings that were produced were then given to the Iris Car Company, which had agreed to undertake its building in return for £250. The majority of the materials for the airframe were purchased from timber merchants and hardware stores. A suitable flying ground with sheds was acquired at Seven Barrows, near Crux Easton; it had been set up by J.T.C. Moore-Brabazon, but then abandoned in favour of Eastchurch.

Here, in December 1909, de Havilland attempted his first flight. His pusher biplane had its engine mounted transversely, with bevel gears driving twin propellers. After numerous engine tests, the replacing of suspect components and

The B.E.1 and B.E.2

The much-maligned B.E. biplanes were in fact very advanced for their day, and it was only the unavoidable extension of their operational use in France beyond their ability to reconnoitre unmolested that led to the vilification of the design. The B.E.1 was a brilliant design for 1911, a time when the pusher configuration was in vogue for biplanes. It had been constructed by October of that year, by the subterfuge of claiming the 'reconstruction' of a Voisin presented to the War Office by the Duke of Westminster, although it did not fly until 4 December. The fuselage was a box-girder structure built on two solid patons that served as anchorages for the lower wings. The only Voisin component was its water-cooled, 60hp Wolseley V8 engine. The use of that engine required a vertical radiator that must have hindered the pilot's view forward. A skid under-carriage was fitted and the rear fuselage supported a semi-circular tailplane and lobe-shaped rudder. There was no fin. The unequal-span mainplanes were un-staggered, two bay structures and lateral control was by wing warping. The engine exhaust was carried to points below the fuselage by twin pipes and the silencing effect of that led to the machine being dubbed the 'Silent Army Aeroplane'.

The B.E.1 was gradually modified, in light of its test flying. Slight negative stagger was incorporated and slight dihedral rigged into the mainplanes. An air-cooled 60hp Renault replaced the original Wolseley engine, its lighter weight both improving performance and, there being no radiator, improving the view forward. This machine lasted until at least 1916, having been rebuilt several times.

The first B.E.2 flew on 1 February 1912 and was, essentially, a B.E.1 airframe fitted with the 60hp Renault. It was used for a variety of test work at Farnborough, including the use of wireless. The replacement of its 60hp engine by one of 70hp improved performance.

As a product of a government organization, the B.E.2 was not eligible for entry in the 1912 Military Trials that were conducted in an attempt to find a machine for standardized reconnaissance use by the RFC. It was, however, present at those trials and was vastly superior to those machines entered by private constructors. Although the competition was won by the outlandish Cody V biplane, the B.E.2 was, quite sensibly,

The B.E.1 was a great advance for 1911. via the author

chosen for quantity production for the RFC's Military Wing. The Naval Wing also ordered the type.

Mass production was beyond the capability of the RAF and so sub-contractors such as Vickers, Armstrong Whitworth and the Coventry Ordnance Works undertook the task. More than seventy B.E.2s were produced and they saw extensive pre-war use by 2 and 4 Squadrons. Production machines were, almost certainly, those designated B.E.2a, and later examples had equal-span mainplanes. 218, a B.E.2a of 2 Squadron, was used by Captain C.A.H. Longcroft to establish a distance record of 650 miles (1,000km) on 22 November 1913.

When the RFC went to war in August 1914, more B.E.2as went to France with the British Expeditionary Force than any other type. They equipped 2 and 4 Squadrons and were later joined by others with 6 Squadron. The type fared well in the mobile campaign that followed, and examples were still in service with the B.E.F. more than a year later.

Further development of the airframe resulted in the series that ended with the B.E.2e, but Geoffrey de Havilland had no part in that story. Edward Busk developed the B.E.2c in the quest for inherent stability and it was that sub-type, and its successors, that were to become the helpless victims of superior enemy machines, as the RFC command retained them in operational use long after their usefulness had passed. There was little wrong with the original design.

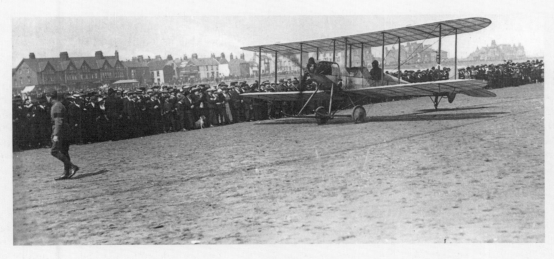

The development of the B.E.1 led to the B.E.2, and that became a standard type with the RFC Military Wing. This machine of 2 Squadron is seen landing on the beach at Seaton Carew during that unit's fateful journey to the 'Concentration Camp' at Netheravon during May 1914. JMB/GSL

A more revolutionary design still was the B.S.1 that was developed into the S.E.2 seen here. Its clean lines were what de Havilland wanted to reproduce for AMC, but initially he was constrained to produce designs for pusher types, the D.H.1 and D.H.2. JMB/GSL

several attempts at take-off, de Havilland finally succeeded in coaxing the machine off the ground – but the strain imposed on the airframe was too great, and he was lucky to escape injury in the ensuing crash.

The engine was utilized in a second machine, where it was mounted longitudinally with a direct drive pusher propeller. The new machine bore some resemblance to contemporary Farman designs and was first flown at Seven Barrows in the summer of 1910. More sustained flights followed, some with a passenger, and de Havilland had soon mastered most manoeuvres. Thus at last he had a successful aeroplane – but he lacked the means of promoting it to a limited market.

A chance meeting with Frederick Green brought a golden opportunity. Green had known de Havilland at Birmingham and had worked for the Daimler Company, a one-time employer of Ivon de Havilland. Green was then working at HM Army Balloon Factory at Farnborough, and he suggested that Mervyn O'Gorman, the superintendent of that establishment who was interested in expanding its remit to include heavier-than-air machines, might be willing to

buy the aeroplane and simultaneously employ de Havilland.

A meeting with O'Gorman was organized, and the arrangement was provisionally confirmed, with the added bonus of employment for Frank Hearle as his assistant. Official confirmation was received before the end of December 1910, with de Havilland receiving £400 for his aeroplane. Financial security was therefore established – which was just as well, because by then he was married to Louie, née Thomas, a former governess of his younger brother Hereward.

The de Havilland aeroplane was tested as airworthy in January 1911 and was named F.E.1 (Farman Experimental No.1, after its pusher layout that was characteristic of the French company's designs). Three months later, on 26 April, the Army Balloon Factory was rechristened the Army Aircraft Factory, reflecting its new involvement with aeroplanes; and a year later it was retitled again, becoming the Royal Aircraft Factory.

Geoffrey de Havilland was employed as designer and test pilot. He developed an improved version of his first machine, the F.E.2, that could be adapted to floatplane

configuration. The remit given to the 'Factory' precluded the construction of original machines, and so the well recorded ploy of reconstruction was used. The first of de Havilland's ventures into this territory, utilizing an ENV-powered Bleriot XII, produced the canard S.E.1 design ('S.E.' for 'Santos Dumont Experimental', Dumont being the leading exponent of the canard design). De Havilland immediately recognized that, in its initial form, the S.E.1 was seriously under-ruddered; but that did not prevent him attempting a flight that ended in a crash.

His next reconstruction led to one of the most successful early designs, the B.E.1 ('B.E.' for 'Bleriot Experimental', meaning a tractor design): it emerged from the remains of a Voisin with a 60hp Wolseley engine, and first flew in December 1911. It was by far the most advanced design of its day, and was developed into the B.E.2, which went into production for the RFC and began the line that was progressed into the B.E.2c by E.T. Busk, and then the B.E.2d and the B.E.2e.

An interest in producing a fast single-seater led de Havilland to produce the B.S.1 ('B.S.' for 'Bleriot – i.e. tractor –

Scout'). The flying surfaces of this scout were, essentially, scaled-down B.E. components, and these were mated to a semi-monocoque fuselage of circular cross-section. Power was from a fourteen-cylinder, two-row, 100hp Gnome rotary that gave a top speed of 91.7mph (147.5km/h) – an astonishing figure for 1913. The type was re-designated S.E.2 by March 1913. It was crashed in a spin on the 27th of that month, hospitalizing de Havilland. The S.E.2 was rebuilt twice, but survived to serve operationally with 3 Sqn in the BEF until March 1915.

The Aeronautical Inspection Directorate was created at Farnborough in January 1914, and de Havilland was transferred to this new body, a move that took him away from design work. This was not to his liking, and he took the opportunity to 'button-hole' George Holt Thomas during one of the latter's visits to Farnborough: in effect, de Havilland offered his services as a designer and test pilot to the Aircraft Manufacturing Company. Holt Thomas had recognized the potential of his firm producing its own designs, and de Havilland's contract was signed on 23 May 1914, coming into effect on 2 July. The salary was a generous £600 per year, plus a commission for each aeroplane sold.

By this time the Aircraft Manufacturing Company had taken over land alongside the Edgware Road in Hendon, on what had been Shoelands Farm. Components manufactured there were taken to Hendon aerodrome for assembly and flight-testing.

War broke out before de Havilland could begin work in earnest for his new employer. Whilst working for the RAF he had joined the RFC Reserve, and he was immediately called up for limited active service – 'limited' because he was still suffering from the effects of the S.E.2 crash. This precluded service overseas, and resulted in a posting to the aerodrome at Montrose where he and a Sergeant Carr were detailed to fly anti-submarine patrols, using a pair of 50hp Bleriots, from Aberdeen to the Firth of Forth. It took less than a month for officialdom to realize that this was a shameful waste of his talents, and by the end of August de Havilland was back at Farnborough. He was released back to AMC in November, with the rank of captain and liable to recall.

AMC's Own Designs

Back in the drawing office, his first thoughts were to produce a tractor biplane, and sketches were made for this; the choice of the tractor layout was undoubtedly the result of his Farnborough experience. But the War Office had different ideas, and wanted a two-seater pusher that would allow the carrying of a machine-gun for use by its observer. De Havilland was obliged to comply, and the resultant machine was the D.H.1. However, the Aircraft Manufacturing Co. was unable to undertake production as it was committed to manufacturing Farman types that had become the standard primary trainers in both the RFC and RNAS; and so the contract was sub-let to Savages of Kings Lynn.

The use of de Havilland's initials for the D.H.1 set the precedent for subsequent naming of AMC designs, and said much about George Holt Thomas' generosity as well as his reticence to having his own name broadcast. Holt Thomas was, however, still firmly in control of AMC, and also had important roles in the infant SBAC, being a member of its management committee and chairman of its aircraft engine section.

He was also to diversify into all aspects of aircraft production. Associated companies then included Peter Hooker Ltd (manufacturing Gnome and Le Rhone engines), the Integral Propeller Company Ltd, Airships Ltd (producing kite balloons and anti-submarine 'blimps') and May, Harden and May (whose Hythe works turned out F.2A flying boats).

Nevertheless, the advantages of the tractor design were still in de Havilland's mind, and after the D.H.1 had emerged in January 1915, he sketched out his ideas for a twin-engined machine of that configuration.

This was put into abeyance in order to design a single-seater pusher scout. That pusher became the D.H.2, which was, essentially, a scaled-down, single-seater D.H.1. It is significant that the possible need for such a scout, one that was capable of mounting a forward-firing machine-gun, had occurred to its designer even before the service introduction by the German Air Service of the Fokker E.I – thus clearly demonstrating de Havilland's understanding of potential service requirements.

As with other successful aeroplane manufacturers, AMC functioned as a close-knit team. George Holt Thomas had the ability to select management personnel of ability and foresight, de Havilland being the classic example. Others, some of whom were recruited by de Havilland, included Hugh Burroughes (general manager), Wilfred Nixon (financial director), Charles Walker (designer), Francis St Barbe (sales), Frank Hearle (experimental department), Frank Halford (engine department) and B.C. Hucks (test pilot). The majority of these formed the nucleus of the de Havilland Company when it rose from the ashes of Airco.

Expansion

Increasing production led to the need for more factory space, and so AMC acquired Grove Park Estate, alongside Stag Lane and half a mile to the south-west of the existing AMC premises. New offices were built on the Hyde, alongside the Edgware Road. By the end of 1915, Airco employed more than 600 personnel and had over 100,000sq ft (9,290sq m) of factory space. Head Office was at 47 Victoria Street, London SW and later 27 Buckingham Gate, London SW1.

The D.H.3 followed in 1916, and although a twin-engined design, it retained the pusher configuration. The D.H.3 was notable as the first de Havilland design to employ extensive use of plywood as a fuselage covering. The use of that material, also favoured by Martinsyde, was to be a design feature of all subsequent de Havilland designs, essentially because it gave great structural strength – there was no need for internal cross-bracing of longerons, and it was found that machines were less prone to loss from combat damage. The D.H.3 was also the first machine to have the characteristic de Havilland shape of fin and rudder, one which was perpetuated right through to the Moths and Rapides of the 1930s.

By 1916 Geoffrey de Havilland had virtually given up test-flying in order to concentrate on design. He had sensibly realized that consideration needed to be given to the thoughts of those who flew service machines in combat, and to that end he was a frequent visitor to France, becoming well acquainted with the command of the in-the-field RFC, F.H. Sykes, and later, H.M. Trenchard. The objective opinions of these men were taken on board, as were ideas for refinements to AMC designs, as postulated by the crews of active squadrons.

It was the D.H.4 that was the bedrock of AMC's fortune. That classic design was flying by August 1916 and went on to be produced in massive numbers, both at home and in the USA. Development of the airframe resulted in the D.H.9 and the D.H.9A.

The other AMC fighting scout was the D.H.5, whose structural strength made it a natural choice as a ground attack aeroplane during 1917. The D.H.6 was designed as an easy-to-produce trainer, and it saw widespread service in that role. Although the D.H.3 did not achieve production, its development, the D.H.10, did, and saw considerable service after the war.

The final de Havilland designs for AMC were not completed until after the Armistice, and so were never likely to achieve production status. The D.H.14 and D.H.15 were merely developments of the D.H.9A.

By the time of the Armistice, the workforce had grown to over 4,400 people and the factory area had increased seven-fold. It was proudly advertised in the 1919 edition of *Jane's All the World's Aircraft* as the 'largest aircraft enterprise in the world'. The parent company was capable of turning out 190 aeroplanes per month.

The increased workforce brought complications, however, as people were recruited from a wider catchment area and found difficulty in travelling to work. The solution was to provide purpose-built housing close to the Hendon factories, and Roe Green Garden Village was created for that purpose. It occupied 24 acres (9.7ha) on the opposite side of Stag Lane to Grove Park, and was a model of its kind. The housing had bathrooms, cookers and water-heaters, shops were located in the village, and a range of recreational activities was catered for. Unfortunately it was not completed until 1920, by which time AMC was about to disappear as a company.

The End of AMC and the Beginning of De Havilland

The Armistice had brought a sudden halt to the need for aircraft. Contracts were either scrapped or reduced, and AMC, like all other manufacturers, found it difficult to stay in business. The imposition by the Treasury of a duty on 'excess war profits' did nothing to alleviate the situation. Although consideration was given to the possible civil market for aeroplanes, the vast and readily available stock of surplus war machines made the design of such types a non-runner. However, with great foresight Holt Thomas had founded a new company in October 1916, Air Transport and Travel Ltd, and this began operations using converted D.H.4s and D.H.9s on services that included cross-Channel mailruns. Meanwhile, manufacturing activity slowed down, and in 1919, AMC was sold to the Birmingham Small Arms Company (BSA), whose directors had no interest in maintaining the aircraft side of the business.

The AMC team was nevertheless convinced of a future for aviation, and after the necessary finance had been scraped together (including a generous £10,000 from George Holt Thomas), Nixon, St Barbe, Walker and Hearle joined de Havilland in setting up the de Havilland Aircraft Company, which was registered on 25 September 1920. The former aerodrome at Stag Lane, only three miles from Hendon, was rented, and the team continued work on the D.H.18 that had been started by AMC. After a patchy beginning the company got into its stride, and its products are all so familiar: the Moth family, the Dragon and Rapide, the incomparable Mosquito and the elegant Hornet, the Vampire and Venom, the Comet, the Sea Vixen and many others besides.

George Holt Thomas maintained his interest in Air Transport and Travel Ltd until the company was subsumed by Imperial Airways. He then forsook aviation and devoted his time and energy to dairy farming. He died, aged 59, at Cimiez in France on 1 January 1929. Today his name is largely unknown, while that of his protege, de Havilland, is world famous; but perhaps that is the way that Holt Thomas would have wished it to be.

The love of flying ran in the de Havilland family. Geoffrey's brother, Hereward, had a distinguished career in the RFC/RAF during the Great War, flying with the BEF in France and also in Mesopotamia and Palestine. After serving as a flight commander in 30 Sqn, he was promoted to major and command of that unit, from 20 January 1917, being made a DSO for his work in Mesopotamia. From 8 July 1918 he commanded 111 Squadron, the principal fighter unit in the Palestine theatre of operations.

Three sons were born to Geoffrey de Havilland – Geoffrey, Peter and John – and all three followed in their father's footsteps: they became pilots and took jobs in the family business, as did their uncle Hereward. Tragically John died in a mid-air collision in 1943 while flying a Mosquito, and Geoffrey was killed on 27 September 1946 in a D.H.108. The shock of these losses contributed to the untimely death of their mother, Louie.

The de Havilland Company was one of the last of the independent manufacturers, in 1960 finally being absorbed into the massive Hawker Siddeley Group, the brainchild of Geoffrey's contemporary T.O.M. Sopwith. Geoffrey himself, who by this time was Sir Geoffrey de Havilland, knighted in recognition of his services to British aviation, then retired. He passed away on 26 May 1965 at the age of eighty-two.

In Conclusion

The following chapters are intended to examine the military products of the Aircraft Manufacturing Company, the majority of which were designed by de Havilland. They are arranged in approximate chronological sequence, and the volume of detail given to each type is a reflection of the quantity built, the duration of its service, or its design significance. Particular attention has been given to two aspects of service, namely the fighting career of the D.H.2, and the operations of the D.H.4s, D.H.9s and D.H.9As with the Independent Force, aspects that have received less than their due measure in print.

CHAPTER TWO

Farmans, Blimps and Flying Boats

Holt Thomas' acquisition of the British manufacturing rights to Farman aeroplanes was a shrewd and timely move. The French aircraft industry was the world leader at the time, and the emerging British air service was deficient in machines. Indigenous equipment for the Royal Flying Corps centred on the output of the Royal Aircraft Factory, notably the B.E. series, with only limited contributions from private manufacturers such as Sopwith, Flanders, Martinsyde and British & Colonial.

The RFC needed machines that were reliable, easy to maintain, and capable of providing an observer with a good field of vision. The pusher designs of Maurice and Henri Farman were ideally suited to these requirements.

The M.F. Serie 7, The Longhorn

The first of the brothers' types to be successfully placed into large-scale production by the Aircraft Manufacturing Company was the Maurice Farman 1912 biplane. It was a large machine. The unequal span mainplanes gave a wing area of 528ft (161m), the lower of these supporting a blunt-nosed nacelle that carried the successful 70hp Renault engine. A rectangular, forward-mounted elevator was carried on long, upswept undercarriage skids and braced to the centre-section and undercarriage struts by further booms.
In its original form, the Maurice Farman had tail booms that curved inwards towards the tail unit. That tail unit comprised twin rudders, a lower tailplane of approximately semi-circular plan, and a rectangular upper tailplane that carried a further elevator, also of rectangular shape. A machine of this form was entered in the 1912 Military Trials, and 207 and 403 were delivered, also in this form, to the Military Wing and Central Flying School respectively.

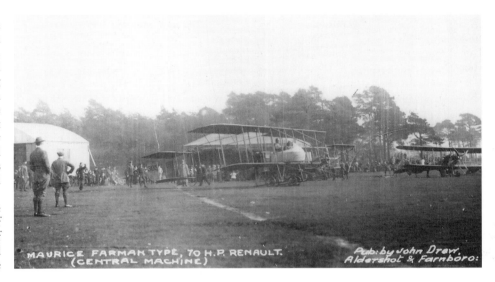

305 was an early M.F. Se.7 that served with the RFC Military Wing. Close examination of this photograph shows that it retained the lobe-shaped lower elevator of the original 1912 design, and had cables connecting the extremity of each tail-skid to the base of the rudder posts. 305 served with 4 Squadron at Farnborough. JMB/GSL

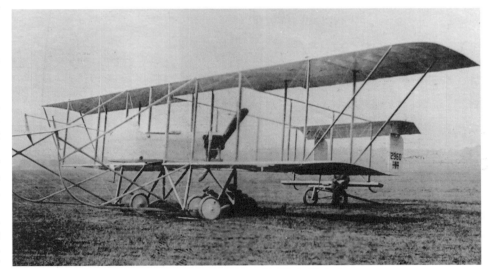

The main features of the M.F. Se.7 are shown in this shot of 2960 of 2 RAS, Brooklands. The forward booms that support the elevator look flimsy, but they served to absorb impact in the event of a nose-in crash. The overhung upper mainplanes are evident, supported by struts from the lower ones. The machine is trestled in flying attitude and the plank-like item under the tailplane was part of a trolley that allowed the aeroplane to be handled on the ground. JMB/GSL

2970, of the same batch as the machine shown in the previous photograph, again shows the booms supporting the elevator; the groundcrew lends scale. A small cockade is carried on the front of the nacelle. JMB/GSL

By 1913 the Maurice Farman biplane was slightly modified, and re-designated the Serie 7. Parallel tail booms were introduced, and the lower tailplane adopted the rectangular layout of the upper one. The nacelle was given a more rounded front, and the corners of the forward elevator were rounded off. Braking skids were added to the undercarriage. All this established the geometry of the type, and it was to remain unchanged for the rest of its service.

Further examples were acquired by the RFC Military Wing and CFS, to be given the serial numbers 214-216, 223-224, 266, 269-270, 302, 305-307, 322, 337-338, 343, 355-360, 376, 410 and 411, 415, 418, 425-429, 431, 450-451, 458-459, 464, 472 and 476-478. Records are incomplete, but it seems likely that a number of these were of French manufacture, or at least assembled from French-built components. Those in the 400 series of numbers were intended for the Central Flying School at Upavon, and some were Military Wing machines that had been renumbered on transfer. Transfer in the opposite direction resulted in 343 becoming 464. In addition to supplying these machines, the AMC (Aircraft Manufacturing Company) was also engaged in the overhaul, repair and

Specification – Maurice Farman Serie 7	
Powerplant:	70hp Renault or 80hp Renault
Weights:	Empty 1,320lb (600kg); loaded 1,925lb (873kg); wing loading 3.64lb per sq ft (17.77kg per sq m)
Dimensions:	Span 50ft 11in (15.53m) (upper), 37ft 9¹/₂in (11.53m) (lower); length 37ft 9¹/₂in (11.53m); height 11ft 5¹/₄in 3.5m); wing area 528sq ft (49.12 sq m)
Performance:	Maximum speed 65mph (105km/h); climb to 3,500ft (1, 068m) c.16 minutes

This rare, in-flight view of a Longhorn well illustrates the type's drag-inducing features that made it slow, sedate and relatively safe to fly. JMB/GSL

Representative Airco-built/assembled Maurice Farman Se.7 with RFC & RNAS Units

1 CFS Upavon – 306, 338, 356, 358, 403, 411, 415, 418, 425,
   426, 427, 428, 429, 431, 450, 451, 458, 459, 464, 472, 476, 477,
   478, 498, 661.
   RAS, later 1 RAS/RS/TS
   Farnborough/Gosport – 342, 343, 344, 345, 360, 464, 610,
   2979, 4006, 6690, 6740.
2 RAS/RS/TS Brooklands/Northolt – 2969, 2970, 2971, 2998,
   4010, 6680, 6691, 6699, 6702, A4102, A7051, A7052.
3 RS/TS Shoreham – 475, 478, 549, 550, 555, 2965, 6904.
4 RAS/RS/TS Northolt – 548, 557, 2017, 2966, 2978, 4002, 4003,
   4005, 4007, 6890, 6900.
5 RAS/RS Castle Bromwich – 2986, A7085, A7099, B3982.
6 RAS Montrose – 2974, 6701.
7 RAS/RS Netheravon – 358, 499, 546, 549, 4019, 6708, 6711,
   A7002, A7054, A7055.
8 RAS/RS Netheravon – 6678, A7003.
9 RAS/RS Norwich – 418, 2957, 2976, 2980, 2982, 2999, 4012,
   4013, 4014, 4015, 5617, 6697, 6698.
10 RAS/RS Joyce Green – 2982, 4008.
11 RS Northolt – 4005, 4007.
12 RAS/RS Thetford – 2528, 2996, 4715, 4716, 4758, 6685,
   A7065, B1989.
14 RAS/RS Catterick – 6682,
   A4064.
15 RAS/RS Thetford/Doncaster – 2964, 4008.
21 RS/TS Abbassia/Moascar – A4091, A4093, A4113, A4114,
   A4122, A4126.
24 RS Netheravon – A4141.
25 RS/TS Thetford – A4077, A4109, A7098.
26 RS/TS Turnhouse – 2985, 6694, 6701, 6706, A7022, A7028,
   A7029, A7030, A7031, A7032, A7033.
31 RS Wyton – A7051.
39 RS Montrose – 2974, 4018, A4069, A4077, A4134, A7007,
   A7008, A7009, A7012, A7013, A7018, A7019, A7020, A7021.
41 RS/TS Bramham Moor/Doncaster – A4075, A4081, A4086,
   A4087, A7035.

47 RS Waddington – A7091, A7094.
48 TS Waddington – A7015, A7046.
49 TS Spittlegate – A7026.
58 RS/TS Suez/Abu Sueir – A4114, A4115, A4117, A4131.
    5 TS AFC Minchinhampton – A4074.
205 TDS Vendome – A4144, A4145, A4146, A7043, A7044, A7045,
    A7046, A7047, A7048, A7049, A7050.
1   Squadron Brooklands – 359.
2   Squadron Farnborough/
    Montrose – 207, 214, 215, 223, 224, 266, 337.
3   Squadron Larkhill/Netheravon – 214, 216, 269, 270, 356, 358,
    359.
4   Squadron Farnborough/Netheravon – 223, 266, 302, 305,
    306, 307, 356, 357, 358, 450, 464, 472, 476, 478, 533.
5   Squadron Farnborough/Gosport – 207, 224, 269, 355, 356,
    358, 359, 360.
6   Squadron Farnborough – 270, 322, 338, 342, 343, 344, 345,
    360.
7   Squadron Netheravon – 223, 338, 355, 360.
9   Squadron Dover – 481, 2982.
18 Squadron Northolt – 2961, 2966.
41 Squadron Gosport – 2979, 4006, 6140, 6690.
RNAS Yarmouth – 67, 69.
RNAS Eastchurch – 23, 69, 70, 188.
RNAS Hendon – 67, 70, 909.
RNAS Grain – 72, 73, 188.
RNAS Eastbourne – 69.
RNAS Leven – 71.
RNAS Dundee – 71.
RNAS Felixstowe – 67, 70.
RNAS Calshot – 71, 73, 188.
RNAS Bembridge – 73.
RNAS School, Chingford – 67, 2973, 2983.
RNAS School, Eastbourne – 2984.

Another in-flight shot that re-enforces the impression of the Longhorn's bulk.
via the author

reconstruction of machines that had become worn or damaged in service.

The Serie 7 saw pre-war service with all squadrons of the Military Wing, though the principal users were 2 and 4 Squadrons. The former unit was transferred to Montrose from Farnborough during February 1913, and several of its Maurice Farmans were flown, in stages, between those bases. In those early days of the RFC the type was nicknamed the 'Mechanical Cow'.

The Naval Wing of the RFC was also interested in acquiring the type, and received AMC-built 23 as early as 12 January 1913. That machine went to Eastchurch and lasted until the end of that year, when it was destroyed in a crash that killed both its crew members, Captains Wildman-Lushington and Fawcett. Further examples of the type were delivered to the Naval Wing during

This shot of 296 was taken at Thetford. The machine may have belonged to either 12 RS or 35 Squadron, both resident at that station during 1916. JMB/GSL

July 1913. Planes nos 67, 69 and 70 had longer careers than the first naval example, serving as front-line types at Yarmouth, Felixstowe and Hendon before being relegated to training duty; 67 lasted in the latter capacity until at least 29 September 1917.

Planes 71-73 were also delivered during the summer of 1913, but these came from AMC as floatplanes. The forward elevator was dispensed with, and a pair of pontoon floats replaced the wheeled undercarriage. At the tailplane end there was no lower elevator, and a further small float had been added under the rear bay of the tail booms. The powerplant was still the 70hp Renault – and this must have left the design seriously under-powered when the increased drag of the floats is considered. These machines were delivered to the early seaplane stations of Leven and Grain.

A further eight were ordered from AMC by the Naval Wing, which was retitled RNAS (Royal Naval Air Service) in July 1914. Only two of these were delivered, however: 91 and 92 were cancelled, but 188 was delivered on 2 June 1914. 909-914 were built, but only the first entered RNAS service, the remaining five being transferred to the RFC. By mid-1914 aeroplane manufacturers were becoming associated with particular branches of the flying services, and AMC became regarded as a supplier to the RFC. The RNAS did receive further examples of the Serie 7, but the majority of these were either bought directly from the French

manufacturers or built under sub-contract at Loughborough by the Brush Electrical Engineering Co Ltd. Six AMC-built examples were transferred from the RFC to the RNAS: 2973, and 2983 and 2984 during the summer of 1915, with A4144-A4146 following at the beginning of 1917. The latter three were for service with the RNAS training school that had been established in France, at Vendome.

By 1914 and the outbreak of war, the Serie 7 was outdated as an operational machine and the RFC was in the process of standardizing on the RAF B.E.2 as its reconnaissance type. Consequently, none of the French type crossed the Channel with the BEF, and those on charge remained at UK bases and were issued as training machines to new squadrons, as those were formed.

Further deliveries, in small numbers, were made in the first months of the war, and the type proved ideal as an initial training machine. The creation of Reserve Aeroplane Squadrons to supply pilots to the increasing number of Service Squadrons ensured a place for the Serie 7, which had by then acquired the nickname of 'Longhorn'. Larger batches were ordered from AMC, and production continued into 1916.

Specification – Henri Farman F.20

Powerplant:	80hp Gnome and 80hp Le Rhone
Weights:	Empty 794lb (360kg); loaded 1,455lb (660kg); wing loading 2.1lb per sq ft (10.29kg per sq m)
Dimensions:	Span 43ft 5¾in (13.26m) (upper); length 26ft 5¼in (8.06m); height 10ft 4in (3.15m); wing area 377sq ft (35sq m)
Performance:	Maximum speed 65mph (105km/h)

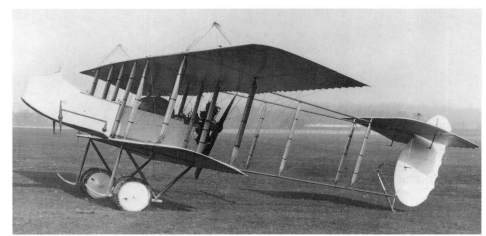

The cleanliness of the H.F. F.20, by comparison with the Longhorn, is clearly shown here. The overhanging upper mainplanes are supported by cables from king-posts, and the undercarriage structure is much simpler. The pilot occupied the rear seat. A connecting rod linked the external cam at the extremity elevator control shaft with the actuating cranks at the front of the nacelle. JMB/GSL

2832 is seen here at Netheravon, where units using the type were 7, 8 and 24 Reserve Aeroplane Squadrons. The F.20 has its serial number marked in a colour that photographed in a light tone, possibly blue. JMB/GSL

2841 served with the CFS; it is seen here on a sunny Upavon aerodrome. The relative lightness of the 80hp Gnome rotary engine is obvious. JMB/GSL

The original Reserve Aeroplane Squadron was created at Farnborough after the departure of the initial squadrons for the BEF, and it was retitled 1 RAS with the creation of a second such unit at Brooklands. Further RAS followed, occupying new bases such as Shoreham, Northolt, Castle Bromwich, Catterick and Norwich. Until the training system was rationalized in 1916, each RAS operated a miscellany of available types – though all had examples of the Longhorn. It proved ideal to its new role: its sedate flying characteristics and low landing speed made it a good instructional machine, and the simplicity of its engine – by then usually the 80hp version of the Renault – made mechanical maintenance easy. Its rigging was complex but straightforward, and manuals were made available to guide that task.

The general shortage of up-to-date machines for service at home meant that types such as the Longhorn were issued as initial equipment to new service squadrons as they formed during 1915 and 1916. 18 Squadron at Norwich and 41 Squadron at Gosport, both of which were intended to fly pusher types operationally, were given small numbers of the type until more suitable machines became available. 9 squadron at Dover also received a few.

When, during 1916, the RFC decided to open training stations in the Canal Zone of Egypt, the initial Reserve Squadrons were numbered 21, 22 and 23, and were, respectively, for initial, intermediate and advanced training. 21 RS was given Longhorns as part of its establishment and

---

Representative Airco-built/assembled Henri Farman F.20 with RFC, RNAS and RAF Units[1]

1 RAS/RS Farnborough/Gosport – 7406, 7407.	199 DS/NTS Rochford/East Retford – (A1189 – GW-built)
2 RAS Brooklands – 513.	200 DS/NTS East Retford – (A1160 – GW-built)
3 RAS Shoreham – 699.	CFS Upavon – 412, 420, 434, 435, 440, 444, 445, 455, 456, 461,
4 RAS/RS Farnborough/Northolt – 2839.	462, 467, 561, 2841, 7401, 7443, (A1166, A1171, A1174, A1175,
6 RAS/RS Catterick – (A1156, A1158, A1159, A1176 –	A1221, A1223, A1224, A1225, A1230, A1231 –
GW-built), A1712, A1717, A1718.	GW-built), A1714, A1719, A3023.
8 RAS/RS Netheravon – 513.	2 Squadron Farnborough – 208, 209, 277, 286.
9 RAS/RS Norwich – 565, 7398, 7399, (A1199 – GW-built).	3 Squadron Larkhill/Netheravon – 268, 274, 275, 277, 284, 286,
10 RAS/RS Joyce Green – 2839, (A1154, A1183 – GW-built).	294, 295, 341, 351, 352, 353, 363.
11 RAS/RS Northolt – 563.	5 Squadron Farnborough/Gosport – 244, 268, 284, 294, 339, 341,
15 RAS/RS Thetford/Doncaster – 7431.	346, 350, 364, 393, 455, 456, 461.
19 RS Hounslow – 7417.	9 Squadron Dover – 560.
24 RS Netheravon – 2838.	18 Squadron Northolt – 558.
26 RS/TS Turnhouse – (A1159 – GW-built), A1717.	28 Squadron Gosport – A1187 (GW-built).
27 RS/TS Gosport – 7419, 7431, A1716.	35 Squadron Thetford – 568, 2845, 2846, 2850, 7398, 7399,
28 RS Castle Bromwich – 7426.	7408, 7409, 7411, 7412.
31 RS Wyton – A1154.	39 Squadron Hounslow – 2838.
45 RS South Carlton – (A1206, A1209, A1210,	40 Squadron Gosport – 7406.
A1240 – GW-built)	41 Squadron Gosport – 7445.

There were few training accidents in the F.20, but this was one of them: the demise of A1216 at South Carlton, the home of 45 RS, and it looks as if its crew would have been lucky to walk away. JMB/GSL

operated these for more than a year. In the heat of that country, it was usually only possible to make flights during the early morning and evening, turbulence during the middle part of the day making sorties dangerous.

More than 300 Longhorns were built for training, and yet, despite the lack of a systematic training syllabus, surprisingly few were involved in fatal accidents. Early casualty reports were often vague with regard to the machine involved, but it would seem that there were fewer than a dozen such incidents. It seems likely that the structure of the machine should take the credit. The majority of accidents at the initial training stage occurred during take-off and landing, and the forward booms and elevator would absorb much of the shock from a nose in crash, while well braced wing cellules would do likewise if a machine side-slipped in.

The Longhorn had become outdated by late 1916. A new generation of front-line tractor aeroplanes was entering service, and the training programme was adapted to cater for this. The Longhorn's successor, the Serie 11 Shorthorn, with its improved performance, was still considered adequate as an elementary trainer; but the days of the former were numbered in the RFC. A few lingered on into 1917, but by the late spring of that year most had been withdrawn. Those of the RNAS – and by then only Brush-built machines survived – lasted longer, but were phased out by the end of the year and replaced with D.H.6s.

No AMC-built example was preserved for posterity in the UK; however, one of Belgian origin is on display at the Musee de l'Air et l'Espace at Le Bourget, where visitors can appreciate the vast size and intricate rigging of the design.

The Henri Farman Biplanes

Almost contemporary with the Maurice Farman 1912 biplane was a somewhat smaller and much lighter-looking design by his brother. Two examples of the Henri Farman 1912 biplane were delivered to the Military Wing, but later transferred to the CFS. They were followed by a machine of similar appearance, but of greater span, that had been purchased from Claude Grahame-White during March 1913. In the meantime Henri Farman had evolved the basic design into the F.20, and that became the standard version to serve with the British air services.

The F.20 was an unequal span, two-bay biplane whose massive upper wing extensions were supported by bracing from king-posts. Those upper wing extensions had full-span ailerons. Its nacelle jutted ahead of the wings and its tail booms tapered in plan-view to the rudder post. That carried a lobe-shaped, balanced rudder of straight trailing edge, and served as the rear support for a single, high-mounted tailplane. The undercarriage was

An in-flight photograph of an F.20, probably 669. The shot shows clearly the overhanging upper mainplanes and the king-posts to support their bracing cables. via K. Kelly

B1960 was a typical wartime production M.F. Se.11 Shorthorn; it served with B Flt of 5 RS at Castle Bromwich. This view illustrates the position of the type's nacelle, supported between the mainplanes. C. Huston via JMB/GSL

widely spaced, with its struts secured to the lower wing at the inner inter-pane struts. A short braking skid and twin wheels were mounted on each side. The engine was an 80hp Gnome Monosoupape rotary that drove a twin-bladed propeller.

Initial deliveries to the CFS and Military Wing were aeroplanes that had either been purchased from a civilian source (435) or from the manufacturer (268). It may have been that French-built F.20s were assembled by AMC, but the Hendon-based company was soon producing examples of its own. Surviving records are incomplete, but it would seem that 274, 328, 350, 351 and 363 were all AMC-built, and it is likely that most of the early examples in service were too. 461 was 328 renumbered, when that Farman and a B.E.2 exchanged identities.

The F.20 was considered a success and was operated pre-war by 3 and 5 Squadrons, in addition to the CFS. Initial deliveries, certainly those intended for the two active squadrons, had single control, with external elevator control cranks protruding from the sides of the rear, observer's, cockpit. Most, if not all, delivered to the CFS had dual control with elevator cables connected to cranks outside the front cockpit and connecting rods to cams that replaced the original cranks. Presumably the control shaft was extended into the rear cockpit, and duplicated rudder controls fitted.

352 was delivered to the Military Wing on 24 April 1913 and went to the RFC Flying Depot at Farnborough, where it was used in experiments with a machine-gun mounted for use by its observer. Both the Maxin and the lighter Rexer weapons were tried.

Further Shorthorns and a Longhorn of 5 RS, B1998 nearest, lined up with A Flight nearest the camera. The higher position of the Shorthorn's nacelle is apparent. JMB/GSL

Specification – Maurice Farman Serie 11	
Powerplant:	70hp Renault or 80hp Renault
Weights:	Empty 1,441lb (654kg); loaded 2,046lb (928kg); wing loading 3.64lb per sq ft (17.78kg per sq m)
Dimensions:	Span 51ft 9in (15.78m) (upper), 38ft 7in (11.77m) (lower); length 30ft 6in (9.3m); height 10ft 4in (3.15m) (without kingposts); wing area 561sq ft (52.19sq m)
Performance:	Maximum speed 72mph (116km/h); climb to 3,500ft (1,068m) c.9 minutes

The Naval Wing was also interested in the type. AMC-built 31, a landplane, was acquired from its manufacturer as early as February 1913. The Admiralty was more interested in acquiring seaplanes and had bought three, 96-98, of French origin. 96 had been a contender in the 1913 Schneider Trophy competition and had the benefit of a 160hp Gnome whose greater power helped compensate for the drag-inducing float undercarriage. It served at Calshot, but lasted only six months before being withdrawn from use prior to its deletion in June 1914. The other two had only the 80hp Gnome, and as such must have been under-powered. Both saw service at Yarmouth, although 97 spent some time at Kirkwall after the

Training accidents with Farman types produced relatively few fatal results, considering the number in service. This example, A6862 of (probably) 48 RS, ended up on a hangar roof at Waddington. JMB/GSL

Colourful training machines usually call to mind Pups and Camels. Here, in the Middle East, an unidentified Shorthorn has been given a striped nacelle, coloured wing-tips and flashes on the inner surface of its rudders. 21 RS was the main Middle Eastern user of the type. JMB/GSL

declaration of hostilities. 98 was deleted before the war was three weeks old, but 97 survived until 1916, latterly at the Calshot seaplane school.

AMC received a contract to build six Henri Farman seaplanes, which were designated F.22H. The F.22 was simply a development of the F.20, with the 'H' for 'hydroplane'. The numbers 139-144 were allocated, but none survived beyond August 1914, having served at Yarmouth, Calshot and Grain. From July 1914 the Naval Wing, RNAS, bought further Henri Farmans of the F.22/22 type; but by

then AMC was committed to production for the RFC.

The Admiralty then turned to the French parent company for deliveries, as well as buying/impressing civilian machines, some of which were AMC-built. Deliveries from France still involved AMC, however: as British representative for the Farmans, AMC had a hand in the assembly of airframes that arrived as components. For example, when 1454, an F.20, was shipped to Southampton and then delivered by rail to Gosforth (Newcastle), AMC sent

a team northwards to assemble and test the machine, a process that took three days.

Eleven F.20s went to war with the Expeditionary Force in August, four with each of the two squadrons and three as reserves with the Air Park. The mobile early weeks of the war, with squadrons operating from makeshift landing grounds, did not suit the F.20. It lacked the strength of other machines, and although further examples had been bought for the BEF from the French parent company, it was soon discarded. 6 Squadron had received a few, but exchanged them before the year was out, as did 3 Squadron. A few remained with 5 Squadron, but they were gone by the early spring of 1915.

If the F.20 had proved unsuitable operationally, its CFS service indicated that it was a good training machine. As the RFC's squadron strength increased and Reserve Aeroplane Squadrons (RAS) were created, the F.20 was ordered from AMC for the training role. The 80hp Le Rhone was sometimes fitted as an alternative to the Gnome engine. Fifty machines were initially ordered, 7396-7445, and these were issued in small numbers to both RAS and service squadrons mobilizing for active duty. More were wanted, but by early 1916, AMC was involved in D.H.2 production and so two batches, totalling 150 machines, were subcontracted to the Grahame-White Aviation Co. AMC received orders for a further 130, A1712-A1741 and B1401-B1500, but the final twenty of the latter batch were cancelled.

At first F.20s were used as part of the diverse equipment issued to the RAS, but by 1916 the rationalization of the training programme led to a more systematic use. Some were still on the strength of Elementary Reserve Squadrons and were used for solo flying after initial training on Maurice Farmans; others went to Higher Training Squadrons that produced pilots for pusher-engined machines, either single seaters such as the D.H.2 and F.E.8 or the two-seater F.E.2b. In that capacity, the F.20 was used to prepare prospective pilots for their operational mounts. Some were also issued to squadrons that were mobilizing, and again, were used as introductory machines to F.E.2bs. When depot squadrons formed for night training during 1917 that role was reprised, with the F.20 leading to instruction (by day

The exact nature of the Shorthorn floatplanes delivered to Loch Doon is not known. They may have borne some resemblance to the seaplane derived from the Longhorn, an example of which (29) is seen here at Yarmouth. JMB/GSL

only) to the D.H.1 and then the F.E.2b. The type was outdated by 1917, and that year saw its withdrawal from RFC service.

The M.F. Serie 11, The Shorthorn

A revision of the Serie 7 design had appeared during 1913, one that dispensed with the forward elevator. This was followed by further modifications to the nacelle position, tail-boom layout and tail unit that resulted in the Serie 11. The new design acquired the nickname 'Shorthorn' at an early stage in its career, the appellation being first used by Charles G. Grey in the journal *The Aeroplane*; the Serie 7 then became known, retrospectively, as the Longhorn.

Representative Airco-built/assembled Maurice Farman Se.11 with RFC, RNAS and RAF Units

RAS later 1 RAS/RS/TS Farnborough/Gosport – 342, 343, 344, 345, 369, 370, 371, 379, 2940, 5904, 7361.
2 RAS/RS/TS Brooklands/Northolt – 516, 523, 536, 556, 2467, 2951, 2958, 4726, 4727, 5718, 5880, 5581, 7351, 7362, 7363, A728, A1711, A2175, A2176, A2447, A6815, A6838, A6850, A6878, A6881, A6883, A9921, B1483, B1962, B1991, B2015, B2043, B4698, B4701, B4741, B4773, B8815, B9443, B9996, C3499, E9998.
3 RAS/RS Shoreham – 514, 2460, 2944, 2946, A2468, A2495, A2501, B2018.
4 RAS/RS Northolt – 515, 533, 540, 2466, 4729, 5885, 5888, 7064, A929, A2177, A2448, A2526, A6805, A6839, A6851, A6900, B1969, B1983, B1992, B3988.
5 RAS/RS Castle Bromwich – 2494, 2948, 2963, 4727, 5887, 7353, 7355, 7392, A915, A916, A933, A953, A1962, A2225, A6808, A6897, B2038, B3981.
6 RAS Montrose – 5900, 7349.
7 RAS/RS/TS Netheravon – 7371, 7372, A2193, A2462, A7055, A7062, B1933, B1953, B1985, B1986, B1994, B4743.
8 RAS/RS Netheravon – 2187, 2195, 4151, 4158, 4160, 4319, 4734, 7003, 7075, 7375, A325, A939, A953, A2208, A2523.
9 RAS/RS Norwich – 535, 2468, 2957, 7364, 7365, A4259.
10 RAS/RS Joyce Green – 5885.
11 RS Northolt – 533, 2466, 7368.
12 RAS/RS Thetford – 2957, 5893, A2209, A2215, A2440, A2459, A2500, A2528, A6825, A6898, B4704, B4728, B4770, B4798, B4801, C4278.
14 RAS/RS Catterick – A329, A331, A6836.
15 RAS/RS Thetford/Doncaster – 5882.
17 RS Croydon – 540, 4729, 5885.
21 RS Abbassia/Moascar – A333, A336, A365, A368, A369, A2449, A2450, A2451, A2452, B4785.
24 RS Netheravon – A346, A362, A373, A934, A2210, A2230, A2442, A2444, A2525, A6859, A6887, A6888, B2041, A7073, A7081.
25 RS/TS Thetford – A945, A2207, A2214, A2466, A2505, A2514, A2528, B2013, B2020, B4662, B4683, B4759, B4760, B4774, B4778, B4807, B9441.
26 RS/TS Turnhouse – 2954, 7349, 7384, A330, A924, A925, A2436, A2437, A2477, A2478, A2479, A2480, A2481, A2482, A2483, A2498, A6819, A6893, B2009.
27 RS Gosport – 514, A913, A914, A921, A2221, A2433, A2434, A2470, B2035.
29 (Australian) TS Shawbury – B1957, B1958, B1960, B4664, B4789.
31 RS Wyton – B4698, B4741, B4773.

35 RS/TS Northolt – B4759.
39 RS/TS Montrose – A2480, A2497, A6818, A6834, A6848, B4682.
41 RS/TS Bramham Moor/Doncaster – 7377, A6810, B1974.
47 RS Waddington – A6892, B4680, B4689, B4795.
48 TS Waddington – A2218, A6841, A6842, A6843, A6852, A6853, A6854, A6861, A6864, B2030, B4657.
49 TS Spittlegate – A2192, A6810, A6812, A6822, B4787.
57 RS Ismailia/Abu Sueir – 7369, A2520, A2521.
64 RS/TS Narborough – A2238.
68 RS Bramham Moor – A6845, A6893.
CFS Upavon – 379, 464, 465, A949, A6817.
5 TS AFC Minchinhampton - B1957.
8 TDS Netheravon – A6890, B4674, B4675, B4690, B4700, B4789, B4796.
204 TDS Eastchurch – B4695.
Wireless School Brooklands – 515.
SAF Loch Doon – A3295, A3296, A3297, A3298, A3299, A3300, A3301, A3302 (MF Se.11 seaplanes).
1 SANBD Stonehenge – A1951, B1993, B2031.
2 SANBD Andover –
3 Squadron Netheravon- 274, 277, 280, 295, 350, 708.
4 Squadron Netheravon/Dover – 342, 379, 464, 465, 633.
5 Squadron Farnborough/Gosport – 342, 369, 742.
6 Squadron Farnborough – 342, 343, 344, 345, 369, 370, 440, 480, 653, 669, 680.
13 Squadron Gosport –
14 Squadron Shoreham – 2943.
22 Squadron Gosport – 514, 535, 2944, 2957.
23 Squadron Gosport – 2948, 2963, 4727.
24 Squadron Hounslow – 545, 556, 2467, 4726.
30 Squadron Basra – 5908, 5909, 7346.
39 Squadron Hounslow – A2196.
41 Squadron Gosport – 5904, 7361.
Experimental Station Orfordness – A2191.
RNAS CTE Cranwell – 7385, A324, A334, A354, B4655.
RNAS School Chingford – B4687.
RNAS School Eastbourne – B4674, B4675, B4690, B4695, B4700.
RNAS School Eastchurch – B4655.
RNAS School Manston – B4705, B4710, B4763, B4764.
RNAS School Redcar – B4676, B4677, B4678, B4713, B4714, B4728, B4729, B4730, B4745, B4746, B4755, B4756, B4771, B4772.
Gunnery School Eastchurch – B4674, B4675, B4687, B4690, B4695, B4700, B4747, B4748.

The Serie 11 was a big improvement on its predecessor although it retained the use of the 70hp and, later, 80hp Renault engine. The wing plan-form was essentially similar to the Serie 7, but of 10in (254mm) greater span. The machine was somewhat heavier, but the increased span served to give it an equal wing loading figure. On early machines the overhanging upper mainplanes continued the use of strut-bracing, although those supporting struts were later replaced by over-wing king-posts that supported bracing cables. The position of the nacelle was raised to a point approximately half way between the mainplanes, and the undercarriage had projecting skids of greatly reduced length. More significantly, the tail booms tapered in the side elevation to converge at a single tailplane. That tailplane's rear spar supported twin rudders that were strut-braced to its leading edge. Simple triangular fins were a later addition.

Military Wing's initial deliveries were made to 6 Squadron at Farnborough. However, when that unit joined the BEF in August 1914 it did not take its Shorthorns with it, most remaining at Farnborough to form the initial equipment of the Reserve Aeroplane Squadron. 4 Squadron took three Shorthorns to France, and another was sent later, but the majority of those used operationally by the squadrons of the BEF were of French manufacture and delivered directly from the parent company.

The outbreak of war led to French output being demanded by that country's air

The Shorthorn-type nacelle is seen in more detail in this view of SS28A's car at Cranwell. JMB/GSL

and of one hundred (A2433-A2532, A6801-A6900, B1951-B2050), and there was even an order for two hundred (B4651-B4850). These large, for the time, orders occupied the AMC workforce, and were the reason for D.H.1 production being subcontracted to Savages.

The training programme was rationalized during 1916, with Reserve Squadrons being designated as either 'Elementary' or 'Higher'. The establishment of all Elementary Reserve Squadrons was set at either eighteen Maurice Farmans or eighteen Grahame-White XVs. As only fifty of the latter were produced for the RFC, the vast majority of primary training was carried out on the former. Most such units operated a mixture of Longhorns and Shorthorns, with the former being used for initial flights leading up to the solo stage, and the latter for solo practice and cross-country work. When the Longhorn was phased out, all initial training was done on the Shorthorn.

The type was popular in its training role, being reliable and safe. Inevitably there were casualties, as there would be in all flying training, but the Shorthorn, like its predecessor, was capable of absorbing a great deal of punishment; only 7 per cent of all fatal training casualties were on Farmans, of all three types. Pilots regarded the type with some affection, and it acquired a further nickname, 'Rumpety', which achieved widespread currency.

Shorthorns joined Longhorns with the Training Wing in Egypt. One pilot who trained there was H.L.V. Tubbs, and his logbook gives a good indication of what contemporary primary training involved. He joined 21 Reserve Squadron and made

Submarine Scout airships built by Airships Ltd were fitted with control cars derived from Shorthorn nacelles. That is obvious in this shot of SS31 that served operationally at Kingsnorth and then, after reconstruction as SS31A, as a training machine at Cranwell. The Airships Ltd craft had wheeled undercarriages that facilitated groundhandling, and the pusher engine not only made life more comfortable for the crew, it also allowed simple inflation of the airbag, via the scoop seen behind the propeller. JMB/GSL

The Shorthorn was almost 10mph (16km) faster than the Longhorn due to its reduced drag, and climbed at almost twice the rate, both of which improvements made it appealing to the British flying services. The new type was acquired by both the Military and Naval Wings. Incomplete records do not make it clear whether all the earliest machines were AMC-built or whether initial deliveries were from the French parent company, either as complete airframes or as components for assembly.

465 was delivered to the Central Flying School on 11 March 1914, followed a week later by 344 to the Military Wing. Others followed, and the majority of the

services. The Shorthorn's dual control made it an ideal trainer, and it was then that AMC production of the type really got into its stride. As the RFC increased in squadron strength there was a need for further Reserve Aeroplane Squadrons. These were retitled Reserve Squadrons from 13 January 1916, and Training Squadrons from 31 May 1917. Initially these units operated a miscellany of available types, but virtually all included Shorthorns on their establishments.

Continuing orders for the type were therefore placed with AMC. Initially these were in small batches, but later orders, from 7346, were for batches of fifty (7346-7395, A324-A373, A904-A953)

his first, 23min, flight in A4113 on 27 March 1917, with Captain Binning MC as his instructor. After a further seven flights in that machine, bringing his total flying time to 3hr 2min, he went solo on 7 April. Apart from control effects, his dual instruction had concentrated on landings, twenty-two being made in those eight flights. After a further 5hr 3min solo time over the next four days, he graduated to 22 Reserve Squadron and intermediate training on Avro 504s.

It was in the Middle East that AMC-built Shorthorns saw operational service; 30 Squadron, in Mesopotamia, operated at least nine (5901, 5907-5909, 7346-7350) in support of General Townsend's offensive against the Turks that began in late 1915. The type proved to be a useful observation machine, and reconnaissance work was carried out effectively in the early stages of the campaign. When a reversal in fortunes led to the besieging of Kut, Shorthorns were among the 30 Squadron machines that attempted to deliver supplies by air. Three machines were involved (5909, 7346 and probably 7348), but were wrecked in a storm at Orah on 2 May 1916. Others soldiered on during that year, and possibly the last in front-line service was 5908, lost in a hangar fire on 14 October.

At home, the introduction of the D.H.6 and the Avro 504 in increasing numbers during 1917 marked the beginning of the end for the Shorthorn as a primary trainer. It did, however, receive two new leases of life, one successful, the other not so. The unsuccessful one involved a reversion of the type to floatplane configuration. By mid-1916 the RFC had realized the need for specialist training, and a 'School of Aerial Gunnery' was planned for Loch Doon in south-west Scotland. Vast expenditure was made in creating the new base, and it was decided to use floatplanes for gunnery practice. For whatever reason, a version of the Shorthorn was selected and AMC received an order for eight (A3295-A3302). No photograph or drawing of these is known, but if the type were similar in layout to the floatplane version of the Longhorn operated earlier by the RNAS, they would have been seriously under-powered. The RNAS was to order further floatplanes based on the Longhorn design (N1530-N1570), and these were to have the 140hp Hispano-Suiza. Perhaps the RFC Shorthorn

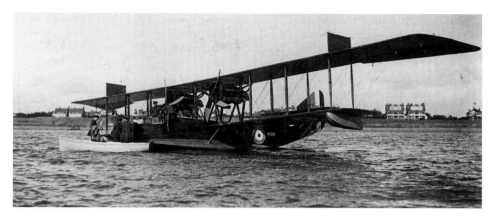

N4534 was a Felixstowe F.2A ordered from AMC but built under subcontract by May, Harden and May. Its service life was spent with 210 TDS at Calshot, and it is seen here moored at Lee-on-Solent. JMB/GSL

floatplanes were intended to have had the same powerplant. As it transpired, the Loch Doon project proved to be a disaster, and a waste of millions of pounds in construction work. Whether the Shorthorn floatplanes were actually used is a matter for conjecture. What is known is that the RFC was looking for replacements by the middle of 1917, and opted for the FBA flying boat.

The successful new lease of life for the Shorthorn was a direct result of the introduction of night bombing. Selected training depot stations were dedicated to the task of turning out pilots for Handley Page 0/400s, and their graduates passed on to two Schools of Navigation and Bomb Dropping, at Stonehenge and Andover, where they were introduced to flying with a crew. Pilots needed an introduction to night flying before being introduced to the twin-engined bomber, and F.E.2bs were selected for that task. The TDS system involved all-through training, and so an introductory type was needed. The logical move was to provide a stationary-engined pusher type, and the Shorthorn was selected. The SNBD also trained observers, and utilized the Shorthorn in a programme similar to that of the TDS.

The RNAS recognized the potential of the Shorthorn and wanted deliveries to fulfil the same roles as those of the RFC. AMC, however, were committed to RFC production, and the RNAS had to look to the parent company for its initial supplies. Later it received machines built under subcontract by the Eastbourne Aviation Co. Ltd. Some AMC-built examples did enter naval service, however: these were

machines transferred from the RFC, and they retained their military numbering. 7385, A324, A334 and A354 were transferred during 1916, all serving at the RNAS CTE at Cranwell, and a further eight, A7043-A7050, followed during the first three months of 1917. These were destined for the training school that the RNAS had opened in France, at Vendome. Twenty-seven others were transferred during the summer and early autumn of that year. The majority went to the RNAS Preliminary Flying School at Redcar, others to Manston, Chingford, Eastbourne and Eastchurch. Most did not last long. Redcar had received the first of its fourteen on 24 July and the last on 13 October. All were dismantled by the end of the year, the school having received D.H.6s as replacements.

It is doubtful whether many Maurice Farmans, Longhorn or Shorthorn, were still in service by the time of the Armistice. The Avro 504J/K was delivered in ever-increasing quantities, and the standardized training syllabus contained manoeuvres that were beyond the Farmans' capabilities. They had served a useful, if unglamorous role in a five-year career, but by 1918 the technological advances during four years of war had made them antiquated. B4674, surprisingly, was registered post-war as G-EAAZ in the civilian register, but its career in that guise was brief. With hundreds of Avro 504Ks and D.H.6s available to potential civilian operators, there was no place for the Shorthorn. None of the type was preserved by the authorities for posterity in the UK.

Airships

Holt Thomas' other early company, Airships Ltd, had been created to produce rigid airships of the French Astra Torres type. Airship production was concentrated at Merton when the aeroplane side of AMC moved to Hendon. It was 1914 before the first rigid was completed, and by then the design was dated. The company therefore turned then to non-rigids, and became involved in the development and production of a new type of machine. The German submarine menace was apparent from the earliest days of the war, and coastal patrol airships were seen as a possible panacea. The Submarine Scout airships were introduced into the RNAS from the spring of 1915. Forty-nine were eventually built, by a small range of manufacturers that included Airships Ltd. The 146ft (44.5m)-long envelope was stabilized by a pair of lateral fins and twin ventral ones. Its crew of two was carried in a B.E.2c fuselage that was suspended underneath by cables that were secured to the envelope by stitched Eta patches. Power was provided by a 75hp Renault engine. Airship Ltd's first attempt at constructing such a machine resulted in the experimental S.S.2, but that craft was not accepted into service because it did not meet operational requirements, and it was scrapped.

A major shortcoming of the S.S. design was the use of the B.E.2c fuselage as a crew car. The slipstream from the tractor-engined propeller caused discomfiture for the crew, and Airships Ltd resolved this problem on their thirteen production airships of that type, S.S.27–S.S.39. AMC supplied Shorthorn nacelles, complete with wheeled undercarriages, and the pusher configuration proved popular with crews, even though it gave a reduced top speed; later the original Renault engine was replaced by the 75hp Rolls-Royce and 110hp Berliet engines, and this restored performance. Dual control was often fitted, and this was another feature that proved popular.

Those S.S. airships produced at Merton entered service in 1915 and served operationally at such stations as Pulham, Luce Bay and Pembroke. S.S.27 did not survive for long – it was deleted on 5 August 1915 – but of the others, only S.S.38 from Luce Bay was lost on operations, on 25 February 1917; in fact

the accident involved only the car, and the envelope was fitted to the car of S.S.23 on the following day. Several S.S. airships were rebuilt, and were noted as such by the addition of the suffix letter 'A'. S.S.32A was involved in mooring experiments at Cavendish Dock, Walney Island, and S.S.34 from Barrow was used for further such experiments from 23 April 1917; it was fitted with floats from a Nieuport seaplane for these. The mooring was to an anchored pontoon. The floats may also have been an experiment aimed at preventing losses similar to that of S.S.38.

By 1917 the S.S. class was becoming outdated, and was gradually replaced at operational stations by the S.S.Z. class of craft. The older design was then relegated to training duties, with several serving at the RNAS Central Training establishment at Cranwell. Some of those training machines were rebuilt as a result of mishaps, the undercarriage unit of the type being particularly vulnerable if there was any side-slip on landing.

Flying Boats

The boat-building firm of May, Harden & May was based at Hythe, on Southampton Water, and became associated with AMC when the Hendon-based company received a contract (A.S.21558) for twenty-five Felixstowe F.2A flying boats, to be given the serial numbers N2530-N2554. During late 1917 AMC was fully occupied with D.H.4 production and the development of the D.H.9. As a consequence, the order was subcontracted to May, Harden & May, which had already received orders for ten of the type under Contract A.S.2697.

Machines built under subcontract followed the Hampshire company's own order from the production line, and were re-allocated the serials N4530-N4554, in order to bring them into the serial block allocated for large flying boats. N4530 was delivered to Felixstowe for acceptance on 14 May 1918, and the last of the order was completed that September.

The F.2A was a development of the Curtiss H.12, with a hull that had been redesigned by Commander John Porte at Felixstowe to accommodate ventral 'steps' that assisted planing prior to take-off. It also utilized a pair of the excellent Rolls-Royce Eagle VIII engines that

---

Known Allocations of SS-Class Airships Built by Airships Ltd

SS27 – Marquise June 1915 and deleted 5 August 1915.

SS28 – RNAS CTE Cranwell 1918 as SS28A.

SS29 – RNAS CTE Cranwell 1918.

SS30 – RNAS Luce Bay. RNAS CTE Cranwell 1918 as SS30A.

SS31 – RNAS Kingsnorth 1916–17. RNAS CTE Cranwell 1918 as SS31A.

SS32 – RNAS Capel 1916. Rebuilt as SS32A. RNAS Barrow 1917.

SS33 – RNAS Luce Bay. RNAS Anglesey. Rebuilt as SS33A at Wormwood Scrubbs.

SS34 – RNAS Luce Bay. RNAS Barrow. Experiments at Walney Island with Nieuport floats fitted.

SS35 – RNAS Luce Bay 1917. RNAS Anglesey. RNAS Pulham for experimental work.

SS36 – RNAS Pulham 1917. RNAS Barrow 1918 for mooring experiments. Envelope to SS32.

SS37 – RNAS Pembroke 1917. Rebuilt as SS37A. RNAS CTE Cranwell.

SS38 – RNAS Luce Bay, lost at sea 25 February 1917. Envelope to SS23.SS39 – RNAS CTE Cranwell as SS39A.

---

developed 375hp. The work of F.2A crews, particularly those from Yarmouth and Felixstowe, on long reconnaissance work over the North Sea has been well recorded in such books as *The Spider Web* and *Story of a North Sea Air Station*.

The bulk of the machines subcontracted from AMC served operationally at the two stations named above, but one or two went to 210 TDS at Calshot to act as training machines. Those used operationally had their share of adventures, with N4533, N4537, N4540, N4549 and N4550 being involved in combats with enemy seaplanes, while N4530 and N4533 made attacks on U-boats.

Some lasted into the post-war years: N4536 was still being used at Calshot during November 1922, and N4535 was at that station a year later. By that time, however, a new generation of flying boats was emerging, and it is doubtful whether any survived beyond the latter year.

CHAPTER THREE

The D.H.1 and the D.H.1A

The Competitor to the F.E.2b

The D.H.1 and its more powerful variant, the D.H.1A, were types that should have been successful operationally; however, due to a combination of circumstances, they were relegated to limited production and mainly second-line service. They were attractive aeroplanes for their size, and serve as good examples of the maxim that 'if a machine looks right, it flies right'.

The Farnborough experience had taught de Havilland that the tractor configuration was the way forward, and after his release from active duty, his first ideas for Airco designs were formulated in sketches for an armed tractor biplane. That was not what the War Office wanted, however, since the early operational experience of the RFC with the BEF in France had pointed up the

need for an armed two-seater, to act as a counter to the Albatros and Aviatics that mounted Parabellum machine-guns and were being employed in increasing numbers by the enemy. The pusher configuration would allow an unrestricted forward field of fire for an observer, and it was this layout that the authorities called for.

Development

Geoffrey de Havilland therefore abandoned his tractor design and set about work on a pusher to meet the military requirement. Simultaneously, the RAF at Farnborough was formulating its own ideas on the subject, and these were expressed in the F.E.2a. That machine had

little or nothing in common with de Havilland's original F.E.2 design.

The Airco design was rolled out during January 1915 and proved to be a compact, two-bay biplane with mainplanes of equal span. Booms of steel tubing supported the tail surfaces. The engine and crew were carried in a nacelle, whose nose and turtle decking were of aluminium. That decking fitted snugly around the cockpits, where the pilot occupied the rear. The undercarriage incorporated hydraulic and spring shock absorbers. A 70hp Renault engine provided power.

A more powerful unit had (apparently) been intended, possibly the 100hp Green, and perhaps in anticipation of a high resultant landing speed, air brakes were subsequently fitted to the nacelle of this prototype. These brakes took the form of

The prototype D.H.1 is seen here at Hendon. The cockpit coamings were very high, so that most of the crew's bodies were enclosed. Stringers were used to give slightly rounded sides to the nacelle, to which air brakes were later fitted. Shock absorbers are visible in the apices of the undercarriage V-struts, as are the pulleys for the rudder, on the lower centre-section, and for the elevators, under the upper one; these were to run cables clear of the propeller arc. Upon acquisition by the RFC, the machine became 4220. JMB/GSL

Contracts for the D.H.1 were given to Savages of King's Lynn and the earliest deliveries were as D.H.1As, with a 120hp Beardmore replacing the 70hp Renault of the original design. 4616 was such a D.H.1A and shows the revised, production-style cockpit openings, the bulkier nature of the Beardmore, with its frontal radiator, and the rounded balance area of the D.H.1A's rudder. This machine saw service with 41 Squadron at Gosport, before that unit was re-designated 27 Reserve Squadron. *JMB/GSL*

There were not enough Beardmore engines to meet demand, and output was therefore directed towards the type's rival, the F.E.2b. As a consequence, 80hp Renaults were fitted to most production machines, making them D.H.1s. This frontal view gives a good impression of the type's considerable span. *JMB/GSL*

small aerofoils that extended from either side of the nacelle and could be rotated on a lateral pivot to increase drag. They were soon removed, however.

Armament was to be in the form of a Lewis gun for use by the observer, and the mounting that de Havilland designed for it comprised a telescopic tube tensioned by rubber cords which permitted sideways movement as well as vertical. Officially it became the No. 4 Mk.1 mounting; it was later patented by de Havilland.

The type was named the D.H.1, and the company name was marked in small characters on the rudder (as 'The Aircraft Mfg Co. Ltd, London'); there was also what appeared to be a large letter H on that same surface. However, in reality the horizontal stroke of that letter was a very small 'de'. Sky Fever, de Havilland's autobiography, records that the designer had wanted the type to be known as the D.H.T1 (de Havilland-Thomas), but that the idea had come to naught.

Test-flying of the D.H.1 prototype at Hendon impressed the military. It was acquired by the RFC, to be given the serial number 4440. A further forty-nine were ordered, but by the spring of 1915, the Airco factory was committed to mass production of Farman types, and the design team under de Havilland was involved in the design of the D.H.2. Consequently, the order was sub-contracted to Savages Ltd of Kings Lynn, a firm that had no prior experience of building aeroplanes.

In the meantime, the F.E.2a had entered limited production; it had the Beardmore-built, 120hp Austro-Daimler engine as its power unit, in place of the original Green. The type proved popular with the RFC in the field, and large orders were placed for a refinement of the design, the F.E.2b.

It was not until early November 1915 that the first Savages-built D.H.1 was delivered to the AID at Farnborough. The seeming delay may have been due to the inexperience of the manufacturers, but several of the earliest machines had the 120hp Beardmore engine, and as such were designated D.H.1A. Design modifications to accommodate the new engine might also have contributed to the delay. The D.H.1A was readily distinguished from the D.H.1 by its taller engine unit, as the Beardmore was an inline while the Renault had a 'V' arrangement of cylinders and a frontal radiator. The D.H.1A also had a gravity tank under its port centre-section, to supplement the supply of fuel for its thirstier engine.

The widespread introduction of the F.E.2b and the natural desire of the RFC to standardize on a single operational type for fighter reconnaissance duties left the D.H.1 in a redundant position. It was decided to issue the type for training, and in that role the D.H.1 eventually became the machine on which prospective F.E.2b pilots gained initial experience of flying larger pusher machines.

Into Service

First deliveries were to squadrons in the process of working up for operational service. The first two production machines were delivered to 28 Sqn at Gosport, and the co-located 41 Sqn, in its original incarnation, also received the type, as did 35 Sqn at Thetford, 57 Sqn at

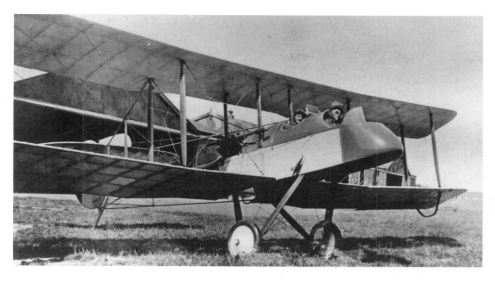

The majority of D.H.1s were issued for training, and this unidentified example is seen at Mousehold Heath, Norwich, the one-time home of 9 Reserve Squadron, which operated the type. Like most early deliveries, this machine has clear, doped fabric areas on its nacelle. JMB/GSL

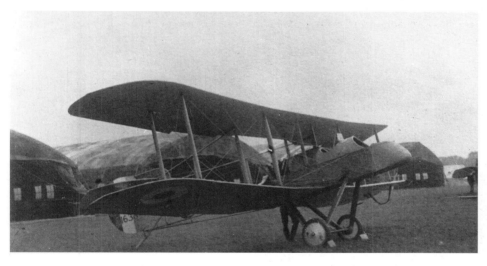

Savages built a second batch which were all D.H.1s. They were delivered in standard camouflage colours of PC 10 brown-doped fabric and battleship grey metal panels. A1638, the subject of this photograph, is seen at Yatesbury, where it served with 59 Reserve/Training Squadron. JMB/GSL

Bramham Moor (Tadcaster) and 59 Sqn at Narborough.

The supply of engines to meet airframe output was always a problem during the Great War, and the 120hp Beardmore engine was in demand for F.E.2b production. The result was that most examples of this first Airco design were delivered as D.H.1s, with the 80hp Renault as the standard engine unit. In that form, the machine was under-powered, and this was most evident in its load-carrying ability, which was

(naturally) inferior to that of the F.E.2b. The D.H.1 was slightly taller than the D.H.1A, probably the result of a small change to the dihedral angle of the wings; otherwise, the two types were identical in other principal measurements. The only other airframe difference between the two types lay in the balance portion of the rudder – the D.H.1 had a straight leading edge to this, while that of the D.H.1A was rounded and of slightly greater area.

When, belatedly in May 1916, the D.H.1A 4605 was placed in comparative

CFS tests with a similarly powered F.E.2b, the Airco design proved the better in every aspect of performance. It was some 10mph (16km/h) faster at sea level, and almost maintained that differential at 10,000ft (3,000m); also the climb to that height took twenty-seven-and-a-half minutes, just over half the time taken by its rival. The D.H.1A was also much more manoeuvrable. The only advantage exhibited by the F.E.2b was its greater load-carrying capability. After these tests were completed, 4605 went to 57 Sqn.

The D.H.1 was destined to become an intermediate trainer, and a further fifty were ordered from Savages. However, only seventy-three of the one hundred machines built were apparently issued for service use.

Hitherto, Reserve Squadrons had each operated a miscellany of types, but during late 1916, the training system was rationalized, with such units being designated as either Elementary or Higher. The Higher Reserve (Training from 31 May 1917) Squadrons were given type specialization, and those for the F.E.2b were 9 RS at Mousehold Heath (Norwich), 19 RS at Hounslow, 46 RS at Bramham Moor and 59 RS at Yatesbury. Each of these was given a mixed establishment of Henri Farman F.20s, D.H.1s and F.E.2b/ds. Thus 46 and 59 RS were intended to have six D.H.1s, six F.E.2bs and six F.E.2ds, whereas 19 RS was scheduled to have nine D.H.1s and nine F.E.2bs. Students arriving at the former from Elementary units were introduced to their intended role on the H.F. F.20, and moved to the D.H.1 for more advanced instruction before graduating to the service machines. Smaller numbers of D.H.1s served with other Reserve Squadrons, such as 6 RS at Catterick and 10 RS at Joyce Green, which were tasked with turning out D.H.2 and F.E.8 pilots.

The withdrawal of the F.E.2b/d from daylight operations during the summer of 1917, led to most of the dedicated Reserve Squadrons being re-equipped to provide D.H.4 pilots. The D.H.1s and F.E.2bs of the Training Brigade were then re-allocated to the training units that were created by the Home Defence Brigade. That organization had the responsibility of providing aircrews for both Home Defence squadrons and the light night-bombing squadrons in France, and had formed Depot Squadrons (later re-titled

A1638 received, at some point, a white-painted lower nose. It is not known whether this is a unit marking, as no documented details have survived of the markings allocated to training units. JMB/GSL

Accidents were inevitable at training units, but there were surprisingly few fatalities on the D.H.1. This example shows one that fell onto the roof of a Besonneau hangar at Yatesbury. The D.H.1 is clear-doped on all fabric surfaces, the translucence of the fabric allowing the upper mainplane cockade to show through. JMB/GSL

Specification – Airco D.H.1	
Powerplant:	70hp Renault (prototype), 80hp Renault (production); fuel capacity 30 gallons
Weights:	Empty 1,356lb (615kg); loaded 2,044lb (927kg); wing loading 4.99lb per sq ft (24kg per sq m)
Dimensions:	Mainplane span 41ft 0in (12.5m) (upper and lower); mainplane gap 5ft 7in (1.7m); chord 5ft 6in (1.68m); length 28ft 11½in (8.83m); height 11ft 4in (3.46m); tailplane span 12ft 5½in (3.8m); wing area 409.3sq ft (38sq m)
Performance:	Maximum speed 78mph (125km/h); landing speed 41mph (66km/h); climb to 3,500ft (1,068m) 11¼ minutes

Night Training Squadrons) for that purpose. Within these, the D.H.1 assumed the same intermediate role as it had in the Reserve and Training squadrons. Available photographs show that these D.H.1s were not fitted with navigation lights and under-wing brackets for Holt's magnesium flares, and so must have been used for day flying only. The principal user was 200 DS/NTS at East Retford, which acted as the preliminary night training unit, and the type proved suited to the task.

There were the inevitable training crashes, but most were minor. Some examples from 200 DS included: A1656, which ran into a Besonneau hangar; A1657, which had its undercarriage removed by a Lt McBlain on 21 September 1917, and after a speedy repair was placed on its nose by a Lt Walsh nine days later; A1647, which was completely wrecked by a Lt Brown on 16 October; and A1653, which ended in a similar state three days afterwards. In all RFC training units there were only eight fatalities on the type.

Operational Use

Not all D.H.1 service was non-operational. The Turkish threat to Egypt and the Suez Canal resulted in a build-up of air power in that region. 14 and 17 Squadrons, equipped with B.E.2cs, had been despatched to Egypt in November 1915, and it was decided to send at six D.H.1As (4606-4607 and 4609-4612) to supplement that force and to act as escort fighters.

These machines were all early production examples, and were armed with a Lewis gun on a pillar mounting in the observers' cockpits. Racks for spare ammunition drums were carried on the sides of nacelles. It would appear that 4607, at least, had a second Lewis for use by its pilots. The D.H.1As had arrived at X Aircraft Park, Alexandria, by June 1916. 4610 went to 1 Sqn Australian Flying Corps on the 28th of that month, but transferred to 14 Sqn exactly a month later. 4611 and 4612 ended up with 17 Sqn at Heliopolis, and moved with that unit to Mikra Bay and the Macedonian theatre of operations. The former machine was struck off charge on 11 October 1916, but the other survived until 13 April of the following year. The remainder of the delivery went to 14 Sqn, and the last of these was not withdrawn

Six D.H.1As were sent to the Middle East during 1916, and one of them is seen here after nosing over on its aerodrome. The gravity tank, added to supply the thirstier Beardmore engine, is visible under the upper port centre-section. JMB/GSL

Specification – Airco D.H.1A

Powerplant:	120hp Beardmore, 6 cylinder inline; fuel capacity 30 gallons
Weights:	Empty 1,672lb (758kg); loaded 2,400lb (1088kg); wing loading 5.87lb per sq ft (28.63kg per sq m)
Dimensions:	Mainplane span 41ft 0in (12.5m) (upper and lower); mainplane gap 5ft 7in (1.7m); chord 5ft 6in (1.68m); length 28ft 11¼in (8.83m); height 11ft 2in (3.41m); tailplane span 12ft 3in (3.74m); wing area 409.3sq ft (38sq m)
Performance:	Maximum speed 89mph (143km/h); landing speed 49mph (79km/h); climb to 3,500ft (1,068m) 6¼ minutes

until March 1917. It was the 14 Sqn crew of 4609 that achieved the first combat success for the RFC in the Middle East, and the only one recorded for the D.H.1A. That event occurred on 2 August 1916, when Lt A. S. C. MacLaren and Lt T. J. West claimed a Fokker that was forced to land after combat near Bir Salmana.

At home, the D.H.1 outlasted those D.H.1As sent to the Middle East. Several were in use as late as 1918, but few survived to be taken on charge by the Royal Air Force. No example of the type was preserved for posterity.

Representative Airco D.H.1 and D.H.1A with RFC and RAF Units

14 Squadron Ismailia – 4606, 4607, 4609, 4610, 4611, 4612.
17 Squadron Heliopolis/Mikra Bay – 4611, 4612.
28 Squadron Gosport – 4600, 4601.
35 Squadron Thetford – 4613, 4614, 4619.
41 Squadron Gosport – 4615, 4616, 4617.
57 Squadron Bramham Moor – 4605.
59 Squadron Narborough – 4631.
1   Squadron AFC Heliopolis – 4610.
6   RS Catterick – 4624.
8   RS Netheravon – 4603.
9   RS Norwich – 4604, 4619.
10 RS Joyce Green – 4629.

17 RS Portmeadow – A1634.
19 RS Hounslow – 4627, 4634, 4637, 4641, 4643, 4644, 4645, 4646, 4647, A5211, B3969.
35 RS Filton/Portmeadow –
46 RS Bramham Moor – A1612, A1614, A1616, A1624.
59 RS Yatesbury - A1618, A1625, A1627, A1630, A1633, A1636, A1638, A1639, A1646, A1648.
68 TS Bramham Moor – A1627.
200 DS/NTS East Retford – A1643, A1647, A1649, A1653, A1656, A1657. CFS Upavon – 4604, 4605.
    Experimental Station Orfordness –

CHAPTER FOUR

The D.H.2

The First True British Fighter

The name 'Fokker Scourge' of late 1915 and early 1916 was given to the period when Allied reconnaissance machines fell vulnerable to attack by the first generation of German armed fighting scouts, initially the Fokker E.I. The German development of a synchronization gear that allowed a fixed machine-gun to be fired forwards through the propeller arc was a significant breakthrough in the first air war, and resulted in mounting, although often exaggerated, Allied losses. The D.H.2 was one of the Allied machines that helped to defeat that 'scourge', although it was not designed specifically for that purpose. In fact, the Fokker monoplane was never as numerous

as service lore would suggest, and armed enemy two-seaters were an equal threat, one that the D.H.2 also helped to counter during 1916. Unfortunately for those who had to fly it, the D.H.2 was then retained in service after the second generation of German scouts had appeared, beginning with the Fokker D.I, then the Halberstadt D.I, and the Albatros D.I.

Then the tables were turned and losses escalated. It was not until June 1917 that the last operational D.H.2s were withdrawn from the Western Front, two years after the prototype had flown – two years that saw massive increases in aeroplane performance and armament. It says much for the pilots who flew the type

that they were still achieving combat successes at that later time.

Development

After completing the design of the D.H.1, Geoffrey de Havilland returned his thoughts to the design of a twin-engined tractor biplane and a tractor scout that would have a performance as good as, or better than, the B.S.1. Sketches of these designs show them to have been very advanced for their day, and both gave prime consideration to the pilot's field of vision and the provision of a clear field of forward fire for a machine-gun. Both also showed some D.H.1 influence – the outline shape of the tailplane on the twin tractor, and the rudder of the scout were almost identical to those of the pusher.

These ambitious schemes were laid aside during March 1915 when de Havilland returned to the pusher configuration with a new single-seat scout design, almost a scaled-down version of the D.H.1. The reasoning behind this retrograde step is not clear. In *Sky Fever*, de Havilland recalled that it was a specific counter to the early Fokker – but that machine did not appear operationally until the early summer of 1915. The Vickers F.B.5 was becoming operational by March 1915, and was to prove itself capable of countering armed German two-seaters. Perhaps it was thought that a faster, more manoeuvrable single-seater would be even more effective.

Once the initial D.H.2 design was established, work on a prototype proceeded apace. There was little innovation in the design, and this helped to speed things up. The nacelle was based around a wooden, wire-braced box-girder. An aluminium fairing formed the nose, and a rounded turtle-decking aft of the pilot's cockpit covered the fuel and oil

The unmarked D.H.2 prototype being run up at Hendon in June 1915. The original high and close-fitting cockpit opening is evident, as is the original small rudder. The whirling mass of its 100hp Monosoupape engine can be seen, and the stick is at its full rearward position to hold the tail down. via K. Kelly

That same prototype after its cockpit area had been modified to accept a Lewis gun armament. An enlarged rudder was fitted by then, with a small union flag marked on each side. The rubber aileron return cords can be seen on the upper mainplanes. JMB/GSL

The prototype was numbered 4732 and was delivered, for evaluation, to 5 Squadron. It was then marked with its serial number painted across the newly applied rudder stripes. Cockades were carried under each mainplane and on the upper centre-section. However, it was lost in action before any evaluation could be reported, and is seen here in German hands. Its captors have removed the tyres for use elsewhere, and a replacement rudder of German manufacture has been fitted. The cut-away port side of the cockpit is obvious, and it reveals the mounting for the Lewis gun. JMB/GSL

tanks. There was a high coaming around the cockpit, similar to that on the prototype D.H.1. Steel engine bearers at the rear of the nacelle carried a nine-cylinder, 100hp Gnome Monosoupape that drove a two-bladed propeller. Tall undercarriage legs carried a single axle that gave a wheel track of 4ft 10in (147mm).

The two-bay mainplanes were of equal span, the upper ones carried on a narrow centre-section of fuselage width. Each mainplane carried a single-action aileron, with the upper one having a rubber bungee return spring. Upper and lower mainplanes were interchangeable. The trailing edge of the inner bay and that of the centre-section was recessed to give clearance to the propeller.

The tail unit was carried on steel booms that led from the rear mainplane spars at the inner struts to converge at the rudder-post. The tailplane was carried on the upper booms and had a plan-form resembling that of the D.H.1. A small fin was mounted above this, and the unbalanced rudder also had a D.H.1-type shape.

The pusher configuration made for a complicated routing of the flying control

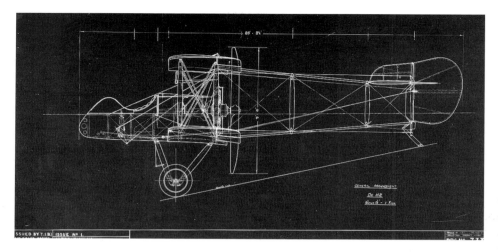

Air Board Office drawing 738 showing the production form of the D.H.2. via the author

wires. The single-action ailerons have been mentioned, and these were actuated from a crank at the forward end of the joystick control shaft via cables that led to pulleys under the lower mainplanes and thence to the aileron control horns. The upper ailerons were actuated by cables that connected them to the lower ones. Elevator action was created by external cranks that attached to a lateral rocking shaft operated from the control shaft. Cables led from those cranks to pulleys under the upper mainplanes, clear of the propeller arc, and thence to the control horns. Rudder cables were similarly led via pulleys above the lower mainplanes.

The prototype D.H.2 made its first public appearance at Hendon on 1 June 1915, the occasion of its first flight. That flight was made by Geoffrey de Havilland, who reported that the machine was tail-heavy. Subsequent flights confirmed that tail-heaviness, and also revealed that there was insufficient area to both fin and rudder. The machine was therefore modified by moving the nacelle forwards by 4in (10cm), and enlarging the vertical tail components. Thought had also been given to arming the machine with a Lewis gun. The de Havilland-patented telescopic gun mounting was added to the port nacelle longeron ahead of the pilot. Access to this demanded that the cockpit opening be enlarged.

Operational Evaluation

The D.H.2 re-emerged with these modifications completed, and performed well on further test flights, reaching a speed of 88mph (142km/h). The RFC hierarchy was aware of the D.H.2 from an early date, and arrangements were made for Captain R. Maxwell Pike of 5 Squadron to carry out an evaluation. Maxwell Pike was an experienced pilot, and he travelled from France to Hendon for that purpose. Although some minor criticisms were made, he reported favourably on the machine after flying it on 22 June; indeed, his closing remarks must have influenced the RFC command into ordering the D.H.2 in quantity: 'I have not seen a German machine which can equal this scout for speed and climbing power.'

Maxwell Pike's report to the OC 2nd Wing RFC was written after his return to France, and its enthusiasm prompted his commanding officer, Major A.G. Board, into adding a covering note that requested the allocation of the D.H.2 to 5 Squadron for operational evaluation. Surprisingly, that request was granted, and the sole example of Britain's latest scout was given the serial number 4732 and delivered to 5 Squadron on 26 July; it was marked with rudder stripes, and cockades under each mainplane and on its centre section. Maxwell Pike recorded an engagement with an Aviatik on 29 July that was frustrated by gun problems, although these did not, apparently, produce any written operational evaluation of D.H.2. By that time 4732 had had the rear decking of its nacelle modified to slope downwards aft of the fuel tank, presumably in an attempt to improve airflow over the engine and assist cooling, though it is not known whether that modification was made at unit level

as a result of operational experience. The lack of any written evaluation was unfortunate, because on 9 August, Maxwell Pike was reported missing in 4732.

He had been shot down by the crew of an Albatros two-seater of 2 Marine Feldfleiger Abteilung from Moorseele, killed by a single shot to the head, and 4732 was captured virtually intact. The D.H.2 was dismantled, transported to Moorseele and re-assembled. Its captors obviously did not know what they had laid hands on, because they referred to the machine as a 'Voisin biplane'. 4732 had overturned on landing, damaging the undercarriage, tail booms and rudder. The undercarriage and booms were repaired, and the rudder was replaced by one of local manufacture, of larger area and more rounded shape. Rubber was a precious commodity to the Germans, and 4732's tyres were removed for use elsewhere. It was exhibited to German higher authority but was apparently not flown, and therefore no documented evaluation of its operational potential was available to either side.

The RFC, however, considered the type suitable for production, and allocated the serial numbers 5335-5383 for forty-nine machines that, along with 4732, made a batch of fifty. Those numbers were allocated in the early summer of 1915 but were not taken up, possibly because they were for machines of 4732's configuration and AMC was already refining the design. Certainly, when the next order for the type was placed – Contract 87/A/36 covering one hundred machines to be numbered 5916-6015 – it was for D.H.2as. The designation never achieved currency, but the production form of the D.H.2 differed from that of the prototype.

The first production D.H.2s began leaving the Hendon factory during late November 1915. Ailerons were lengthened by one rib space, and the control cables for them were led from a quadrant at the rear of the control shaft and exited the nacelle just ahead of the lower mainplane leading edge. A gravity tank was fitted under the upper port mainplane, which increased endurance to two-and-three-quarter hours. Streamlined RAF wires replaced cable bracing, and the undercarriage was shortened, with its track increased by 11in (280mm) to improve stability on the ground. The most significant alteration was to the positioning of the Lewis gun. The nacelle decking in front of the cockpit was given a central slot in which the gun was carried on the telescopic No.4 Mk.1 mounting that allowed for upward, downward and sideways movement. A small windscreen was fitted to the gun ahead of its magazine.

The First Fighter Squadron

Even before the first production D.H.2s had left the factory, the RFC had made a significant decision about the use of the type. Hitherto, there had been no squadron with homogenous equipment of scouts; instead, such machines had been allocated in ones and twos to all squadrons, to serve in an escort role when needed. 24 Squadron, which had formed at Hounslow on 1 September 1915, was intended to be wholly equipped with the new type, and to join the BEF during February 1916. Although its first D.H.2s were allocated during November 1915, 24 Squadron did not receive any until after the New Year. Instead, several of the earliest deliveries to the RFC went to existing units of the BEF, possibly for evaluation purposes, since there were no performance reports for 4732.

5917 and 5918 were the first D.H.2s intended for the BEF, but their allocation was changed to the CFS at Upavon, possibly for comparative trials with the F.E.8, the RAF's pusher scout design. Both later joined the RFC in-the-field. 5919 was the first to reach France, arriving at 1 AD St Omer on 8 January 1916; it went to 18 Squadron at Treizennes on the following day. That squadron operated Vickers F.B.5s that also used the 100hp Monosoupape engine, and maintenance of that may have been a consideration. 5920 arrived in France three days after 5919, going to 5 Squadron, which was still at Abeele and also operating some Vickers F.B.5s. 5 Squadron also had the second F.E.8 prototype, and it is likely that both pusher scouts were allocated to the same unit to allow a comparison of the two at operational level. 5920 was returned to St Omer after a week with 5 Squadron, but that unit received a further example of the type when 5917 was delivered on 7 February; 5916 had arrived in France three weeks before, on 16 January, joining

5919 on 18 Squadron. The last of the early D.H.2s with the BEF was 5918, delivered to 11 Squadron at Bertangles on 9 February.

These early D.H.2 allocations to squadrons of the BEF gave operational pilots the opportunity to test the new type, and several used them in action. The first was probably Hereward de Havilland, then serving on 18 Squadron. He had indecisive encounters in 5919 with an Albatros and then an Aviatik on 19 January. The first D.H.2 'victory' was achieved on 5 February by Captain J.A. Cunningham of 18 Squadron, in 5916. He attacked an Albatros two-seater and forced it to land, smoking, near Carvin. Four days later Captain R. Lorraine, in 5 Squadron's 5917, attacked an Aviatik and reported his fire hitting the fuselage of the enemy machine. That day, 9 February,

also saw 24 Squadron commence operational flying.

24 Squadron had begun to replace its training machines with D.H.2s at Hounslow on 10 January. The unit had been under the command of Captain L.G. Hawker VC, DSO, since 1 October 1915, and that officer was one of the ablest and most inventive in the RFC. He had served in 6 Squadron and had been made a DSO for a determined attack on the airship station at Gontrode on 18 April 1915. His VC was awarded, less than four months later, on 24 August, and the citation noted his success in shooting down an enemy two-seater on 25 July, as well as his sustained efforts in reconnaissance work. Hawker's majority was announced on 2 February 1916, the day that he accompanied the ground party of 24 Squadron across the Channel.

Specification – Airco D.H.2	
Powerplant:	100hp Gnome Monosoupape or 110hp Le Rhone; fuel capacity 25 gallons
Weights:	Empty 943lb (428kg); loaded 1,441lb (654kg); wing loading 5.78lb per sq ft (28.24kg per sq m)
Dimensions:	Mainplane span 28ft 3in (8.62m); mainplane gap 4ft 9in (1.45m); chord 4ft 9in (1.45m; length 25ft 2$\frac{1}{2}$in (7.69m); height 9ft 6$\frac{1}{2}$in (2.91m); tailplane span 10ft 3in (3.13m); wing area 249sq ft (23.16sq m)
Performance:	Maximum speed 93mph (150km/h); landing speed 50mph (80km/h); climb to 6,000ft (1,830m) 11 minutes

8725 was 6014 during its brief period with the RNAS for evaluation. Its existence in naval service was for a mere fourteen days. F. A. Yeoman

A naval aviator in the cockpit of an unarmed 8725. F. A. Yeoman

operational loss: 5922 spun in on approach to landing at St Omer, and 2nd Lt E.A.C. Archer was killed. For those first three days the squadron had been under direct control of GHQ RFC, but it was transferred to the 12th (Corps) Wing and moved to Bertangles on the 10th.

That move was followed by ten days of practice flying, to familiarize pilots with the new area of operations. Sadly that practice was marred by another loss, when three days after arrival at Bertangles 5926 spun in near the aerodrome, killing 2nd Lt E. A. Cave.

This second loss in the same circumstances caused concern among 24 Squadron pilots regarding the safety of their new machines. At that time spinning was not on the training syllabus, and few pilots understood the procedures for recovery from one. Hawker, demonstrating his leadership, proceeded to give a demonstration of spinning the D.H.2, followed by an explanation of recovery technique. Practice at this soon allayed the pilots' fears. Hawker also realized the dangers of cold at high altitude in the D.H.2's large cockpit, and devised the fur-

The ground party had arrived at St Omer, the unit's initial base, on the 7th, and were joined there by its aeroplanes which flew across from Hounslow, via Folkestone. One D.H.2 had crashed on take-off, and another was damaged en route. Unfortunately, the squadron's first day of operations coincided with its first

Representative Airco D.H.2 with RFC and RNAS Units

5 Squadron Abeele – 4732, 5917, 5920.
11 Squadron Bertangles – 5918.
14 Squadron Deir-el-Belah, Palestine – A2623, A2628, A2629, A4788.
17 Squadron Macedonia – A2586, A4768.
18 Squadron Treizennes/Auchel/Bruay – 5916, 5919.
24 Squadron Hounslow/St Omer/Bertangles/Chipilly/Flez – 5904, 5918, 5919, 5922, 5924, 5925, 5926, 5927, 5928, 5929, 5930, 5931, 5932, 5939, 5948, 5949, 5956, 5958, 5962, 5963, 5964, 5965, 5966, 5967, 5968, 5988, 5989, 5990, 5991, 5992, 5997, 5998, 6000, 6007, 6008, 6010, 6011, 6016, 7850, 7842, 7850, 7864, 7865, 7873, 7876, 7878, 7880, 7884, 7885, 7887, 7901, 7909, 7910, 7911, 7918, 7930, A305, A2538, A2540, A2541, A2542, A2544, A2549, A2553, A2554, A2555, A2556, A2459, A2563, A2577, A2581, A2592.
29 Squadron Gosport/St Omer/Abeele/Le Hameau – 5917, 5934, 5935, 5936, 5937, 5940, 5943, 5945, 5946, 5947, 5950, 5951, 5952, 5953, 5955, 5956, 5957, 5959, 5961, 5970, 5972, 5973, 5974, 5975, 5976, 5977, 5979, 5980, 5984, 5985, 5987, 5994, 6002, 6009, 7844, 7849, 7855, 7857, 7858, 7872, 7875, 7876, 7915, 7917, 7925, 7927, 7928, 7929, A2543, A2552, A2555, A2557, A2565, A2571, A2572, A2608, A2614, A5010.
32 Squadron Netheravon/St Omer/Auchel/Treizennes/Vert Galant/Lèalvillers – 5941, 5942, 5954, 5979, 5981, 5983, 5986, 5993, 5995, 5996, 5999, 6001, 6002, 6003, 6004, 6005, 6006, 6007, 6012, 6015, 7840, 7845, 7847, 7851, 7856, 7857, 7858, 7859, 7860, 7861, 7862, 7863, 7874, 7877, 7879, 7881, 7882, 7883, 7886, 7888, 7890, 7891, 7892, 7894, 7895, 7897, 7898, 7899, 7903, 7907, 7914, 7916, 7923, 7926, 7932, 7937, 7938, 7941, A2533, A2534, A2535, A2536, A2539, A2545, A2546,

A2548, A2553, A2570, A2583, A2604, A2607, A2622, A2627, A4800, A5012, A5025.
40 Squadron Gosport – 5951.
41 Squadron Gosport –
47 Squadron Macedonia – A2584, A2586, A2616, A2617, A2619, A2625, A2631, A2632, A4764, A4765, A4766, A4767, A4768, A4769, A4770, A4771, A4772, A4774, A4776, A4777, A4781, A4782, A4784.
63 Squadron Cramlington – 7866.
111 Squadron Deir-el-Belah, Palestine – A2585, A2616, A2617, A2625, A2628, A4782.
X Flt Aqaba – A4778.
1 RS Gosport – 5921.
6 RS Catterick – 7912, 7913, A2561, A2562, A2575.
10 RS Joyce Green – 6008, 7866, 7867, A2550, A2559, A2560, A2597, A2602, A2613, A4786, A4789, A4798, A4800, A4802, A4988.
13 RS Dover – A4991.
15 RS Doncaster – A2633.
20 RS Wye – 5921.
22 RS Aboukir – A2585, A2618, A4778.
34 RS Ternhill – 7942.
45 RS South Carlton – 7886, 7940, A2538, A2588, A2609, A2620, A4796, A4992, A4993, A5034, A5035, A5051.
CFS Upavon – 5901, 5911, 5917, 5918, 5923, 5937, 5938, 5941, 5954, 5982, 6001, 7843, 7853, 7868, 7912, 7934, A2576, A4994.
Pilots School 1 AD St Omer – 5916.
1 SAF/1 SAFG/1FS Ayr & Turnberry – A5058, B8824.
2 (Aux) SAG Turnberry – 5938.

lined, thigh-length 'fug boot' to help counter that distraction. Those boots were put into production commercially and advertised in the aviation press.

D.H.2 losses through inadvertent spinning were nothing in comparison to those following engine failure. The 100hp Monosoupape had a tendency for its tappet rods to shear, a failure that at best produced irregular running, and at worst threw the metal into the propeller or tail structure. Numerous forced landings were attributed to this. More disastrous was the loss of a complete cylinder, which could result in greater airframe damage, and often fatalities. These engine problems were never satisfactorily resolved, and later, attempts were made to provide an alternative engine for the D.H.2.

24 Squadron resumed its operational flying on 20 February, and sorties became a combination of escort work for B.E.2c reconnaissance and bombing missions, and line patrols against incursions by enemy machines. 5930, 5931 and 5932 were all damaged in accidents during the first week of operations, and further mishaps during March and April caused 5927, 5928, 5948 and 5965 to require repair work. A more serious loss occurred on 25 March when 5930 failed to return from patrol: 2nd Lt O. Lerwill had been obliged to make a forced landing behind enemy lines and was made POW – and the Germans were presented with another example of the new scout.

Further Squadrons

Meanwhile, a second D.H.2 squadron was being readied for active service with the BEF: this was 29 Squadron, which had been 'working up' at Gosport under the command of Major L. Dawes. Its mobilization period began with the arrival of its first three D.H.2s (5935, 5936 and 5946) during the last week of February 1916. Others were taken on charge over the next three weeks, so that the unit had its full complement of twelve by the date of its scheduled departure for France, the 24 March.

29 Squadron's early experience with the D.H.2 was not, however, a happy one. Three of its aeroplanes were unable to start the journey to France because of engine trouble and an outbreak of illness among its mechanics. The remaining nine set out for Dover on the first leg of their flight to the continent, but only four arrived. One of the others had successfully force-landed, but the others were wrecked, with two pilots injured. The four survivors set out for St Omer: all arrived, but 5935 was crashed on landing.

The remainder of the unit had a two-week wait while replacement machines were delivered and prepared. Further misfortune followed, with 5974 being ditched in the Channel en route for France. Once collected together at St Omer, the unit moved to its operational base at Abeele – but lost another D.H.2 (5976) on the journey. When they were settled at the new base, 29 Squadron pilots began a series of familiarization flights before commencing line patrols. A further five D.H.2s were wrecked during April, including 5934 whose crash on the 24th resulted in the unit's first fatality – 2nd Lt J.E.H. Freeman.

5, 11 and 18 Squadrons had continued to operate the first four D.H.2s, with Cunningham of 18 Squadron and 2nd Lt J.D. Latta of 5 Squadron proving particularly aggressive on the type. In 18 Squadron, 5919 was wrecked on 18 February, but 5916 was not withdrawn to 1 AD until 16 April, and was used at St Omer by the Pilots School attached to the depot. 5918 went from 11 Squadron to 24 Squadron on 5 April, and 5917 left 5 Squadron for 29 Squadron on the 26th of that month.

As well as flying escort missions, the main duty allocated to the D.H.2s of 24 and 29 Squadrons was line patrol, aimed at preventing enemy reconnaissance machines observing activity behind the front line. Initially these were performed by single machines, and there were encounters with enemy aircraft. However, operational experience soon showed that engagements usually resulted in the enemy being turned back, but without a decisive result. That was largely attributed to the poor standard of gunnery, but also to the fact that return fire from two-seaters distracted the attacking pilots. Patrols were increased in strength to two, and later four machine formations, the idea being that one D.H.2 could distract the enemy while another attacked unseen.

The gunnery problem was resolved by practice – on 24 Squadron, this was on an aeroplane outline shape cut into the chalk that underlay the aerodrome. The telescopic gun mounting also contributed to inaccurate fire as the Lewis was not braced against its recoil action, and another 24 Squadron innovation was a clamp that could hold the weapon steady, and yet be released if the operator needed to fire outside the line of flight.

Gunsights were also introduced. Some of the more aggressive members of 24 Squadron experimented with fitting twin Lewis guns to their D.H.2s during the spring of 1916, including Lts J.O. Andrews, N.P. Manfield and A.M. Wilkinson. For some reason both the clamp and the twin gun armament were frowned upon by higher authority – but were still used surreptitiously. Not all pilots liked the central positioning of the Lewis gun, as it interfered with forward view, and some machines – for example 5929 – had the central 'slot' faired over and the gun repositioned to starboard.

On other machines – such as 5930 – the Lewis was clamped externally to the upper port longeron, and the twin gun installation may have been a variation on this (there is no photographic evidence to corroborate this). The 97-round 'double drum' was not initially available, and many pilots found the single 47-round magazine too readily exhausted. As a consequence, the fitting of an external rack for spare magazines, on the nacelle outside the cockpit, became a widespread modification to the D.H.2.

A potentially dangerous airframe defect of the D.H.2 was soon revealed, namely that the lower longeron of the nacelle had a tendency to split at the point where the forward undercarriage strut was attached, a failure no doubt caused by the shock the frame received when the plane landed. Fortunately, its early discovery meant that remedial action was taken before any accident could result, namely the fitting of reinforcing plates and bolts around the longeron at the weak point.

Many of the early combats by both 24 and 29 Squadron pilots resulted in moral victories only, with enemy machines being 'driven off' or 'driven down' without any confirmation of either damage or destruction. What soon became evident, however, was the superiority of the D.H.2 over the Fokker monoplane, especially in terms of manoeuvrability. Probably the first destruction of an enemy machine occurred on 2 April, when 2nd Lts S.J. Sibley (5948) and D.M. Tidmarsh (5924) of 24 Squadron brought down an Albatros C type. The squadron had limited contact with the enemy during the remainder of

5954 was a typical early-production D.H.2; it was issued to 32 Squadron prior to that unit seeing operational service. This photo shows it unarmed, on 16 January 1917, during a period when it served with the CFS at Upavon. It retained the original two-bladed propeller. Its upper surfaces were left in natural finish, but the metal panels of the nacelle were doped in PC10 Khaki. *JMB/GSL*

6001 also served with 32 Squadron, but on an operational basis. It had the four-bladed propeller that was soon introduced. Here, attention is being given to its nasal area – the aluminium nose panel can be seen on the ground below the machine. 6001 was returned to the UK after use by 32 Squadron, and went to the CFS on 25 January 1917. It crashed on 20 February, killing 2nd Lt J.L. Fry. *JMB/GSL*

that month, although an escort mission on the 25th by Lts Andrews, Manfield and Wilson provided some excitement when three Fokkers attempted to intervene. The D.H.2 pilots drove off the attacking machines, one of which received eleven hits, its pilot being the noted Ltn Max Immelmann. 5968 crashed during an engine test on the 28th, killing Captain E.H. Mitchell; but Tidmarsh, in 5965, provided a boost for the squadron when two days later his aggressive flying caused a Fokker to fall out of control and crash into housing at Bapaume – without Tidmarsh firing a single shot!

On 4 May, 2nd Lt S.E. Cowan of 24 Squadron, in 5966, caused a two-seater to land, and fired on its crew as they ran from the machine. Then on 16 May, Captain A.M. Wilkinson claimed two 'hits', sending an AGO C type and a Fokker E type down, out of control; these were the first of ten accredited 'victories' that would make him the top-scoring D.H.2 pilot. On this occasion he was also using 5966. 24 Squadron continued this successful run on the 20th when Tidmarsh (5965) and Lt D. Wilson (5918) destroyed an LVG and an Albatros C type respectively, with the LVG falling in flames.

May was a quiet month for 29 Squadron. It opened its scoring on the 1st, when Lt H.O.D. Seagrave (5977) drove an Aviatik down into a forced landing with at least one of its crew wounded; Seagrave was later to achieve greater fame as the holder of both the world land- and water-speed records. Then on 19 May Sgt J. Noakes (noted post war for his 'crazy flying') used 5961 in a possibly decisive combat with an LVG. But ten days later the unit had its first operational fatality, when 5946 was shot down in combat and Captain E.W. Barrett killed.

The RNAS showed an interest in the type, possibly because of difficulties in obtaining greater numbers of the Nieuport 11, that it already had. Accordingly, 6013 and 6014 were allocated for transfer from the RFC to that service. 6013 was scheduled to be at Guston Road, Dover, by 20 May, but its transfer did not take place. 6014's did, and it was renumbered 8725, in a serial block reserved for RNAS machines, and delivered to the RNAS site at Hendon for an evaluation that took place on 28 May. The upshot of this was that RNAS authorities decided against the acquisition of further examples, and

8725 was returned to the RFC at Farnborough.

The date of 28 May was also when the third, and final, fully equipped D.H.2 squadron joined the BEF, namely 32 Squadron. It had had a long 'working up' period at Netheravon, a period that had been extended because larger numbers of the type and its pilots had had to be replaced in 24 and 29 Squadrons than had been anticipated. A few D.H.2s had been received by April, but it was not until 20 May that the squadron had its allotted total of twelve. It was also issued with a pair of Vickers E.S.1s for evaluation. The unit's machines, led by its CO Major L.W.B. Rees MC, left for St Omer on the 28th; five had the journey interrupted with engine trouble. By 4 June the squadron and all its machines was temporarily established at Auchel, before moving to Treizennes three days later.

Operational experience had led to some airframe and equipment modifications. The position of the gravity tank under the port upper mainplane necessitated a long feed-run to the carburettor, and so its position was transferred to the upper surface, at first further inboard on the mainplane, and then above the centre-section. Some machines had a balance cable that ran via pulleys across to the top surface of the upper mainplane, added as a replacement for the bungee return cords to the upper ailerons.

Variations in machine-gun mountings have been mentioned, but it would seem that the centrally mounted Lewis was eventually more or less fixed to the line of flight. The central slot in the nacelle

L.W.B. Rees – the Victoria Cross Winner

L.W.B. Rees, VC. Frank Cheeseman

Lionel Wilmot Brabazon Rees was a professional soldier, with eleven years' service, most of it in Africa, when the First World War broke out. He was still a Lieutenant when he learned to fly, at his own expense, during 1913, and requested a transfer to the RFC. That request was granted in August 1914 and was followed by a posting to the Central Flying School at Upavon, where Rees became a flying instructor. A further posting to 7 Squadron at Netheravon saw him become a flight commander, and his flight became the nucleus of 11 Squadron when that unit formed on 14 February 1915.

Rees went to France with 11 Squadron, which had equipped with the Vickers F.B.5 Gunbus, and he became one of the more aggressive pilots in that famous unit. He was credited with driving down four enemy machines, destroying another and causing a sixth to be captured. His gunner on many of his flights and in five of his successful combats was Flight Sergeant J.M. Hargreaves. His actions brought the award of a Military Cross. Rees was posted home to the CFS in November 1915 and promoted to Major the following month. On 1 February 1916 he assumed command of 32 Squadron and steered that unit through its mobilization period and its initial active service. After his wounding in action on 1 July, he was posted home. His recuperation was followed by a posting to the command of 1 School of Aerial Fighting at Ayr and, as a Lieutenant Colonel, he commanded 1 Fighting School at Turnberry, when 1 SAF merged with 2 (Auxiliary) School of Aerial Gunnery. He was granted a permanent commission in the peacetime RAF and rose to the rank of Group Captain, having also been awarded the Air Force Cross. He commanded units in the Middle East before leaving the service in 1931. Having been made an OBE, Rees died in 1955.

front was faired over, and the gun raised to the upper limit of the No. 4 Mk.1 mounting. Some lateral movement may have been possible, but a downward chute for ejected cartridge cases was installed, supporting the idea that the gun was fixed. And because there was a chance that those cases might strike the propeller, a small fairing that acted as a collector bin was also added; this became evident on D.H.2s from the summer of 1916. The supply of 97-round magazines for the Lewis gun dated from about that period, and was welcomed by pilots whose offensive actions had been curtailed when the loads of the 47-round version had been quickly exhausted.

Operations in the Summer of 1916

Fine weather at the start of June 1916 soon gave way to unsettled conditions that prevented much flying. Conditions improved on the 8th, however, and both 29 and 32 Squadrons were out – but only to suffer casualties. Captain A.C. Clarke of the former unit was wounded in combat with an enemy machine while flying 5976, and 32 Squadron suffered its first combat loss when 6005 was wrecked in a forced landing, with 2nd Lt R.A. Stubbs fatally wounded.

Further inclement weather followed, but cleared by the 17th, and then 24 Squadron had a very successful day. Lt G.H. Gray forced an enemy machine to a crash-landing, the D.H.2 pilot then firing into the wreckage. Captain A.M. Wilkinson (in his usual 5966) continued his successful run by sending a Fokker monoplane down to crash, and then forced an Albatros C type to land. He attacked a third E.A., but it managed to reach its own aerodrome. Wilkinson used the same D.H.2 on the following day to destroy another E.A., one of six that were attacking F.E.2bs of 23 Squadron. 2nd Lt W. E. Nixon of 32 Squadron was wounded that day, and 5983 damaged, as he attacked a formation of five Aviatiks. But then Wilkinson made his own successes three in a row by sending a Fokker monoplane down out of control on the 19th.

Three days later, however, 32 Squadron lost 6003, though 2nd Lt O.V. Thomas escaped unhurt from a crash-landing

after the machine had been hit. The final eventful D.H.2 combat of June occurred on the 28th, a day of increased enemy air activity. Lt N.P. Manfield of 24 Squadron confirmed the D.H.2's superiority over the Fokker when he sent one down in an apparently disintegrating condition.

1 July 1916 will always be remembered as the opening day of the Somme bloodbath, but it was also the day on which a D.H.2 pilot won the Victoria Cross. An enemy formation of eight to ten machines had been reported, and these were intercepted by a patrol led by Major W.L.B. Rees MC in 32 Squadron's D.H.2 6015. Rees single-handedly attacked a sub-formation of four, driving them off but being wounded in the process. His squadron had already had a casualty that

captured virtually intact. Four days later, on the 15th, Lt G.H. Lewis (7859) scored the first of his two 'victories' for 32 Squadron, destroying another Fokker E type; he was helped in this by an F.E.2b crew from 25 Squadron.

Although a majority of patrols were inconclusive, the D.H.2 squadrons were by then confident of their machines' superiority over the enemy, and had proved that they were more than a match for the Fokker E types. This was shown by a growing aggression, with solitary D.H.2s being noted as taking on formations of enemy machines with seeming impunity. 2nd Lt J. Godlee (7874) of 32 Squadron was, however, fatally wounded in destroying one of the monoplanes on 19 August – but then 24 Squadron showed the way on the 20th,

7850 was a later production machine that was delivered in PC10 camouflaged upper and side surfaces, with a small cockade marked on each side of the nacelle. A rack for spare ammunition drums is fitted below the cockpit opening, and a collector bin for spent cartridge cases has been added below the nose. It was photographed at 2 AD Candas, before delivery to 24 Squadron. JMB/GSL

day – Captain S.G. Gilmour (6002), who had been wounded in action. The increased enemy activity attracted 24 Squadron, and Lt S.E. Cowan added to his existing 'victory' by sending a C type out of control.

On the 'down' side, that unit lost Lt D.H. Gray on the 3rd, when 7850 was hit by AA. The D.H.2 squadrons undertook many escort missions for bombing raids, though clashes with the enemy were few. A solitary 32 Squadron machine avoided one such encounter with three Fokkers on the 9th; but on the 11th, 2nd Lt C. Kerr of 24 Squadron was brought down in 6011, the pilot made POW, and the D.H.2

when a patrol of four took on an eleven-strong enemy formation, dispersing it while destroying three of its number. Furthermore, the unit followed up this success on the next day, when five D.H.2s dispersed a ten-strong formation, and after being joined by Major Hawker, did the same to another of four machines. Lt Pither was reported to have shot at a downed enemy with Buckingham ammunition, suggesting that the D.H.2s were also looking for enemy observation balloons.

A later patrol by the squadron that day saw three D.H.2s team up with a Morane Parasol and a pair of F.E.2bs to disperse

7851 was marked across its centre-section, as 'C-1' of 32 Squadron. Its gravity tank was placed centrally above the centre-section, and it had the refinement of double-action ailerons – the balance cable for these can be seen running above the upper mainplanes. The wheel discs are marked in a dark colour, probably red, and have a small white central dot. This D.H.2 was lost in action on 7 January 1917. JMB/GSL

fifteen E.As. Lt S.E. Cowan continued the unit's run of success by single-handedly driving off five enemy machines on the 27th; and he followed that achievement two days later with the destruction of a Roland C.II with fire from 6000. That E.A. had been one of four that tangled with an equal number of 24 Squadron machines. 32 Squadron was also in action that day, claiming no successes, and indeed having 2nd Lt E. Lewis (6002) wounded in combat. But July ended with a further 'victory' for 24 Squadron, when Lt R. H. M. S. Saundby (5967) sent a Fokker out of control; however, he was slightly wounded in the process.

The D.H.2 was in its heyday during August 1916. By that time the pilots of the three active squadrons were confident in the capabilities of their mounts, and willing to tackle enemy machines whenever possible. The month was to see those units continue their run of success, with minimal casualties. 24 Squadron had become the most successful of the three, and on 3 August one of its patrols attacked seven E.As. Captain J.O. Andrews (5925) was credited with sending one out of control, and Lt S.E. Cowan (5904) another. 29 Squadron was equally successful three days later, with 2nd Lt W.V. Sherwood (5976) sending down an L.V.G. Lt Yates of 24 Squadron took on two from a group of five E.As on

the 7th, apparently wounding or killing the observer of one. However, 7878 from the same unit was damaged on the following day, 2nd Lt H.C. Evans having attacked a formation of four enemy machines and sustaining return fire, and 5998 on the next when S.E. Cowan was wounded.

On the 'up' side, 32 Squadron claimed its first positive 'victory' for August on the 11th, Captain H.W.G. Jones (7859) sending down a Fokker monoplane. But the unit lost two machines on the 12th, when Captain S.G. Gilmour wrecked 7894 in a forced landing, having been hit by AA shrapnel, and Sgt E.H. Dobson was shot down and killed in 6015. Also, Captain R.E.A.W. Hugh-Chamberlain was wounded during a combat in 5929 four days later. However, the squadron had a moral victory on the 21st, when a patrol attacked ten bomb-carrying E.As and prevented their mission, the enemy jettisoning the bombs, some of which fell in German lines. 24 Squadron had a more tangible claim the following day, with Captain A.M. Wilkinson destroying an enemy C type, with assistance from 2nd Lts H.A. Wood and S.J. Sibley.

2nd Lt W.G.S. Curphey (7851) opened his score as a 32 Squadron pilot on the 22nd when he sent an L.V.G. down out of control. Sibley was slightly wounded on the 25th, but 29 Squadron was more

unlucky, losing 5994 when it came down after combat with enemy scouts; 2nd Lt K.K. Turner was made POW. On the 28th, Wilkinson (7880) destroyed another E.A. – and then on the 31st, he joined with 24 Squadron in a day of epic achievement. First, Captain J.O. Andrews and Lt A.E. Glew fought a half-hour combat with three enemy scouts of a new design that were superior in speed and climb rate; only the manoeuvrability of the D.H.2s saved them.

After the enemy had withdrawn, the British pair attacked another of the same type, seeing it descend in a steep dive. Wilkinson (again in 7880) and Lt R.S. Capon (7873) then attacked eleven Roland C.IIs that were engaging a formation of F.E.2bs and B.E.12s, and Wilkinson sent one down – but Capon was wounded and forced to return home. Wilkinson then found and attacked an L.V.G., sending it out of control – even as he was attacked by another four Rolands. He retaliated and the E.A. made off, but 7880 had been damaged: two struts and two main spars had been shot through, and six bracing wires cut. Nevertheless, his 'victory' tally had reached ten, and that placed him as the leading exponent of the D.H.2, even though the type was to remain in front-line service for another eight months.

The 100hp Gnome Monosoupape 9B

Monosoupape translates as single valve, and the 100hp Gnome engine of that name was seen as a useful aero engine during the first half of the First World War. Developed from pre-war engines by its designers at the Société des Moteurs Gnôme et Rhône, it was an air-cooled rotary engine that, not needing a water jacket, offered a relatively high power-to-weight ratio. The engine weighed only 270lb (122kg) 'dry'. Its nine cylinders distributed stress via a firing order of 1, 2, 3, 4, 5, 7, 9, 2, 4, 6, 8. Induction was via the crankcase and the single valve was for exhaust only. That valve was operated by a central, frontal push-rod, activated via a cam on the stationary crankshaft. Ignition was via a single spark plug on each cylinder. Fuel consumption was 72lb (33kg) per hour, and lubrication needed a quarter of that figure. The engine was used in a variety of designs, both French and British, was built under licence in Britain, America and Italy. Its drawbacks were tendencies to shed cylinders and suffer from the shearing of push-rods, both liable to cause significant, if not fatal, airframe damage.

Improving Enemy Opposition

The new design of E.A. engaged by Andrews and Glew was the Albatros D.I., and its arrival at the front signified the beginning of the end for the D.H.2's supremacy as a scout. The Albatros scout, along with other D types from Fokker and Halberstadt, was issued in increasing numbers, and as the air war escalated during September, their presence was soon felt. 32 Squadron lost 7895 on 2 September, Captain R.E. Wilson falling victim to a Fokker D.III flown by Ltn Oswald Boelcke, the CO of the newly formed Jasta 2. On the other hand, 24 Squadron had more luck that day, Captain Andrews and Lts Glew and Byrne each sending down an enemy machine, one of which crashed. The unit was in action again the next day, with Lt A.G. Knight (5931) claiming success – but 2nd Lt H.C. Evans (7887) was killed in combat with three enemy machines. On the same day, 2nd Lt N. Brearley attacked an enemy kite balloon using a clever ruse: approaching at over 11,000ft (3,350m), he put 5961 into a series of manoeuvres that made it look as though he had lost control, to fool ground gunners, and descended to 1,500ft (460m) before diving to fire at his target. He was carrying Buckingham ammunition, which set the balloon alight. His unit colleague, 2nd Lt G. H. Bowman was lucky that day, his D.H.2 (5984) touching a Fokker E.III during combat, with a resultant loss of aileron control. Bowman made a careful – and successful – return to base.

A patrol of three from 32 Squadron, led by Curphey, ambitiously attacked thirteen E.A. on 5 September – but they lost 2nd Lt E.F. Bainbridge (7916), who was killed. The following day saw the first success in a distinguished combat career for J.T.B. McCudden, who had joined 29 Squadron almost a month earlier as a Flight Sergeant pilot. In 5985, he attacked an Aviatik at 14,000ft (4,270m) and sent it down to crash. 24 Squadron was also active that day, claiming another two enemy machines, one crashed and one out of control. However, on the 7th the unit's 6010 was damaged, although it claimed an enemy driven down; but a patrol of its sister unit on the Somme, 32 Squadron, drove off an enemy formation. On the 9th, a four-machine patrol of the latter unit almost lost Captain L.P. Aizlewood when he hit the tail of an enemy during combat, breaking the undercarriage and propeller of his D.H.2 and damaging its tail booms. Aizlewood was lucky to land safely: his opponent crashed. 24 Squadron had the misfortune to meet Jasta 2 that day and lost 2nd Lt N.P. Manfield (7842) to Oswald Boelcke. That unit lost 7901 (Lt L.R. Briggs) on the 11th, and 7873 two days later, the latter falling to Boelcke; its pilot, 2nd Lt J.V. Bowring, was made POW.

There was some redress on the 14th when Sergeant S. Cockerell and Lt A.G. Knight sent a Fokker D.II down in flames, and more when Lt Byrne sent down another on the 15th. Knight scored again that day, and a further 'flamer' was credited to 2nd Lt Mare-Montembault in A2539 of 32 Squadron. 2nd Lt S.E. Cowan (5964) got another in flames for 24 Squadron on the 16th, and a patrol from the unit crashed yet another the next

day. Further north, 2nd Lt G.T.R. Hill (7939) of 29 Squadron flamed a balloon on the 21st, while two more enemy machines were claimed by 24 Squadron, one shared with a 32 Squadron D.H.2. And there was more action the next day, when Captain H.W.G. Jones scored his second 'victory' in 32 Squadron; 24 Squadron was less fortunate, however, having a pair of D.H.2s (7910 and 7911) damaged in combat. Further successes were claimed on the 26th and 28th by 32 Squadron. At the end of the month, however, 2nd Lt C.P.V. Roche of 24 Squadron was wounded in combat. Thus September had seen continued success for the D.H.2, but a rise in combat casualties.

The occasional attack on enemy kite balloons, such as that by Brearley, relied on the use of Buckingham incendiary ammunition to ignite the gas-bag. A French innovation of 1916 was the Le Prieur rocket. Named after their inventor and resembling the firework variety, these rockets were carried in launching tubes attached to interplane struts, and were fired electronically. Attempts were made to fit the weapon to the D.H.2, an early fitting being made to 5956 of 29 Squadron during late September. However, the rockets were erratic in flight and very inaccurate, and so their use was limited.

29 Squadron claimed another balloon on 1 October, 2nd Lt I. Curlewis (A2551) using Buckingham ammunition, as was traditional, to destroy that target. 32 Squadron was heavily engaged that day, and although able to claim two E.A.s, two of its machines (7892 and A2533) were shot down. Both pilots survived, though A2533 (Captain H.W.G. Jones) became another of Boelcke's victims. Unsettled weather precluded most patrol work for more than a week, but both 24 and 32 Squadrons were in action on the 10th – and both suffered. The former lost A2540 (2nd Lt N. Middlebrook: POW) and A2556 (Sergeant S. Cockerell: wounded), and 32 Sqn lost A2539, miraculously force-landed by Mare-Montembault after its controls had been shot away. All three had tangled with machines from Jastas 1 and 2. From 24 Squadron, 2nd Lt W.E. Nixon (5965) was wounded on the 15th and lost A2542 on the following day, and Lt P.A.L. Byrne was killed as Boelcke continued a successful run against the D.H.2. As consolation, J.O. Andrews had been credited with a success on the 16th, and A.G. Knight drove down two E.A. on

the 18th. 29 Squadron had been having a relatively quiet month, but lost 2nd Lt J.N. Holthom (5952) on the 22nd, the D.H.2 falling to a machine from the new-formed Jasta 5.

24 and 32 Squadron had more luck that day, encountering formations of enemy two-seaters and successfully dispersing them, claiming two 'victories' each. A combat on the 26th revealed that the D.H.2, properly handed, could hold its own in the right circumstances. Five of 24 Squadron took on about twenty E.A. in three formations that included Halberstadt scouts, and by committing the enemy to a 'dogfight', the manoeuvrability of the D.H.2 compensated for its lack of speed, and the patrol was able to return to base with claims of five enemy 'driven down'. The only D.H.2 casualty was A2549 whose pilot, Lt K. Crawford, was wounded. The patrol had included Lt A.G. Knight and Lt McKay, and that pair was involved in a combat two days later that saw the death of Boelcke. They were attacked by more than six E.A.s, and these were re-enforced by a further six – and two of the enemy collided in the ensuing melee, one crashing and killing the great German pilot. The British pair held out for twenty minutes until the enemy withdrew.

The persistent problems caused by the 100hp Monosoupape engine led to the trial installation of a 110hp Clerget 9Z, reportedly in 5994 during June 1916. That installation must have proved impractical because a further attempt at improving performance was made, namely the fitting of a 110hp Le Rhone in an un-numbered D.H.2, received at 1 AD St Omer during the last week of October. It is not known whether the machine was a private Airco venture, but its lack of a serial suggests so. That lack was made good by 1 AD, whose painters applied the number A305 from the block of numbers reserved for aeroplanes acquired from French sources. That may have been the unidentified D.H.2 with the same engine installation that was tested at the CFS, Upavon. At least two further attempts were made to mate that engine to the D.H.2 airframe but none was successful, the performance of machines so equipped being inferior to that of the Monosoupape version, due no doubt to the Le Rhone's greater weight and because increased fuel tankage had to be provided for the thirstier engine. A305 was therefore subsequently re-engined

with a Monosoupape; it went on to serve, with some distinction, in 24 Squadron until it was lost in action on 21 March the following year. Those attempts at improving performance by upgrading the engine were abandoned, but an earlier modification was adopted: the original two-bladed Integrale 70 propeller was replaced with the four-bladed T7928 type that had been adopted for the F.E.8.

November began with mixed fortunes for the D.H.2. Captain J.O. Andrews (5998) claimed 24 Squadron's first 'victory' for that month by destroying a Halberstadt D.II on the 2nd; but also on that day 32 Squadron lost A2546, when 2nd Lt R. H. Wallace was wounded in combat, and the machine was wrecked in the ensuing crash. Poor weather then curtailed operations for much of the next week, but on the 9th, Lt A.G. Knight (A305) added to 24 Squadron's score with a 'victory' over an enemy scout. 29 Squadron, however, was much less fortunate that day, losing four machines to enemy scouts. 2nd Lt N. Brearley force-landed 7928 in no-man's-land after being wounded, and spent a nervous four or more hours waiting for dark and the opportunity to reach British lines, which he did. Captain A.C. Bolton (7915), and 2nd Lts I. Curlewis (A2543) and H.A. Hallam (7925) all tangled with Albatros D.I/D.IIs of Jasta 1, and were all brought down to become POWs.

Lt A.E. McKay (7884) continued 24 Squadron's successful run on the following day, when a 32 Squadron patrol failed to finish an enemy two-seater, as its observer took control when its pilot was hit. A further spell of poor weather followed, but on the 16th both 24 and 32 Squadrons had successes. During the course of a patrol by the former, 2nd Lt E.C. Pashley (7930) sent an enemy scout down, and then Captain S.G. Long (A305) followed suit with a Roland C.II. Captain H.W.G. Jones (7882) of 32 Squadron combined with Lts M.J.J.G. Mare-Montembault (7899) and P.B.G Hunt (7938) to send a pair of two-seaters down, out of control.

17 November was a much less happy day. 24 Squadron lost A2577 when 2nd Lt W.C. Crawford was killed in combat with Jasta 2; and a pair of 29 Squadron machines collided when attacking the same enemy machine: Captain S.E. Cowan (A2555) had recently been promoted to flight commander and transferred from 24 Squadron, and had

just sent an enemy scout down when he hit A2565 (2nd Lt W.S.F. Suandby). Both were killed. 32 Squadron was also active that day, with 2nd Lt M.J.J.G. Mare-Montembault (again in 7899) claiming a C type out of control. That 'victory' for his squadron was countered five days later, when Lt R. Corbett (A2607) was brought down as a POW, probably by an Albatros scout of Jasta 1. Furthermore, RFC morale suffered even more on the following day.

Hawker was one of the RFC's greatest assets, a skilled leader of men and a technical innovator. His duties as 24 Squadron CO prevented him from participating in most patrols, and it is a fact that he did not add to his 'victory' tally of seven after taking over the unit. He had participated in a patrol of five D.H.2s on 31 July that broke up a ten-machine enemy formation; but the nature of air fighting was changing by the late autumn of that year, and it may be that he was unused to the opposition then being encountered. He joined a defensive patrol on 23 November, alongside Captain J.O. Andrews and Lt R.H.M.S. Saundby. The patrol attacked two enemy machines, which followed them into German airspace. It was then unfortunate to encounter eight Albatros D.Is of Jasta 2. Hawker became involved in a combat with the rising 'star' of the enemy unit, Ltn M. Fr von Richthofen. The German had the advantages of doubled firepower, speed, and therefore height.

Hawker made for the lines, using the tighter turning circle of the D.H.2 (5964) to evade repeated attacks by the Albatros. Edging nearer to safety in a fight that lasted more than thirty minutes, Hawker had almost made it when his engine began to miss. He put the nose of the D.H.2 down to gain speed, and made straight for the lines. This was the first opportunity of a straight shot that had been presented to Manfred von Richthofen, and he took it immediately: thus Hawker was shot dead, counting as the German's eleventh combat 'victory'. Hawker was not the only 24 Squadron loss that day: 2nd Lt H.B. Begg had failed to return from an earlier patrol, having being shot down and killed in A2554 while escorting an F.E.2b reconnaissance by 22 Squadron.

Inclement weather then predominated for more than a week, virtually preventing patrols and allowing 24 Squadron to come to terms with its loss. However, another unnecessary D.H.2 loss occurred on 26

November when 2nd Lt W.B. Clark was made POW in 5947: he had been ferrying the machine from Abeele to Bertangles when he landed on the wrong side of the lines.

24 Squadron was back in the fray on 11 December, when Captain S.H. Long (A305) and 2nd Lt E.C. Pashley (7930) combined with a 22 Squadron F.E.2b crew to destroy an Albatros D.I. 32 Squadron was also active that day, but lost 5986, Lt B.P.G. Hunt being taken as a wounded POW – another of von Richthofen's victims. Poor weather again set in, but on the 16th, Captain A.G. Knight of 29 Squadron (A2614) sent down an Albatros D type out of control.

The morale effects of that encounter were short-lived, however, because four days later the squadron suffered the loss of Knight, in 7927, to von Richthofen. On that same day 29 Squadron pilot 2nd Lt W.K.M. Britton (A2614) was wounded, and two other D.H.2s damaged in combat: 5956 (2nd Lt A.N. Benge) and A2552 (2nd Lt H.B. Hurst). S.H. Long of 24 Squadron continued to use A305 as his usual mount, and claimed an enemy two-seater on Boxing Day, sharing the credit with 2nd Lt F. Rr Sedgwick. However, that success had to be set against the loss of 2nd Lt E.L. Lewis, who was killed in 7885, probably by an Albatros pilot of Jasta Boelke. Nevertheless, Captain S.H. Long continued a successful run on the following day, sending down an Albatros D.II with fire from 7930.

Thus concluded the year's successes for the D.H.2.

The Final Months of Service

The build-up of the German fighter force over the winter of 1916-17, and the quality of its equipment, were beginning to place the British air services at an even greater disadvantage. New scout types for the RFC were in the pipeline, Nieuport 17s were being delivered from the French, and the first Sopwith Pup unit had arrived during December – but the three D.H.2 squadrons, along with two of F.E.8s, had to soldier on and fulfil the offensive stance demanded by Trenchard. Despite this, the New Year started quite well.

The weather conditions for much of January 1917 prevented flying, but patrols

were sent out whenever conditions allowed. Thus patrols from 24 and 32 Squadrons went out on the 5th and each suffered a pilot wounded in combat, Lt W.F.T. James (A2581) and Lt D. Faure respectively. 32 Squadron was in action two days later, with a patrol encountering a formation of the enemy. One of the German machines was hit, but 2nd Lt E.G.S. Wagner in 7951 was reported missing, and later as killed. A period of cloud and snow followed that lasted until the 20th, preventing patrol work although some practice flights were possible. 2nd Lt G.A. Exley of 29 Squadron was killed in 7929 during one of these on the 14th. Conditions had improved by the 23rd, when a 24 Squadron patrol encountered the enemy, and Lt. E.C. Pashley, in his usual 7930, forced an Albatros D.II to crash-land in British-held territory.

The squadron repeated this success the following day when Captain H.A. Wood (7918) and Lt A.E. McKay (7884) forced an Albatros C type down and its crew was captured. The growing aggression of the enemy was clearly manifested by the fact that these machines had been operating over the British lines, as they were on the 25th, when 24 Squadron notched up a third successive 'victory', Captain S.H. Long (A305) sending an L.V.G. down in flames, its crew being seen to jump or fall out. That same pilot, in the same D.H..2, repeated his success two days later, when a seven-strong 32 Squadron patrol, led by Captain L.P. Aizlewood, also destroyed a C type. Recently commissioned 2nd Lt J.T.B. McCudden MM had rejoined 29 Squadron on 21 January, and five days later claimed his second 'victory' when he used 7858 to destroy an enemy two-seater. Lt A. N. Benge of the same unit secured the final January success for the D.H.2 on the 29th.

February was another month of mixed fortune for the D.H.2 squadrons. 29 Squadron lost Captain A.P.V. Daly on the 1st, his D.H.2 (A2614) falling to Ltn W. Voss after an engagement with Albatros scouts of Jasta Boelke; Daly was taken POW. McCudden, again in 7858, and Major A.W. Grattan-Bellew somewhat compensated for his loss when on the following day they shared the destruction of an enemy C type. 32 Squadron was also in action that day, though they were less fortunate: they lost A2570 in a combat with nine E.A.s, and 2nd Lt H. Blythe was fatally wounded. Two days later 24

Squadron fared better, Captain H.W. von L. Poellnitz sending one enemy aircraft out of control, and Lts E.C. Pashley and R.H.M.S. Saundby sharing in the destruction of another. A third was claimed jointly by 2nd Lt S. Cockerell (A2541), Lt Begbie (A2544) and Lt Evans (A2563). A 32 Squadron patrol was also in action that day, with Captain W.G.S. Curphey (A2536) claiming an Albatros D.II. Combat damage to its machines forced the patrol home, but Curphey went out again and destroyed a second enemy scout, although he was wounded in the process.

24 and 29 Squadrons had further successes on 6 February, with Cockerell (in A2581) and McCudden (7858) each claiming a C type. Curphey's run of successes for 32 Squadron ended with his sixth 'victory' on the 7th, another Albatros D.II, shared with 2nd Lt H.D. Davis. His squadron was in action again on the 9th. However, on the next day Captain L.P. Aizlewood (A2548) was wounded in an affray, though he did manage to send one enemy machine out of control. But the unit suffered two further casualties on the 15th, with Captain H.W.G. Jones (A2535) wounded in the course of an otherwise successful combat, and 2nd Lt C.H. March (7932) being forced down to become POW. McCudden achieved his final 'victory' for 29 Squadron that day: flying 6002, he destroyed a Roland C.II. Deteriorating weather then restricted service flying until 25 February, on which date 2nd Lt R.J.S. Lund in A2557 of 29 Squadron was wounded when in combat with Ltn W. Voss, who was emerging as a leading German scorer. On the following day 2nd Lt L.L. Carter of the same unit was also wounded, though Lt C.E.M. Pickthorne (7898) of 32 Squadron achieved the final D.H.2 combat success for that month.

The air war intensified during March as German troops withdrew to the Hindenburg Line and British forces advanced to occupy their vacated territory. That intensification saw escalating British air losses as the German fighter force began to dominate, with increasing numbers of Albatros-equipped Jastas beginning to receive the improved D.III version of that scout. 29 Squadron contributed to the Allies obtaining an example of that machine when Lt A.J. Pearson and an F.E.2b crew from 11 Squadron forced a Jasta 5 machine to land intact behind

Thirty-two D.H.2s went to the Middle East; some were briefly with 14 Squadron in Palestine. This shot of a D.H.2 was taken either when it was with 14 Squadron in that region, or after it had been passed – like others – to 111 Squadron, the scout squadron for the region. JMB/GSL

Australian lines on the 4th.

Unfortunately for the unit, on the same day 2nd Lt V.M. Bowling was killed in an accident in A5010. An estimated seventy enemy machines were active on the 6th, and both 24 and 32 Squadrons had encounters with some of these. Pashley and Long of the former unit shared in the destruction of a C type, the final 'victory' for both. 32 Squadron was less fortunate, losing 2nd Lt M.J.J.G. Mare-Montembault (7882) and Captain H.G. Southon (7941) as POWs, and having Lt C.E.M. Pickthorne (7938) wounded. 29 Squadron lost A.J. Pearson on 9 March, when A2571 went down in flames after a combat with von Richthofen, now commanding Jasta 11; Pearson was the last D.H.2 combat casualty for his squadron.

The increasing combat inferiority of the D.H.2 was confirmed by an affray involving a 32 Squadron patrol on 11 March. Although Pickthorne, in his usual 7898, destroyed an Albatros D.I, and others were claimed as out of control by 2nd Lts G. Howe and A.C. Randall (A2548), the patrol had six machines badly damaged, with four pilots wounded:

Randall, Howe, Captain J.M. Robb (A2535) and 2nd Lt W.A.G. Young (7903). Pickthorne wrecked his machine in a forced landing, and A5025 was similarly damaged by 2nd Lt J.H. Cross. A2583 of that unit was wrecked after a combat with Werner Voss on the 17th, when Lt T.A. Cooch was wounded. However, on 11 March, 29 Squadron began to re-equip with Nieuport 17s, and the unit recorded no further D.H.2 claims. Its old machines were returned to 2 AD Candas – though on the 21st, A2572, the last D.H.2 on charge, crashed on such a flight, fatally injuring Major Grattan-Bellew. Pickthorne scored the final D.H.2 success on that day, when he forced Albatros D.I 210/16 to land intact in British territory; this was particularly significant because the aircraft carried Prince Charles Frederick of Prussia, who was taken prisoner. 24 Squadron was also active, but lost A305, and Captain H.W.G. Jones was wounded by the crew of a German two-seater. The final D.H.2 combat casualty of the month was 7862 of 32 Squadron, damaged on the 28th; however its pilot, 2nd Lt A.V.H. Gompertz, was uninjured.

April 1917 became known as 'Bloody April' to the RFC, because the service suffered its greatest monthly casualties since the start of the war; it also marked the swan-song for the D.H.2. Although both remaining squadrons were up to their full establishment of eighteen machines each, they were almost anachronisms in a force that included SPADs, Nieuport 17/23s, Pups, D.H.4s and Bristol Fighters, supported by RNAS machines that included Sopwith Triplanes. RFC authorities must have realized this, because after the first week of that month the units were required to make fewer offensive patrols into enemy airspace, and instead were tasked for line patrols and escort work when needed, and for re-equipment as soon as possible. This policy resulted in relatively little action for the D.H.2, and therefore surprisingly few losses in that month of high casualty rate. As regards re-equipment, delays in D.H.5 production were all that prevented this.

On 2 April, a 24 Squadron line patrol joined in a melee between five F.E.2bs and an estimated eighteen Albatroses. Lt K. Crawford (5925) sent one down in flames, and Lt S. Cockerell (A2581) sent another down to crash. The only action for 32 Squadron was on the following day, when a five-machine patrol tangled with Albatros scouts from Jastas 3 and 5. Lt E.L. Heyworth was wounded and shot down in A2536 to become a POW, while Lt L.W. Barney was lucky to bring A5012 back to crash in British-held territory. 24 Squadron made a further claim on the 6th, Lt C.R. Kerry and 2nd Lt T.C. Arnot sending a C type down out of control; but they lost 2nd Lt E. Kent in a flying accident with 6007 two days later. The final D.H.2 combat of the month was on the 23rd, when 24 Squadron machines acted as escort for F.E.2bs of 22 Squadron. 2nd Lt M. A. White was killed in 7909 when he collided with an F.E.2b while avoiding the attentions of an Albatros scout.

24 Squadron received the first of its replacement D.H.5s on 1 May, but deliveries were slow and the D.H.2s had to soldier on a little longer. Also on the 1st, Captain Taylor and Lt C.G. Eccles of 32 Squadron shared in the destruction of an Albatros two-seater. Their unit's re-equipment began a week later, so it, too, had to continue operations with D.H.2s. On the 6th, A2627 was hit by a shell, and its pilot, Lt T.A. Cooch, was lucky to walk away from the forced landing that wrecked the machine. 24 Squadron suffered its final D.H.2 casualty on the 10th, Lt H.C. Cutler being killed when A2581 was shot down. And six days later 32 Squadron lost a leading pilot, too: the squadron's patrol was detailed to attack enemy observation balloons, and succeeded in forcing their targets down, with observers taking to their parachutes. But the patrol was then attacked by Albatros scouts, one of which was sent down by 2nd Lt C.C. Tayler in A4800, the D.H.2 suffering combat damage. Another Albatros brought down A2622 in flames, killing Captain W.G.S. Curphey MC.

Both squadrons were largely re-equipped by the end of May, though a few D.H.2s lingered on in 32 Squadron. Mixed D.H.2/D.H.5 patrols were then being flown, and one of these, on 3 June, saw the last D.H.2 combat loss in France when 7926 was badly damaged and its pilot, Lt F.J. Martin, wounded, possibly by ground fire. The D.H.2 was taken back to 2 AD, and its return, followed by those of the remaining few, marked the end of the D.H.2's role as a fighting scout on the Western Front.

Training

There were three home-based Reserve Squadrons dedicated to training D.H.2 pilots: 6 RS at Catterick, 10 RS at Joyce Green and 45 RS at South Carlton. Pupil pilots who had graduated from Elementary Reserve Squadrons and were deemed to possess the qualities required in a scout pilot were posted to these units. After initial refresher flying on Henri Farman F.20s, trainees were moved onto the Vickers F.B.5/9 and then to the de Havilland scout. D.H.2s were never very numerous on these training units; flight strength was the norm, and even then they could be operated alongside F.E.8s.

Other home-based training units had smaller numbers on charge. Individual examples appeared with such units as 13 Reserve Squadron at Dover and 15 Reserve Squadron at Doncaster. Specialist training units began to form from early 1917, and D.H.2s – though again in very small numbers – served with fighting schools and gunnery schools such as those at Ayr, Turnberry and Loch Doon. The latter base was intended for seaplane operations, but had a nearby aerodrome at Bogton from where Y Squadron operated a B.E.2c, an AW F.K.3 and D.H.2 A2610. The home-based unit that used the greatest number of D.H.2s was the CFS at Upavon, a unit that also provided pilots for active service overseas. However, the withdrawal of the D.H.2 from front-line service during the late spring and early summer resulted in home-based Reserve Squadrons being given new type specializations. 10 and 45 TS began to operate D.H.5s, 6 TS went over to training pilots for the Sopwith Pup, and the CFS concentrated on the S.E.5a.

The decision to withdraw the D.H.2 from front-line service had some rapid effects. On 17 April, G.B. Anderson, instructing with 45 RS, recorded in his logbook: 'Pushers washed out. Flying stopped until we get our tractors. Avros, Bristols and D.H.5s'. His next flight was not until the 25th, and that was on one of the dozen new Avro 504As received by his unit. Such few D.H.2s as remained with Reserve Squadrons were scrapped, although their engines were retained for reconditioning and use in Pups and Avro 504s.

The Destruction of L.48

After his service in 24 Squadron, R.H.M.S. Saundby was promoted to the rank of captain, to command a flight in 41 Squadron, flying F.E.8s. However, he added another 'victory' to the three credited to him in 24 Squadron before being posted to Home Establishment in March 1917. His posting was to the Armament Experimental Station at Orfordness, and there he re-acquainted himself with the D.H.2. A Zeppelin was reported in the vicinity of that station in the early morning of 17 June, and Saundby took off in A5058, following an F.E.2b, B401, crewed by 2nd Lt F.D. Holder and Sgt S. Ashby. 37 Squadron, from bases further south, also had machines in the vicinity. Ground observers saw incendiary fire from three machines directed at the airship, which caught alight and came down at Theberton, some 10 miles (16km) north of Orfordness. The airship proved to have been the L.48, and the third attacking machine had been a B.E.12 from 37 Squadron, flown by 2nd Lt L.P. Watkins. The three officer pilots were awarded the MC for this action, and Ashby an MM.

Overseas Service

Some D.H.2s operated further afield. At least twenty-eight of the thirty-two sent to the Middle East Brigade were delivered for use on the Macedonian Front, where 17 and 47 Squadrons operated a miscellany of types against Bulgarian forces that were bolstered by German aviation units. Each squadron was required to perform both reconnaissance and bombing duties, mainly flying B.E.2cs and AW F.K.3s during 1917. These were vulnerable to attack by enemy aeroplanes, and the D.H.2s were provided to allow the provision of fighter escorts. The first were received at Salonika Aircraft Park by February 1917, and others followed – A2585, A2630, A4778 and A4779 were recorded as being delivered there on the 5 May. Most of those issued for service went to 47 Squadron, which operated from Mikra Bay; they helped comprise a fighter flight within that unit, and had the occasional success. For instance, on 30 May Captain E.E. Clarke claimed a

Halberstadt D.II as out of control after a combat in A4771, and 2nd Lt H.J. Gibson put in a similar claim on 29 June, with A4772. A third possible D.H.2 'victory' occurred during November, after Lt G.C. Gardiner had a brief combat with an Albatros D.III. Gardiner's gun jammed after a few rounds and he did not claim any success, but ground troops later reported the E.A. as crashed. 17 Squadron is reported as having received A2586 and A4768, but nothing is known of their service in that unit.

Even by the standards of that 'forgotten front', the D.H.2 was outdated in Macedonia by the summer of 1917 and gradually withdrawn from service. Six (A2585, A2616, A2617, A2618, A2625 and A4782) were packed and shipped to X Aircraft Depot at Alexandria in Egypt on 16 August, and others followed later.

Some D.H.2s had already passed through X AD and been issued for escort work to 14 Squadron in Palestine. These included A2623, A2628, A2629, and A4788. 111 Squadron formed at Deir-el-Ballah on 1 August 1917 as a dedicated scout unit for the RFC in Palestine and its initial equipment included the D.H.2s from 14 Squadron. A week after the new unit's formation, 2nd Lt R.C. Steele, in an unidentified D.H.2, claimed its first 'victory', an enemy machine that was possibly driven down out of control. That initial success was marred by the loss of A2628 on the same day, in a crash that killed 2nd Lt R.A. Davey. 111 Squadron also received some of the ex-Macedonian D.H.2s, but by the end of 1917 these had been withdrawn and replaced by more up-to-date Bristol F.2Bs and S.E.5as. A4779 was detached to serve with X Flight, a semi-autonomous unit that worked with the irregular Arab forces and was based at Aqaba. After return to X AD, some, including A2585, A2618 and A4778, were issued to 22 TS at Aboukir, for use as advanced training machines. It seems unlikely that these lasted long into 1918.

At home also, very few D.H.2s remained by 1918. It is known that A2569 was at the RAF Farnborough as late as 20 March of that year. Appendix XLI of the *Official History*, *The War in the Air*, records that on 31 October the RAF had two obsolete machines in use at its schools. One of these was A5058 that was still in flying condition at 1 Fighting School, Turnberry – it must have been the last in service. It was still there and flying almost three months later, no doubt providing pilots with an indication of the massive contrast between its performance and that of the Snipes and Buzzards that had recently been received. The date of its demise is not known, but none of the type survived for preservation in the post-war period.

CHAPTER FIVE

The D.H.4

The First Effective Day-bomber

The D.H.3 design, a twin pusher-engined bomber, is discussed in the chapter on the D.H.10, in the development of which it played an important part. The next de Havilland design was a radical departure from those that had gone before, and was developed into one of the great aeroplanes of World War One. At last de Havilland was free to express one of his ideas about the tractor configuration that he had been advocating, and the resultant D.H.4 took Airco designs a generation further. In fact, such was the integrity of the design that the D.H.4 had the versatility to operate as a bomber, a reconnaissance machine, an escort fighter, an anti-submarine aircraft, an anti-airship machine and a floatplane – indeed, that versatility has resulted in its being regarded as the Great War equivalent of de Havilland's later design, the Mosquito.

Development

During the initial design stage the 160hp Beardmore was in production, and was considered as the powerplant for the new machine. Perhaps it was his experience with the D.H.1, and the precedence given to the F.E.2b for that engine, that caused de Havilland to opt for a new and experimental powerplant: the 200hp BHP. Such an engine (1 WD7820) was allocated and fitted to the first prototype D.H.4 that emerged in mid-August 1916, and given its first flight by its designer. There is no doubt that the authorities were aware of, and impressed by, the design even before it had flown, as Contract 87/A/496 for fifty machines (A2125-A2174) had already been signed on 13 July.

It was a large, two-bay biplane, with wings of equal span and chord. The mainplanes were slightly staggered and set with 3 deg of dihedral, and all four carried ailerons. The upper mainplanes were carried on a narrow centre-section, of fuselage width, and a gravity tank was mounted inboard on the port surface.

The D.H.3 had made extensive use of plywood in its fuselage structure, and that characteristic was continued in the D.H.4. The fuselage frame was made in two parts, which joined at the rear of the observer's cockpit. Both parts employed typical spruce longerons with ash spacers, but only the rear section incorporated wire cross-bracing to maintain alignment. Even then, the rear three bays of that unit were ply-covered to give strength for tailplane support. The frame of the

The first prototype D.H.4 showing the initial engine cowling, the small observer's cockpit, and the wing disposition that was later altered. JMB/GSL

The second prototype with its Rolls-Royce engine in a modified cowling, a redesigned observer's cockpit, and wings in a more forward position that caused a re-alignment of the centre-section strutting. JMB/GSL

Much of the D.H.4's success was due to the superb Rolls-Royce engines that were fitted to many examples. That engine went through a series of developments that took output from 250hp to 375hp in the Eagle VIII shown in this photograph. JMB/GSL

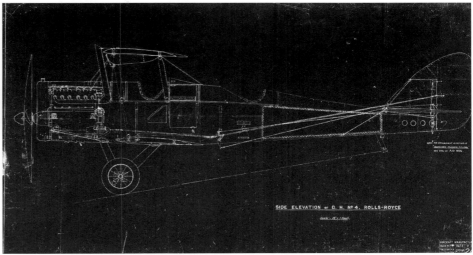

Air Board Drawing 2445, dated 9 January 1917, shows the original shape intended for the observer's cockpit and the disposition of the dual controls. via the author

forward fuselage lacked internal bracing and was ply-covered on its sides and on all except the front three lower bays. The use of plywood in this manner was not novel: it had been used in several earlier machines, notably by the Martinsyde concern. What it provided was an exceptionally strong structure that was capable of maintaining its integrity after sustaining damage.

The fin and rudder employed a graceful shape similar to the one that had appeared on the D.H.3, and it would become a hallmark of de Havilland designs. The incidence of the large tailplane was adjustable via the use of a worm gear that connected to a control wheel in the pilot's cockpit. Flying controls were duplicated, with primary runs for the elevators and rudder leading to the observer's cockpit, and then linked to that of the pilot. Aileron control cables led from a quadrant on the pilot's end of the control shaft to the lower surfaces; the cables then connected to the upper ailerons. The first prototype employed single action ailerons, but a balance cable was subsequently employed.

The BHP engine was of inline configuration and its enclosing aluminium top cowling was above the level of the pilot's head. That cowling tapered to its top to allow some forward vision, but it was far from satisfactory from an operational viewpoint. The water-cooled Beardmore, which drove a four-bladed propeller, necessitated the use of a frontal radiator. The propeller was created by the simple expediency of bolting together a pair of two-bladed units, and it was fitted with a small spinner.

Initial D.H.4 deliveries to the RFC had the decking about the observer's cockpit cut down to the fuselage longerons to allow the installation of a Scarff ring. That modification is shown here on an unidentified machine of 51 TS Waddington that was named 'Wullypug'. JMB/GSL

A major shortcoming of the B.E.2 series that was then in wide operational service was the fact that the pilot occupied the rear cockpit and the observer sat under the centre-section, from where the use of a defensive gun was difficult. Geoffrey de Havilland acknowledged that short-coming, and reversed those crew positions in the D.H.4. The only flaw was the wide spacing of the cockpits: they were separated by the main fuel tank, which made communication between crew members difficult.

The first prototype was passed to the CFS testing squadron at Upavon during September 1916. After completion of its trials, it returned to Airco at Hendon on 12 October; three days later it flew out to France. CFS reports 64 and 64A recorded performances for the D.H.4 that were far superior to those of existing types. Without a bomb load, it could achieve 113mph (182km/h) at 10,000ft (3,050m), and it took only 16min 20sec to reach that altitude. The additional weight of 262lb (118kg) of bombs reduced that speed by only 4mph (6km/h), and increased the climb rate by less than 3min.

That first D.H.4 spent only three days in France, but it must have impressed the Trenchard and HQ RFC in the field. And during that visit, Trenchard received notification from de Havilland that a second prototype was almost ready, and that he would like the BHP replaced by the new 250hp Rolls Royce twelve-cylinder engine. That engine was to become known as the Eagle: Marks I-IV in its 250hp form, and later developed through 275hp (Mks V-VII) to 375hp in the Eagle VIII.

The second prototype, carrying no markings save rudder stripes, flew in that same month. The adoption of the new powerplant had necessitated revisions to the design: thick plywood formers supported the engine bearers, that were set at a lower level; this reduced the height of the top-decking ahead of the pilot, increasing forward vision. The new engine was also water-cooled and employed a radiator of revised, lozenge-shaped design. The greater weight of the Rolls-Royce unit meant that the wings had to be brought forward, and this affected the positioning of the centre-section struts. A new, very low undercarriage was fitted, though its four-bladed propeller was similar to that on the first machine.

The observer's cockpit opening had been very small on the first prototype, presumably no thought having been given to defensive armament. The second machine had that aperture enlarged, and cut down to the level of the top longerons. It went to the new experimental station at Orfordness, by which time the characters 'DX' and 'D4' were painted over its rudder stripes, the latter presumably representing 'de Havilland 4'. By then the propeller had acquired a small spinner. The decking about the observer's cockpit was altered to incorporate a plywood windshield, apparently in anticipation of the potential difficulties in operating a defensive gun in the slipstream at high speeds. A mounting for a Lewis gun was fitted at either end of that cockpit.

The first prototype was re-engined with a 250hp Rolls-Royce, and interestingly, because Airco was seen as a contractor for the RFC, was acquired by the RNAS along with the second machine. In that service the pair were numbered 3696 and 3697, and were brought up to operational standard. 3697 had been intended for transfer to the RFC as B394, but that was not implemented. Both prototypes saw service in France. 3697 lasted until 1 October 1917, when it was destroyed by fire at the Dunkerque depot. 3696 lasted longer, being finally deleted on 31 August 1918, because of 'general fatigue'.

Production D.H.4s of the first batch began leaving the Airco factory during January 1917 and were initially delivered to Hendon AAP for distribution to RFC units. The vast majority had the 250hp Eagle fitted. Their appearance was similar to that of the second prototype in its original guise, although they were, of course, armed. A Scarff ring was fitted for the observer's Lewis gun, and a forward-firing Vickers was mounted, slightly to port of centre, ahead of the pilot's cockpit and synchronized to fire through the propeller arc by the Constantinesco hydraulic gear. Fuel feed was initially by a Rotherham wind-driven pump, mounted on a convenient strut, but later, a pair of 'windmill'-driven pumps was fitted above the fuel tank on the fuselage decking.

The initial contract with Airco was extended to cover a further 690 machines (A7401-A8090), and at the time, was the

The Rolls-Royce Eagle Engines

The Eagle series of engines were regarded as the best aero engines pro-duced in Britain during the First World War. The original design, known as the Rolls-Royce Series 1, was produced at the request of the Admiralty during 1915 and the RFC was quick to realize the potential of the type. The Series 1 and its developments, the Series III and IV, produced 250hp and were manufac-tured alternately as left- and right-hand tractor engines. The RFC first used them in the F.E.2d, fitting engines of the right-hand type. It had, however, also acquired left-handed engines, which were fitted to the first D.H.4s. The basic Series 1–IV was renamed Eagle I–IV; it was developed further to produce 275hp, and then known as the Eagle V–VII. The ultimate development, the Eagle VIII, had an output of 375hp and was fitted to most late-war D.H.4s.

The Eagle engines were very smooth-running, due partly to the adoption of the V12 configuration but also to the manufacturing method and ignition system. The twin banks of six cylinders were set at the customary 60 deg and all components were made from metal that had been carefully selected and tested for consistency. Careful balanc-ing of parts, such as the crankshaft and connecting rods, helped to improve the smoothness already bestowed by the twelve-cylinder arrangement. Dual ignition was fitted to both cylinder banks, using four magnetos and ensur-ing consistent burning. The Rolls-Royce lubrication system added further evenness to the running, and the epicyclic reduction gear took strain from the crankshaft bearings. The rec-ommended fuel was a mixture of 80 per cent petrol and 20 per cent benzole.

Carburation allowed for the pilot to adjust mixture control to suit condi-tions, whether it be starting or running at high altitude. The engine could be started by a battery pack. Each cylin-der bank had its own water jacket.

In the Eagle VIII, the bore was 4½in (114mm) and the stroke 6½in (165mm), giving a compression ratio of 5.3:1. The engine ran at 1,800rpm but the reduction gear allowed the airscrew to turn at 1,080rpm. Fuel and oil consumption was 204lb (93kg) per hour.

Specification – Airco D.H.4

Powerplant:	255hp Rolls-Royce Eagle I–IV, 200hp BHP, 230hp Siddeley Puma, 200hp RAF 3a, 260hp Fiat A12, 275hp Rolls-Royce Eagle V–VII, 375hp Rolls-Royce Eagle VIII, 230hp Galloway Adriatic; fuel capacity 66 gallons (300l)
Weights:	Empty 2,197lb (996kg) with Puma, 2,304lb (1,045kg) with RAF 3a and 2,387lb (1,083kg) with Eagle VIII; loaded weight 3,162lb (1,434kg) with Puma, 3,340lb (1,515kg) with RAF 3a and 3,472lb (1,575kg) with Eagle VIII; wing loading 5.5lb per sq ft (27kg per sq m) empty and 8lb per sq ft (39kg per sq m) loaded (Eagle VIII)
Dimensions:	Mainplane span 42ft 4in (12.91m) (upper and lower); mainplane gap 5ft 6in (1.68m) ; chord 5ft 6in (1.68m); length 30ft 2in (9.2m) with Eagle and 30ft 8in (9.35m) with Puma; height 10ft 1¾in (3.09m) with Eagle and 11ft 4½in (3.47m) with Puma; tailplane span 14ft (4.27m); wing area 434sq ft (40sq m)
Performance:	Maximum speed 120mph (193km/h) with Puma, 117mph (188km/h) with RAF 3a and 126mph (204km/h) with Eagle VIII; landing speed 52mph (84km/h); climb to 10,000ft (3,000m) 9 minutes with Eagle VIII

largest order so far placed by the RFC. B1482, with an RAF 3a engine, was belatedly added to that contract. The RNAS also wanted the type, but the Airco factory was committed to production for the RFC. Consequently, orders were placed in January 1917 with the Westland Aircraft Works at Yeovil for two batches of fifty D.H.4s, the first to have Rolls-Royce engines and the second BHPs. Other contracts followed and included those awarded to F. W. Bewick, the Vulcan Motor & Engineering Co, the Glendower Aircraft Co, Waring & Gillow and Palladium Autocars, as well as the two existing suppliers.

Service With the RFC

55 Squadron was selected as the unit to take the D.H.4 into operational service with the RFC. The squadron had formed at Castle Bromwich on 8 June 1916, and moved to Lilbourne two days later. It had operated a miscellany of second-line types, but began to mobilize with the new D.H.4 in early February 1917. It was intended to move to France as a fighter-reconnaissance unit, and as a result of this, bomb ribs were not, at first, fitted to its machines. The squadron's 'working up' period was not uneventful, and A2143 was lost in an accident on 10 February; its pilot, Lt W.H. Legge, succumbed to his injuries on the following day.

A2142 went, via 2 AD, to the French government on 11 February, for evaluation at Villacoublay. Its new owners took the opportunity to replace the Rolls-Royce engine with a twelve-cylinder Renault.

55 Squadron was fully equipped with operational machines by March, and flew to its designated base at Fienvillers on the 5th, where it came under the 9th (HQ) Wing; as such it was available for duty in support of action on any Army Front. Its initial machines all had the 250hp RR Eagle engine and were from the first Airco-built batch, A2125–A2174; it was a month before the unit became operational. Its machines were fitted with bomb ribs, and its pilots underwent familiarization flights around their sector of the front. The unit was brought into the air war that accompanied the Arras offensive, and made its first bombing attack on 3 April, a raid on Valenciennes. It suffered its first combat

A2170 was a machine from the first batch of D.H.4s built by AMC with a 250hp Rolls-Royce. It went to 55 Squadron, was crashed, rebuilt, and then damaged in combat. After repair it was issued to 25 Squadron, where it was marked with that unit's crescent symbol and given the individual letter L. It was lost in action on 23 November 1917, and its crew of 2nd Lt R. Main and AM1 G.P. Leach were both made POW. JMB/GSL

The GHQ of the RFC with the BEF was keen to appraise the new type, and asked for two examples to be sent for evaluation, in advance of 55 Squadron's expected arrival date. These would seem to have been A2132 and A2142, which were delivered to 1 AD at St Omer on 15 and 9 February respectively; the latter crashed on arrival, but was reconstructed and later served with both 55 and 57 Squadrons.

casualties two days later, in an ambitious raid on a German HQ at Hardenpont, near Mons. The target was bombed, but on the return journey, the formation encountered Albatros scouts of Jasta 11. Two (A2140 and A2141) were shot down, with one crew killed and the other made POW; a third, A2160, was hit by AA and came down near Amiens, with its crew fatally wounded. A2140 was captured intact,

The rear decking of D.H.4s was subsequently modified to raise the height of the observer's Scarff ring. Most then had a rectangular section rear fuselage, as seen here on A7779 – with the individual letter X – that served at Catterick with 52 TS and then 49 TDS. JMB/GSL

D.H.4 sub-types can be identified by the shape of the radiator; the one shown here was characteristic of those fitted with Rolls-Royce engines. JMB/GSL

which enabled the German Air Service to evaluate the new bomber. The fact that this D.H.4 was given German national markings suggests that it might have been flown by its captors.

By the early summer of 1917 the F.E.2b and F.E.2d were totally outdated for the day fighter-reconnaissance role, and their replacement in 18, 20, 22, 23, 25 and 57 Squadrons was a priority. 20 and 22

Although scheduled for the Expeditionary Force, A2168 went to the CFS at Upavon for evaluation. Its testing took place on 10 April and the results were promising. Its speed at height, its service ceiling and its rate of climb were superior to those of the 250hp Rolls-Royce version. The RAF 3a type could be easily distinguished by the higher thrust-line of its engine, its exhaust stack that

discharged over the centre-section, and its frontal radiator aperture, which was of greater radius at the top. A second experimental installation of the RAF 3a was made in A7436, and that machine eventually went to the experimental station at Martlesham Heath. The installation of the RAF 3a was finally authorized for production machines – although problems were to emerge that

A shortage of Rolls-Royce engines led to alternative powerplants being installed. The RAF 3a was one, and D.H.4s so fitted can be identified by that engine's higher thrust line and the central exhaust stack. This RAF 3a D.H.4 served with 19 TS Hounslow. **H.S. Clarke via** JMB/GSL

Squadrons received Bristol Fighters, although it had been intended that they had D.H.4s, and 23 Squadron was to become a single-seat scout unit with SPAD S.VIIs. The remaining three F.E. units were to be re-equipped with the D.H.4. However, it was one thing to decide upon such a policy and have the airframes available, but another to find sufficient engines. The Rolls-Royce Eagle was in demand by both the RNAS and the RFC, and there were simply not enough to go round; and so thought was given to finding an alternative powerplant. The scarcity of Eagles was largely due to government reluctance to allow Rolls-Royce either to expand its existing production and reconditioning facilities, or to license production in the USA. The untried RAF 3a, which developed 230hp, was seen as a possible solution, and a trial installation of that engine was made in A2168; this D.H.4 was delivered to Hendon AAP by the end of the first week in March 1917.

The other major alternative engine was the 230hp BHP in its Puma form. D.H.4s so fitted had the radiator shape shown here, and a single exhaust stack on the port side of the cowling. This particular D.H.4 was at Harling Road, the home of 10 TDS. JMB/GSL

plagued those units flying the type operationally.

Available engine supplies made it possible to re-equip 25 and 57 Squadrons with the Eagle D.H.4 – no doubt the Rolls-Royce engines from the withdrawn pusher type were reconditioned and ended up in the replacement aeroplane. 57 Squadron, which shared the Fienvillers base with 55 Squadron, was the RFC's second operational D.H.4 unit, and received the first of its new machines on 28 March; it was also attached to the 9th (HQ) Wing. Its re-equipment was delayed by the need to replace losses in 55 Squadron, and it was June before it was fully converted to the new type. Crashes had accounted for a number of those losses, with most occurring on landings. 25 Squadron, at Lozinghem, began to re-equip during June.

55 Squadron had mounted further raids during 'Bloody April', and attacks on Boue and Lechelle on the 23rd, in conjunction with 27 Squadron Martinsydes, resulted in further casualties and the unit's first claim for an enemy aeroplane. Despite having an escort of Nieuports, the bombers were attacked on their return journey. Lt I.V. Pyott, DSO, and 2nd Lt A.D. Taylor, in A2147, came under fire: Taylor was wounded, but fire from his Lewis gun was thought to have sent a red Albatros down OOC. Pyott had been made a DSO for his destruction of the Zeppelin L.36 the previous November. Two other crews came under attack, but managed to cross the lines before crash-landing: Captain A.T. Greg in A7408 had been killed, but his observer was safe, as was the crew of A7410.

The squadron's employment was established as one of bombing interspersed with photo-reconnaissance. For the latter, a camera was mounted vertically behind the observer's cockpit. It was on such duty on 10 May that the unit suffered its next casualties, losing three of its replacement machines: A7413, A7416 and A7419. The two latter were brought down by AA, their crews killed; the pilot managed to land A7413, though the observer was dead, but was shelled on the ground. Another D.H.4, A2150, was damaged, and a further casualty was incurred later that month. The unit then moved north to Boisdinghem for the forthcoming Flanders offensive, followed by 57 Squadron which had reached operational status with its new machines; it

transferred to nearby Droglandt. Both units were in action during the Battle of Messines. Remarkably, 55 Squadron came through June 1917 without fatalities, although one observer was wounded. 57 Squadron was detailed for similar operations to its sister unit, and began these with some success: for instance on 17 June an Albatros scout was driven down by Sgt A.T. Rose, the observer in A2173. However, that early success was tempered with the loss of two machines in the second half of the month, both on photographic duty: A7473 was shot down on the 24th by Ritt M. von Richthofen, and A7488 five days later. Both crews were killed.

25 Squadron, the third Eagle-engined D.H.4 squadron, began to receive the first of its new machines during June. A7486 was delivered on the 17th, and others followed slowly until the last of its F.E.2ds was withdrawn in August. However, operations began before re-equipment was complete, and A7479 became its first operational loss on the D.H.4, being shot down on a photographic mission on 27 July with its crew, 2nd Lts W.L. Lovell and W.W. Fitzgerald, killed.

The RAF3a could not be fitted into the existing D.H.4 fuselage without modifications to the engine bearers. This necessary work delayed delivery of production machines with that engine and it was not until 12 June that the first two were accepted. These were A7457 and A7459 and they were delivered for RNAS service. The Navy wanted an aerial photo-reconnaissance of the Keil Canal and the greater ceiling and longer endurance of the RAF-engined machine, compared with existing Eagle-engined variants, made it the preferred choice. The RFC agreed readily to the transfer of those two machines; in return the military was to receive two RNAS Eagle-engined D.H.4s from the Westland factory. The projected reconnaissance was never undertaken and the two aeroplanes, still in a special camouflage scheme, were delivered to Yarmouth and Grain.

18 Squadron had also begun to relinquish its F.E.2s in June, but its replacement D.H.4s had the RAF 3a engine. Its first new machine was A7466, delivered on 26 June, and others followed over the next two weeks. The unit had its first fatalities on the type on 2 July: Lts W.H. Ryder and E.G. Rowley were killed when A7474 broke up on a practice flight.

Re-equipment was slow, and the squadron was still operating a few F.E.2bs as late as 19 August. Operations with the D.H.4, from its base at La Bellevue, had started in July, and another loss occurred on the 15th of that month when A7490 was shot down on a flight to familiarize its crew with the lines: Lts V.C. Coombs and H.M. Tayler were made POW.

55 and 57 Squadrons had, meanwhile, been heavily involved in the build-up to the Battle of Ypres, photographing and bombing enemy supply dumps and communications centres. Such operations were made against determined enemy opposition, inevitably resulting in casualties. During July, 55 Squadron lost four machines and 57 Squadron five.

The battle finally opened on 31 July, and after an initial lull due to adverse weather, all three Eagle-Four units resumed operations. Rail junctions and ammunition dumps continued to be targeted, and raids were usually made at flight strength. Units of the German Air Service, particularly the recently formed JG1 (the grouping of Jastas 4, 6, 10 and 11 under von Richthofen) were becoming increasingly successful, and so enemy aerodromes were added to the target list. Targets for 16 August – and this was a typical day's operations during this period – included railway stations and sidings at Courtrai, Ingelmunster and Seclin; aerodromes at Dorignies, Heule and Recklem; and dumps at Carvin, Auby and Raimbeaucourt. Such intensive operations inevitably produced losses, 55 Squadron losing A7495 (crew POW) and 57 Squadron suffering damage to A7424, with Sgt C. R. Goffe being wounded.

At that time 18 Squadron was drawn into the scheme that co-ordinated ground-attack work with infantry advances. On the 18th, its D.H.4s were loaded with eight Cooper bombs apiece, and they attacked German trenches from low level, following up the bombing with machine-gun attacks. Fortunately there were no casualties, but Lts Byron and Foord were lucky to return after putting an enemy machine-gun out of action; their machine had been hit no fewer than forty-two times. 55 and 57 Squadrons were also in action that day, but they were were less fortunate, the former losing A7471, and the latter A7454 and A7510 as they bombed various targets in the German rear areas. On the credit side, 2nd Lts A.B. Cook and R.N. Bullock, in A7561 of

57 Squadron, destroyed one of fifteen enemy scouts that had attacked their formation. Similar casualties were suffered three days later, but again, an enemy scout was sent down by Captains H.R. Harker and W.E.B. Barclay MC in A7568. That successful crew had been lucky on 7 July, escaping injury when their D.H.4 (A7492) was attacked in error by a Belgian Nieuport 17.

The Ypres battles petered out, temporarily, during late August. Fourteen D.H.4s had been lost to enemy action during that month, with many others damaged. The type was, however, proving itself to be superior as a bomber to the outdated Martinsyde G.100/102s of 27 Squadron, and capable of limiting the effects of attacking EA through the adoption of formation flying that allowed for mutual defensive fire.

The four D.H.4 squadrons resumed operations when the ground war re-

5 October when one from 25 Squadron was attacked after bombing the aerodrome at Chateau de Sart: three of eight attacking Albatros scouts were sent down OOC, without loss to the D.H.4s. And it was not just the observers who claimed enemy machines: three days previously, a 57 Squadron formation encountered fifteen Albatroses after bombing Abeele aerodrome. 2nd Lt F. Martin and Lt J. O'Neill, in A7424, sent one down in flames, while other EA attacked A7568, crewed by Captain D.S. Hall and 2nd Lt E.P. Hartigan. Hartigan's fire caused one of the enemy to break up, then another crossed the pilot's line of fire and was sent down in flames. Hall fired on a third, which went down OOC, and Hartigan had similar success with yet one more. Tragically that aggressive crew was killed on 20 November, when A7568 crashed on a routine test flight.

55 Squadron also demonstrated the

new base at Ochey, near Nancy. The new wing's brief was the bombing of targets inside Germany, as retaliation for the night bombing raids on London and south-east England that had begun the previous month.

The RAF 3a suffered from its unreliability, and in any case it was in relatively short supply. Other power units were considered, and the 200hp BHP selected as a second alternative to the Eagle. A trial installation was made in A7456, which was delivered in June 1917. It had a two-week stay at Martlesham during July, but was returned to its makers, presumably for further modifications. A second such installation was made in A7519, which went to Farnborough for tests that took place in late November. The BHP was developed into the 230hp Puma, but that engine was often referred to by the name of the original. Its lower thrust line called for a revision to the

2N Squadron was the RNAS photographic squadron on the Channel coast. It operated a few BHP-engined D.H.4s alongside those fitted with Rolls-Royce engines, and here, three of the latter are flanked by two of the former. The taller undercarriage fitted to later D.H.4s is evident on the BHP machines. JMB/GSL

opened in early September. Their targets were similar to those of August, and raids were interspersed with reconnaissance missions. Machines on the latter type of mission were not encumbered with bombs, and relied on the type's high speed to complete their sorties. They were not, however, immune to attack: A7480 of 25 Squadron was lost on a photographic mission on the 4th, its crew killed in a combat with ten enemy scouts. A further eight D.H.4s were lost during September, most during the course of bombing missions.

The defensive capabilities of a good formation were amply demonstrated on

ability of its D.H.4s to defend themselves. Enemy scouts intercepted a bombing raid on Courtrai station on 7 October. All the British machines returned to base, but not before two of the enemy had been sent down in flames and a further two out of control. Captain D. Owen and his observer, Gunner W.G. Osborne in A7586 were credited with one in each category, Sergeant P. O'Lieff and Corporal A. Walters (A7703) got the other 'flamer', and Sergeant M. J.C. Weare and AM2 S. Moreman accounted for the fourth. 55 Squadron was withdrawn from operations on the Flanders Front four days later; the unit transferred to the 41st Wing and a

radiator, and a shell of inverted kite shape was adopted. By late 1917, production machines with the BHP engine were entering service. 27 Squadron began relinquishing its Martinsyde G.102 Elephants on 21 September, and was the sole squadron of the BEF to receive the new variant. By that time Airco had succeeded in making the airframe capable of accepting any of the versions of the Eagle engine and its alternatives, and machines left the production line fitted with the type of engine available at the time. 27 Squadron's re-equipment was slow, however, with a further three D.H.4s arriving during October, and most of the others the following month. Martinsydes continued to be flown as this re-equipment took place.

Further ground offensives in the third Battle of Ypres continued through October and into November, as weather conditions permitted. 18, 25 and 57 Squadrons continued to contribute to the British effort with the usual combination of bombing and reconnaissance sorties; although heavily involved, the three units suffered surprisingly few total losses. Only nine D.H.4s were lost to enemy action during October, but those losses were disproportionate. 57 Squadron suffered six, and 25 Squadron the other two.

The departure of 55 Squadron was compensated for when the RFC with the BEF received its penultimate D.H.4 squadron on 12 November. 49 Squadron arrived at La Bellevue from Dover, where it had spent an extensive 'working-up' period. Its D.H.4s also had the RAF 3a.

The Ypres battle finally petered out on 10 November, but the short lull that followed was merely the calm before a new offensive further south. In anticipation of this, 49 Squadron had been based at La Bellevue. As well as its bombing duties, 18 Squadron was delegated reconnaissance duties in the northern part of the new sector, while 25 and 57 Squadrons were to target railway centres more distant from the lines. The latter two units were to operate with 27 Squadron, which was in the process of re-equipping with the D.H.4 and was flying examples of the type

alongside a diminishing number of Martinsydes. 27 Squadron had suffered its first D.H.4 casualties on 7 November, when 2nd Lts W.J. Henney and P.S. Driver lost their bearings on a test flight, accidentally crossed the lines, and had their machine, A7633, shot up by enemy ground fire.

The D.H.4 squadrons dutifully went about their business when the Battle of Cambrai opened on 20 November. 49 Squadron was the only such unit involved in the actual battle zone, and lost a single machine (A7704) in the fighting, that continued until 7 December. The other squadrons with the type incurred similar minimal losses and that pattern continued to the end of the year.

The 260hp Fiat A-12 engine had a similar configuration to the BHP, and was seen as a further alternative to power the D.H.4. A trial installation of that engine was made in A7532 by June 1917; however, when it was tested at Martlesham during the following month it returned a poorer performance than variants with other types of engine. The Imperial Russian Air Service had ordered fifty D.H.4s, and the Fiat was the engine specified for these. A deal was struck whereby the machines intended for Russia would be delivered to the RFC in 1917, on the understanding that seventy-five would be delivered the following spring. The October Revolution served to make this deal unnecessary. The forty such machines that had been completed were accepted

onto RFC charge as C4501-C4540, and it would seem that the airframes of the order's balance were delivered for use as spares. The Fiat-Four dispensed with the frontal radiator layout. Its nasal contours were still quite blunt, but its semi-retracting radiator was located under the forward fuselage, in a similar position to that on the later D.H.9.

The majority of the completed Fiat-Fours were delivered to the BEF during the early winter of 1917-18, and were placed in storage at 2 ASD. 49 Squadron was issued with the variant, its first four such machines (C4502, C4505, C4526 and C4530) arriving on 11 February. Although eighteen machines passed through its hands, the squadron was never fully equipped with the type. Until mid-March, an average of six was flown, sufficient to equip one flight. The number on charge peaked at twelve during the last week of that month, but diminished thereafter until the last three (C4521, C4523 and C4524) were withdrawn on 12 April. The use of the variant had not been a success, and given the impracticality of trying to maintain two types of engine on one squadron, the known quantity that was the RAF 3a was preferred.

1918 began relatively quietly for the RFC's D.H.4 squadrons. Reconnaissance and bombing continued, and indeed increased, to counter preparations for the German spring offensive that everyone expected. And when that offensive opened on 21 March, the squadrons were

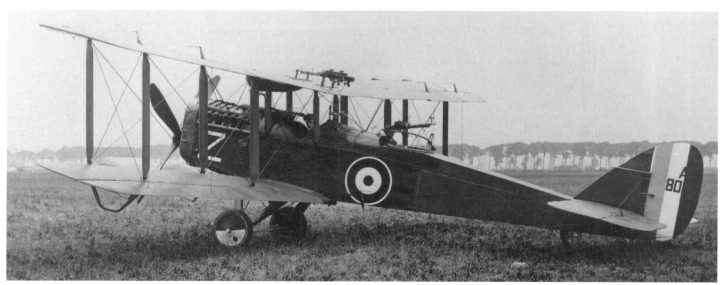

C Flight of 2N/202 Squadron was its escort flight, and A8025 is seen suitably armed for that role. It, too, had the taller undercarriage. It was issued to 202 Squadron on 6 June 1918, and was lost in action on 28 September. JMB/GSL

tasked with undertaking attacks on advancing enemy troops; only 49 Squadron was reserved for distant bombing. The RFC units were reinforced by the arrival of 5N Squadron's D.H.4s at Villers-Bretonneux. Low flying on ground-attack sorties increased casualties, and 27 Squadron suffered worst in the opening days of the offensive, losing two machines through combat damage on the 24th (B2079 and B2108) two more on the 26th (B2076 and B2101), with another (B2111) missing on the latter date. The low-flying D.H.4s were vulnerable to attack by enemy scouts, but with an experienced crew they could also hold their own. N6001, flown by Flt Comm C.P.O. Bartlett, was attacked by five EA on the 28th, but his observer, A.G.L.W. Naylor, shot one of the Pfalz down. A pair of Fokker D.R.1s then collided while trying to manoeuvre onto the tail of the D.H.4.

Service With the RNAS On the Channel Coast

D.H.4s for the RNAS, from the batch N5960–N6009, began to leave the Westland Aircraft Works during March 1917. Westlands machines differed in detail from early RFC deliveries: all had

the 275hp Eagle engine (Mks V, VI and VII), and the majority of that first batch had a revised upper rear fuselage. The original design, with the Scarff ring mounted on the upper longerons, had a restricted field of fire for the observer's gun; however, that situation was remedied by raising the gun ring to the level of the inter-cockpit decking. Plywood faired the ring into the contours of the decking. The rear turtle-decking was rounded on early machines of the batch, but some later deliveries were given the slab-sided and flat-topped rear fuselage that characterized later RFC deliveries. The original design also had a very short undercarriage, and led to the possibility of the propeller catching the ground on take-off. This was remedied from N9559 onwards by the fitting of a taller unit. Frontal firepower was doubled with the fitting of a second fixed Vickers machine-gun.

The 200hp BHP engine was specified for Westland's other batch of fifty D.H.4s, N6380-N6429, that was delivered from August 1917. This was no doubt due to the increasing scarcity of Rolls-Royce engines. Several, however, were issued to units in France, but the majority served in either the UK or the Aegean.

By this time the Sopwith 1½ Strutters of 2N and 5N Squadrons were becoming hopelessly outdated, and from April onwards the de Havilland machine began

to replace them. The squadrons were not withdrawn from service for re-equipment: instead, D.H.4s were delivered as production allowed, and flew alongside diminishing numbers of Sopwiths until replacement was completed. 2N Squadron, the first of the two to receive D.H.4s, flew from St Pol, and 5N from Bray Dunes. Initially their duties were those inherited from the Sopwiths, reconnaissance for the former unit and bombing for the latter. 2N Squadron introduced its D.H.4s to operations as they arrived, and an early success was achieved on 12 May, when FSL L.N. Glaisby and OSL V. Greenwood (in N5963) downed an enemy biplane that attempted to interfere with their spotting for a monitor attack on Zeebrugge.

The unit suffered its first operational loss on the new type when N5963 failed to return from escorting a reconnaissance of Ostende on 26 May. FSL W. Houston-Stewart and Lt C.L. Haines were both killed. Spotting for monitors was another duty allocated to 2N Squadron, and its first success in this role was on 5 June. A pair of the unit's D.H.4s, with a further pair as escort, called the shots for the monitors *Terror* and *Erebus* as they shelled the Ostende dockyards. Although smoke-screens were quickly laid, three dozen shots were registered and the results – as revealed by a later reconnaissance – were

5N Squadron was the RNAS bombing squadron until its transfer to RFC duty in March 1918. N6000 was issued to the squadron in July 1917, and had a distinguished combat career with the unit that lasted nine months. Like most Westland-built machines, it had twin fixed Vickers guns for its pilots' use. Various crews used this machine in six successful combats with enemy scouts. Its elevators were marked in national colours, and the rear fuselage was doped in a colour that photographed in a dark shade, possibly red. *via K. Kelly*

good, with destroyer repair facilities hit and the submarine UC70 sunk.

The introduction of the D.H.4 into 2N and 5N Squadrons coincided with the closing stages of the Battle of Arras and the transfer of British attention to a possible advance on the Flanders Front. The two units were drawn into the preparations for this, and one of 2N Squadron's duties was an exhaustive photographic reconnaissance of the Belgian coast from Nieuport to Middelkerque. That reconnaissance entailed making a series of photographic mosaics to show the fall of the tide and, consequently, the submarine contours of the shoreline. The reason for this was that an amphibious landing to occupy the coast was intended, should the British advance in Flanders draw German troops away from that area.

The completion of 5N Squadron's re-equipment with D.H.4s coincided with the preparations for the Ypres battles, and the unit was diverted from naval duties to assist tactical bombing by the military. Its usual targets were enemy aerodromes and railway junctions, which had the desired effect of diverting German scouts from front line operations to defensive ones. Increasing aerial opposition to 5N Squadron's activities led to the provision of fighter escorts, usually in the form of Bristol F.2Bs from 48 Squadron RFC. Aerodromes in the vicinity of Thourout, such as Aertrycke, Varssenaere, Ghistelles and Sparappelhoek, were subjected to high-level attacks from July to September 1917, all made without loss to the bombers. 5N Squadron's first casualty on the D.H.4 came about as a result of a raid on Ghistelles on 7 July. Leading mechanic W.J. Edwards, the observer in N5974, was killed when an Albatros scout attacked the machine on its return flight.

A temporary lull in the offensive at the beginning of September meant that 5N Squadron could be used for a short bombing campaign against the dockyards at Bruges, which were being developed as a major submarine base with ferro-concrete pens under construction.

Ostende dockyard was a frequent target for British monitors, and their activities usually resulted in German torpedo boats making for the open sea during bombardments. This activity had been noted, and a bombardment on 15 September was made with 5N Squadron waiting near the target. When the

German vessels left port, the D.H.4s attacked them, hitting a destroyer and an armed trawler.

A variation in the type of aerodrome attacked by 5N Squadron was made for six days from 27 September. German night-bombing of London led to raids being mounted against the main Gotha bases of Gontrode and St Denis Westrem. The raids were in conjunction with night attacks by HP 0/100s and had two results: the positive one was the dispersal of the Gotha units – but there was a down side, in that they caused retaliatory raids to be made on RNAS at St Pol.

2N Squadron maintained its reconnaissance role, its Eagle Fours being supplemented by six of the BHP-powered variety from mid-September. The situation of a squadron's mechanics having to maintain two completely different engines can have been far from satisfactory, but may have been a necessity demanded by the transfer of a fifth of the first Westland-built batch of D.H.4s to the RFC.

The reconnaissance squadron plied its trade on a daily basis, photographing the enemy-held coastline and adjacent inland areas (to a depth of 4 miles/6.4km) from Nieuport to the Dutch border. Its composite flights had dedicated duties. A Flight had photographic responsibilities, and B Flight was dedicated to target registration work with naval monitors and its machines were fitted with WT. C Flight provided escorts for the other

two. The D.H.4s were modified accordingly. Photographic machines usually operated at altitudes of over 18,000ft (5,500m), at which heights oxygen equipment was a necessary fitting: this involved mounting an oxygen cylinder under the fuselage, with crews using simple, perforated rubber pipes to inhale an oxygen/air mixture.

The RNAS asked for twenty D.H.4s fitted with large cameras, and these may have been intended for 2N Squadron, several of whose machines showed modifications for photographic work. The cameras used for high-level work had long focal lengths and protruded through the cockpit floor. The lens was often protected by the addition of a streamlined fairing attached to the underside of the fuselage. The camera occupied the space immediately behind the main fuel tank, but its bulk meant that the rocking shaft for elevator control had to be moved forwards. B Flight machines carried simple spark transmitters with trailing aerials that could be let out from, or wound in a drum in the rear fuselage. The primitive nature of the equipment meant that it could be easily jammed by the enemy and so an Aldis lamp was also carried. The C Flight escort machines were often armed with as many as six machine guns. Several had the twin Vickers armament and that could be supplemented with a pair of fixed Lewis guns, carried above the centre-section. It

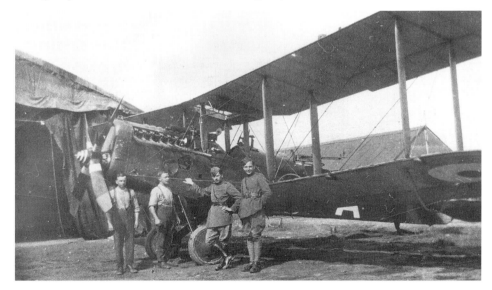

A typical late-production Rolls-Royce D.H.4 in RAF service showing all the major features of the type. The windmill-like propellers that drove the fuel pumps are clearly visible behind the pilot's cockpit. C. Cousins via K. Kelly

Representative D.H.4s with RFC, RNAS and RAF Units on the Western Front

18 Squadron Baizieux, La Bellevue, Auchel, Treizennes, Serny, Maisoncelle, Le Hameau – A7466, A7474, A7478, A7483, A7490, A7498, A7500, A7501, A7512, A7514, A7517, A7523, A7524, A7526, A7527, A7528, A7544, A7548, A7550, A7553, A7572, A7573, A7593, A7594, A7596, A7597, A7598, A7602, A7630, A7634, A7635, A7646, A7653, A7658, A7682, A7709, A7719, A7745, A7747, A7767, A7769, A7770, A7795, A7797, A7798, A7799, A7800, A7808, A7809, A7815, A7816, A7818, A7833, A7839, A7847, A7851, A7852, A7853, A7854, A7855, A7887, A7899, A7907, A7981, A7984, A7989, A7990, A7991.

25 Squadron Lozinghem, Boisdinghem, Serny, Villers-Bretonneux, Beauvois, Ruisseauville, La Brayelle, Maubeurge, Bickendorf, Merheim, South Carlton – A2144, A2145, A7442, A7464, A7470, A7486, A7489, A7503, A7505, A7507, A7536, A7543, A7547, A7561, A7562, A7595, A7599, A7600, A7657, A7664, A7672, A7680, A7683, A7733, A7775, A7776, A7805, A7820, A7822, A7823, A7834, A7838, A7865, A7882, A7895, A7968, A8016, B7911, D8372, D8379, D8380, D8381, D8383, D8389, D8395, F5832, F6076, F6103, F6120, F6127, F7598.

27 Squadron Serny, Villers-Bretonneux, Beauvois, Ruisseauville, Fourneuil, Ruisseauville, Chailly, Beauvois – A7519, A7622, A7625, A7631, A7633, A7640, A7677, A7706, A7707, A7740, B2053, B2068, B2071, B2072, B2073, B2074, B2075, B2076, B2077, B2078, B2079, B2080, B2081, B2082, B2083, B2084, B2085, B2086, B2087, B2088, B2090, B2091, B2092, B2093, B2094, B2098, B2099, B2101, B2102, B2103, B2104, B2105, B2107, B2108, B2109, B2110, B2111, B2112, B2113, B2132, B2133, B2135, B2144, B2145, B5506, B9460, B9461, B9470.

49 Squadron Dover, La Bellevue, Les Eauvis, Boisdinghem, Petite Synthe – A7682, A7693, A7694, A7700, A7704, A7705, A7708, A7712, A7715, A7720, A7722, A7724, A7740, A7758, A7801, A7812, A7842, A7861, A7957, A8034, B2059, B2060, B2062, B2063, B2067, B7747, D8364.

55 Squadron Lilbourne, Fienvillers, Boisdinghem – A2133, A2135, A2136, A2137, A2138, A2140, A2141, A2142, A2143, A2144, A2145, A2147, A2149, A2150, A2153, A2155, A2157, A2158, A2159, A2160, A2161, A2163, A2166, A2170, A7401, A7408, A7409, A7410, A7411, A7493, A7495, A7530, A7575, A7775, A7791, B3955, B3961, B3962, B3965, B3966, B3967.

57 Squadron Fienvillers, Droglandt, Boisdinghem, Ste-Marie-Cappel, Le Quesnoy, Vert Galand, Mory, Beauvois, Vert Galand, Le Casteau, Spy, Morville – A2155, A2157, A2173, A2174, A7402, A7403, A7404, A7405, A7406, A7480, A7481, A7484, A7485, A7492, A7525, A7529, A7533, A7535, A7537, A7538, A7540, A7542, A7554, A7555, A7637, A7687, A7811, A7876, A8017, A8070, B3963, B3964, D8398, D8406, D8415, D8416, D9267, E4625, E4626, E4628, F1552, F5718, F5727.

2N/
202 Squadron St Pol, Bergues, Varssenaere – A7632, A7665, A7768, A7845, A7849, A7868, A7930, A8025, A8079, B7986, D1754, D1757, D8390, D8391, D8402, D8409, D8418, D8420, D8422, F2643, N5960, N5961, N5963, N5964, N5965, N5966, N5969, N5972, N5979, N5981, N5983, N5985, N5989, N5997, N6389, N6390, N6391, N6392, N6394, N6402, N6403.

5N/
205 Squadron Petite Synthe, Villers-Bretonneux, Mons-en-Chaussée, Champien, Bertangles, Bois-de-Roche, Bovelles, Proyart East – A7486, A7487, A7518, A7587, A7644, A7663, A7739, A7742, A7790, A7908, A7915, A7933, A7964, A7976, A7985, A8029, A8030, A8071, A8084, A8089, A8090, D8387, D8401, D8405, D8412, D8421, D8429, D9232, D9234, D9238, D9241, D9243, D9250, D9253, D9255, D9256, D9260, D9269, E4624, N5962, N5967, N5968, N5971, N5978, N5996, N6009.

6N Squadron Dover, Petite Synthe – B9499, D1751, D1752, D1753, D1754, N6390, N6404. 11N/211 Squadron Petite Synthe – B9497, B9498, B9499, D1751, D1752, D1753, D1754, D1757, D1758.

12N Squadron Petite Synthe – A7863, B9497, D1758, N5961, N6391. 17N/217 Squadron Bierne, Bergues, Crochte, Varssenaere – A7760, A7762, A7772, A7773, A7829, A7846, A7863, A7867, A7870, A7875, A7878, A7917, A7920, A7924, A7925, A7941, A7945, A7969, A7996, A8006, A8013, A8022, A8023, A8046, A8050, A8056, A8059, A8061, A8063, A8065, A8066, A8067, A8072, A8074, A8081, A8082, B7941, D8353, D8363, D8366, D8370, D8374, D8376, D8393, D8394, D8399, D8400, D8403, D8417, F2640, F2643, F2645.

was not uncommon for the observers to mount paired Lewis guns on the Scarff rings.

2N and 5N Squadrons continued their respective duties through the winter of 1917–18 and suffered surprisingly few casualties. Until the end of February 1918, 2N squadron's only operational loss was N5963, mentioned earlier. Others had been lost in the inevitable crashes and forced landings that occurred in all units, three of these (involving N5973, N5983 and N6402) resulting in fatalities. The unit's minimal operational losses can be attributed to the performance of the Eagle Four, and the fact that photographic missions usually involved flying at 18,000-plus ft (5,500m), making interception difficult. 5N Squadron's bombing missions were usually carried out at altitude and in formation that

allowed for mutual defence. Consequently, its operational losses in the same period were similarly negligible. Only N5982 and N6008 were lost in that manner, but the squadron also had its share of accidents, an example being that involving N5968: that D.H.4 crashed at Petite Synthe on 13 January 1918 with its pilot FSL H. Willis fatally injured. Its observer, AM2 A. Foster, escaped the burning machine, but a member of the groundcrew, AM1 A.L. Jeffries, was killed trying to salvage the machine's Lewis gun from the flames. Wastage of machines, and the transfer of Westland-built Eagle Fours to the RFC soon depleted reserves, and so RFC machines from the A7401-A8090 batch were made available to the two units.

In early 1918 the RNAS contingent in the Dunkerque area was strengthened by

the formation of new squadrons and the reformation of others; these included some that operated D.H.4s. 17N Squadron was formed with the type, for anti-submarine work, while 6N and 11N Squadrons (scheduled for bombing duties with D.H.9s) each operated some as initial equipment during their working-up periods. 12N Squadron at Petite Synthe served in the role of a finishing school with a miscellany of types that included a few D.H.4s, as well as scout types.

Plans for the forthcoming formation of the RAF were well in hand by January 1918, and the Air Council had considered the future of the RNAS units in the Dover-Dunkerque Command. Its decision was that one of the three existing Wings would be permanently retained on existing naval duties, but the other two would come under military command and

A BHP-powered D.H.4 showing the radiator shape and the carburettor intakes on the starboard cowling. JMB/GSL

be available for operations anywhere along the Front, as circumstances dictated. 1 Wing RNAS (later 61 Wing RAF) was to be the naval wing, and its composition was intended to include one D.H.4 squadron for reconnaissance (2N Squadron) and another for anti-submarine work (17N Squadron). 5N Squadron was destined for military duty before the formation of the RAF came about.

The expected German 'push' in the spring of 1918 called for a reinforcement of RFC units in the Amiens/Albert area. On 6 March 5N Squadron transferred to Villers-Bretonneux, and moved to Mons-en-Chaussee five days later. It immediately became involved in operations aimed at disrupting the anticipated offensive, bombing ammunition dumps and railway junctions in the German rear area. Enemy opposition was intense and casualties inevitable. The first occurred on 16 March, with the loss of the experienced crew of A7908, when Flt Comm L.W. Omerod was killed and his observer, OSL W.L.H. Pattison fatally wounded. On 21 March, the first day of the German advance, the squadron was shelled out of its aerodrome and hasty moves were made to Champien, Bertangles and, finally, Conteville.

Service With the RAF

The formation of the RAF, on 1 April 1918, brought little change to the daily routine of the D.H.4 squadrons. Naval squadrons had 200 added to their unit numbers, so that, for example, 5N Squadron became 205 Squadron RAF. Apart from that, life continued as before, with an all-out effort being made to halt the German spring offensive on the Somme by the units already so detailed. As the assault on the Somme petered out, another on the Lys had to be countered.

The D.H.4s so employed by the RAF flew reconnaissance missions to identify enemy troop concentrations and bombing raids to disperse them. Casualties were inevitable in the latter work, particularly as missions were of shorter duration and thus more could be launched in a day. Low flying left the D.H.4s vulnerable to attack from above, but there were frequent occasions when attacking enemy scouts were brought down. The number of D.H.4s lost during April's fighting was surprisingly few, and only four were brought down – but numerous others returned to base with damage, and crew members wounded or killed. By the end of the month the German advances had been stemmed. The D.H.4 was also

beginning to be replaced by the D.H.9. 49 Squadron had received its first examples of the new type in early April, and was completely re-equipped by May. The choice of 49 Squadron was not a random one, since its mixture of RAF 3a and Fiat-powered machines represented the least effective forms of the D.H.4.

With the pressure of the German advances relieved, the D.H.4 units resumed their normal duties during May 1918, raiding enemy rail centres, ammunition dumps and aerodromes. The return to high-level bombing enabled a return to effective formation flying and fewer casualties. Occasionally things went wrong, however: on 9 May, for example, a pair of 57 Squadron machines (A8068 and D8411) on a photo-reconnaissance were caught by enemy scouts and severely damaged, with one observer wounded. Losses were more serious during a raid on Roye by 25 and 27 Squadrons on 16 June, when opposition was encountered from Jastas 2 and 15; the affray resulted in the loss of three D.H.4s, with two crews killed and another wounded. A similar raid on Bapaume, seven days later, ended with similar losses. By this time 27 Squadron had begun to receive D.H.9 replacements and was operating these alongside its D.H.4s, and two were also lost. The re-equipment of 27

Squadron was slow, and it was not until July that it was completed.

The fitting of dual control to the D.H.4 was done with the intention that the observer could take over should a pilot be incapacitated. Such a situation arose on several occasions, and a good example is one that involved D9277 of 205 Squadron on 17 June 1918. Captain J. Gamon was on a bombing mission to Chaulnes with Major S.J. Goble, the unit's CO, as observer. Gamon was hit in the head by AA shrapnel and passed out. The AA fire had also hit the engine and severed a petrol pipe, and the leaking fuel caused a fire to break out; the D.H.4 fell for 1,000ft (300m) before this went out and Goble was able to exert control of the machine. He released the bombs and turned to glide for home – a Pfalz scout attacked the D.H.4, without success, before the lines were reached. Gamon recovered consciousness in time to bring D9277 in to land at Conteville.

The D.H.9 was becoming available in ever-increasing numbers, and the addition of squadrons so equipped to the strength of the BEF took some of the pressure off the remaining D.H.4 units. Perhaps it was the difference in bombing altitudes that was the cause, but the D.H.4 suffered fewer casualties than its lower-flying replacement. The D.H.4, particularly in its Eagle-engined form, was by no means obsolete and could still give as good an account of itself in aerial combat. During July 1918 only seven D.H.4s serving with the BEF were brought down with fatal or POW consequences, whereas the comparable figure for the D.H.9 was seventeen.

D.H.4 squadrons were heavily involved in the great Allied offensive of the summer 1918, the Battle of Amiens. The work of the day bombers was part of the battle plan for the opening day of that offensive, 8 August. RAF reinforcement in the area was quietly prepared and involved 18, 25, 57 and 205 Squadrons; they were to help open the offensive at daybreak by attacking enemy aerodromes and, hopefully, cause damage by surprise and limit enemy aerial opposition. 57 Squadron was to bomb Moislains aerodrome, and 205 Squadron that at Bouvincourt. German reaction to the offensive was calculated to involve bringing in reserves by train, and so evening raids were then to be made against railway centres. That day was a bloody one for the RAF, though only one

D.H.4 (F6059, a reconstructed machine of 57 Squadron) was lost. Against this, 57 Squadron claimed three enemy scouts and 205 Squadron another. The British push gained more ground on the first day than had been expected, and the enemy was forced to bring in reinforcements across bridges over the Somme. Destruction of, or damage to those bridges would leave opposing German troops cut off, and so an all-out series of attacks was ordered, and those against railway targets cancelled. These bridge raids continued from the 8th to the 10th, but the targets were very difficult to hit from high altitude. 205 Squadron managed to achieve one hit on the bridge at Brie when a formation of seven of its D.H.4s attacked from only 2,000ft (600m).

The raids against the Somme bridges were curtailed from 10 August, and those on railway centres reinstated. An indication of the intensity of operations during the first few days of the offensive can be gathered from an examination of the work done by 205 Squadron. In the first four days (the 8th-11th) its pilots flew 324 hours and 13 minutes on operations, without casualty to aircrew. Sixteen tons of bombs had been dropped, and only one machine so damaged in combat that it had to be sent away for repair. The reliability of its Eagle engines was such that only three-and-a-half hours were spent on air-testing the machines; the comparable figure for a D.H.9 squadron was 21hr.

The success of the offensive continued throughout August and into September, and the D.H.4 squadrons resumed more distant bombing raids, primarily against railway centres. Many raids passed without incident, but mishaps could occur, and 57 Squadron was particularly unfortunate. The unit lost a pair of machines (F5825 and F6167) on 29 August in a fight near Douai – although there were claims for an equal number of enemy machines – and another (F6096) three days later. Deteriorating weather after the first week of September restricted the number of missions flown, but conditions improved again by the middle of the month, and so the intensity of the air war increased. 16 September was the first day of this renewed heavy fighting, and it saw losses for 25, 57 and 205 Squadrons. Three D.H.4s were lost with crews killed or POW, and another six severely damaged in action, with crew members wounded or killed.

By the late summer of 1918 the D.H.4 was being seen as a poor alternative for the D.H.4, but its successor, the D.H.9A with a 400hp Liberty engine, was coming into service and held great promise. 205 and 18 Squadrons were scheduled to re-equip with the new type. The former squadron had received its first D.H.9A (E9662) on 12 August, and re-equipment progressed throughout that month and into September; however, it continued to fly its diminishing number of D.H.4s on operations until that re-equipment was completed. 18 Squadron followed suit, beginning to re-equip during September, until eventually 25 and 57 Squadrons were the sole D.H.4 units with the BEF. The retention of those two squadrons was undoubtedly due to the fact that they flew the Eagle-powered version, and were by then receiving machines with the ultimate form of that engine, the 375hp Eagle VIII.

Enemy aerial opposition to the Allies' offensive escalated as the summer progressed, and it became common for formations of D.H.4s on bombing duty to be given an escort from scout (Camel/S.E.5a) or fighter-reconnaissance (Bristol F.2B) squadrons.

The signing of the Armistice signalled the imminent end for most squadrons. 25 and 57 Squadrons, however, were allocated to post-war policing duties with the Army of Occupation in the Rhineland. 202 and 217 Squadrons kept their machines until March 1919, when they were handed over to 98 (Demobilization) Squadron. Cadres of the two units then returned to the UK and disbandment. Apart from their policing duties, the BEF's other two D.H.4 units served in a communications role, often being employed in mail flights. 57 Squadron began to re-equip with D.H.9As at Morville during February 1919, and relinquished the last of its Fours three months later. 25 Squadron had received some D.H.9As during November 1918, and operated these alongside its remaining D.H.4s until 2 September 1919, when it returned to the UK, prior to disbandment and after giving up its machines. There was no place for the D.H.4 in the post-war RAF; accumulating stocks of D.H.9As and a shrinking number of squadrons made it redundant. Three (G-EAEW, G-EAEX and G-EAMU) came onto the British Civil register with some intent of permanence, the latter later being converted to D.H.4A standard. A further twenty-one also acquired civilian registrations, but their issue was only made to expedite sale abroad, mainly to the Aviation Militaire Belge.

The Strategic Bombing of Germany

The German raids on London and the south-east of England that had begun during May 1917 brought much pandemonium, especially when night raids began in September. A War Cabinet meeting on 1 October raised the issue of retaliation in kind, and a further meeting the next day, attended by Trenchard, agreed the detachment of units to the area around Nancy, from where targets in southern Germany would be in range.

Ochey aerodrome, used previously by 3 Wing RNAS, was the initial base for units of the 41st Wing RFC that was created to conduct those bombing operations. The RNAS was to contribute A Squadron, whose HP 0/100s had been engaged on anti-submarine duties but would engage in long-range night bombing. 100 Squadron, with F.E.2bs, would perform similar duty against targets closer to the lines. Day bombing was to be performed by 55 Squadron, with Eagle-engined D.H.4s. The choice of a squadron equipped with the excellent Rolls-Royce engine was not a random one. Fifty D.H.4s, intended for the Imperial Russian Air Service, were made available to the BEF and would make good any deficit resulting from 55 Squadron's withdrawal from tactical operations. The Fiat D.H.4, with its poorer performance, was not considered suitable for long-range penetration of German territory, but it could be used as a stop-gap tactical bomber, pending the anticipated arrival of D.H.9s in the spring of 1918. Deliveries of the Fiat machines to France began in late October, and they were held in storage at 2 AD Candas.

55 Squadron moved into Ochey on 11 October. It and the other two units of the 41st Wing, had a primary function of disrupting German supplies of iron ore, essential to the war effort. Germany relied on the ore fields of Lorraine and Luxembourg for some 80 per cent of its iron. The French had the railway centres for ore transportation as primary targets,

A beautifully clear shot of an Eagle Four going about its business at high altitude. The inaccuracy of strategic bombing can be understood when flying at such heights is considered alongside the primitive nature of contemporary bomb-sights. JMB/GSL

D.H.4s of 55 Squadron resembled this machine, here seen having its radiator topped up. It is not known who owns this particular machine. JMB/GSL

and requested that the 41st Wing join in that campaign. The British view was that its machines were for the bombing of targets in Germany, but that railway centres could be bombed as part of a process whereby targets of progressively greater range were attacked until those on the Rhine were reached.

55 Squadron made its first raid from Ochey only six days after its arrival. Its machines' range had been increased by the addition of extra 20gal (90l) fuel tanks. Eleven D.H.4s set out for the Burbach ironworks near Saarbrucken. Three had to turn back with engine trouble, but the remainder found their target and bombed successfully. Bous was the target four days later, and that raid saw 55 Squadron's first loss in its new role: enemy machines intercepted the twelve D.H.4s and succeeded in driving down B3961 to make Captain D. Owen and Lt B. Harker POWs.

The squadron's D.H.4s adopted a six-machine formation for its operations; usually two such formations comprised a raid. The D.H.4s flew in a triangular formation with a leader, a pair in echelon to both port and starboard, with the sixth machine behind the leader; this meant that bombs could be dropped together on the leader's signal, and it also made best possible use of the observers' guns for defence of the formation. The bomb load carried usually comprised a pair of 112lb (50kg) weapons. Great emphasis was placed on the maintenance of formation. A straggling machine was considered too vulnerable, and this accounts for the numbers of machines that returned to base with engine trouble, rather than carrying on alone.

Pirmasens, to the east of Saarbrucken, was attacked without incident on 30 October, and Kaiserlautern two days later. German scouts intercepted one formation on the latter raid, compelling the D.H.4s to drop their bombs prematurely. The weather conditions deteriorated rapidly in November, precluding any further raids that month. 55 Squadron moved base to Tantonville on the 7th, and this became its home for the next seven months.

Operations resumed on 5 December, but the persisting weather conditions made the primary target of Mannheim impossible to reach. One formation attacked Saarbrucken and another Zweibrucken, both causing damage. Eleven D.H.4s returned to Saarbrucken on the following day, and seven attacked Pirmasens on the 11th, but neither of these excursions was of any great military significance. However, the final raid of the year, against Mannheim on Christmas Eve, was the deepest penetration into Germany yet accomplished by the 41st Wing. Ten D.H.4s made it to the target, two having returned to base with engine trouble. The bombs dropped did little real damage; furthermore A7465 was lost, with 2nd Lts G.F. Castle and A.F. Turner being made POWs.

These early raids were well covered in RFC communiques of the period, meriting a separate section in each for the 41st Wing's activities. This reflects the novel nature of long-distance bombing to the service, and the recognition of the arduous nature of such raids for participating crews.

A significant sortie had been made on 6 December. It is not always realized that most techniques applied by the RAF in World War Two had been pioneered in the earlier conflict; photographic reconnaissance was one such technique. 55 Squadron was intended to operate against uncharted targets, and so sorties by individual machines were dedicated to both gathering target information and gaining assessment of raid results. The unit's first such sortie in its new area of operations was made on that date. Good weather conditions were necessary for such missions, and the D.H.4s involved would fly at altitudes of up to 19,000ft (6,000m). Interception by enemy scouts was unlikely at such heights, but to achieve that altitude meant that all superfluous equipment had to be stripped from the machines and ammunition kept to a minimum. On occasions where EA did make contact, the D.H.4s were usually able to outrun them – an ability shared with the great de Havilland design of World War Two, the Mosquito. During its period with the 41st Wing, 55 Squadron made ninety-eight such flights and lost only one machine in the process. Improvement in the performance of the unit's D.H.4s was achieved over the winter of 1917-18 by the replacement of the original 250hp Eagle III engines with 275hp Eagle VIIs. The replacements were made at unit level.

55 Squadron mounted only two raids in January 1918, as adverse weather conditions continued to hamper operations. Karlsrule was successfully attacked on the 14th, causing considerable damage, but the raid on Treves on the 27th encountered cloud and rain, which caused one formation to abort the mission.

Conditions were only slightly better in February. Offenburg was attacked on the 12th, but rain and cloud on the 17th made it impossible to reach Mannheim, so all twelve participating machines returned to Tantonville with bombs still aboard. Single formations attacked both Treves and Thionville on the following day. Further attempts to reach Mannheim were made on both the 19th and 20th, but each time the Rhine Valley was filled with mist, making navigation impossible. On the 19th Treves was therefore attacked instead, though A7468 was lost in the process: it was seen turning for home before the target was reached, but did not make it. Presumably it had suffered engine trouble and came down in enemy territory; its crew became POWs.

During March 1918 atmospheric conditions were more stable, and so there was a corresponding increase in the number of missions flown. More significantly, most of the targets were at a greater range than those previously attacked; for instance Mainz was bombed on the 9th, and Stuttgart the following day, and both were more than 100 miles (160km) beyond the lines. The attack on Mainz was particularly successful, with riverside warehouses hit and all ten participating machines returning safely. That on the Daimler works at Stuttgart was less fortunate, resulting in the loss of A7569 to EA, with its crew (2nd Lts R. Caldicott and G.P.F. Thomas) made POWs. Lt J.M. Carroll, the observer in A7556, was wounded in that encounter, and another D.H.4 was damaged that day. A7418 set out on a photographic mission, but caught fire while climbing to operational altitude; Captain J.B. Fox made a rapid descent and crash-landed, and was pulled from the burning machine by his observer Lt S.S. Jones.

Koblenz, at the junction of the Rhine and Mosel, was the target for the 12th, and this was even further than the targets of the previous raids. Only nine D.H.4s out of twelve that departed made it to the target, but their bombing was successful, with a barracks hit, as well as civilian areas. All returned safely, and an enemy scout was claimed as being sent OOC. The increase in the number of missions flown was bound to bring increased losses, and during an attack on Freiburg the following day three D.H.4s (A7489, A7579 and B5966) were lost, with two crews killed and another made prisoner. Zweibrucken was visited on the 16th, Kaiserlautern on the 17th, and Mannheim on the 18th, and all three missions were accomplished without loss, although A7548 suffered extensive combat damage. After a five-day break, Mannheim was again attacked on the 24th, and in the course of this another two machines (A7562 and A7661) were lost, with their crews made POWs; also the gunner of another crew was killed. However, all crews had reached and bombed the target,

were bombed instead, resulting in the loss of A7555 on the first of these missions, with its crew made POWs. A further abortive attempt was made on the 12th, but this too was thwarted by weather conditions.

Railways were the target in the first half of May 1918, and four raids were mounted between the 2nd and the 15th, with one of these being abandoned due to poor weather. However, the one on the 3rd was estimated to have caused 25,000 marks worth of damage. Railways and factories at Saarbrucken were targeted on the 16th, but the twelve D.H.4s were attacked by enemy scouts. A7477 went down in

far. Landau was bombed on 20 May, and more distant railway targets at Charleroi/Namur and Liege on the next two days; A7791 was lost on the 22nd. Thionville and its railway system were attacked on the 29th and 30th, and on the last day of the month a sortie was made by twelve D.H.4s against Mannheim; they were obliged to divert to Karlsruhe, and had the misfortune to lose A7825 in flames, with the pilot fatally wounded and the observer killed.

55 Squadron flew its first mission of June on the following day when eleven D.H.4s made for Karthaus and encountered enemy opposition. A7482 was seen to break up in mid-air with fatal consequences for its crew, but the remaining ten bombed and returned successfully. Attempted raids on the 3rd and 4th were diverted to attack secondary targets when thick cloud prevented machines from reaching their primaries. The squadron had been joined at Tantonville by 99 Squadron, which had begun flying bombing missions with its D.H.9s, and both units transferred base to a new aerodrome at Azelot on 5 June. There, the two units joined 104 Squadron, newly arrived and also with D.H.9s, to bring all three squadrons of the 41st Wing to a common base.

There was no respite, however, because ten 55 Squadron machines were sent on a raid to Koblenz on the following day; they completed their mission without loss. Cloud prevented accurate bombing of that same target on the 7th and prevented it being reached again on the 8th, when Thionville was attacked as an alternative. Another attempt was made five days later, but the twelve attacking machines had to divert to bomb Treves, and lost A7466 in the process; its crew, 2nd Lts W. Legge and A. McKenzie, were killed. Cloud did not interfere with an attack on Metz-Sablon on the 23rd, but it did prevent ten D.H.4s from reaching Mannheim the day after; on this occasion the formations were separated, and so they bombed Dillingen and Metz-Sablon instead. Saarbrucken was targeted on the 25th, with B7866 going down to enemy fighters and its crew killed. A further loss was suffered the next day, when A8073 was seen to land in enemy territory after bombing Karlsruhe, and its crew taken prisoner. After bombing Thionville again on the 27th, 55 Squadron was sent to attack chemical works at Mannheim on the penultimate

The 51 TS D.H.4 'Wullypug', shown earlier, is seen here after coming to grief on a visit to its neighbouring base at Scampton. The rear fuselage marking was used by 51 TS on its D.H.4s and Martinsyde G.102s. JMB/GSL

the first time for six weeks. March ended with raids on the 27th and 28th against railway targets, probably in an attempt to disrupt the movement of material to support the German offensive in the west that had begun six days earlier.

Only three raids were mounted in April, the first two, on the 5th and 11th, being aimed at a German HQ in a chateau near Spa. But on both these occasions weather conditions prevented the D.H.4s from reaching the target, and railway targets

flames, with 2nd Lt R.C. Sansom and AM2 G.C. Smith killed, and the observers of two other machines were wounded. On the 17th, Metz-Sablon railway targets were successfully hit; and on the following day six D.H.4s were sent against targets in Cologne. Enemy aeroplanes intercepted the D.H.4s, but two were shot down out of control; however, A7595's observer was killed. Significantly, this raid was the furthest north that 55 Squadron had penetrated so

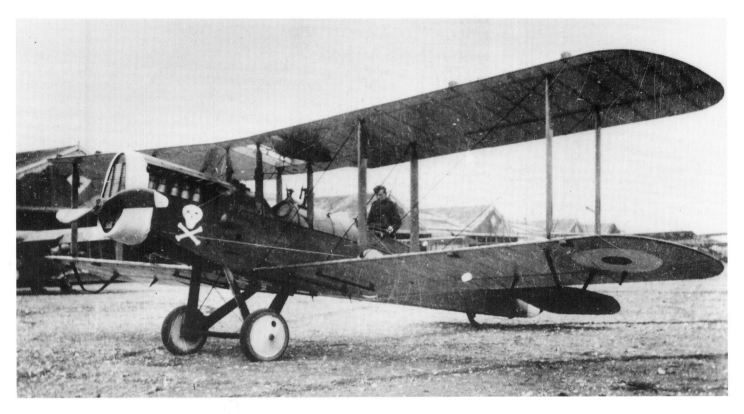

This BHP-engined D.H.4 had an unusual skull-and-crossbones marking on its nose. It was photographed at Thetford, in 1918 the home of 4 School of Navigation and Bomb Dropping. JMB/GSL

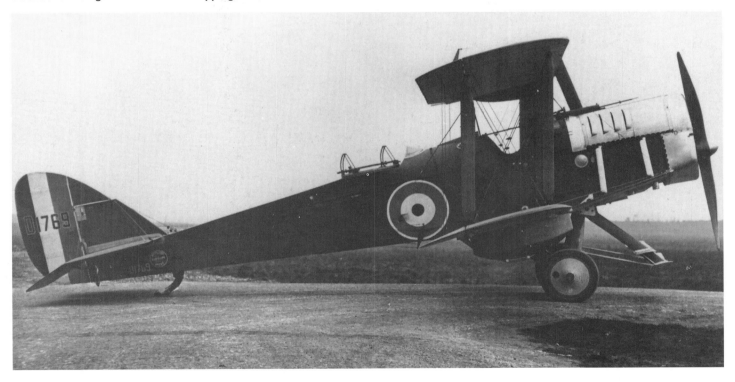

D.H.4s used on Marine Operations units had to face the added hazard of being forced to ditch in the event of engine failure or combat damage. Experiments were conducted at Grain to find ways to minimize the risks involved; one was to add inflatable flotation bags at the sides of the engine cowling, also a hydrovane and wing-tip floats. D1769 was one machine used. JMB/GSL

THE D.H.4 – THE FIRST EFFECTIVE DAY-BOMBER

day of the month. It was a successful raid, with all eleven of the attacking machines returning, and a claim for two enemy machines being shot down out of control. Damage was estimated at 151,000 marks.

The pace increased even further during July 1918, when 55 Squadron mounted fifteen raids. The majority of these were relatively uneventful, but most were still made by formations that had lost machines after engine troubles. Karthaus, Koblenz (twice) and Duren (twice) were attacked during the first nine days of the month, followed by raids on railway targets on three occasions between the 11th and the 15th.

On the 16th the squadron was scheduled to attack Stuttgart, in conjunction with 99 Squadron, but thunderstorms made the outward leg impossible and twelve D.H.4s bombed Thionville instead. A second attempt on the following day ended with the same result. Four machines dropped out of a raid on Oberndorf on the 19th, but the remaining eight bombed. A return to the same target was made next day, but the D.H.4s were intercepted over the target: fighters shot down A7876 (pilot wounded and taken POW, and its observer killed) and D9275 (both crew killed), and A7427 returned with its pilot, Lt A.D. Keep MC, wounded and its observer dead. Stuttgart was brought back onto the target list, but attempts to reach it on both the 22nd and 30th were impossible, and secondary targets were bombed instead.

The final raid of the month was more successful: ten D.H.4s, from twelve that took off, reached and bombed Koblenz without incident. Thus 55 squadron had fared well in a month that averaged a raid every two days; much better than 99 Squadron, whose D.H.9s had flown on ten raids for the loss of eight machines down in enemy territory, or 104 Squadron, with four such losses in four missions.

The July losses suffered by 99 Squadron meant that the unit was kept back from raids for much of August. 55 and 104 Squadrons continued the 41st Wing's effort, and both units suffered increased losses – but again, the D.H.4s came off more lightly that the D.H.9s. 55 Squadron could not reach its allotted targets at Cologne on the 1st, bombing Duren instead, but a week later eleven D.H.4s bombed Wallingen successfully. Nine out of ten machines that had been detailed to attack Mannheim on the 11th had turned

back, and the remaining crew wisely bombed the Metz-Sablon railway triangle instead. However, the full force of twelve machines reached and bombed Frankfurt the next day. Extensive cloud banks prevented Cologne being reached on the 14th, and the squadron claimed three enemy scouts destroyed and a further two shot down out of control over the Offenburg, which had been selected as an alternative target. Another attempt was made to reach Cologne four days later, but again cloud interfered; at first the leader of the eleven attacking D.H.4s decided to attack Mannheim, but then it was decided to press on to Darmstadt. Enemy scouts attacked, and although three were claimed as driven down, three D.H.4s were also lost. Furthermore the crews of A7781 and D9273 were killed, and 2nd Lts J. Campbell and J.R. Fox brought A7813 down to become POWs.

Cologne was again the location of targets when twelve machines set out on the 22nd, but again it was not reached, the eight that had made formation bombing the alternatives at Koblenz. It was a similar story on the following two attempts, with ten (out of twelve) D.H.4s bombing Treves when cloud banks prevented their reaching Cologne on the 23rd, and six attacking Luxembourg when high winds were the problem on the 25th. Cloud was again a problem two days later, when railway targets at Bettembourg were abandoned in favour of attacking Conflans. Yet another attempt to reach Cologne was aborted on the 30th, but as the eleven D.H.4s bombed Thionville, they were attacked by enemy scouts and lost four of their number: the crews of A7589 and A7708 were lucky to be brought down as POWs; those of A7972 and D8396 were killed. The POW pilots were both Americans learning their trade before posting to units of their own air service. Also on this raid, 2nd Lt P.J. Cunningham brought A7783 down in Allied territory and was killed, and his observer fatally wounded. The observers of a further two aeroplanes were wounded, one fatally.

It took the squadron time to recover from such a mauling. On 7 September just six machines tried to get to Cologne, but again the target could not be reached. The unit was back to full strength after a further week, however, when twelve machines had a relatively easy raid on railway targets at Ehrang. Twelve set out

for Stuttgart the following day, and the nine that achieved formation bombed successfully, causing considerable damage and returning safely. The unit was less fortunate on the 16th, losing one (F5712) of five machines that bombed Mannheim in conjunction with 110 Squadron, that was making its first strategic raid. After an eight-day respite from strategic missions, 55 Squadron was detailed to attack Kaiserlautern on the 25th. All twelve D.H.4s that set out managed to bomb the targets, but heavy AA fire was encountered and enemy scouts attacked the formations. Two of those scouts were claimed as destroyed and a further pair as driven down – but four of the de Havillands also failed to return. The crews of D8388 and F5714 were made POW, those of D8356 and D8413 were killed, and both D8386 and D8392 returned to Azelot with their observers dead. However, the squadron must have drawn on its reserve of six D.H.4s because it was able to send up another twelve the next day, when it was detailed to attack railway targets at Adun-le-Roman. Only six made it to the targets, four having to turn back, and two making forced landings after engine trouble.

Only four strategic raids were made by 55 Squadron during October, and the same number in the last eleven days of the war. That does not imply that the unit was otherwise idle, and small formations were detailed for tactical work. It was 21 October before Cologne was again revealed as a target, and twelve machines set out. Only seven made formation, and their incursion into Germany was again prevented by thickening cloud – and so Thionville, as so often, was the recipient of the bombs. A further attempt was made two days later, but was aborted after the leader had engine problems over Metz; the railway network around that city was attacked before the D.H.4s returned to base. Enemy scouts attempted to interfere with eleven D.H.4s bombing Longuyon on the 29th, and one was claimed as driven down; the D.H.4s, however, suffered no losses.

On the final day of October yet another attempt was made to reach Cologne, but as ever, adverse weather intervened and so railway targets around Bonn were selected instead. The same bad luck applied three days later on 3 November when D.H.4s bombed the Burbach works at Saarbrucken, because the formation was then attacked by enemy fighters: two were claimed as destroyed, and another as driven down. On 9 November only one D.H.4 from a force of six reached the target, the railway system around Bensdorf; and the squadron made its final raid on the 10th. Inevitably that was aimed at Cologne, but the attempt was no more successful than previous ones. Ehrang was bombed instead, but the unit lost F5725; its crew was made POW, but the pilot died the next day.

Had the war continued into 1919, 55 Squadron would have re-equipped with D.H.15s, but with the signing of the Armistice there was no need for this. The D.H.4s flew west to Le Planty Farm on 16 November, and thence to St-Andre-aux-Bois. After being reduced to a cadre, the unit returned to the UK in February 1919, and disbanded the following year.

The D.H.4 In UK Service

Even before the first D.H.4 had been delivered, the RFC planned for a supply of pilots trained on the type. 44 RS, at Harlaxton, was the first unit devoted to the task, and had a paper establishment of six Avros, six R.E.7s and six D.H.4s on 23 December 1916. As the first D.H.4s entered service, they were allotted to 44 RS; thus A2125-A2127 and A2131 were all earmarked for that training unit. Trainee pilots, fresh from Elementary RS, were introduced to tractor machines on the Avro; moved on to the R.E.7 to experience large, single-engined machines; and then finally graduated to the D.H.4. Martinsyde G.100/102s soon replaced the R.E.7s. The single unit was considered sufficient to supply 55 Squadron. However, when the planned replacement of F.E.2s in 18, 25 and 57 Squadrons by D.H.4s was scheduled for the summer of 1917, it was realized that 44 Training Squadron (as 44 RS had become on 31 May) would be unable to cope with the extra demand. 52 TS at Stirling had been intended to equip with twelve B.E.2es and twelve D.H.4s, but that did not happen until later in 1917. Consequently, 51 TS at Wye – later Waddington – was then given similar equipment and duty to 44 TS. The final withdrawal of the F.E.2 from daylight operations meant that there was no further need for that type in the existing training squadrons, and several of those dedicated to F.E. training were transferred to training D.H.4 pilots. 9 TS at Norwich (later Sedgeford), 19 TS at Hounslow and 46 TS at Bramham Moor, later Catterick, were the units involved. 52 TS received D.H.4s, after moving to Catterick, as did 31 TS at Wyton.

2 TDS at Lake Down was one of the handful of such units formed experimentally in 1917 to provide all-through pilot training. It was dedicated to turning out day-bomber pilots and received some D.H.4s, in addition to B.E.2es and R.E.8s, to fulfil that task. The unit's existence was brief: it disbanded to form 1 SNBD after moving to Stonehenge. D.H.4s formed only a small part of the new unit's equipment, the same being true of the other two UK-based SNBD. Further TDS were formed in 1918, and many of those scheduled to turn out D.H.9 pilots had some of the earlier type on strength. Squadrons mobilizing for active service with the D.H.9 also received D.H.4s, pending the arrival of their operational equipment.

19 TS was one of the few such units to survive the almost wholesale transfer to the TDS system in mid-1918. It moved to the Curragh, in Ireland, but the gradual replacement of the D.H.4 with the D.H.9 made its operation of the earlier type increasingly less urgent. By 31 October there were only six D.H.4s with the Irish group, not all of which may have been on 19 Training Squadron's books.

Small numbers of D.H.4s served with the Fighting Schools at Turnberry, Marske and Bircham Newton, and others with 1 (Observers) SAG at New Romney, but

This rear view shows the flotation bag mountings and the other attachments. It is not known what effect such drag-inducing features had on the machine's performance. JMB/GSL

A more ambitious idea for a Marine Operations D.H.4 was the fitting of floats. This was done to A8044 at Felixstowe during October 1918. JMB/GSL

the type was never numerous with those units. Some were also operated by squadrons mobilizing for service with the D.H.9, notably 99, 105, 106 and 109 Squadrons.

A majority of the D.H.4s issued to 44 and 51 TS had the Eagle engine. The 230hp BHP/Puma powered most of those issued to other training units, and this was obviously a consequence of the scarcity of Rolls-Royce engines.

During 1917, most RNAS D.H.4 pilots were not introduced to the type until they reached operational squadrons. 12N Squadron at Petite Synthe served as a 'finishing school' for pilots posted to naval squadrons in France, and operated a few D.H.4s alongside its predominant scout equipment. The situation was remedied by the formation of the D.H.4 school at Manston, on 19 January 1918. That school operated both D.H.4s and, later, D.H.9s, providing an earlier introduction to the type for those destined to fly it operationally. The unit was retitled 203 TDS upon the RAF's formation, and was subsequently designated 55 TDS to bring it into the main TDS numbering system. As 1918 progressed, fewer D.H.4s and more D.H.9s were operated, reflecting the

increasing availability of the latter type. The same was true at 202/57 TDS Cranwell, a former component of the RNAS Central Training Establishment.

Service at home was non-operational. The introduction of German aeroplane raids from May 1917 resulted in all available machines being made available for interception. As early as 5 June, 2 AAP at Hendon had dispatched A7471, being readied for delivery, against that day's raid. The same unit launched A7486 and A7487 against a further raid eight days later, with A7481, ready for dispatch to France, rising from 8 AAP at Lympne. A2129 was undergoing tests at Orfordness and it, too, made sorties, but its pilots failed to make contact. Contact was made against the raid of 4 July, when four D.H.4 sorties were made from Hendon and one from Martlesham Heath; the latter was by A7436, and was flown by Captain J. Palethorpe, with AM1 J.O. Jessop in the observer's seat. They were on a routine test of the new machine when the Gotha formation was sighted. Palethorpe attacked, but his Vickers jammed, and Jessop was hit and killed. Palethorpe landed and then took off again, with another gunner, in a vain search for the

enemy. He was awarded the MC for his actions.

Further contact with the enemy was made three days later. 2 AAP sent five D.H.4 sorties against the attacking force of twenty-two Gothas. Lt D.W. Clappen in A7483, with A.M. Wills as his gunner, made contact, but his Vickers gun also jammed. Clappen followed the raiders, with Wills firing his Lewis when possible. Engine trouble then necessitated a return to Hendon, where it was discovered that enemy fire had damaged the D.H.4's tail surfaces. A7508, also from Hendon and crewed by Lt F.L. Hambly and 2nd Lt M.A.E. Cremetti, had a similar adventure with a jammed Vickers, failing engine and the Lewis gun hit by enemy fire. A7436 from Martlesham was again airborne, but this time made contact. Captain J. Palethorpe, with A.M.F. James manning the Lewis, attacked the Gothas over Essex. Again the Vickers jammed, but James fired all his ammunition – though without observed effect. Retaliatory fire from a Gotha hit Palethorpe, who nevertheless managed to land at Rochford.

Eight uneventful D.H.4 sorties were made against the raid of 22 July, two on 12 August and one on the final daylight raid

Representative D.H.4s with RFC/RAF Training Units and Squadrons Mobilizing

9 TS Norwich/Sedgeford – A7496, A7656, A7752, A7793, B5452, B9951.
19 TS Hounslow/The Curragh – A7433, A7714, B2054.
26 TS Narborough – A7932, B2121, B5463, B5469, B5476.
44 RS/TS Harlaxton/Waddington – A2125, A2126, A2127.
51 RS/TS Wye/Waddington – A2128, A2134, A2136, A2146, A7698, B3960.
46 TS Catterick – A7499, A7576, A7585, A7588, A7611, A7617, A7623, A7636, A7696, A7729, A7746, A7748, A7983.
52 TS Stirling/Montrose/Catterick – A2127, A7435, A7438, A7752, A7779, A7826, A7986, B2126, B5502, B5514, B5516.
61 TS South Carlton – A7787, A7813.
69 TS Narborough – A7590, B5465.
75 TS Cramlington – A2128, A7814.
2 TDS Lake Down/Stonehenge – A7659, A7669, A7678, A7686, A7758, B2055, B2056, B2061, B2096, B5451, B5458.
5 TDS Easton-on-the-Hill – A7590.
6 TDS Boscombe Down – B5497, B5521, B5525, B5526, B5527.
10 TDS Harling Road – A7667, A7714, A7752, A7753, A7938, A7974, B5512.
11 TDS Old Sarum – A7827, A7962, A7994, B5467.
31 TDS Fowlmere – B2115, B5538.
35 TDS Duxford – B5539.
49 TDS Catterick – A2127, A7779, A7826, B2127, B5517, B5546, B5549, B5550.
55 TDS (ex-203 TDS) Manston/Narborough – A7884, A7962, B9480, B9482, B8486, B9487, B9490, B9491, N6414, N6425.
57 TDS (ex-202 TDS) Cranwell – A7726, B9478, B9479, B9488, B9489, B9496, D1767, N6427, N6429.

204 TDS Eastchurch – A7817, A7831, A7832, A7841, A7843, N6426.
1 SNBD Stonehenge – A7890, A8011, B5482, B5483, B5484, B5485, B8091, B8125.
2 FS Marske – B5522, B5528.
3FS Bircham Newton – B2089, B2100.
MAFIS Lilbourne – B2114.
Pool of Pilots Joyce Green – A7992, B5453.
WEE Biggin Hill – A7689, A7890, B2052, B5549.
Medical Flight Hendon – A7993.
49 Squadron Dover – A7571, A7678, A7693, A7722, A7758.
83 Squadron Wyton – A7462, A7520.
98 Squadron Old Sarum – A7741, B2096, B5451, B7891, B9456.
99 Squadron Old Sarum – A7755, B2051, B2096.
103 Squadron Old Sarum – A7460, A7659, A7741, A7755, A7777, B2057, B2097.
104 Squadron Andover – A7765, A7980, B2096, B5491.
105 Squadron Andover – A7765, B5460, B5466, B5468, B5473, B5487, B5490.
106 Squadron Andover – B5472, B5489, B5492.
108 Squadron Lake Down – B2096.
109 Squadron Lake Down – B2055, B2057, B2096, B5481, B5486, B5499, B5508, B5509, B5542, B5543, B5544, B5545.
110 Squadron Sedgeford – A7734, A7965, B9994.
121 Squadron Narborough – A7721, A7948.
125 Squadron Fowlmere – A7952.
126 Squadron Fowlmere – B2095, B5504, B5520, B5539, B7818, B7857.
127 Squadron Catterick – B5515.

of 22 August. Subsequent raids by Gothas and Giants were made at night.

The RNAS had established a chain of coastal aerodromes for operations against enemy submarines and airships, and some of these received D.H.4s. Yarmouth and its satellites at Bacton, Burgh Castle and Covehithe were the principal stations for operations over the Dogger Bank.

A7457 and A7459, the two RAF 3a-engined D.H.4s acquired by the RNAS for the proposed reconnaissance of the Keil Canal, were delivered to Bacton on 9 August 1917. The pilots' impression of that machine can be deduced from the nickname bestowed upon the former: 'Non-Starter'. A7459 was lost in the North Sea on 5 September. Yarmouth received a pair of BHP-engined Fours (N6395 and N6396) during that month. These were employed on a variety of duties that included the escort of Felixstowe F.2A flying boats on their incursions along the German coast. Such flying boat patrols often encountered enemy opposition in the form of fighting seaplanes, and the D.H.4s were intended to provide escort cover. In addition, North Sea patrols were likely to encounter enemy airships, and the use of the D.H.4 in these various roles led to trials that would maximize the type's effectiveness.

A7457 went from Bacton to the Experimental Station at Grain on 30 September; there it was fitted with flotation gear and a hydrovane. The flotation gear was successfully tested after a ditching on 28 January 1918, and a further such test involved BHP-engined D1769. The purpose of such tests was, of course, to provide an element of safety for crews employed on over-water operations. The question how to attack German airships was also addressed by the staff at Grain. At least three D.H.4s (A2168, A7879 and A7894) were fitted with COW guns: these were 37mm cannon, and on A2168 the gun was mounted at the front of the observer's cockpit to fire upwards at about 80 deg to the thrust line. Its positioning necessitated modifications to the centre-section structure.

A more ambitious conversion was that made to A8044. The Brandenburg seaplanes that were employed by the German Navy had a vastly superior performance to the F.2As used on reconnaissance duties, and were held in high regard by British pilots. A8044, fitted with an Eagle VIII, had served at Bacton and Covehithe and was delivered to the seaplane station at Felixstowe, where it was fitted with long pontoon-type floats and flown successfully by 18 October 1918. The end of hostilities presumably ended the requirement for any further development.

The greatest success of home-based D.H.4s came on 5 August 1918, a date that saw the final airship raid against Britain. It was led by Fregattenkapitın Peter Strasser, the commander of the German Naval Airship Service, who flew in the new Zeppelin L70 (commander Kapitınleutnant von Lottnitzer) alongside L53, L56, L63 and L65. Slackening wind conditions led to the airships approaching landfall by 8pm. After a delay, the raid was notified and L56 and L63 were clearly visible from Yarmouth.

Aircrew rushed for available machines, and these included two D.H.4s with Eagle VIIIs fitted. Lt R.E. Keys took off in A8039, with AM1 A.T. Harman as gunner. A8032 had a more experienced crew, Major E. Cadbury and Captain R. Leckie, both with previous experience of attacking airships: Cadbury was involved in the destruction of L21 on 28 November 1916, and Leckie in that of

L22 on 14 May 1917. Other Yarmouth-based machines joined the chase as the airships turned north into thickening cloud. The D.H.4s independently found the other three Zeppelins at about 18,000ft (5,500m), and both attacked the nearest, L70. Unaware of each other's presence, both D.H.4 crews attacked, using incendiary and explosive ammunition. The airship soon caught fire and came down off the north Norfolk coast, eight miles (13km) from Wells-next-the-Sea.

Cadbury and Leckie then made for L65, but the D.H.4 was below and at its ceiling. Leckie's Lewis gun soon jammed, and although Keys and Harman also joined the attack, the airship escaped. Both D.H.4 crews were lost in cloud, and were lucky to find safe landings: A8032 came down at Sedgeford, and A8039 on the landing ground at Kelstern in Lincolnshire. The loss of Strasser had a devastating effect on the morale of the German Naval Airship Service, and its activities were thenceforth confined to fleet reconnaissance.

Yarmouth's D.H.4 element, part of a formation known a 'D Flt', was titled '490 Flt' on 20 August 1918, becoming a component of the newly reformed 212 Squadron. The Covehithe-based element of D Flt became 534 Flt of 273 Squadron. BHP-engined N6395 was still at Yarmouth, on the strength of 490 Flt, and it saw action on 16 September when, in company with a D.H.9, it escorted a pair of F.2As on a long reconnaissance. The British machines encountered five of the enemy's near the Shipwash light vessel, but managed to escape unscathed from the ensuing combat.

Home-based D.H.4s disappeared rapidly after the signing of the Armistice: only eighty-three remained with training units, and the majority had the BHP (Puma) engine. A mere twenty-three remained in storage, all with the Eagle engine, an indication perhaps of the intention to relinquish the type. The Fiat-Four had virtually disappeared, only two remaining with 'Areas', a generic term that covered the training depot stations and the few remaining training squadrons. The D.H.9

had supplanted the type at training depot stations, and the marine operations units were disbanded during the spring and early summer of 1919. Apart from a handful at experimental establishments, the only users by late 1919 were the communications squadrons, whose work is discussed below.

Anti-Submarine Operations

A third D.H.4 unit had been added to the RNAS force in the Dunkerque area. This was 17N Squadron, formed on 23 January 1918 from elements of the RNAS Seaplane Base at that port. It was properly established in 1 Wing RNAS at Bergues by 1 February, and was tasked with anti-submarine work. Its D.H.4s were also of the Eagle-engined variety, whose greater reliability was considered essential for operations over the Channel.

17N Squadron became 217 Squadron RAF on 1 April and, like other units of 61 Wing (ex-1 Wing RNAS), was dedicated to continue existing naval operations. Units of the former 4 and 5 Wings RNAS

B7941 served with 217 Squadron on anti-submarine duties. American pilots for the Northern Bombing Group were posted to this unit to gain operational experience, and this connection may account for the rear fuselage decoration. The aeroplane returned to the UK after the cessation of hostilities; it is seen here at Netheravon during 1919. F. A. Yeoman

were taken under military control. The squadron's main duty was to catch surfaced U-boats as they made to enter or leave the ports of Zeebrugge and Ostende. For this the usual bomb load was a pair of 230lb (104kg) weapons. When necessary, however, 17N/217 Squadron was also called upon to participate in bombing raids on land targets, particularly the installations at those two coastal ports and those at the inland port of Bruges, the main submarine base.

The anti-submarine patrols entailed flying a regular 'beat' off the Belgian coast, and on 13 March, A7863 (FSL J.N. Rutter and Gunlayer A.W. Vidler) found a surfaced vessel north-east of Dunkerque. They dropped a single 230lb bomb, apparently without result. A further such attack was made on 3 April, by A7846 and A7867.

On 23 April, A7773 and A8059 caught a surfaced U-boat, escorted by four destroyers, twelve miles (19km) north of Zeebrugge. Each dropped its pair of bombs, but without any observed result. There was a similar negative result on 19 May when A7846 and A8065 attacked four destroyers off Ostende; A7934, A7945, A7996 and A8067 also attacked the same target, and two days later A8065 attacked a single destroyer.

217 Squadron participated in a raid on Zeebrugge on 28 May, as part of an attempt to block the entrance to that harbour and its canal link to Bruges. A8065 was lost in the process, being shot down by an EA of the Seefrontstaffel. Two days later A7772 and A7935 attacked a submarine NNW of Dunkerque, without any positive result. A7772 was in action again on 1 June, attacking a U-boat off Ostende, with the help of A7846.

Units of 5 (Operations) Group were fortunate in that machines being damaged in combat were not always obliged to land in enemy-held territory. The neutral Netherlands was just to the north of the main targets of Zeebrugge and Ostende, and crews of stricken machines could make for that safe haven and face internment for the war's duration, a much better prospect than being made POW. 2nd Lt G.B. Coward and Lt J.F. Read took that option on 17 June after A7935 had been attacked by four EA. Coward succeeded in landing the D.H.4 on a Dutch aerodrome; it was taken on charge by the Luchtvaartafdeeling (LVA), but returned to the RAF after the war.

A further Zeebrugge raid on 30 June resulted in the loss of A8013, and Lt C.J. Moir and Sgt Mechanic Hunnisett were killed as the machine broke up in mid-air. Three days earlier A7867 and A8022 had bombed a U-boat, and another was bombed on the 29th by A7773 and A8022.

Enemy aerial opposition to 217 Squadron's activities often came from Brandenburg seaplanes based at Zeebrugge, and land-plane scouts of the Seefrontstaffel at Ostende. The D.H.4s were able to hold their own on many occasions, and had several combat successes. One example of this was when A7643 and A7941 were attacked by eight seaplanes during the course of an anti-submarine patrol on 29 July. The combined fire of the observers (Lt N.S. Dougall and Lt U.G.A. Tonge) sent one of the EA down to crash. Another involved A7846, whose observer, Gunlayer Hunnisett, sent an Albatros scout down on 28 June.

217 Squadron had moved to Crochte on 10 July, and that remained its base for the duration of hostilities. Its duties began to incorporate more bombing raids, but there were occasions when its continuing marine operations resulted in vessels being bombed. A7772 and A8850 attacked a surfaced submarine off Middelkerke on 12 August. Each dropped four bombs, presumably the 112lb (50kg) type, but no claim was made for damage. The squadron suffered minimal casualties during its operational period. Other than the loss of A8013, mentioned earlier, the only other fatalities involved three D.H.4s, all on 28 September 1918: A7924 was lost in a bombing raid on Staden when it was attacked by sixteen EA, and Lt J.E. Gregory and 2nd Lt E. Martin Bell were killed; F5704 crashed on return from bombing Ostende, killing Lt A.R. Padmore and Sgt Mechanic F.W. Shufflebotham; and finally 2nd Lt A.F. Tong was killed in a flying accident on D8374, and his observer, Sgt Mechanic M. Connolly, was injured.

Service In the Mediterranean, Aegean and Mesopotamia

The Sopwith 1½ Strutters that served with the RNAS 2 Wing in the Aegean, and 6 Wing in southern Italy, were rapidly becoming outdated by late 1917. Sixteen D.H.4s had been shipped by the end of that year to enable 2 Wing to maintain bombing operations, but only two of those (N5975 and N5976) had the Rolls-Royce engine; the others were BHP-powered. Units serving in France had priority in delivery of the more powerful version of the type. The number of D.H.4s was considered insufficient, as were the existing numbers of fighter and seaplane types. The situation was communicated to the Admiralty in a telegram from Vice-Admiral the Hon. Sir S.A. Gough-Calthorpe, dated 5 December 1917. One effect was the diversion of further D.H.4s to the Mediterranean area. Needless to say, those D.H.4s also had the BHP engine.

2 Wing RNAS had operated in the Aegean since 1915, and comprised A–G Squadrons that flew from a selection of island bases. Its duties were various, and included reconnaissance of the German-Turkish fleet as well as bombing raids on targets in Turkey, Bulgaria and Macedonia. The arrival of the D.H.4s provided welcome replacement for the ageing Sopwiths, and the first were brought into use shortly after their arrival in October.

C Squadron at Gliki, on the island of Imbros, received the first two D.H.4s, and flew them on missions during November that included attacks on the Sofia-Constantinople railway, and objectives on the Gallipoli peninsular. Such attacks, interspersed with reconnaissance of mainland Turkey, remained the regular work of the unit.

F and G Squadrons were based on Mudros from late 1917 and were well placed to counter a sortie by the German cruisers Goeben and Breslau that was notified on 20 January 1918. All available aircraft were brought to readiness, and these included D.H.4s of the two squadrons. The German vessels succeeded in sinking a pair of monitors before air attacks caused the Breslau to manoeuvre and stray into a minefield – and so to meet her fate. The Goeben attempted to continue the sortie, but turned back after striking mines. The ship ran aground and was spotted and bombed by a pair of D.H.4s. Further D.H.4 attacks resulted in one 112lb (50kg) bomb hitting the vessel; but such weapons were too light to inflict serious damage. The Goeben eventually floated off and made for Constantinople, where she remained moored for the rest of the war. Her presence in the area was still a cause for concern, and regular reconnaissance was made by D.H.4s to confirm that she was 'bottled up'. N6410 was lost on such a reconnaissance on 22 March, its crew being made POWs.

2 Wing RNAS became 62 Wing RAF on 1 April 1918, but the formation of the new service had little effect on the everyday activities of the unit – at first its squadrons did not even adopt the numbers in the 200 series that had been allotted to the Aegean Group. The D.H.4s with C, D, A and B Squadrons continued their established tasks for the rest of the war, and adopted the squadron numbers 220-223 respectively during September. By that time the majority of D.H.4s were with 220 Squadron (for reconnaissance) and 221 Squadron (for anti-submarine work). 223 Squadron (a mobile bombing unit) also operated a few, but the D.H.9 had replaced most of the earlier type by the time of the Armistice. D.H.4s lingered on in the Aegean into 1919, and some were transferred to the Greek government. Most, however, were broken up as the squadrons disbanded, so that all had gone by July 1919.

6 Wing RNAS had been established in southern Italy to reinforce the Otranto Barrage, the latter a response to German and Austrian submarine operations in the Mediterranean. British forces in Egypt, Macedonia and Mesopotamia, as well as more eastern parts of the Empire, depended upon supply from Britain by sea. The Mediterranean sea-lanes provided ample targets for U-boats, whose Austro-Hungarian bases were in the Adriatic, notably at Cattaro, Pola and Durazzo. The wing's Sopwith 1 1/2 Strutters had been employed to attack submarines passing through the Straits of Otranto, but from late January 1918 the supply of D.H.4s meant that plans could be made for raids against their home ports.

The formation of the RAF saw the creation of 66 and 67 Wings from the former naval unit. D.H.4s were delivered to a squadron in each Wing, namely 224 Squadron in 66 and 226 Squadron in 67. The majority of those D.H.4s were handed to 224 Squadron, comprising 496, 497 and 498 Flights, at its Alimini base, it being intended that 226 Squadron at Pizzone receive D.H.9s. The latter did, however, operate a few D.H.4s until September.

An initial raid was made on 23 April when five D.H.4s bombed Durazzo, their missiles exploding among anchored shipping. Cattaro was a more ambitious target, raids involving a round trip of some 400 miles (650km). 224 Squadron first visited that port on 11 May, when six D.H.4s attacked shipping in the harbour. The bombing was accurate, but the *Official History* reports that one D.H.4 was lost to enemy action, with its crew made POWs.

Towards the end of August 1918 there were a further twelve raids on Cattaro and seven on Durazzo, usually by formations of six, and damage was caused to both vessels and shore installations. Enemy air opposition was slight, and so casualties were few; for instance, B9500 was caught by Austrian seaplanes during a raid on 13 June, and returned to base. However, on the 12th the crew of D1761 (2nd Lt J.P. Corkery and Lt E.C. Bragg) were drowned when their D.H.4 went down in Trieste Bay.

The units of 66 and 67 Wings had been given a secondary duty during July, when the Italian offensive opened on the Albanian Front. The bombing elements were tasked with attacking enemy supply lines and aerodromes, duties that were successfully carried out.

Raids on Durazzo had caused damage, but their objective had not been fully achieved. The destruction of the enemy base was planned using bombers in conjunction with a naval bombardment by an Anglo-Italian fleet. The operation was conducted on 2 October, with eight D.H.4s of 224 Squadron opening the attack. Follow-up raids by D.H.9s and naval gunfire had the desired effect of leaving much of the port in flames.

With the end of hostilities on 4 November there was little further need for the Otranto-based units. 224 Squadron relinquished its D.H.4s during January 1919, and disbanded three months later.

31 Wing RFC, operating in Mesopotamia, had flown a miscellany of types, mainly B.E.2 variants, but it began to receive more efficient machines during late 1917: these included R.E.8s for reconnaissance, SPAD S.VIIs for fighting, and four D.H.4s for bombing (A7591, A7601, A7621 and A7623). As with the RNAS in the Mediterranean, there was never a chance of units in that far-flung theatre of war receiving Eagle Fours: instead the four delivered had the RAF 3a engine. They were shipped on 19 November 1917. A7591 and A7621 were issued to 30 Squadron during December and January, but both were lost before the end of that latter month. A7591 was one of twelve machines detailed to attack the German advanced aerodrome at Kifri on 21 January; it was hit by an AA shell and Lt W.S. Bean and AM3 R.G. Castor were killed. That raid was one of a series of tit-for-tat attacks on aerodromes, and the German raid on Baghdad three days later warranted retaliation. 30 Squadron again attacked Kifri the following night, using five machines that included A7621. The engine of the D.H.4 caught fire at 1,000ft (300m) and its crew, Captain F. Nuttall and Lt R.B.B. Sievier, was obliged to force-land behind enemy lines. After retrieving the D.H.4's two Lewis guns for self-defence, they made for British-held territory, a march of 24 miles (38km). But they reached their goal, and were picked up by armoured cars. On 31 October Nuttall rescued a downed B.E.2c pilot after landing a Martinsyde G.100 in a feat that resembled the one that resulted in McNamara being awarded a VC.

More RAF 3a-powered D.H.4s were delivered to 31 Wing during 1918, and an extraordinary incident involved the crew of one, whose identity remains elusive. Lt Col J.E. Tennant, commanding the RFC in Mesopotamia, had undertaken a reconnaissance of the soon-to-be-attacked Turkish positions at Khan Baghdadi with Major P.C.S. Hobart as passenger. Groundfire brought the D.H.4 down; the crew was made POW and sent northwards under armed escort. The GOC Mesopotamia issued orders for an armoured car column to effect the rescue of the two prisoners. This was done after a dash of 32 miles (51km) into enemy-held territory, and a fighting return.

Sixteen D.H.4s were taken onto charge by 31 Wing after the original four, and deliveries continued into 1919. A7695 and A7756 are known to have served with 72 Squadron's A Flight, and 63 Squadron had A8004, A8005 and A8008 in the post-war period. A8008 was probably the last D.H.4 with the RAF in that theatre: it was not struck off charge until 3 December 1919.

The D.H.4A and Communications Work

An often overlooked fact is that the RFC and RAF operated dedicated communications units for the transport of high-

The D.H.4A H5898 served with 1 Communication Squadron and, like others of the unit, was doped in an overall aluminium scheme. The rear fuselage band was light blue, with dark blue borders and a red central stripe. The realignment of the centre-section struts, to resolve stagger to the mainplanes, is evident in this photograph. J. Meaden via JMB/GSL

ranking officers. The BEF had its own Communications Flight that was expanded to squadron status, and the two original Aircraft Depots also had their own communications aeroplanes. At home, a miscellany of machines was attached to 2 AAP at Hendon, on the northern outskirts of London, for use by Air Ministry officers. These machines were subsumed by the Communications Squadron when it formed on 23 July 1918. The squadron's A Flight was equipped with D.H.4s. These were standard machines, such as A8032, but some did have the refinement of a fully equipped rear cockpit that dispensed with the Scarff ring.

The open cockpit for the single passenger was not considered satisfactory from the viewpoint of comfort, and the D.H.4A was an attempt both to remedy this, and to double the carrying capability of the type. It is often assumed that the conversion entailed nothing more than the addition of a rear cabin, but that was not the case.

The D.H.4A employed a standard fuselage frame, and was fitted with the 375hp Rolls-Royce Eagle VIII; the greater power of that engine was needed for the increased passenger load. The raised and glazed rear cockpit cabin

Known D.H.4A Conversions

F2644, F2655, F2663, F2664, F2665, F2666, F2694, F2699, F2702, F2704, F5764, H5894, H5895, H5939 (H5939 a post-war conversion).

hinged to port, to allow passengers access to tandem seats. That access was facilitated by the provision of a short ladder that was fixed to the starboard fuselage side. The D.H.4 petrol tank was retained, but dual control was dispensed with. The traverse rocking shaft for the elevator control was moved forwards, and a small cut-out made in the root of the lower wing to allow this.

The fuselage modifications altered the position of the centre of gravity and so the wings had to be re-rigged to an unstaggered layout. This was achieved by the use of new sockets for the centre-section struts, which then assumed a rearward sweep.

The first D.H.4As entered service as the war drew to a close and were issued to the Communications Squadron, which then operated a detachment at Buc, near Paris, for use by politicians engaged in peace negotiations. The parent unit was

retitled as '1 Communications Squadron' in March 1919, when its detachment became 2 Communications Squadron. The original unit moved to Kenley on 13 April and was re-designated 24 Squadron on 1 February 1920. Internal mail flights were added to the home-based unit's duties.

D.H.4As used by the RAF were usually finished in an overall high-visibility scheme of aluminium-pigmented dope; this gave them an attractive appearance when seen alongside the drab-finished machines of other units. That attractive appearance was often enhanced by the addition of a broad fuselage band of RAF colours – a light blue band with thin, dark blue borders and a central, thin red band.

The two Communications Squadrons plied their trade in D.H.4s and D.H.4As until mid-1919, when the types started to be withdrawn in favour of Bristol F.2Bs. Not all of their seemingly mundane flights were uneventful, and at least two with D.H.4s ended in a fatal crash: for instance, F5743 crashed in Kent during a Paris run on 26 February 1919 when bad weather necessitated a forced landing; its passenger, Lt Graham of the Ministry of Shipping, was seriously injured, and Lt L.A. Hacklett, the pilot, was killed. And

F2699, another D.H.4A, photographed at Marske. The over-painting of the tail suggests civilian use, and it may be that the machine retained its military number until its registration of G-EAHF was allocated. JMB/GSL

on 3 May, D8355 crashed after take-off from Hendon because its radiator had not been filled, and its engine overheated and seized. Captain E.M. Knott AFC, its pilot, was killed, and the passenger, Sir Frederick H. Sykes, the Controller of Civil Aviation, was injured.

The withdrawal of the D.H.4A from military service began in mid-1919, and the surplus machines found a ready market in the burgeoning civil aviation business. Air Transport & Travel Ltd, a George Holt Thomas enterprise, acquired F2694, F2699, F2702 and F2704, as well as D.H.4s F2670 and F2671. The D.H.4As became G-EAHF (F2699), G-EAHD (F2694), G-EAJC (F2702) and G-EAJD (F2704), and they achieved two 'firsts' for British aviation: on 25 August 1919, G-EAJC became the first British aeroplane to carry fare-paying passengers to France, on a Hounslow-Le Bourget flight that cost the (then) princely sum of 20 guineas. And G-EAHF became the first British machine to carry civilian air-mail to the continent, on a service that was inaugurated on 10 November of that year. Other D.H.4As were operated by Instone Airlines of Hendon and Handley Page Transport of Cricklewood. Most civilian D.H.4As were withdrawn by the end of 1920. G-EAMU, a post-war conversion, was the last, serving with Imperial Airways until at least 1924.

Post-War Foreign Service

Considerable numbers of D.H.4s were used abroad after the war. Greece was the first foreign recipient, when it was handed at least five BHP-engined machines from 62 Wing RAF in the weeks after the Armistice. Those supplied to other governments were powered by the Rolls-Royce Eagle. During 1919, Canada and New Zealand received twelve and two respectively as part of imperial gifts to those dominions.

At least eight RAF 3a D.H.4s had joined the RAF Expeditionary Force in North Russia during 1919. The Imperial Russian Air Service may not have received its intended D.H.4s, but the Bolshevik forces went on to operate the type. Some may have been survivors from RAF stocks after

---

D.H.4s AND D.H.4As Serving with RAF Communications Squadrons

1 Communications Squadron Hendon/Kenley: D.H.4 – A8032, A8040, B7895, D8351, D8352, D8355, D8359, F5734, F5736, F5743, F5744, F5745, F5748, F5759 and F5783; D.H.4A – F2644, F2655, F2666, F5764, H5894 and H5895.

2 Communications Squadron Buc: D.H.4 – F5707, F5721 and F5784; D.H.4A – F2663, F2664 and F2665.

---

the British withdrew from Murmansk, and others perhaps captured from American interventionist forces, but most in Russian service during the 1920s and 1930s were built in that country. Production had been planned before the October Revolution, and some drawings had been supplied; these were used in 1920 to produce the first D.H.4s from the State Aircraft Factory No.1, and were given, appropriately, Fiat A12 engines. It would appear that more than eighty were produced. However, the type was found wanting, and the D.H.9 was selected to replace it on the production line.

Belgium received the first of more than sixty Eagle D.H.4s for the Aviation Militaire Belge during 1919. These served until 1925, and were joined by at least eight civilian machines. Two went for civilian use in Australia during 1920. The vast majority of D.H.4s during the 1920s were of American manufacture, and the subject of a later chapter. And although examples of those survive, none of British manufacture managed to.

South Africa received ten as an imperial gift during 1920, and towards the end of a decade of service, some were re-engined with radial engines – Jaguars and then Jupiter VIIIs – before replacement Wapitis arrived in 1930. This was the year when the majority of air services with the D.H.4 finally relinquished the type, and despite the large numbers produced, none of British manufacture has been preserved.

CHAPTER SIX

The D.H.5

Air Fighting and Ground Attack Work

Geoffrey de Havilland's initial idea for a fighting scout had been abandoned in favour of the D.H.2, due partly to the contemporary lack of a suitable gun synchronization mechanism.

That aborted design had several notable characteristics: it was to have been powered by a rotary engine, and to have been of tractor configuration with a fixed and forward-firing machine-gun, and the range of view of the pilot was given prime consideration. These same considerations were given to his next design, which emerged as the D.H.5.

Development

The prototype appeared during the autumn of 1916 and was flying, without armament, by that October. It was a compact, single-bay biplane. As with the D.H.3 and D.H.4, its fuselage was manufactured in two parts: the rear half was a wire-braced box girder, and the forward section was again built on a pair of substantial routed patons that carried the spars of the lower wing centre-section. Vertical and diagonal timber spacers connected the patons to the upper longeron and acted as supports for the fuel

tank, the pilot's seat and the rear engine bearer. The two halves of the fuselage were joined by fish-plates. A 110hp, Le Rhone 9J was enclosed in a circular aluminium cowling, and this was contoured into the slab-sided fuselage with a triangular fairing. The vertical tail surfaces were relatively small, and employed a balanced rudder.

The cockpit was positioned well forward, ahead of the fuel and oil tanks, with a small headrest behind, that contained filler ports for fuel and oil. The lower wing was mounted centrally under the cockpit, and good forward and upward

The D.H.5 prototype in its original guise, unarmed and fitted with a small rudder. The slab-sided nature of its fuselage is most apparent, as well as the fairing that blended the cowling to the fuselage shape. It became A5172, and after a brief visit to France, had a gun fitted and was tested at Upavon. JMB/GSL

A9186, an early D.H.5, was tested at Martlesham Heath; this shot shows the full fuselage fairings and enlarged rudder of production machines. The rubber return cords for the single-action ailerons can be seen on the upper plane. JMB/GSL

visibility was achieved by mounting the upper planes with 27in (685mm) of negative stagger. That brought the leading edge of the top plane to a point above the centre of the cockpit.

The wings were of conventional construction, but employed a wide centre-section of approximately one-fifth of the span. The mainplanes were rigged with a marked dihedral angle of 4½ deg. Ailerons were carried along most of the span on all four mainplanes. There was no balance cable between the ailerons: return action was by the use of rubber cords. Good ground-handling was ensured by the provision of a wide-track (5ft/1.5m) undercarriage that employed a single axle, sprung by the use of bungee cord. The forward port undercarriage strut mounted a wind-driven fuel pump.

This prototype was acquired by the military and given the serial number A5172. It was flown, still in its natural finish, to France for service evaluation; its only national markings, at this time, were rudder stripes, onto which the serial was superimposed. A5172 arrived at 1 AD, St Omer, on 26 October and proceeded to 2 AD, Candas, on the 28th. It is not known whether the machine was allotted to any squadron for evaluation, or whether pilots were brought to Candas to

fly it. What is known is that the D.H.5 created a very favourable impression with the RFC hierarchy, and as a result it was ordered into quantity production. A5172 returned to the UK in mid-November, by which time consideration was being given to the acquisition of sufficient engines to allow production to take place.

As ever in the Great War, engine supply ran behind demand. The Le Rhone 9J was a scarce commodity, being required by the French for use in their Nieuport series of scouts and Morane two-seaters. Manufacture, under licence, was to be in the UK, but the tooling-up process could be time-consuming. This placed the large-scale production of the D.H.5 in jeopardy.

The RFC with the BEF had suggested that the proposed Vickers gun armament of the D.H.5 be mounted in such a way as to allow elevation of up to 60 deg from the horizontal, although the reasoning behind this is not clear. It will be remembered that the movable gun-mounting on the D.H.2 had been clamped to allow more accurate fire by pointing the machine at the enemy during combat manoeuvres; thus the seemingly retrograde step of installing the elevating mechanism in the D.H.5 defied combat experience. The gun was mounted to port, allowing the installation of as large a magazine as

possible (all Vickers guns at that time had right-hand feed).

Nevertheless, A5172 was fitted with such a mounting and was passed to the CFS Testing Squadron for evaluation. By that time it had been fitted with new and enlarged vertical tail surfaces that retained a balanced rudder, and whose profile resembled a scaled-down version of those in the D.H.4. Testing took place on 9 December, and the ensuing report (M.76) was quite favourable.

As a result, 400 D.H.5s were ordered, 200 from the parent company and the same number from the Darracq Motor Engineering Co. Ltd; both orders were placed on 15 January 1917 – that from Airco included the prototype. Later, further orders were placed with the British Caudron Co. Ltd and with March, Jones & Cribb for fifty and 100 machines respectively.

Initial delivery was slow, and it was not until some ten weeks later that the RFC received its first examples of the new type. That delay may have been due to the introduction of modifications to the fuselage and fuel systems, as well as a shortage of Le Rhone engines.

The fuselage was strengthened and streamlined. The basic fuselage frames remained as on the prototype, but the complete forward section and the tail end

This rear view of A9186 shows the shape bestowed by the fuselage fairings and the location of the gravity tank. The Vickers gun was capable of being raised, and is seen here in its elevated position. JMB/GSL

of the rear one were reinforced with plywood that was nailed and glued over the existing framework. The ply sheets were fretted to save weight, and the webbing followed the shape of the existing fuselage structure. Angular side fairings were added to the fuselage spacers, and these carried full-length stringers, over which the fabric was stretched and secured before doping. The D.H.5's structure proved immensely strong, and when Farnborough performed the standard loading tests, using sand on the flying and control surfaces, it was the metal attachments (securing plates for the flying wires and elevator control horns) that sheared.

The fuel system then incorporated a gravity tank that was mounted to starboard above the upper centre-section. The Vickers gun was, sensibly, fixed, and was synchronized to fire through the propeller arc by the Constantinesco CC gear. The mechanical Kauper gear was scheduled to be standardized for rotary-engined machines with the BEF, but was not available in sufficient quantities. The Constantinesco gear was hydraulically operated and, as such, allowed a greater rate of fire. However, early sets of the gear were plagued by problems, and some time was taken in refining the design to a state in which it could be issued for operational purposes.

Delays were also caused by an unaccountable vibration during flight. It was assumed that this was due to the use of an unbalanced engine, but tests with different machines produced the same result. Engine bearers were reinforced as a counter-measure, but this did not fully alleviate the problem. Stiffened engine cowlings with reinforcing ribs were also introduced, and some machines had the lower segment of that cowling removed.

Into Service

The RFC units scheduled to introduce the D.H.5 into service were those still operating the, by then, obsolete pusher

scouts – 24 and 32 Squadrons with D.H.2s, and 41 Squadron with F.E.8s. It was 1 May 1917 before the first D.H.5 was issued to 24 Squadron, later that month before 32 Squadron received examples, and July by the time 41 Squadron began to re-equip. Among 24 Squadron's early D.H.5s was the prototype, A5172, that had returned to France during April and had, presumably, been brought up to production standard.

May was the month that the Camel entered service, and a month after the S.E.5 had arrived in France with 56 Squadron – and in comparison to those two famous scouts, the D.H.5 was already outdated, in particular its single gun armament placing it at an immediate

Specification – Airco D.H.5	
Powerplant:	110hp Le Rhone or 100hp Gnome Monosoupape (some training machines); fuel capacity 25 gallons
Dimensions:	Mainplane span 25ft 8in (7.83m); mainplane gap 4ft 9in (1.45m); chord 4ft 6in (1.45m); length 22ft (6.71m); height 9ft 1½in (2.78m); tailplane span 8ft 4½in (2.55m); wing area 212.1sq ft (19.73sq m)
Weights:	Empty 1,012lb (459kg); loaded 1,492lb (677kg); wing loading 7.03lb per sq ft (34.3kg per sq m)
Performance:	Maximum speed 102mph (164km/h); landing speed 50mph (89km/h); climb to 5,000ft (1,500m) 4 minutes 55 seconds

disadvantage to the latest generation of enemy scouts, the Pfalz D.III, Albatros D.III and D.V. The D.H.5 was quite manoeuvrable, and capable of performing all the gyrations necessary in combat – but it had other failings. For instance, the pilot's rearward view was non-existent, and that made it a liability in the 'dogfight' combats that persisted at that time. It may have been an improvement on the D.H.2 and F.E.8, but the operational units destined to fly the D.H.5 never achieved the combat successes that they had on pushers.

It was not, however, comparable with the Camel and the S.E.5, nor even with the Sopwith Pup when it came to performance at height. The service ceiling

'victory' occurred on 25 May, when Lt S. Cockerell of 24 Squadron, on A9363, sent down an Albatros D.III that was following 2nd Lt H.W. Woollett. Cockerell's only D.H.5 success (he was a veteran of fighting on the D.H.2) came two days after his unit had suffered the first operational loss on the type when Lt J.H.H. Goodall was made POW in B343. Goodall was not the first D.H.5 casualty, however: the units had lost A9364 on the 19th, when Captain W.T. Hall was killed in a flying accident. In 24 Squadron, Woollett was credited with the destruction of three enemy machines (including a 'double' on 23 July), and with sending another down out of control; all were claimed while flying A9165. These

Walter also claim an enemy scout OOC. However, those three 'victories' were offset by the loss of 2nd Lt K.G. Cruikshank in B344, who was shot down and made POW after accidentally joining a formation of enemy machines. Over the next nineteen days, Coningham had a further eight successes, all except one being scouts. His machine for all those claims was A9179.

Despite the best efforts of its pilots, the D.H.5 was never to become noted for widespread success in combat with enemy aeroplanes, largely because of the limitations mentioned above. The type did have its strong points, however, and they were brought to the fore with the opening of the Third Battle of Ypres. The

D.H.5s suffered from severe in-flight vibration and various attempts were made to counter this, including the fitting of stiffening ribs to the cowling, as seen here. *via G. Simmons*

of the D.H.5 was only 16,000ft (5,000m), and its performance was sluggish at that height. Operational experience found that the type performed best as a scout at 9,000–10,000ft (2,700–3,000m), and so D.H.5 formations were at the permanent disadvantage of being liable to attack from above; a common panacea was to send out co-ordinated patrols comprising a 'top cover' of Pups at 15,000ft (4,500m) with Bristol Fighters below and D.H.5s as the lowest formation.

Some of the D.H.5's more aggressive pilots did find success. The first recorded

were added to a previous 'victory' on the D.H.2. His colleague, Captain B.P.G. Beanlands did even better, achieving six 'victories' between August and November. The first two (both claimed on 25 August) were also achieved in A9165.

The leading exponent of the type was Captain A. Coningham of 32 Squadron, who was made a DSO and awarded an MC for his determined use of the D.H.5 during July 1917. He sent an Albatros scout down OOC on the 11th, a day that had seen Lt St C.C. Tayler open the unit's score-sheet for the D.H.5, and Lt S.R.P.

D.H.5 was a stable machine at low heights, and could be dived steeply and steadily. These attributes lent themselves well to ground attack work.

An Introduction to Ground Attack Work

Until the summer of 1917, RFC scouts had not made co-ordinated attacks on ground targets. Such targets had been attacked, but on an individual basis and without any pre-planning. Preparations for the Ypres offensive included the use of scouts to attack enemy strongpoints and troop concentrations, both at the front line and behind it. The D.H.5 was one of the types chosen for the task, and 32 Squadron was involved from the opening of the offensive on 31 July, being joined by 24 and 41 Squadrons from mid-August. Two D.H.5s were designated to work with each division and to engage in ground attack work – but of course low flying brought machines into the range of enemy groundfire and increased the risk of damage or loss.

31 July was rainy, with the cloud base at 1,000ft (300m), but in spite of this, RFC scouts set about their work, with Lt St

attachment to 32 Squadron from 68 Squadron, crashed in A9372 after it was hit by groundfire; fortunately he was unscathed, as was 2nd Lt W.R. Fish two days later when A9396 suffered similar damage. Fish was one of a number of 32 Squadron pilots mentioned in RFC communique no.100, for dedication in attacking enemy trenches. 2nd Lt E. Seth-Ward was less fortunate, and was killed when A9213 was hit. 2nd Lt G.A. Wells was wounded the next day, and on the 12th, Captain R.M. Williams was killed, apparently being attacked from above by an enemy scout. By this time the squadron's D.H.5s were fitted with under-fuselage carriers for four 20lb (9kg) bombs, and indeed bombs had been used to great

type of work, but on the 26th they suffered a further loss when 2nd Lt J.G. White was killed when A9178 was hit by groundfire. This low work was interspersed with 'offensive patrols', and it is recorded that 41 Squadron had lost A9212 on such a mission the previous day, its pilot Captain J.S. de I. Bush falling into enemy hands; he was fatally injured.

Until this time aileron control had been of single action, and had retained the use of rubber return cords. However, several machines of 32 Squadron had been modified at unit level to have dual-acting ailerons, with a spanwise balance cable running across the upper surface of the top mainplane. That sensible modification was ordered to be repeated on machines undergoing overhaul at the St Omer and Candas depots, and was standardized on production machines from the early autumn of 1917.

September opened quietly enough for the three D.H.5 squadrons. 32 Squadron lost A9374 on the 5th, but 41 Squadron claimed its first combat success the following day – after almost two months of using the type. The return to patrol flying did not lead to a reduction in casualties, however, and on 17 September 41 Squadron lost two machines – the consecutively numbered A9409 (2nd Lt R.E. Taylor) and A9410 (Lt G.C. Holman), both falling to enemy scouts. Three days later 32 Squadron was almost as unfortunate, losing 2nd Lt W.O. Cornish in A9179, and having A9434 and B345 severely damaged in combat.

The D.H.5 element of the BEF was reinforced on 21 September by the arrival of 68 Squadron; this unit was manned by Australian personnel and had formed at Harlaxton on 30 January. After a period of working up with a variety of obsolete types, the squadron was mobilized for active service: it received D.H.5s and set up base at Baizieux, and its pilots spent the rest of the month on familiarization flights – nine days that saw further casualties in the other three squadrons, with 32 Squadron suffering the most.

The weather during October was far from ideal for war flying, but the continuing ground offensive meant that operations were flown whenever conditions allowed, and offensive patrols, mainly in the vicinity of the lines, occupied the four D.H.5 squadrons. 68 Squadron had its first operational casualty on the 2nd, losing 2nd Lt C.F. Agnew

Souvenir-takers left this D.H.5 in an unidentifiable condition; however, stripping off the fabric allows inspection of the heavily fretted plywood re-enforcement in the forward fuselage. JMB/GSL

C.C. Tayler of 32 Squadron scattering an enemy concentration of 500 troops, and 2nd Lts T.E. Salt, St Clair and H.J. Edwards attacking trench systems around Langemarck. Tayler was wounded by enemy groundfire. By then Tayler had accumulated a victory tally of six, and he was later awarded an MC for his work with the squadron; Edwards was almost as successful, and rose to command a flight of the unit.

A further deterioration in the weather prevented flying during the first four days in August, but as conditions improved, operations were resumed – and further casualties were sustained. On the 7th, Captain R.C. Phillipps, an Australian on

effect by Edwards on the 10th, when he had succeeded in hitting an enemy strong-point before attacking troops from 100ft (30m) with machine-gun fire.

A less hectic spell followed as the initial offensive drew to a close, but the situation intensified again as attacks resumed on 16 August, and 32 Squadron was once more in the action. They had one successful day, but then on the 17th B368 was lost, with 2nd Lt W. Chivers KIA, and on the next day so was A9438, with 2nd Lt T.R. Kirkness also killed. 41 Squadron had joined in low attack work, and on 19 August in particular helped out Lt M. Thomas in A9168 in attacking enemy troops. 24 Squadron was also active in this

Representative Airco D.H.5s with RFC Units

24 Squadron
Flez/Baizieux/Teteghem/Marieux –
A5172, A9165, A9166, A9167, A9175,
A9176, A9178, A9182, A9183, A9220,
A9222, A9232, A9239, A9248, A9249,
A9257, A9272, A9289, A9291, A9304,
A9329, A9339, A9363, A9364, A9367,
A9389, A9431, A9435, A9471, A9494,
A9495, A9496, A9512, A9509, A9514,
B331, B334, B341, B343, B348, B349,
B357, B359, B361, B362, B4906,
B4918.

28 Squadron Yatesbury – A9216, A9417,
B365.

32 Squadron Léalvillers/Abeele/
Droglandt – A9179, A9185, A9193,
A9194, A9199, A9200, A9207, A9209,
A9211, A9213, A9219, A9233, A9235,
A9251, A9258, A9269, A9280, A9283,
A9300, A9311, A9312, A9315, A9317,
A9331, A9337, A9340, A9357, A9366,
A9372, A9374, A9385, A9386, A9396,
A9398, A9399, A9404, A9407, A9412,
A9414, A9421, A9422, A9424, A9429,
A9431, A9434, A9438, A9439, A9445,
A9450, A9470, A9500, A9511, A9513,
A9515, A9517, A9522, A9529, B336,
B344, B345, B349, B353, B368, B369,
B4912, B4914, B4916, B4923, B4924.

41 Squadron Léalvillers – A9212, A9168,
A9196, A9208, A9212, A9218, A9225,
A9241, A9276, A9278, A9371, A9375,
A9406, A9408, A9409, A9410, A9426,
A9440, A9444, A9465, A9474, B340,
B360.

64 Squadron Sedgeford/St Omer/
Le Hameau – A9177, A9201, A9235,
A9236, A9237, A9256, A9295, A9298,
A9299, A9301, A9305, A9307, A9313,
A9316, A9335, A9384, A9393, A9405,
A9407, A9458, A9481, A9482, A9485,
A9486, A9487, A9489, A9490, A9491,
A9492, A9499, A9507, A9508.

65 Squadron Wye – A9163, A9184,
A9377, A9379.

68 (Australian) Squadron
Harlaxton/Baizieux – A9197, A9224,
A9226, A9228, A9242, A9245, A9257,
A9258, A9263, A9265, A9271, A9273,
A9275, A9277, A9278, A9279, A9283,
A9284, A9288, A9294, A9326, A9328,
A9341, A9344, A9378, A9395, A9399,
A9415, A9420, A9428, A9432, A9445,
A9449, A9451, A9457, A9459, A9461,
A9462, A9464, A9466, A9469, A9473,
A9477, A9483, A9517, A9532, A9542,
A9544, B377.

88 Squadron Harling Road – A9394.

30 (Australian) TS Ternhill – A9205,
A9287, A9415, A9467, B4905, B4911.

40 TS Croydon – A9163, A9172, A9266,
A9377, A9452, B373.

43 TS Ternhill – A9205, A9234, A9413,
A9418, A9420, B359.

45 TS South Carlton – A9189, A9441,
A9454, B4908.

54 TS Castle Bromwich – A9197.

55 TS Yatesbury – A9413, B364, B365.

61 TS South Carlton – B4908.

62 TS Dover – A9163, A9250, A9254,
A9357, A9377, A9388.

63 TS Joyce Green – A9206, A9215,
A9252, A9387, A9395, A9442.

3 TDS Lopcombe Corner – A9330,
A9416, A9526, B365, B366, B4920,
B4943, B7762, B7792.

CFS   Testing Squadron Upavon –
A5172.

RAF   Farnborough – A9403.

Experimental Station Martlesham
Heath – A9186.

Experimental Station Orfordness –
A9186, A9403.

School of Instruction Watford –
A9545.

(POW) in A9271. 41 Squadron lost B360 on the 10th, and three days later 68 Squadron suffered its second operational loss, when Lt D.G. Morrison was wounded in combat: his D.H.5, A9277, made a forced landing, but was destroyed by shelling.

The following day saw the arrival of the fifth, and last, operational D.H.5 squadron. 64 Squadron flew into St Omer and departed the next day for Le Hameau, and a further move was made nine days later to Aniche, from where its first operations were flown. The squadron had mobilized at Sedgeford, and part of its final training was in formation flying at low altitude, a pointer to the intended further application of the D.H.5 in the ground attack role.

41 Squadron had little success on the D.H.5, and so 18 October was one of its better days: A9406 was lost in action, but two of its pilots claimed combat success, 2nd Lt R.M. Whitehead (A9408) and

Lt R. Winnicott (A9218) each being credited with an Albatros scout sent down out of control. These were the last of the unit's few D.H.5 'victories'; its final D.H.5 casualty came eleven days later when 2nd Lt F.S. Clark was made POW in A9474. The squadron was scheduled to re-equip with S.E.5as, and the first of its new machines began to arrive in November; this meant that the unit escaped the massive losses that were to be inflicted on the remaining D.H.5 units.

Early November saw the final stages of the Third Battle of Ypres; this conflict finally petered out on the 10th, and although the D.H.5s were involved in patrol work, activity was slight. Even so, combats still developed, and first successes were claimed on the 15th by two pilots who would achieve respectable 'victory' scores: 2nd Lt I.D.R. McDonald (A9471) and 2nd Lt P.A. McDougall, both of 24 Squadron, were each credited with an Albatros D.III sent down out of control.

Cambrai and Systematic Ground Attack

The relative inactivity of mid-November was abruptly interrupted on 20 November, the stalemate that had been reached in Flanders to be replaced by a further ground offensive aimed at breaching the Hindenburg Line near Cambrai. For the first time a massed tank attack was to be attempted, and preparations took place in great secrecy. The application of air power as a support to advancing troops had been tried and proven at the beginning of the Ypres offensive, and that support was to be extended at Cambrai. 64 and 68 Squadrons were to be used primarily in that role, with other D.H.5 squadrons flying close offensive patrols, aimed at keeping enemy aeroplanes at bay. They could and would, however, be given dedicated special missions against ground targets, as and when the need arose.

Early morning fog and mist on the 20th did not prevent the offensive from opening – indeed, the weather helped the attacking British troops. And when those conditions gave way to low cloud and rain, equally that did not prevent the two dedicated D.H.5 units from entering the fray: 64 Squadron was out first, sending machines out from 7am to attack gun positions near Flesquieres that could hold

This D.H.5 was photographed at Harlaxton and was undoubtedly with 68 (Australian) squadron during its mobilization period. Its presentation inscription reads 'AUSTRALIA NO17, NEW SOUTH WALES NO16, "THE UPPER HUNTER BATTLEPLANE", Presented by residents of Upper Hunter District' – though here it may have been scratched onto the negative of this photograph. Two D.H.5s, namely A9107 and A9245, carried such an inscription, although the presentation and wording was different on A9245 to that shown here. *JMB/GSL*

up the advance. However that, and subsequent missions, demonstrated the dangers associated with such work: flying at low level, the D.H.5s were relatively easy targets for ground gunners, and three of 64 Squadron's first sortie (A9201, A9298 and A9335) were lost, with another pilot, 2nd Lt L.B. Williams in A9486 wounded, and two further D.H.5s (A9235 and A9492) severely damaged. And the Australians of 68 Squadron fared little better when they were led out by Captain J. Bell an hour later: 2nd Lt L.N. Ward in A9399 was shot down to become a POW, and a further five aeroplanes were shot up. Bell, in A9473, received fatal wounds.

The weather conditions made flying impossible on the following day, but 68 Squadron was out again on the 22nd, attacking the enemy positions that defended the tactically important higher ground around Bourlon Wood. A further two D.H.5s were severely damaged by groundfire during this offensive, and a third, A9477, was shot down and its pilot, 2nd Lt D.G. Clark, killed. Nevertheless, the unit claimed its first combat victories on this day: Lt F.G. Huxley, in A9461, had attacked an infantry column at low level,

A D.H.5 Pilot

A pilot who trained and fought on D.H.5s was 2Lt H.L.V. Tubbs. After basic training in Egypt, he returned home to 63 TS at Joyce Green for finishing as a scout pilot. His initial flights from the Kent base were in Avro 504As, these being gradually interspersed with others on Pups. Tubbs made his acquaintance with the D.H.5 on 21 August 1917, with a 55-minute flight on A9215. After a further fourteen such flights – his last involving firing practice into Staines Reservoir – he graduated. With ten hours on the type, he was posted to active service with 24 Squadron and made his first flight with that unit on 11 September. The squadron was then based at Baizieux and Tubbs' lack of combat training was apparent. His first nine flights were non-operational and all except one involved target practice, the other being a flight to take temperature readings for the artillery. It was not until the 19th that he crossed the lines, then being forced to make an emergency landing after the magneto of his D.H.5 failed. Between then and the New Year, Tubbs flew more than ninety-four hours on operations, plus more than seventeen hours on practice and test flights. His logbook entries show that the vast majority of patrols were carried out at less than 10,000ft and were of under two hours' duration. Occasionally, a higher one was flown, such as on 28 September when 15,000ft was reached in A9248. He saw his first enemy aircraft when on patrol at 13,000ft two days later, but the shortcomings of his mount are revealed by the log entry '12 EA over Leike, too high to engage'. Tubbs only encountered the enemy on a further seven occasions, four of which resulted in combat. His patrol attacked a pair of enemy two-seaters on 21 October and Tubbs recorded that he did not think that they had crashed. However, he subsequently added '1 confirmed later' to his logbook entry. That was not his last combat, but most of his further D.H.5 patrols proved uneventful, except for those when mechanical trouble intervened. The majority of such cases centred on 'pressure trouble', suggesting problems with fuel feed. Tubbs' last D.H.5 flight was on 3 January 1918. 24 Squadron had begun to receive S.E.5a fighters to replace the D.H.5 and he had made a practice flight on the new type the previous day, that final D.H.5 flight being made to return A9289 to 2 AD at Candas.

and as he climbed away he saw an Albatros D.V. immediately ahead. He fired before the German pilot had seen him, and the Albatros went down to crash. Later that morning, Lt R.W. Howard, in A9294, encountered a D.F.W. C.V. over the battlefield – the enemy was using two-seaters to attack the advancing British troops. Howard's attack caused the D.F.W. to land in British-held territory, and its crew was captured.

The attacks against Bourlon Wood continued on the 23rd, with both 64 and 68 Squadrons sending out patrols. Again casualties were high, with a further six machines being forced down and lost. Fortunately most pilots were able to return to the squadron, although two, including a flight commander, were wounded. Enemy scouts were involved in the action, and Lt J.A.V. Boddy in A9299 may have fallen to the guns of Rittmeister Manfred von Richthofen, the commander of J.G.1. Enemy aircraft accounted for A9326 flown by Lt L.H. Holden of 68 Squadron, when that unit sent out late morning missions, though Holden was uninjured – and that was his second lucky escape, because his mount of the 20th, A9278, had also been shot down. But the unit lost another two D.H.5s (A9263 and A9428), with both pilots fatally wounded.

Final Operations

The pace of the air war around Cambrai slowed down as the offensive was halted; fewer patrols were flown, and those tended to be against aerial opposition. This did not preclude losses, however: Howard, of 68 Squadron, had his D.H.5, A9517, damaged in combat on the 29th; and 2nd Lt H.C. Cornell was lucky to walk away after A9532 was shot down on the following day.

64 Squadron had then been in France for more than six weeks, but it was not until 30 November that it made its first claims for successful aerial combats: on that day Captains J.A. Slater (A9458) and E.R. Tempest (A9507) respectively sent a D.F.W. C.V. and an Albatros D.V. down out of control. In fact, Slater had two previous 'victories' to his credit, both

A9418 of 43 TS being refuelled in the snow at Ternhill during the winter of 1917-18. It is marked with a broad white rear fuselage band. via the author

A9416 was issued for training and served with 3 TDS at Lopcombe Corner. That unit replaced its D.H.5s with Camels when the type was withdrawn from active service. JMB/GSL

Unarmed A9377, that served with 40 TS at Croydon. Its fin must have been replaced or re-covered, because the serial number presentation is non-standard. JMB/GSL

This line-up of 40 TS includes three D.H.5s, with B373 and A9172 nearest the camera. JMB/GSL

A9413 served with 55 TS at Yatesbury, where this photograph was taken. It later served with 43 TS at Ternhill. JMB/GSL

gained on Nieuports with 1 Squadron, and like Tempest, he went on to greater things with the S.E.5a. These, however, were the only D.H.5 successes for those pilots.

That day saw the start of the German counter-attack at Cambrai. It was supported by low-flying aeroplanes, particularly two-seaters, with enemy scouts working above to provide protection. 24 Squadron was working in support of the British ground attack work, flying patrols over the front line, and as always, it experienced mixed fortunes: on the down side, 2nd Lt I.D Campbell (A9509) was lost on such a patrol on the 30th; but then Captain B.P.G. Beanland scored a final D.H.5 'victory' in A9304 when he sent down an Albatros D.V. near Bourlon Wood.

But the day of the D.H.5 was drawing to a close. 41 Squadron had re-equipped with the S.E.5a, and 24, 64 and 68 Squadrons began to receive that scout type during December. 32 Squadron continued to operate the type into the New Year, but then it, too, received the S.E.5a. Even so, it was still operating the D.H.5 as late as 29 January, on which date it made its last combat claim on the type, 2nd Lt C.J. Howsam being credited with the destruction of an Albatros D.V.

Training

The limited production of the D.H.5 meant that relatively few had served with training units in the UK. During the early summer of 1917, 40 Training Squadron at Croydon, 62 Training Squadron at Dover and 63 Training Squadron at Joyce Green were all issued with small numbers of the type. These Higher Training Squadrons flew the D.H.5 alongside Avro 504s and Sopwith Pups, and all three were detailed to make contributions to the Home Defence organization during that summer, bringing their front-line types into support of the largely inadequate BE variants that equipped many of the HD squadrons. Anti-Gotha sorties were made by D.H.5s from these units, but none met with any success. There may have been a Home Defence connection with a modification made to A9186: this D.H.5 had been delivered to the Experimental Station at Martlesham Heath, and from there, went to the Armament Experimental Station at Orfordness where it was fitted with its Vickers gun mounted to fire upwards at 45 deg. It had been discovered that bullets fired at such an angle retained a straight line trajectory, and the application to aeroplanes attempting to

intercept raiding bombers was therefore most appealing.

A9403 was also used in experiments at Orfordness. It had been fitted with a plywood-skinned fuselage, but this added 35lb (16kg) to its all-up weight, which in turn necessitated a reduction in the military load of ammunition, and this was unacceptable for operational usage. Equally unacceptable was the vibration suffered. Vibration had plagued early D.H.5s, and it may have been that the plywood fuselage accentuated the resonance that was generated in the engine bearers. A9403 was then fitted with a Lloyd-Lott fuel tank that could be jettisoned in the event of fire, but although tests with this device were successful with the machine suspended from a crane, the system was not adopted operationally on the type.

55 TS at Yatesbury also received that D.H.5, as did 43 TS at Ternhill. Some D.H.5s that served on training units were given the 100hp Gnome Monosoupape engine in lieu of the Le Rhone, which was often in short supply: this was because deliveries from France were often withheld, and engines were required for Nieuport and, later, Camel units with the BEF.

Many training unit D.H.5s retained their Vickers guns. This machine was photographed at Gosport and again shows the re-enforced cowling, as well as the fuel pump fitted to the port undercarriage strut. JMB/GSL

Some D.H.5s were also issued to UK-based squadrons in the process of 'working up' for operations with the BEF. For example, 65 Squadron at Wye flew several, and was also brought into temporary HD work during the summer of 1917. 28 Squadron from Gosport exchanged bases and equipment with 55 TS on 23 July 1917, inheriting some of the latter's D.H.5s. Both 28 and 65 Squadrons were scheduled to receive Clerget-engined Sopwith Camels, and the D.H.5s served to give their pilots experience of flying a rotary-engined scout of greater power than the Pups that were also operated. The two units were both operational with Camels by that October.

The rationalization of the home-based training organization began in the summer and autumn of 1917 with the creation of the first training depot stations. However, of the first seven created in 1917, only one was for training pilots of fighting scouts: this was 3 TDS at Lopcombe Corner, and it received some D.H.5s; it also continued to operate them well into 1918, and so well beyond the date of the last being withdrawn from operational squadrons. Its machines were probably the last in service, but all were withdrawn by the summer of 1918, in favour of the Camel.

Few, if any, of the D.H.5's operational pilots will have regretted its passing, because the replacement S.E.5a was far superior. It is interesting that the change from rotary- to stationary-engined scouts did not necessitate a change of squadron personnel. The D.H.5 squadrons were withdrawn from operations, provided with their new equipment, and then given a short familiarization period before being returned to operational status. The D.H.5 may not have been the quality scout that was hoped for, and its combat successes may have been limited – but it was the machine on which many of the RFC/RAF's high-scoring pilots of 1918 learned their trade.

And although the D.H.5 may not have been remembered as a fighting scout, it has its place in history as the first British single-seater to be associated with ground-attack work. The dangers associated with such operations were first realized by D.H.5 squadrons and those operating Camels in the same role. During the Battle of Cambrai, the daily loss rate had been as high as 66 per cent, and the fact that low-flying operations were continued says much for the bravery and determination of the pilots involved. The value of such work was beyond doubt, but the unsustainably high casualties created a demand for a specialized, armoured machine that could absorb the punishment that the D.H.5 could not. That demand was to result in the Sopwith Salamander.

No example of the D.H.5 exists today. A9340, recently withdrawn from 32 Squadron, was returned to England for exhibition during the YMCA Blue Triangle week of March 1918. It was on display in Trafalgar Square, but was not preserved for posterity, and it seems likely that it, along with other contemporary survivors, was scrapped. The 110hp Le Rhone engines were not, however: they were in demand, favoured above the 130hp Clerget, for Sopwith Camels with the BEF.

CHAPTER SEVEN

The D.H.6

Simplicity For Mass Production

The Avro 504 is usually thought of as the first standardized training aeroplane used by the British flying services during the Great War, but this was not the case, as the Avro did not enter service in large numbers until 1918. It was preceded by the Airco D.H.6, a de Havilland design that succeeded the Shorthorn as an *ab-initio* trainer and served as a stopgap until the Avro was available in sufficient quantities to allow for its widespread introduction. It was only towards the end of the conflict that the D.H.6 was beginning to disappear from its primary role – but even then another, more war-like duty had been found for it. The type did much useful, if unspectacular work, and it is often overlooked by aviation enthusiasts.

In 1916 there were major changes to the structure and equipment of the RFC. A massive planned expansion in the number of operational squadrons, coupled with

the introduction of machines with greater performance, had implications for the training programme of the RFC at home. The M.F. Longhorn was, by then, virtually obsolescent and the Shorthorn was not far behind. Safe as these pushers were, their performance and handling were nowhere near that of the new generation of operational aeroplanes, and the complexity of their assembly and rigging was a handicap on training units where minor crashes were frequent. As the main producers of Farman types, Airco must have seen the writing on the wall – and it was against this background that de Havilland designed the D.H.6. His intention was to produce a training machine of tractor configuration that had docile handling characteristics and was easy to assemble, rig and maintain – and in that he succeeded. Circumstances beyond the designer's control conspired to delay the type's introduction, but

eventually almost all training units, both at home and in Egypt, were issued with the D.H.6.

Development

Two prototype D.H.6s (A5175–A5176) were ordered, but it would seem that only one was built. It was of typical contemporary construction: thus, as with the D.H.4 and the D.H.5, the fuselage was based around a pair of basic timber box girders that were joined immediately behind the cockpit. The forward part was ply-covered, and this alleviated the need for internal wire bracing. The rear section of the fuselage was cross-braced, and had a rounded turtle-deck. The vertical tail surfaces employed the sweeping profile of those on the D.H.4, while the horizontal ones were of rectilinear form. The blunt nose housed a 90hp RAF 1a engine, a power unit that was readily available and familiar to mechanics. The engine partly protruded from the nose, and a pair of vertical stacks carried its exhaust gases over the top wing.

The wings were the key design features of the D.H.6. Docile handling was considered essential in a training machine, and de Havilland employed a wing section of extreme camber that produced high lift, albeit at the expense of high drag. The mainplanes were also of rectilinear planform, and were inter-changeable between the upper and lower surfaces; this interchangeability some-times led to cockades being visible on the upper surface of the lower wings and the undersides of the upper ones. There was no stagger to the mainplanes. A cylindrical gravity tank, suspended under the centre-section, gave an endurance of two-and-three-quarter hours. The aircraft was inherently safe as a flying machine, especially in its intended role as a primary

The prototype D.H.6 looks deceptively small in this photograph, which was taken without anything or anyone to lend scale. In reality it was of considerable size. The photograph clearly shows the heavily cambered and unstaggered mainplanes, as well as the typical de Havilland tail unit. JMB/GSL

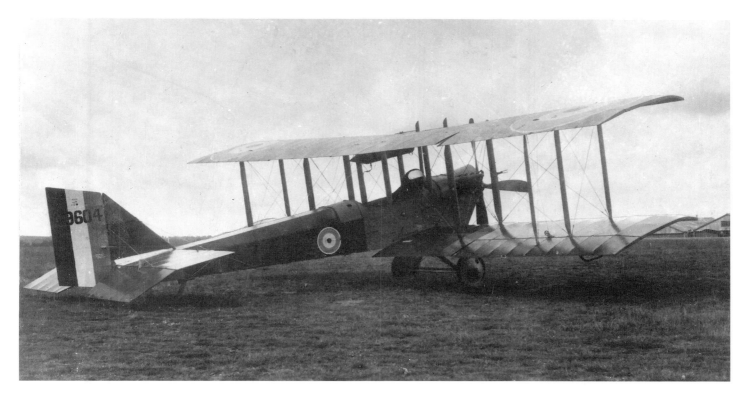

A9604, a very early D.H.6, shows the parallelogram-shaped rudder and triangular fin adopted for production machines. JMB/GSL

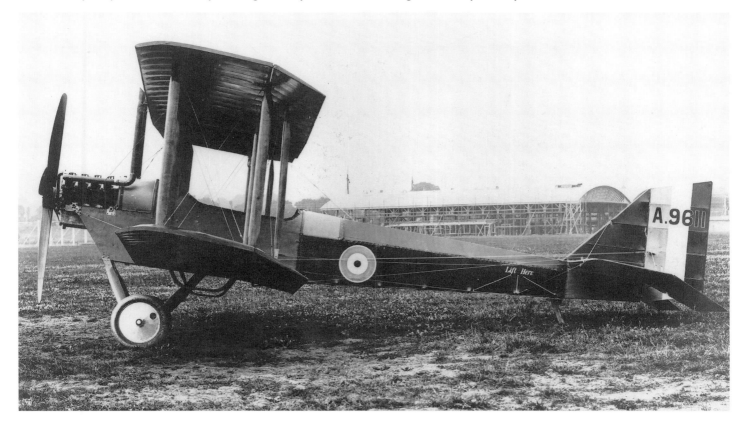

A9611 at Hendon before delivery. It saw service with 121 Squadron at Narborough. The hangars in the background now form part of the RAF Museum main building. JMB/GSL

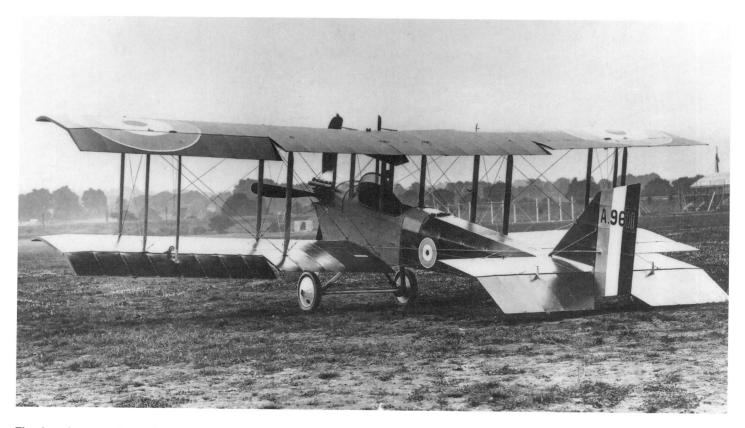

The drooping port aileron, in this further view of A9611, exaggerates the camber of the wing section. JMB/GSL

This view from the rear shows the massive elevators that almost touched the ground when the stick was pushed fully forwards. The square-cut upper and lower mainplanes were interchangeable, hence the cockades on the upper surface of the lower ones. JMB/GSL

trainer. It was slow, with a maximum speed of 66mph (106km/h) and a stalling speed of only 35mph (56km/h); it was landed at 39mph (63km/h). It was also impossible to stall it inadvertently, and so it was ideal for circuit flying. The problem was that trainee pilots needed experience of aerobatic flying, and the D.H.6 was unsuited to this. Even basic manoeuvres such as looping created control problems, and there were the inevitable crashes as a consequence. Systematic modifications to the design eventually overcame these problems.

The initial production order, for 200 machines, was given to the Hendon-based Grahame-White Aviation Co. Ltd on 13 January 1917. The parent company was, at that time, too heavily involved in the output of D.H.4s and D.H.5s to have the capacity for that extra production. Output from Grahame-White was slow, with only thirty-seven machines accepted into service by June 1917, and these were beset by problems of structural integrity. Those problems centred on timber supplies. Longerons and spars in the D.H.6 were, as in other contemporary machines, of spruce. Silver spruce from the west coast of the USA was the preferred material, but the entry of the USA into the war had resulted in the American government requisitioning all the supplies for its domestic aeroplane industry. As UK stocks of spruce were diminished, the use of swamp cypress as an alternative was promulgated. That alternative was a much shorter-grained wood, however, and less suited to absorbing the stresses imposed. The problem was compounded by the fact that the supplies of swamp cypress to Grahame-White had not been fully seasoned, and this resulted in the situation where airframes soon became distorted and weakened as the timber shrank, then twisted as it dried. Claude Grahame-White notified the unsuitability of the timber to the authorities, but his protestations were initially ignored.

Into Service

The first D.H.6s were issued to some of the higher training squadrons in lieu of intended Avro 504s: during mid-1917, these were in relatively short supply. Production machines differed from the prototype by the employment of a triangular fin, a rudder of parallelogram

shape and an angular turtle decking. Some had exhaust manifolds that ejected sideways. 68 TS at Bramham Moor, 20 TS at Wyton and 16 TS at Beaulieu were early recipients of the type. The latter unit incurred the first fatalities with the D.H.6 when, on 11 July, A9579 crashed in a dive and burst into flames, killing Captain H.E. van Goetham and 2nd Lt I.M. Tatham.

Casualties on the type were comparatively few – there were only a further seven fatal crashes during 1917 – but the concerns over the design's nose-heaviness were investigated, and resulted in modifications that eventually produced a panacea to the problems encountered when diving. Concurrently, the substandard nature of the timber was acknowledged, and production was temporarily halted, pending supplies of spruce. Further contracts were placed and included batches of 500, 100, 200 and 96 from the parent company, although 296 of these were cancelled. Grahame-White

was given orders for a further 550 and others were placed with Kingsbury Aviation, Harland and Wolff, Morgan & Co, Savages, the Gloucester Aircraft Co and Ransomes, Sims & Jeffries. In all, 3,046 production machines were ordered from UK manufacturers, and 2,300 were delivered. Production continued until September 1918.

A9605 was delivered to the Royal Aircraft Factory at Farnborough and subjected to structural tests. The results of these, combined with an adverse report from the CFS, provided a spur to the modification of the airframe. These modifications, under the auspices of the RAF, centred on the mainplanes and control surfaces. The heavily cambered aerofoil of the mainplanes was the first aspect to receive attention. The simple expediency of foreshortening the leading edge by some 4in (10cm), markedly reduced that under-camber. The mainplanes were then re-rigged with various

Specification – Airco D.H.6	
Powerplant:	80hp Renault, 90hp RAF 1a, 90hp Curtiss OX-5; fuel capacity 26 gallons
Weights:	Empty 1,460lb (662kg); loaded 2,027lb (989kg); wing loading 4.64lb per sq ft (24.35kg per sq m)
Dimensions:	Mainplane span 35ft 11in (10.95m) (upper and lower); mainplane gap 5ft 8½in (1.74m); chord 6ft 4in (1.93m); length 27ft 3½in (8.32m); height 10ft 9½in (3.29m); tailplane span 12ft (3.66m); wing area 436.3sq ft (40.6sq m)
Performance:	Maximum speed 66mph (106km/h); landing speed 39mph (63km/h); climb to 6,500ft (2,000m) 29 minutes

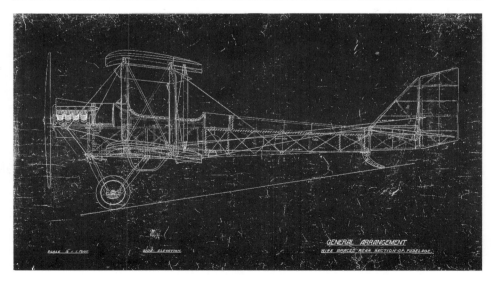

Air Board Office Drawing 2149 shows the original layout of the D.H.6. via the author

C6534 was photographed at Lake Down and probably served with 109 Squadron at that station. Its mainplanes are unstaggered, but it has the modified smaller fin and rudder. via D. Brown

amounts of negative stagger until the best results were obtained, at about 11in (28cm). The chord of the elevators was narrowed, as was that of the rudder, and the angle of the tailplane incidence was reduced. The alterations produced a much safer machine, but by the time they had been determined, more than half of the orders had been fulfilled. Introducing these changes on production lines would have serious implications for delivery rates, and so relatively few D.H.6s incorporated them all.

More than 600 D.H.6s were delivered during 1917, and over 1,000 in the first quarter of 1918. The type was issued to nearly every training squadron, including those that had, hitherto, been equipped with Maurice Farmans. It was also part of the equipment of the training depot stations that had begun to form in the autumn of 1917 as an attempt to rationalize the training system. 1 TDS at Stamford, for example, used large numbers of the type as initial trainers for R.E.8 pilots, and they survived well into the summer of 1918, when Avro 504J/Ks began to arrive as replacements. It would appear that the TDSs to use the D.H.6 were those designated to produce corps and day-bomber pilots, and that those for prospective scout pilots had priority for supplies of Avro 504s.

The study of pilot logbooks by this writer has revealed very little comment

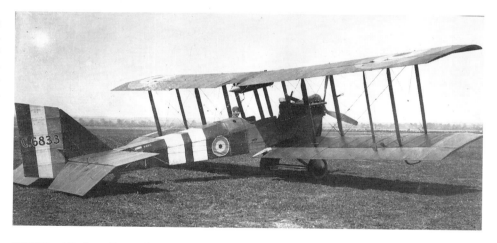

C6833 had its heavily cambered mainplanes set with negative stagger, but it retained the large fin and elevators. Photographed at Harling Road, the home of 10 TDS. JMB/GSL

about the D.H.6, either positive or adverse. For the most part, the type soldiered on, taking student pilots to the solo stage of their training, from where they passed to more warlike machines. There were, of course, the inevitable forced landings, but few seem to have resulted in any serious damage. One intriguing comment appears in the log of D.M. Hambley, who recorded a flight in A9598 at Chingford on 5 December 1917, namely 'Balanced rudder, lighter on controls...'. Other logs show that the D.H.6 could be fitted with a camera gun. Pilots were required to pass four air tests in order to graduate from Category A

Training. The fourth of these tests was for 'aerial gunnery' and required taking two successful photographs from under 1,500ft (460m) while diving at a ground target. Perhaps the difficulties of diving the D.H.6 were responsible, but on 26 August 1918, W.R. Parkhouse of 37 TDS Yatesbury recorded against C5484: 'Camera gun, eleven exposures, eleven photos – no hits'. Category B Training included aerial fighting, and pilots had to take sixteen successful camera-gun photographs of another machine from a maximum of 150yd (137m). Again, the D.H.6 could be used for this, and from 16 August 1918, G. Dixon of 49 TDS

C5155 had all the modifications recommended to make the D.H.6 safe. It had negative stagger to its mainplanes, whose leading edges had been reduced to decrease the camber of the wing section. The small fin and elevators were also fitted. JMB/GSL

Catterick recording doing so. The type was not manoeuvrable, however, and its use for fighting practice led to some fatalities – C7251 of 47 TS Waddington was lost in this way, colliding with D.H.9 C1201 of the co-located 44 TS on 7 June 1918; and similar incidents accounted for A9704 and C2028 of 5 TDS Easton-on-the-Hill on 4 June, and C3506 and C6602 of 1 TDS Stamford on 24 July.

VI Brigade, responsible for home defence, also used the D.H.6, but only in a training capacity. That organization had its own training programme, turning out pilots (and initially observers) for both its own squadrons and the light night-bomber units flying F.E.2bs in France. The D.H.6 was employed with those night training squadrons that had a preliminary training role, for example 190 NTS, and smaller numbers went to selected Home Defence squadrons, which were also charged with pilot training. Others served with 2 Wireless School at Penshurst, to which VI Brigade pilots were posted for training in the use of wireless telephony.

Service squadrons that were working up in the UK also used the D.H.6. – 119, 121, 123, 124, 125, 126, 127 and 131 Squadrons are among those which had

the type in small numbers during the early summer of 1918. These units also served in a training role, and were disbanded when the training system was re-organized to allow the widespread introduction of training depot stations.

RNAS Service

RFC stocks were so great that it was possible to transfer machines to the RNAS, directly from the parent manufacturer. During the latter part of 1917, the RNAS Preliminary Flying Schools at Chingford and Redcar received D.H.6s to replace M.F. Shorthorns, and the school at Eastbourne was similarly re-equipped in the New Year. Subsequent recipients were the schools at Manston and Eastchurch. These RNAS units became training depot stations upon the formation of the RAF: 203 TDS, Manston; 204 TDS Eastchurch; 206 TDS Eastbourne; and 207 TDS Chingford.

Four RNAS machines, B2658-B2661, were shipped (without engines) to 2 Wing in the Aegean. They were erected, fitted with engines, and after some unspecified use by F Sqn, eventually used for training Greek naval aviators.

Overseas Service

Others served further afield. The RFC had realized the potential of Egypt as the location for training units: the climate of that country would cause little interference to flying, and a chain of stations was built in the Canal Zone. Large numbers of D.H.6s were shipped there for use by training squadrons and schools; indeed, the whole of the Grahame-White batch D951-D1000 was shipped there as components for assembly at X Aircraft Depot. When the Schools of Aerial Gunnery at Aboukir and Heliopolis were established, some of these assumed a more war-like appearance, with the fitting of pillar mountings for Lewis guns to their observers' cockpits. On 31 October 1918, the RAF in Egypt and Palestine still had sixty-nine of the type on charge, and a further forty were awaiting shipment to that destination.

An extensive training scheme was also established in Canada during 1917, and the locally built Curtiss J.N.4 (Can) was standardized as the aeroplane for issue to units of the 42nd-44th Wings. The RFC's less-than-happy experience of the earlier Curtiss J.N.3 may have been the reason why Canadian Aeroplanes Ltd at Toronto

Representative Airco D.H.6s with RFC and RAF Units

61 (HD) Squadron Rochford – B2869.
76 (HD) Squadron Copmanthorpe/Helperby/Catterick – A9571, B3018.
77 (HD) Squadron Penston -
98 Squadron Old Sarum – A9612.
119 Squadron Duxford – C7248.
121 Squadron Narborough – A9738, A9739, A9611, C6581, C6607, C9365.
123 Squadron Duxford – B2677, C5586.
124 Squadron Fowlmere – C6540, C6569, C7258, C7259.
125 Squadron Fowlmere – C5482.
126 Squadron Fowlmere – C5483, C5489, C6547, C6548, C7241, C7462, C7677, C7835.
127 Squadron Catterick – B2717, B2725, B2729, B3048, B3049, C6510, C9349.
131 Squadron Shawbury – C7864, C7866, C7874.
4 TS Northolt – C5724.
5 TS Wyton – B2734, C5453.
13 TS Dover/Yatesbury – A9576, A9690, A9692, C5451, C7663.
16 TS Beaulieu – A9579, A9580, A9633, A9659, C9337, C9338.
17 TS Portmeadow/Yatesbury – A9582, A9583, A9626, A9628, A9635, A9637, C1753, C1999, C2105, C2120, C2127, C2129, C2130, C2135, C2136, C5452, C5501, C6516, C6588, C6591, C6822, C7226, C7276, C7666, C7670, C7672, C7673.
20 TS Wye/Wyton/Spittlegate/Harlaxton – A9588, A9590, A9591, A9593, A9594, A9627, A9637, B2632, B2633, C9388, C9434.
21 TS Ismailia – C2046.
23 TS Aboukir – A9644.
24 TS Netheravon – B2003, B2008, C5469, C5471.
25 TS Thetford – A9611, A9617, A9623, A9625, A9628, A9633, A9663, A9721, A9744, B2675, C5144, C5482, C5483, C5504, C6558, C6836, C6843, C6844, C7244, C7245, C7246, C7252, C7253.
26 TS Harlaxton/Narborough – A9731, A9733, B2645, B2668.
29 TS Stag Lane – C7212.
31 TS Wyton – A9717, A9719, A9720, A9721, A9722, A9723, B2663, B2714.
35 TS Portmeadow – B2817, C7222.
37 TS Scampton – A9595, B2635.
39 TS South Carlton -
42 TS Hounslow – A9611, A9616, A9666, A9667, A9678, A9679, A9705, B2609, B2610, B2677.
44 TS Waddington – A2830, A7546, A7652, A7884, A7886.
46 TS Catterick – A9753, B2711, B3051, B3054.
47 TS Waddington – C7251, C7274, C7363.
48 TS Waddington – A9761, C2018.
50 TS Narborough – A9590.
51 TS Waddington – A9647, A9758, C6823, C6837, C7224, C7300, C7864, C9385.
52 TS Cramlington/Catterick – A9391, B2683, B2700, B2701, B3050, C1986, C6654, C6804, C6853, C6857, C7280, C7289, C7322, C7323, C9391.
53 TS Narborough – A9607, A9608, A9610, A9669, A9733, A9754, B2634, B2667, B2668, B2669, B2763, C2020, C6806.
54 TS Harlaxton – C5813.
56 TS London Colney – B2614, B2650.
59 TS Yatesbury – B2811, C1994, C9345.
61 TS South Carlton -
64 TS Narborough – A9760, B2673.
66 TS Yatesbury – A9619, C5503.
68 TS Bramham Moor – A9564, A9565, A9571, A9573, B2601, B2603, B9034, C6509, C9336.
69 TS Bramham Moor – A9724.
75 TS Cramlington – C7220.
186 NTS East Retford -
187 NTS East Retford -
188 NTS Throwley -
189 NTS Sutton's Farm -
190 NTS Newmarket – B2835.
191 NTS Marham – B2864, C7708, C9381, C9401, C9470.
193 TS Amria – A9651, A9652, A9653, A9656, A9681, C1969, C1971, C2033.
194 TS Amria – C2033.
5 TS AFC Minchinhampton – C1991, C1992, C1993, C1994, C5141, C5142, C6550, C6560, C7215, C7216, C9342, C9343, C9344.
7 TS AFC Leighterton – B2775, B2819, B3057, C6815.
RAE Farnborough – B2840, B2963.
2 Wireless School Penshurst – B3004, B3006, B3010, B3011.
Artillery Observation School Almaza – A9699.
1 SANBD Stonehenge – A9669.
2 SANBD Andover -
3 SANBD – Helwan – A9713.
4 SANBD – Thetford.
Marine Observers School Aldeburgh – F3389, F3390, F3391.
School for Marine Operations Pilots Dover – A9633, B2645, B3056, C2147, C6577, C6578, C7378.
1 TDS Stamford – A9610, A9668, A9669, A9671, A9672, A9673, A9675, A9703, A9706, A9708, A9751, B2618, B2629, B2631, B2653, B2656, B2671, B2713, B2722, B8799, B8800, C2013, C2030, C5076, C5134, C5176, C5455, C6529, C6531, C6603, C6619, C6620, C6621, C6627, C6628, C9355, C9359.
2 TDS Gullane – C3506.
3 TDS Lopcombe Corner – A9621.
5 TDS Easton-on-the-Hill – A9703, A9704, A9706, A9708, A9736, C2028, C7677.
6 TDS Boscombe Down – B2742, B2745, B2746, B2753, C6801.
8 TDS Netheravon – A9690, B3042, B3045, B3046, B3053, B3056, C2002, C2100, C2147, C2150, C5133, C5137, C5138, C5486, C6518, C7351.
9 TDS Shawbury -
10 TDS Harling Road – C6633, C6635, C6636, C6833, C6839, C7254, C7257, C7822, C7833.
11 TDS Boscombe Down – A9604, C6559, C7870.
12 TDS Netheravon – C7354.
13 TDS Ternhill – B3027, C7657.
14 TDS Lake Down – B2758, C6829.
15 TDS Hucknall – B2606.
16 TDS Amria – C2033.
18 TDS Abbassia – C2045, C5540.
20 TDS Shallufa -
21 TDS Eastburn – A9564, B2970.
31 TDS Fowlmere – B2666, C5483, C6842, C6843, C7260, C7261, C7674.
35 TDS Duxford – A9611, A9617, A9623, A9625, A9628, A9633, A9663, A9721, A9744, B2675, B2715, C2093, C5144, C5482, C5504, C6558, C6841, C6843, C6844, C7244, C7245, C7252, C7253.
36 TDS Yatesbury – B3059, C7713, C9337.
37 TDS Yatesbury – B2612, C2105, C2129, C5154, C5454, C5463, C5484, C6815, C7666, C9337, C9405.
40 TDS Harlaxton – C9434.
41 TDS London Colney – B2614, B2650.
48 TDS Waddington – C6826, C7238, C7728, C7743, C7751, C7867.
49 TDS Catterick – B2701, B3052, C1986, C6510, C6834, C6849, C7232, C7235, C7302, C7303, C7324, C7329, C9349.
51 TDS North Shotwick –
52 TDS Cramlington – C7218.
202 TDS Cranwell -
203 TDS/55 TDS Manston/Narborough – B2773.
202 TDS/57 TDS Cranwell – C2128.
204 TDS Eastchurch -
206 TDS/50 TDS Eastbourne – A9672, B2760.
207 TDS Chingford – A9598, A9599, A9603, A9612, A9613, A9634, A9640, A9641, A9650, B2612, B2613, B2614, B2615, B2616, B2625, B2626, B2637, B2638, B2639, B2640, B2641, B2647, B2648, B2650, B2651, B2657, B2680, B2681, B2682.
213 TDS/58 TDS Cranwell – B2787.

produced a single D.H.6. That D.H.6 had the Curtiss OX-5 engine and the flying controls of the J.N.4 (Can), and is assumed to have been the prototype of a safeguard against any major problem with the American design. It transpired that the J.N.4 (Can) was perfectly adequate for the task, and the modified D.H.6 was not needed. However, that D.H.6 would appear to have seen service with a Canadian-based training unit.

Training squadrons of the Australian Flying Corps based at Minchinhampton and Leighterton in the UK were issued with the D.H.6, but others were sent to Australia for use by the AFC's Central Flying School at Point Cook. An initial eight (B2801-B2804 and C9372-C9374) were shipped out, but two were lost en route when their transport was sunk; they were later replaced.

Marine Operations

During 1918, the D.H.6 assumed the role for which it is best known: it became a coastal patrol machine, and began to undertake front-line tasks. This situation arose because of the German decision to apply unrestricted submarine warfare. By late 1917, the UK was dependent upon imports of food and raw materials, and merchant shipping was easily intercepted as it approached home waters. Minefields constricted that shipping to swept channels that extended to some 10 miles (16km) from the coast, and this made targeting them easier. The RNAS had employed airships in the anti-submarine role, and had also experimented with the use of aeroplanes for the task. Sopwith 1 ½ Strutters had been operated from RNAS bases in the South West during the spring of 1917, and Handley-Page 0/100s were flown from RNAS Redcar that autumn. Both detachments had indicated that the mere presence of aeroplanes was sufficient to keep submarines submerged below periscope depth, and therefore less harmful. The RNAS did not, however, have the capability to maintain such operations.

Shipping losses were greatest in the South-West Approaches and the North-East War Channel. The closure of the RNAS school at Redcar, upon the formation of the Royal Air Force, made D.H.6s available, and it was decided to try these machines on coastal patrols. Two Special Duty Flights were formed at Cramlington by 27 April 1918; their machines were delegated to fly specific

B2929 had all the wing and tail modifications and was fitted with a Curtiss OX-5 engine. It was used at Grain to test flotation gear that was intended for D.H.6s in Marine Operations units. JMB/GSL

patrol 'beats' along the War Channel off the Tyne, and although their presence had yet to indicate that the desired effect could be achieved, plans were already in hand to expand the scheme by forming 250, 251 and 252 Squadrons on 1 May.

It was soon realized that the best coverage could be achieved if each squadron was not concentrated on a single aerodrome. The flights that comprised each unit were therefore dispersed, some taking over VI Brigade landing grounds that were upgraded to temporary aerodromes. Conditions for the flights were primitive, with (usually) canvas Bessoneau hangars for the machines, billets for officers, and tented accommodation for other ranks. This situation was compounded by the fact that the flights were seldom up to strength in personnel, and the aircrews were often those unfit for active service overseas. Yet despite these handicaps, the Marine Operations units went on to do sterling service that prompted the Lords Commissioners of the Admiralty to state, in a letter to the Air Council dated August 1918:

... considerable credit is due to pilots who first undertook the anti-submarine work, flying land machines over the sea, particularly in the case of those using D.H.6 type, a training machine of poor performance, and by no means suited to this type of work. If the Air Council see no objection, My Lords suggest that an expression of appreciation be conveyed to the officers concerned ...

Further Marine Operations squadrons were formed. Most were wholly equipped with the D.H.6, while others had one or two flights operating the type alongside flights of seaplanes or other land-planes. Eventually fifteen squadrons operated the D.H.6 on marine operations, covering shipping in the Irish Sea as well as off the north-east, south and south-west coasts.

The flights that comprised the Marine Operations Squadrons were at first known by letters within individual units (A Flt, B Flt etc); then from 25 May 1918, a numbering system came into effect. Discrete blocks of flight numbers were allocated for specific duties, and nos 500-533 were reserved for D.H.6 units. Although subject to minor changes, small blocks of consecutive flight numbers were given to each squadron. The intended establishment of each flight was six machines.

250 Sqn had its HQ at Padstow, and comprised 500 and 501 Flts at that station; and 251 Sqn, HQ Hornsea, had 504 Flt at Atwick, 505 Flt at Greenland Top and 506 Flt at Owthorne. 252 Sqn had its HQ initially at South Shields, with Cramlington as its aerodrome until its flights were dispersed – 507 & 508 Flts to Tynemouth, 509 Flt to Seaton Carew and 510 Flt to Redcar.

254 Sqn continued the build-up in the South West. It operated 515 and 516 Flts from Mullion, and 517 and 518 Flts at the parent base of Prawle Point. 255 Sqn was next to form, on 25 July. It had its HQ at Pembroke and controlled six flights that covered the Irish Sea. 519 and 520 Flts were at the parent station, 521 and 522 Flts operated from the Anglesey airship station, and 523 and 524 Flts were at Luce Bay.

256 Sqn followed in early June, extending coverage of the north-east coast to the Scottish border. Its HQ was at Belford, and initially its component units were 525 Flt at Rennington, 526 Flt at New Haggerston, 527 Flt at Seahouses and 528 Flt at Cairncross. 253 Sqn was formed to provide coverage of the south coast, with four D.H.6 flights on 7 June. 511 and 512 Flts were at Brading, on the Isle of Wight, 513 Flt used Chickerall and 514 Flt at Telscombe Cliffs extended the patrol line eastwards.

258 Sqn formed at Luce Bay, on 25 July. It took over 523 and 524 Flts from 255 Sqn, and formed 529 Flt. All three shared accommodation on that airship station. 244 Sqn formed at Bangor on the same date, receiving 521 and 522 Flts from 255 Sqn, and forming 530 Flt. This transfer of flights between squadrons was a forerunner of similar movements the following month, when new Marine Operations units formed.

236 Sqn formed at Mullion, taking over the existing 515 and 516 Flts at that station. 241 and 242 Sqns were primarily seaplane units, but they subsumed 513 and 514 Flts respectively. The final D.H.6 coastal squadron was 272 Sqn, which came into being at Machrihanish on August 15. It comprised 531, 532 and 533 Flts. That day also saw 525 and 528 Flts of 256 Sqn transfer bases, to Ashington and Seahouses respectively.

The disposition of the D.H.6 units remained fairly static until the Armistice. 530 Flt was briefly detached to Tallaght (Dublin) in October, and 510 Flt

transferred units, as noted below. An anomaly exists with 404 Flt. That unit number was in a block reserved for Short seaplanes, but it is recorded as operating from North Coates Fitties with the D.H.6. 404 Flt had operated Shorts from Hornsea, but the coastline at the Lincolnshire base was unsuitable for operating such machines. At this distance in time it is difficult to discover whether the entry was a typing error for 504 Flt, or whether 404 Flt really did re-equip.

It is not possible to give a detailed account of the histories of each unit, but an understanding of their operations can be gained by examining the role played by one Marine Operations flight. On 23 May 1918, 252 Squadron at Cramlington had seventeen D.H.6s. Its 'C' Flight was re-designated as 510 Flight two days later, and under the command of Captain M.A. Simpson, flew in formation from Cramlington to its new base at Redcar on 29 May 1918. Its machines were A9573, A9694, B2686, C5130, C9383 and C9403. The flight, which came under the control of 18 (Operations) Group, shared its new base with 2 SSF (which became the NEAFIS in July), and its personnel had the luxury of permanent accommodation. The flight immediately resumed patrols and convoy escorts over the North-East War Channel. That channel was marked, at its outer edge, by a series of buoys, each of which was identified by letter. The usual operating height for patrols was 800ft (250m), and most were along the Yorkshire coast as far south as Robin Hood's Bay, Whitby and Scarborough. The duration of patrols varied, but some lasted over three hours. C9403 flew 195min on a patrol to Scarborough on 10 June, and that was with an observer on board. From 11 July, the flight came under the control of the 68th Wing, still in 18 Group. The flight had the inevitable accidents, and replacement machines were collected from the Marine Aircraft Depot sub-station at South Shields. That was a seaplane station, but the D.H.6s were flown off from the large apron that fronted its hangars.

The arrival of 63 Training Squadron at Redcar, from Joyce Green, in early October resulted in that station becoming overcrowded, and so 510 Flt transferred to West Ayton. The move to the new base also meant that the flight transferred to the parentage of 251 Sqn, whose HQ was at Hornsea. West Ayton was a new site near Scarborough, not the Riggs Head racecourse that had earlier been used by the RNAS, but a field alongside the River Derwent, some 3 miles (5km) south-west of the town. Patrols were then made in a northerly direction, usually as far as Skinningrove. The Armistice saw a noticeable reduction in flying, however, and in March 1919, the flight was reduced to cadre status and its machines disposed of. That cadre transferred to Killingholme during March 1919; here, along with other 18 Group units, it disbanded on 30 June.

Production of the RAF 1a engine had ceased before 1918, and available supplies were insufficient for the number of D.H.6s on order. Some machines were fitted with the 80hp Renault, a process that involved little modification, but that engine, too, could only be obtained second-hand. Perhaps the installation of the 90hp Curtiss OX-5 in the solitary Canadian-built D.H.6 served as a precedent, because that engine and the similar OX-2 were brought into use. Although of similar V8 configuration to the RAF 1a, these were water-cooled engines, and as such required the use of a radiator. A frontal radiator was mounted, and this served to lengthen the nose of the machine. The OX-5 was fitted to production machines as supplies became available. Morgan & Co began fitting the engine to machines when about two-thirds of its batch C6501-C6700 had already been delivered with the 80hp Renault. Other manufacturers were in the same situation, but the transition to the new engine does not appear to have caused any delays in deliveries. The vast majority of D.H.6s with the Curtiss engines were delivered to Marine Operations units.

D.H.6s on marine operations could be flown with either one or two crew. A signaller was sometimes carried, if communication with vessels was intended – that communication was by signal lamp, although some D.H.6s were fitted with wireless. The *Official History* records that the ratio of single- to two-crew patrols was in the region of 75 to 25 per cent. When the type was flown as a single-seater, allowing a bomb load to be carried, a 100lb (45kg) bomb was mounted on an under-fuselage carrier, though aiming was a matter of guesswork. Drawings dated 11 July 1918 were prepared by the Grahame-White company for a single-seat bomber

version, specifically for marine operations. These were to involve alterations to the disposition of the spacers in the frame of the forward fuselage to accommodate a clear-view floor panel to starboard, a central floor opening with a sliding shutter that allowed the use of a Low Height Mk. IIA bomb-sight. The bomber was to be flown from the rear seat position, and the design of the rudder bar was to be altered to accommodate the bomb-sight. Purpose-designed bomb-fusing and release gear was to be fitted within the cockpit. The bracing was to be strengthened by the use of extra wires that ran from the upper fuselage longerons to the bases of the inboard mainplane struts. However, it seems unlikely that any operational D.H.6 was so modified.

It was inevitable that engine failures on coastal patrols could lead to D.H.6s coming down in the water. In calm conditions it was found that the type could float for a considerable length of time (up to ten hours was possible), and there are many recorded instances of ditched machines being towed to a convenient landfall, and even being

returned to service. B2933 of 510 Flt West Ayton, for example, landed in the sea off Whitby on 11 October 1918, was salved, and was still with its unit a calendar month later. Some machines were unsalvageable in such situations, but there were few instances of pilots being lost. This was undoubtedly due to the fact that the convoy patrol system meant there was usually a vessel nearby to pick up the ditched crew. Despite the D.H.6's tendency to remain afloat of its own accord, experiments were conducted at Grain to fit flotation gear that would ensure this situation. Several D.H.6s were delivered to that experimental station, and at least two were used in trials of this gear, namely B2929 (Curtiss OX-5) and C2098 (RAF 1a). The gear comprised a pair of flotation bags that were fitted under the inboard ends of the lower mainplanes and projected forwards to the level of the front undercarriage struts. The forward projections were supported by struts. In their deflated condition, the bags were flat and presented little resistance to airflow; inflated they became pontoons that bore the weight of the heaviest parts

---

Representative D.H.6s with Marine Operations Units

236 Squadron 515–516 Flights Mullion – C6516, C6519, C6561, C6588, C6664, C7645, C7649, C7799, C7834,C7840.

241 Squadron 513 Flight Chickerall – C6513, C6892, C6899, C6900, F3414.

242 Squadron 514 Flight Telscombe Cliffs – C6886, C6891, C6893, C6895, F3421, F3425.

244 Squadron 521–522 & 530 Flights Bangor & Tallaght – B2791, B2976, B2979, B3020, B3023, B3025, C6560, C6655, C6656.

250 Squadron 500–501 Flights Padstow – B2847, B2848, B2851, B2857, B2896, B2897, B2963, C2114, C5191, C5193, C5194.

251 Squadron 504–506 & 510 Flights Atwick, Greenland Top, Owthorne & West Ayton – B2800, B3051, B3061, B3064, B3065, B3067, C5170, C5212, C5215, F3392.

252 Squadron 507–510 Flights Tynemouth, Seaton Carew & Redcar – B2709, B2719, B3031, B3037, B3081, B3089, C2078, C2079, F3373, F3433.

253 Squadron 511–513 Flights Brading, New Bembridge & Chickerall – C6513, C6565, C6566, C6593, C6897, C7877, C6892, C7877, C7883, F3417.

254 Squadron 515–518 Flights Mullion & Prawle Point – C5199, C5200, C5204, C5208, C5210, C6521, C6562, C6564, C6566, C6567.

255 Squadron 519–524 Flights Pembroke, Bangor & Luce Bay – B2781, B2786, B2789, B3020, C2067, C2076, C9415, C9523, F3351, F3353, F3357.

256 Squadron 525–528 Flights Cairncross, Rennington, Seahouses, New Haggerston & Ashington – B2842, B2844, B2845, B2853, B2883, B3033, B3035, C2084, C6686, C6687.

258 Squadron 523–524 & 529 Flights Luce Bay – B2965, B2967, B2970, B2972, C5520, C9407, C9411, C9413, C9416, C9438.

260 Squadron 502–503 Flights Westward Ho! – A9659, C2087, C2112, C6671, C6672, C6680, C7418, C7419, C7422, C7423.

272 Squadron 531–533 Flights Machrihanish – B2960, B2961, C2085, C2111, C2115, C2121, C5499, C7780, C7782, F3380.

---

of the machines. There must have been faith in the gear because 200 sets for D.H.6s were ordered in May 1918, a month before C2098 was tested with the equipment. Despite the success of the tests, there is little evidence of the gear being used operationally.

In spite of the primitive operating conditions and its mediocre performance, the D.H.6 acquitted itself well on marine operations, and there were several occasions when contact was made with the enemy.

The remaining D.H.6s from Cramlington moved to Tynemouth on 8 June 1918 as 507 and 508 Flts – but not before an encounter. Two days previously Captain F. W. Walker DSC sighted a submarine whilst on patrol in Curtiss-engined C6883, and attacked it at a position 7 miles (11km) south-east of Cresswell, though without causing damage. It was the first recorded instance of a D.H.6 making contact with the enemy, and there were to be a further sixteen such incidents.

C6882 was another early OX-5-powered D.H.6, and it was issued to 510 Flt of 252 Sqn at Redcar. On 24 June 1918 it was being flown by Lt L.M. Burton, who sighted a U-boat near the H Buoy off Hartlepool. A bomb was dropped, but no damage was observed. On 15 July the same D.H.6 was involved in a further encounter with a submarine. On the 14th, Lt F.R. Giradot of the same unit used C6881 to drop a 100lb bomb on an enemy vessel a mile east of the P Buoy off Runswick Bay. HMS *Calvier* followed up the attack, but the enemy managed to elude her.

Captain H. Goodfellow of 250 Sqn Padstow was near his aerodrome on 23 July when he sighted an enemy submarine 3 miles (5km) off Trevose Head. He dropped what was given as an 85lb (38kg) bomb from C5206, but without result.

On 26 July 1918, C5189 was flown from Atwick by Lt S. Markussen of 504 Flt, 251 Sqn, and after sighting a U-boat the pilot descended to drop his bomb. It had no effect, and the submarine was lost. The following day Lt A.C. Tremellen of 250 Sqn Padstow dropped a 65lb (24kg) weapon from C7849 on a submarine at 5055N 0450W, but again without result.

On 13 August Lt H.H. Shorter from 250 Sqn Padstow, flying C5207, found a submarine 2 miles (3km) off Newquay: he dropped his 60lb (27kg) bomb, but to no

Several D.H.6s came onto the British Civil Register. Here, Captain B. Martin, the proprietor of Martin Aviation, is seen in front of one of his machines. The photograph shows well the very basic mounting of the engine. via the author

avail. Then on the following day Lt A.J.D. Peebles of 255 Sqn Pembroke was patrolling in C9439 and sighted a submarine, which he bombed – but although bubbles rose to the surface after his attack, no claim was allowed.

During the course of a patrol on 17 August 1918, Lt Whitmore in B3082 of 252 Sqn Tynemouth sighted a German submarine 25 miles (40km) east of Druridge Bay. His 100lb (45kg) bomb was dropped, but without any observed result.

B2917, in use post-war, retained its military number. The remains of a cockade can be seen under its upper mainplane. JMB/GSL

Beaches were favourite locations for 'barn-storming' pilots to use as landing grounds. G-EARJ is seen in such a setting.

G-EARJ's upper wings and tailplane had white dope applied to accept the registration and national letter. This machine had negative stagger, but retained the large tail control surfaces. JMB/GSL

B3090 took over the search, but there was no further trace of the enemy vessel.

Four days later, Lt C.B. Gibson in C2079 of the same unit attacked another U-boat, this time 3 miles (5km) south-east of Sunderland. The single bomb dropped did little apparent damage – though some oil was seen on the surface – and although the attack was taken over by naval vessels, the enemy escaped.

At 12.30pm on 24 August 1918, B2789, flown by Lt R. Nicholson of 255 Sqn Pembroke, attacked a submarine, but his bomb failed to explode. A further patrol was sent out, and F3351 flown by Lt S.J.D. Peebles had his second contact with the enemy when he found the U-boat at 2.45pm. He dropped his bomb, but again with no positive result. On that same day, C5172 of 527 Flt 256 Sqn, from Seahouses, was flown on patrol by Flt Sgt Douglas, and that pilot sighted a submarine at 5535N 0130W – but again, no damage was observed.

On 11 September, 2nd Lt W.U. Kennedy of 526 Flt 256 Sqn flew C7336 on patrol from New Haggerston and attacked a U-boat – but yet again without result. Twelve days later Lt R. Wimpenny of 254 Sqn Prawle Point attacked a submarine at 5015N 0334W, but his 65lb (30kg) bomb did no apparent damage. On the 29th, 2nd Lt H.C. Cook in C7657 of 510 Flt Redcar dropped a 100lb (45kg) weapon on a submarine at 5428N 0030W, but the outcome was again negative.

The lack of damage as a result of these contacts can be attributed to several factors. The pilots had no formal training in bomb dropping, and their machines were not fitted with bomb-sights. The munitions themselves were suspect, as few of the flight stations had any proper bomb stores, with ordnance often being kept exposed to the elements. Trained armourers were in short supply, and so the fusing of the bombs was often a matter of guesswork. None of this can, however, detract from the bravery shown by the pilots of the D.H.6 on marine operations.

The D.H.6 soldiered on in this role until the Armistice, but had the war continued into 1919, the type would have been replaced by Vickers Vimys and D.H.10s. It had been intended that, as a stop-gap measure, D.H.9s would temporarily replace the D.H.6 in some units; 506, 507 and 527 Flts were mentioned in the weekly *Dispositions of Naval Aircraft* as being scheduled to receive that light bomber, but it is most unlikely that any were ever delivered. The Marine Operations flights were run down after the Armistice, and all were disbanded by the following summer.

On 31 October 1918 the RAF had 1,050 D.H.6s on charge. More than a quarter of these were in storage, and 571 were with 'Areas', a generic term that included Marine Operations Units and Training Depot Stations. A further sixty-nine were in Egypt, with another forty destined for service there. Small numbers were with other operators, such as 6 Brigade and various schools. On that same date the RAF had three times as many Avro 504s as it had D.H.6s, and the de Havilland design was rapidly withdrawn from service after the Armistice was signed.

Post-War

Civilian aviation mushroomed in the immediate post-war years, and many ex-service pilots saw a future in providing demonstration and air-experience flights. Barnstorming companies came and went, but surprisingly few chose the easily maintained D.H.6 as a vehicle for their activities. A good number did enter the Civil Register, but the Avro 504J/K was preferred, due no doubt to its superior performance and the ease of maintaining rotary engines. Probably the first civilian D.H.6 was marked as K-100 in the initial register, later re-registered as G-EAAB. That machine was unusual in that it was fitted with vertical tail surfaces, apparently from a D.H.4 or D.H.9. The D.H.6 received certification as a three-seater conversion during 1920, but its performance with two passengers must have bordered on the dangerous, and few survived for very long.

An even more unlikely conversion of a D.H.6 was made by the Blackburn

Known D.H.6 Registered as UK Civilian Aeroplanes
(Original Identities Given Where Known)

G-EAFT (B2943)	G-EAFY (C7390)	G-EAFZ (C7320)	G-EAGE (C5224)
G-EAGF (C5220)	G-EAGG (C2101)	G-EAHE (B2917)	G-EAHH (F3435)
G-EAHI (C6889)	G-EAHJ (C9432)	G-EALS (C7620)	G-EALT (B3094)
G-EAMK (C9448)	G-EAML (C9449)	G-EAMS (B2689)	G-EANJ (B2861)
G-EANU (C5230)	G-EAOT (C7434)	G-EAPG (C7430)	G-EAPH (C7739)
G-EAPW (C6503)	G-EAQB (C7815)	G-EAQC (C7436)	G-EAQY (B2885)
G-EARA (C5527)	G-EARB (C5533)	G-EARC (C5547)	G-EARJ (B3061)
G-EARK (B3065)	G-EARL (B3003)	G-EARM (B3068)	G-EARR (B3067)
G-EAUS (C7763)	G-EAUT (C9436)	G-EAVR (C7797)	G-EAWT (F3437)
G-EBPN (C7823)	G-EBWG (C7291)	G-AARN (B2868)	

Aeroplane & Motor Co during 1920 to test the parasol fitting of a novel wing design, the brainchild of Dutchman A.A. Holle, which he claimed gave increased lift in proportion to airspeed. This incorporated a curved leading edge and straight trailing edge. The wing thickness-chord ratio decreased dramatically towards the tips, and the angle of incidence changed from positive at the centre to negative at the tips. Aileron control was fitted. The variant was given a 200hp Bentley B.R.2 rotary engine.

Registered G-EAWG, the machine was first flown on 2 January 1921 when the operation of the ailerons was found to be ineffective. Holle then modified the wing by replacing aileron control with leading-edge slats, a modification that caused the design to become known as the 'Alula Wing', so named after the alula bone in the leading edge of a bird's wing that extends to modify camber at low flying speeds.

The noted pilot Frank T. Courtney was engaged to test the modified design during April of the same year, however the results were little better, and the project was abandoned. Holle went on to try a further version of the wing on the Martinsyde Semiquaver, but that, too, was not successful.

Some D.H.6s found civilian buyers overseas. When the Australian flying service relinquished its machines, beginning from 1921, seven – including C1972, C7625 and C9374 – came onto that country's Civil Register. C9474 (as G-AUBW) survived the longest, finally being destroyed in a hangar fire on 7 August 1931. Five of the other six had been destroyed in crashes.

Others were operated in South Africa, Belgium, Canada, the USA and Spain. The previous identities of the Spanish M-AAAB and M-AAEE are not known, but these were unusual in that they were fitted with Hispano-Suiza engines, most likely of the 150hp variety. It is in South Africa that the sole known remains of a D.H.6 can been seen: parts of C9449 are held by the South African Air Force Museum in Pretoria.

CHAPTER EIGHT

The D.H.9

That Machine or Nothing

The D.H.9 has always been compared unfavourably with its precursor, the D.H.4; however, its shortcomings can be attributed to the enforced use of an engine that had insufficient power for a machine that was designed to have both a longer range and a greater bomb-carrying capacity than the earlier type. Although 130lb (59kg) lighter when empty, a loaded D.H.9 was 490lb (222kg) heavier than a similarly powered D.H.4. Despite the D.H.9's inferiority to both the D.H.4 and its successor, the D.H.9A, it outlived both in service, and converted examples were still flying as late as 1939.

Development

Despite the D.H.4's superb – for its time – performance, it was realized at an early stage that there were also shortcomings in its design. Most significantly, the position of the pilot's cockpit, under the centre-section, impaired the field of vision and made rapid communication with the observer difficult – and such immediate contact between the crew of a two-seater was essential in combat. The redesign, named the D.H.9, was an attempt to remedy this situation, and its development was authorized at the early date of 23 January 1917, under Contracts AS17569 and AS21273/1/17.

Because the D.H.9 incorporated many D.H.4 components, naturally its structure bore a close resemblance to that of its antecedent. Extensive use was again made of sub-assemblies, with the fuselage being in two parts. The forward section followed the de Havilland practice of utilizing a pair of heavy patons to carry the lower mainplanes, and also ply-covering that eliminated the need for internal cross-bracing.

C6051 was the first production D.H.9 from AMC, and was tested at Martlesham Heath in November 1917. It was allocated to 27 Squadron, for evaluation, that December. It then went to France, but was wrecked in a ground collision. It is seen here with its radiator retracted and fitted with the original style of exhaust manifold and header-tank pipe-work. via K. Kelly

F1258 is a D.H.9 that went to France for evaluation by that country's authorities; it is preserved at Le Bourget. This view shows the clean lines of the nose that were marred when the radiator was in its extended position. It features revised header-tank pipe-work and a long exhaust pipe to deflect gases and the resultant haze from the pilot's line of vision. via the author

A further view of F1258 showing the carburettor intakes in the starboard side of the cowling, and the aperture between the rear undercarriage legs, for the internal bomb compartment. It also has a pair of ribs, for bomb carriers, under each mainplane. *via the author*

The positions of the main fuel tank and the pilot's cockpit were not directly transposed – the tank was mounted further forwards, and the space behind it was used to accommodate compartmentalized cases for internally carried bombs. These cases could be of differing internal configuration, the most common being designed for six, but Air Board Office drawing 7002 shows one for twelve weapons, and at least one report mentions the internal stowage of fourteen bombs. Naturally, the greater the number of bombs, the smaller the weight of each, and the smaller the compartments. The undercarriage, resembling the taller Mk.2 undercarriage of the D.H.4, again employed a single cord-sprung axle, and had the same 6ft (2m) track as its predecessor.

The water-cooled engine was carried with its cylinders and cylinder head exposed in order to assist cooling. The rounded contours of the nose were designed to reduce drag, and so a ventral radiator was fitted. This was semi-retractable, again as a drag-saving device, and was extended for take-off and landing. The pillar-like header-tank for cooling water was mounted behind the engine and supported from the centre-section. Access to the engine's ancillaries was facilitated by the use of top panels that were hinged along the upper longeron and folded downwards.

The main fuel tank was pressurized, and fuel was pumped by the action of two small windmill propellers that were fitted on the forward fuselage decking. There was a gravity tank within the centre-section. These tanks gave a combined fuel load of 74gals (336l), 12 per cent more than that of the BHP-engined D.H.4.

As with the D.H.4, full dual control was fitted. A pair of control columns (the observer's was detachable for stowage so that it would not interfere with the use of his gun) was mounted on a longitudinal shaft that led into both cockpits; in the observer's, this connected to a transversely mounted rocking shaft that passed out through the fuselage sides to control horns to which the elevator cables were attached. A quadrant on the forward end of the longitudinal shaft secured aileron cables that passed, via a series of pulleys, along the lower wing leading edges to those lower control surfaces. The upper ailerons were attached by cable to these, and balanced by a lateral cable along the

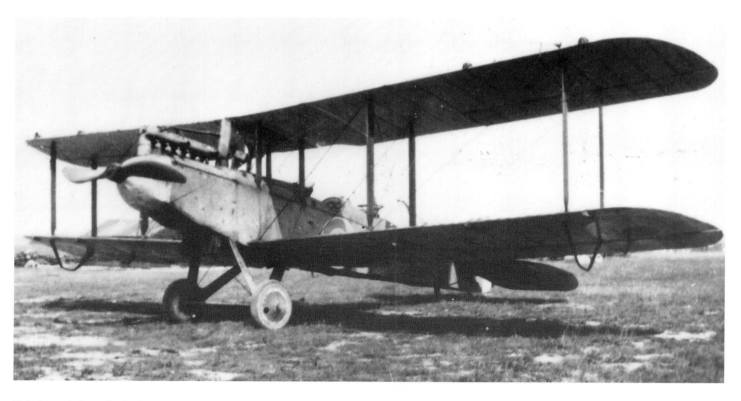

This frontal shot of a D.H.9 at Netheravon during 1919, shows the wing plan-form that was identical to that of the D.H.4. via F. A. Yeoman

Another view of the D.H.9 seen in the previous photograph, showing the blisters on the leading edges of the upper mainplanes that housed the pulleys for the aileron balance cable. via F. A. Yeoman

upper wing leading edges. The rudder cables connected to a rudder bar that protruded through the sides of the pilot's cockpit, and by further cables to another in the observer's cockpit.

Internal fuselage fixtures comprised a wicker seat for the pilot, and a rotating stool for the observer. A negative-lens bomb-sight was fitted, the sighting being through a panel in the cockpit floor that could be slid open when needed. Defensive armament comprised a fixed Vickers machine-gun, mounted externally in a channel to port of the pilot's cockpit, and a Lewis gun carried on a Scarff ring in the observer's cockpit. The Vickers was synchronized to fire through the propeller arc by the use of the Constantinesco CC hydraulically operated timing gear. Occasionally two Lewis guns were carried, but their combined weight made the use

limited the size of bombs carried.

An enormous increase in the squadron strength of both the Royal Flying Corps and the Royal Naval Air Service was sanctioned on 2 July 1917. The recently introduced daylight raids on London and the South East provided the impetus for this decision, and it was planned that the majority of the new squadrons would operate day-bombing aeroplanes. These were intended to carry the war to the enemy by raiding the industrial towns in the south of that country.

Massive orders had been placed for the D.H.4, but as ever, engine production lagged behind that of airframes. This lag was exaggerated in the case of Rolls Royce power units, whose precision engineering prolonged manufacture. The matter was compounded by the fact that the same engines were also needed for F.E.2d and

Felixstowe F.2A production. The design of the D.H.9 was concurrent with these events, and certainly on paper, the machine was seen as a panacea to the supply problem. It was decided that orders recently placed for almost 700 D.H.4s would be replaced by ones for a similar number of the new type.

These machines were to be provided by sub-contractors. The Westland Aircraft Works at Yeovil were to deliver B7581-B7680 (100) as D.H.9s, as were The Vulcan Motor & Engineering Co of Southport with B9331-B9430 (100), C & J Weir of Cathcart with C1151-C1450 (300), Mann Egerton & Co of Norwich with D1651-D1750 (100), and F.W. Berwick & Co of London with C2151-C2230 (80). On 29 September, Airco received an initial order for 300 of the type (C6051-C6350), and further massive orders followed.

It was anticipated that there would be little problem with engine supply, as similarly huge orders had also been placed for the 230hp BHP engine with the Galloway Engineering Co, Siddeley-Deasey and Crossley Motors. Those from Galloway were named 'Adriatic' and had cast-iron cylinder banks, but the others, named 'Puma', were an attempt to reduce weight by the use of steel-lined aluminium components. The Galloway and Puma were not interchangeable. Unfortunately, the anticipation of smooth delivery was ill-founded, and production difficulties

Specification – Airco D.H.9	
Powerplant:	230hp Siddeley Puma, 230hp Galloway Adriatic, 260hp FIAT A12; fuel capacity 74 gallons
Weights:	Empty 2,200lb (998kg); loaded 3,890lb (1,764kg); wing loading 8.96lb per sq ft (43.7kg per sq m)
Dimensions:	Mainplane span 42ft 4in (12.91m) (upper and lower); mainplane gap 5ft 6in (1.68m); chord 5ft 6in (1.68m); length 30ft 10in (9.4m); height 11ft 2in (3.41m); tailplane span 14ft (4.27m); wing area 434sq ft (40.37sq m)
Performance:	Maximum speed 102mph (164km/h); landing speed 57mph (92km/h); climb to 10,000ft (3,000m) 20 minutes

of the Scarff ring difficult at high altitudes.

The tailplane, fin and rudder were taken directly from the D.H.4, but the incidence of the tailplane could be adjusted. A worm-gear device, similar to that used in Sopwith designs, was connected by cables to a chain that passed around a hand-wheel in the pilot's cockpit; this allowed trim changes to be made in flight, to allow for alterations to the centre of gravity as fuel and armament were used.

The mainplanes and centre-section were standard D.H.4 components, set at the same incidence and stagger as on the earlier type. A pair of bomb ribs was a common fitment under each lower mainplane, and an under-fuselage carrier for a 230lb (104kg) bomb was another. Internal bomb stowage seems to have found little favour – certainly it would have been more awkward to load than external ordnance, and would have

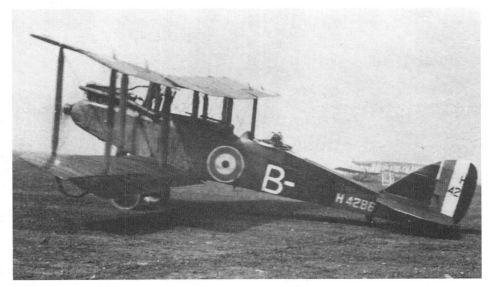

H4286 carried a small rectangular marking aft of its individual letter B similar to that used by 104 Squadron. It featured a lengthened exhaust, and another variation in header-tank pipe-work. JMB/GSL

H4288 was aircraft G of 49 Squadron during the post-war period. RCB Ashworth via JMB/GSL

B7632 was built by Westland and served with 211 Squadron. It is seen here fitted with a 230lb (100kg) bomb on an under-fuselage carrier. The weapon would not fit the internal bomb compartment that seems to have had little usage on any operational squadron. JMB/GSL

emerged with the aluminium castings of the engine crankcase and cylinders; by the end of 1917, less than 300 of the 4,000 engines on order had been delivered.

However, the Air Board had taken the precaution of ordering an alternative powerplant: the 260hp Fiat A-12, another six-cylinder, vertical inline engine. Half of the 2,000 on order were for installation in D.H.9s. Unfortunately, the alternative engine had the disadvantage of being considerably heavier than the BHP unit.

Airco created the first D.H.9 by converting the airframe of D.H.4 A7559. It was flying during August 1917, and initially was reported as having a superior performance to the Rolls Royce-engined D.H.4. Its engine was a Galloway Adriatic, delivering 230hp. A7559 did not undergo official assessment until after 5 October,

and externally. However, the results, published as M156A and M156B, were very disappointing; for instance, maximum speed at 15,000ft (4,500m) was less than 100mph (160km/h), and that height was about the service ceiling for the type. The problem for the RFC hierarchy was the lack of an alternative to the D.H.9, and Trenchard was informed that the BEF would have to accept that machine or nothing.

C6053 joined the first production machine at Martlesham on 22 December, and was used in a comparative series of propeller tests. Disappointment with the BHP-engined type resulted in C6052 arriving at the experimental station with a Fiat A-12 installed, a modification that delayed delivery until 8 January 1918. Report M171A, compiled the following month, showed a greatly improved

performance without bomb-load – but when fully armed, C6052 returned performances that were inferior to those of A7559 and C6051. Externally there was little to distinguish the Fiat D.H.9 from the one with the BHP engine, the only significantly recognizable feature being the starboard positioning of the exhaust manifold: a pair of triple induction manifolds led to the cylinder bank at its port side, and were fed by a single carburettor intake in the side panelling below. C6055 was to have joined these machines for further tests, but crashed on delivery from Hendon, killing Lt F.H.V. Wise and 2nd Lt A. Payne. The cause of the accident was to be a common one on the type: C6055 stalled on a turn and spun into the ground.

It had been intended that the Fiat A-12 would be fitted to those D.H.9s that

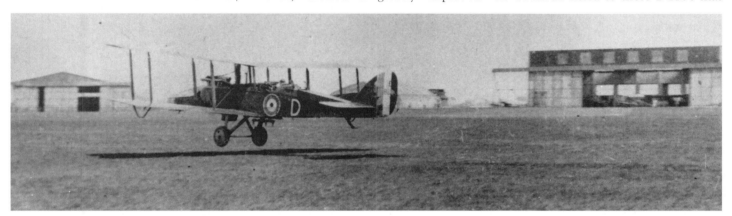

E8873 of 206 Squadron taking off from Bickendorf in 1919. It too had a carrier for a 230lb (100kg) bomb. A. Thomas via JMB/GSL

when it was delivered to the testing squadron based at Martlesham Heath. Testing was delayed while it underwent an exchange of engine, and a further delay was incurred by its temporary detachment to Orfordness, presumably in connection with assessment of its armament. Trial Report M146D, dated 3 November, was not totally unfavourable, and the repositioning of the cockpits, its manoeuvrability and landing characteristics were praised. However, the trials had been conducted without bomb-load.

Airco was quicker to respond to the production orders for the D.H.9. Its first production machine, C6051, was ready by early November, and was delivered to Martlesham Heath on the 6th of that month. It was tested with full military loads that included alternative combinations of bomb sizes, carried both internally

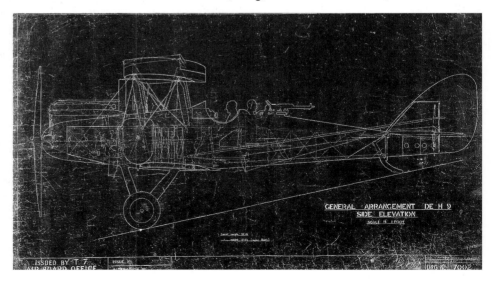

The location of the internal bomb compartment and the dangerous proximity of the main fuel tank to the engine are shown in Air Board Office drawing 7002. via the author

had been ordered from the Westland Aircraft Works, in lieu of its D.H.4 contract; but delays in the provision of drawings, and the lack of a specimen engine, served to delay production. It was anticipated that sufficient engines would be available to permit fitting the first ten machines (B7581-B7590) with the Fiat, but this never materialized. Instead the BHP was fitted to all 100 machines, namely B7581-B7680. The Westland concern was regarded as a naval contractor, and its machines were intended for delivery to RNAS units. B7581-B7583 were ready for delivery during January 1918, and a further twenty-six were handed over during the following month. The contract was fulfilled on 20 May.

6 Squadron RNAS. That squadron had reformed at Dover (Guston Road aerodrome) on 1 January 1918, and it moved to Petite Synthe, for service with 5 Wing RNAS, thirteen days later. The original 6(N) Squadron had flown Nieuports and Camels, before disbanding in August 1917 to provide pilots for other naval units. The reformed squadron operated some D.H.4s, but re-equipment with Westland-built D.H.9s began in mid-February.

6(N) Squadron had been joined at Petite Synthe by a further D.H.9 unit: 11(N) Squadron, which reformed on 11 March. Its previous existence had mirrored that of 6(N) Sqn. Also initially issued with a few D.H.4s, 11(N) Sqn had been fully equipped with D.H.9s during March, but was not attached to the RFC.

training types, and had moved to the Wiltshire base fifteen days after formation, coming under the parentage of the 33rd Wing. Its equipment had included some D.H.4s, but it began to receive D.H.9s from 6 February 1918, when C6062 was delivered from 2 AAP at Hendon. Most of its initial establishment comprised D.H.9s from the first Airco-built batch. The first to be delivered were intended as training machines. After a few weeks of training, 98 Sqn moved to Lympne on 1 March, to work up to an operational footing; here it received its full complement of service aeroplanes. The unit moved to St Omer on the day of the RAF's formation, and then to its first operational base, Clairmarais, on 3 April.

The training D.H.9s that had been

A D.H.9 marked 'N' and trailing a tail streamer flying low over an aerodrome occupied by a Bristol F.2B unit. via K. Kelly

Into Service

In terms of quantities used, the D.H.9 was one of the four principal types used by the British air services on the Western Front during 1918. Its service in that theatre of operations can be divided into three categories: bombing in support of army operations; reconnaissance and bombing of the German-held ports in Belgium; and strategic bombing with the Independent Force.

The unit destined to introduce the D.H.9 to operational use with the BEF was

It remained in 5 Wing RNAS. 11(N) Sqn became 211 Sqn RAF on 1 April, and its parent formation was re-designated 65 Wing. Initially the squadron's duties mainly comprised bombing missions against the German-occupied ports on the Belgian coast, which were bases for U-boats operating in the Channel. It shared these tasks with the other components of the Wing, 214 and 215 Squadrons, both equipped with Handley-Pages.

The first RFC squadron scheduled for operations was 98 Sqn, formed at Harlaxton on 15 August 1917. It was initially equipped with a miscellany of

discarded at Old Sarum were used to help bring 99 Sqn to operational status. That squadron had formed on the same day as 98 Sqn and had likewise moved to Old Sarum, also known as Ford Farm, on 30 August 1917. It received further machines to those handed down from its sister squadron, and after mobilization was completed, set out for St Omer on 25 April and thence to Tantonville nine days later. Many of its discarded training D.H.9s went to other units, notably 11 TDS at Old Sarum and the co-located 103 Sqn. 103 Sqn underwent a similar mobilization to the two previous units,

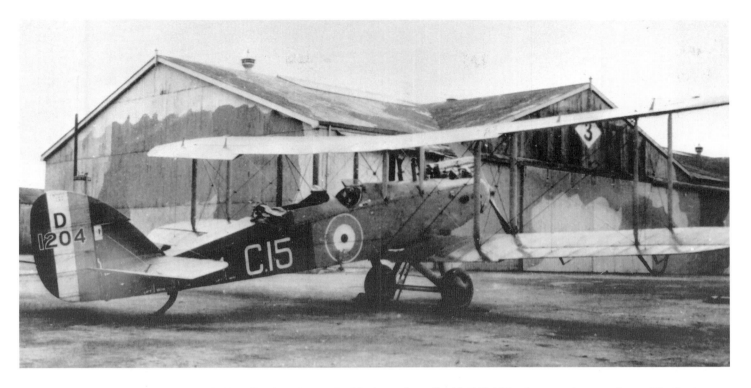

D1204 went to 120 Squadron at Bracebridge Heath and served with that unit until mid-1919. This photograph was taken at Thetford, however. A. Thomas via JMB/GSL

and joined the war at Serny on 12 May. These three squadrons were the first of the planned new bombing units that were to help bring the RAF up to its intended 1918 strength of 200 squadrons.

Salisbury Plain was the initial centre for the mobilization of D.H.9 squadrons and associated training units. 104 Sqn worked up at Andover and went on to operations from Azelot. Lake Down was the eventual UK home to 107, 108 and 109 Sqns; all three worked up on the type during the early summer of 1918, although the last was disbanded in the rationalization that created many training depot stations. The first two became operational with the BEF, and 6 TDS at Boscombe Down and 14 TDS at Lake Down were to become two of the many D.H.9 training units.

Also in the UK, 105 Sqn at Andover and 110 Sqn at Sedgeford began receiving examples of the type, though neither was fated to fly the D.H.9 operationally. 105 Sqn was fully equipped with R.E.8s by May 1918, when it moved to Ireland with the similarly equipped 106 Sqn for policing duties against the Republican movement. 110 Sqn was scheduled to be the first unit to fly the D.H.9A operationally, and relinquished its D.H.9s

after moving to Kenley on 15 June.

Airco-built machines, from the batch C6051-C6350, were also issued to existing units with the BEF. 49 Sqn, at Petite Synthe, had been flying D.H.4s operationally for five months, and began to receive D.H.9 replacements at the beginning of April. Another D.H.4 unit, 27 Sqn at Ruisseauville, accepted C6109 on 31 March, although it was not fully re-equipped with the D.H.9 until July.

Tactical Bombing On the Western Front

The pandemonium created by the German advance that began on 21 March led to some naval units from the Dunkerque area being attached to the RFC. 6(N) Sqn was one of these, and on 31 March, moved to Ste-Marie-Cappel and joined II Brigade RFC as part of the defence against the German push on Arras. Even before entering operational service, the squadron had suffered its first fatalities: D.H.9 B7622 had crashed on a flight on the day of its transfer to RFC control, and its pilot, FSL L.E. Oakeshott, and his observer, AC1 W.H. Dray, both

fatally injured after stalling in a flat turn on their flight to their new base. The following day the RAF came into being, and 6(N) became 206 Sqn. Its duties mainly comprised bombing raids against troop concentrations, ammunition stores and railway centres to the rear of the German lines.

98 Squadron had initially been based at Clairmarais, and flew its first bombing missions on 11 April. It moved to Alquines the following day, and continued in support of the efforts to prevent a German breakthrough. Its first operational casualty was suffered on the 21st, the observer of C6199 being wounded in a combat that resulted in two enemy scouts being claimed at driven down. The first loss occurred four days later, when C6089 went down with its crew made POW, and the second (D5571) with a similar result on the 29th. Both 98 and 206 Squadrons had been intensively involved in low bombing work, and yet the latter unit had yet to suffer an operational loss. 49 Squadron had begun to re-equip with the type, and 103 Squadron was to join the BEF on 12 May. 27 Squadron had also started to receive some machines that flew alongside its D.H.4s during a lengthy re-equipment process. The D.H.9 had a

This D.H.9 based at Thetford was painted with a swastika, a mark that, at the time, was nothing more than a good luck symbol. JMB/GSL

seemingly successful future.

The D.H.9 squadrons with the BEF performed duties similar to those undertaken by D.H.4s, and the same operational practices were adopted. Raids were usually carried out by formations of flight strength, with machines being flown in defensive units that allowed mutual protection by observers. Despite the, sometimes, high losses suffered, many D.H.9 squadrons often gave as good as they got, and accounted for a considerable number of 'victory' claims.

On 3 May, 98 Squadron lost C6085, when Lts R.A. Holiday and C.B. Whyte were killed, and an observer was wounded. 206 Squadron suffered its first operational loss that same day, when the crew of C2157 was killed. 49 Squadron had started using D.H.9s on raids, losing its first of the type (C6094) on the 9th. Enemy scouts were not the only hazard faced, as many targets behind the lines were well defended by AA – 98 Squadron found this out to its cost on 17 May, when three of its machines were shot up by German gunners. All three returned, but the crew of D5630 was less fortunate when they were shot down and killed that day in

the course of a reconnaissance. Fortunes turned for 206 Squadron two days later, when three machines (B7594, C6159 and C6161) were lost, with two crews killed and the third made POW. Another D.H.9 returned badly shot up and with its observer wounded. 103 Squadron was in action by 20 May when C6179, crewed by Captain J.S. Stubbs and 2nd Lt C.C. Dance, flamed an enemy kite-balloon. But 27 Squadron's impression of the new type would have been thoroughly subdued after the loss of D5616 three days later: its engine fell out in flight and the crew was killed in the ensuing crash.

The D.H.9 force available to the BEF was temporarily reduced on 25 May. Part of the agreement that released 6N Squadron had allowed for the detachment of a D.H.9 squadron for operations with 5 Group when needed. A planned campaign against the U-boat facilities on the Channel coast resulted in 98 Squadron being detached to Coudekerque for almost a fortnight. The remaining D.H.9 units went about their routine business for the rest of the month, with few casualties resulting.

The first days of June passed without

much incident as the Battle of the Aisne petered out. 107 Squadron arrived from England on the 5th, and 98 Squadron returned from its detachment the following day. Except for 206 Squadron, the D.H.9 units with the BEF came under IX Headquarters Wing and were to be used as a mobile bombing force, being moved along the front to support offensives or bolster defensive forces. Consequently, 27, 49 and 103 Squadrons had moved bases on the 3rd, being detached to the French front in anticipation of a new German attack. They bombed troop concentrations at Roye on the 5th, when 103 Squadron lost C6203 in a combat with enemy scouts, Ham and Chaulnes on the 6th, and Flavy-le-Martel on the 7th. 103 Squadron successfully attacked ammunition dumps at that last target, but 49 Squadron lost C6184 to enemy scouts which were operating in formations of up to forty machines. The D.H.9s were then provided with fighter escorts. The Battle of the Matz opened on 11 June, and all RAF squadrons involved were dedicated to making low-flying attacks on enemy troops. Several D.H.9 crew members were

---

Representative D.H.9s with the B.E.F

27 Squadron Chailly-en-Brie, Beauvois, Villers-les-Cagnicourt, Bavai – B9336, B9338, C1212, C1316, C2152, C2194, C2212, C6109, C6169, C6247, C6340, C6346, C6347, D469, D475, D490, D535, D570, D572, D1092, D1676, D1678, D1702, D1719, D1726, D2867, D2873, D2874, D3161, D3163, D3172, D3173, D3214, D3229, D3237, D3266, D5600, D5616, D5622, D5704, D5710, D7222, D7317, D7347, D7355, D7356, E634, E8857, E8866, E8933, H4270.

49 Squadron Petite Synthe, Conteville, Fourneuil, Beauvois, Rozay-en-Brie, Beauvois, Villers-les-Cagnicourt, Bavai – B7636, B9334, B9335, B9340, B9344, B9349, B9395, C1172, C1173, C1176, C1178, C2185, C2196, C2202, C2222, C6110, C6121, C6138, C6146, C6160, C6162, C6175, C6183, C6184, C6209, C6315, D457, D461, D462, D463, D502, D648, D1002, D1075, D1097, D1108, D1680, D1715, D1723, D1727, D2861, D3046, D3054, D3056, D3058, D3085, D3164, D3165, D3170, D3198, D3223, D3227, D3260, D3265, D3269, D5554, D5563, D5576, D5585, D7201, D7221, D7231, D7234, D7321, E623, E635, E636, E658, E695, E8865, E8971, E8981, F1294.

98 Squadron St Omer, Clairmarais, Alquines, Coudekerque, Ruisseauville, Drionville, Chailly, Blangemont, Abscon, Marquain, Alquines – B7634, B7641, B7657, B7674, B9332, B9345, B9421, C1166, C1174, C1177, C1180, C1205, C1208, C2151, C2158, C2174, C2178, C2184, C2203, C2206, C2221, C6073, C6079, C6081, C6083, C6085, C6166, C6199, C6204, C6210, C6211, D460, D467, D504, D506, D1010, D1665, D1667, D1717, D1720, D1721, D1724, D1731, D2805, D3051, D3052, D3053, D3060, D3078, D3079, D3082, D3096, D3169, D5723, D7325, D7335, E622, E672, E8867, F6057.

103 Squadron Marquise, Serny, Fourneuil, Serny, Floringhem, Ronchin, Maisoncelle – B9333, B9343, C1213, C2177, C2195, C2200, C2204, C2224, C6150, C6151, C6157, C6172, C6179, C6185, C6186, C6192, C6194, C6200, C6203, C6207, C6251, C6253, C6344, D464, D480, D484, D485, D489, D496, D539, D550, D1003, D1023, D2877, D3047, D3162, D3254, D5569, D5571, D5572, D5577, D5594, D7337, E631, E8884, F1224.

107 Squadron Le Quesnoy, Drionville, Chailly, Moislains, Bavai, Francwaret, Maubeuge – B9331, B9350, C1179, C2181, C2182, C2183, C2217, C6165, C6252, C6269, C6319, C6320, C6324, D477, D478, D488, D566, D607, D1016, D1038, D1049, D1055, D1064, D1107, D1111, D1722, D1725, D1734, D2956, D3036, D3057, D3059, D3098, D3106, D3160, D3236, D3274, D5629, D7339, E621, E633, E660, E661, E8861, E8862.

206 Squadron Ste Marie Cappel, Boisdinghem, Alquines, Ste Marie Cappel, Linselles, Nivelles, Bickendorf, Maubeuge – B7654, B7658, B7668, B7678, B7680, C1341, C2154, C2156, C2157, C2175, C2176, C2193, C2199, C6136, C6159, C6161, C6163, C6240, C6245, C6275, D459, D560, D569, D1012, D1015, D1051, D1663, D1688, D1689, D1695, D1728, D1730, D2783, D5590, D5606, D5607, D5609, D5782, D7315, E8873, E8874.

---

wounded on such missions, and 27 and 103 Squadrons suffered heavily on the 16th, the former losing three machines (including D.H.9s C6109 and C6346) and 103 Sqn two (C2200 and C6192). Three of the D.H.9 crews were killed, and the other made POW. The squadrons returned to BEF control on 21 June, but were still based to cover the French front, where Foch expected the next German attack to be mounted. The four D.H.9 units of IX Brigade (49, 98, 103 and 107 Squadrons) were given specific targets for intensive bombing, around Valenciennes, Tournai, Lille and Coutrai. Only 27 and 206 Squadrons were left operating against other targets along the British-held front, the latter losing D1012 (crew killed) on the 24th, and C1177 five days later, with its crew made POWs.

Although there was much poor weather at the beginning of July, that did not often prevent D.H.9 operations. 206 Squadron flew several useful reconnaissance patrols, and the other units continued in their bombing routine. But enemy scouts were active, and 107 Squadron suffered its first casualty on the 10th, when the observer of D1725 was killed. The next day was worse: the unit lost a further three machines (C2182, C2183 and D5647),

although two enemy machines were claimed. 98 Squadron also suffered that day, losing D1724 with its crew killed.

Foch's initial idea regarding the location of the next German offensive proved to be misguided, and by 12 July there was concrete evidence that it would be in the Champagne sector. 27, 49, 98 and 107 Squadrons were therefore hurriedly moved to that region on the 14th – and none too soon, because the enemy bombardment began that midnight, and its troops advanced four hours later. The D.H.9 crews were given low-flying attacks as their primary duty, and were frequently attacked by enemy scouts while undertaking these missions. 27 Squadron lost D469 on the first day of the offensive, when a 49 Squadron observer was wounded. It was worse on the 16th, however: 49 Squadron lost B9335, and had observers in three others killed or wounded; 98 Squadron lost D1717; and 107 Squadron had three observers wounded. The last unit lost a further two D.H.9s on the 20th. After this the Allied counter offensive got into its stride, and the threat on the Marne was effectively subdued within three days.

Plans were in hand for a subsequent Allied attack at a different point on the

front: the objective was the taking of Amiens, and air power was to be used to the full. There was to be no preliminary bombardment – instead, aeroplanes and tanks would be used to 'soften up' the enemy ahead of advancing infantry. The scheduled date for the attack was 8 August. The day bombers, mainly D.H.9s, were to attack enemy aerodromes in the morning and railway stations in the afternoon, with the aims of preventing German aeroplanes counter-attacking and denying battlefield access to German troops from other parts of the front.

206 Squadron had been active during the interlude in ground fighting, and had suffered what might be considered routine casualties involved in bombing and reconnaissance; these included C6289, lost the day before the Amiens offensive began. The attack on the 8th, however, proved more successful than anticipated, and the German retreat across certain bridges on the Somme attracted attention; it was rapidly deduced that successful bombing of those bridges would serve to trap the enemy, and an all-out effort was made to accomplish that goal. The D.H.9s, like the D.H.4s, were detailed to attack. They were provided with fighter cover – but despite that escort, losses on

the first day were high: 27 Squadron lost two machines (D1719 and D7317), 49 Squadron three (C2152, C6110 and D7231), 98 Squadron two (C2203 and D3078) and 107 Squadron one (D5668). The day-bomber force made 205 sorties that day.

The bridge targets were revisited on the following day, and again there were heavy casualties. Six D.H.9s were lost, five of those from 107 Squadron (C6320, D1722, D5666, E621 and E633), and many other crew members were wounded. And at the end of this offensive, the bridge bombing was largely ineffective, so on the 10th the D.H.9s were switched to railway targets; these were bombed from greater altitude, and only one machine (B9344 of 49 Squadron) failed to return. The air war was losing its initial intensity, but rail bombing continued, and 98 Squadron lost D1721 and D3097 in an attack on Clery on the 11th, with another two machines badly shot up. 206 Squadron was still undertaking reconnaissance tasks and lost C2199 that day. The offensive slowed down after a week of hard fighting, and was followed by a lull until the attack on Bapaume began on the 23rd. Day bombing and reconnaissance work continued.

German night bombers had raided Bertangles on the night of 24/25 August, causing extensive damage, and retaliatory raids were ordered on Etreux and Mont d'Origny aerodromes. 27 and 49 Squadrons were allotted the former target, 98 and 107 Squadrons the latter. Fighter cover was provided, but enemy scouts managed to attack 49 Squadron, which lost two machines. Bombing was from over 10,000ft (3,000m), and it was impossible to assess accurately the damaged inflicted. The D.H.9 units then returned to bombing railway centres, often without incident but sustaining losses when enemy scouts made contact. 98 Squadron suffered that way on the 29th, and 49 Squadron on the 30th.

September 1918 was a month of hard fighting for the RAF, a month in which it suffered its greatest number of losses against an enemy that, although short of material, was still not beaten. The D.H.9 squadrons went about their routine work for most of that month, and their losses, although inevitable, were relatively low in comparison to those suffered by scout squadrons and their counterparts with the Independent Force. The squadrons of IX

Brigade increased their efforts against rail centres in support of a further Allied advance during that month, 98 and 107 Squadrons losing two machines each, on the 2nd and 4th respectively. 103 Squadron suffered a similar loss on the 16th, a day when 98 Squadron had a hard-fought mission to Valenciennes, losing D3267 in combat with German scouts, but claiming at least two of the enemy in return. Allied hopes of delivering a final blow to the German armies centred on attacking the Hindenburg Line, an offensive planned to begin with a bombardment on 28 September, and D.H.9s were again involved in the bombing of rail centres that could be used by enemy reinforcements, both before and after the offensive opened. But on the 24th, 49 Squadron took a mauling in the course of a preparatory raid on Aulnoy: three machines were lost, and the crew of another three were wounded in an intensive combat with enemy scouts. The neutralization of enemy machines was considered, and to this end the IX Wing squadrons raided aerodromes at Bevillers, Bertry and Ermerchicourt on the 27th, followed by others on Busigny and Montigny as the offensive opened on 29 September.

The Puma engine had never been reliable, and many sorties were aborted due to its mechanical failings. That unreliability was well demonstrated on 1 October, when the D.H.9 squadrons of IX Wing were detailed to attack Aulnoy station in two morning raids. However, of the forty-nine D.H.9s that set out, no fewer than twenty-one returned with failing engines – only eleven bombed the target. A further attempt made in the afternoon was more successful, and eighteen out of twenty-one starters made the target.

The Allied advance continued throughout October, but enemy aerial opposition was still strong, and D.H.9 raids were nearly always given fighter escort. But targets were often at greater distances, and that sometimes stretched the fighter cover; for instance, on 9 October 107 Squadron lost D1107 and F5846 on a raid to Mons. Poor weather then closed in for four days, until the 23rd when raids resumed: on this day, 98 and 107 Squadrons were involved in a furious air battle, when their D.H.9s were attacked while bombing Hirson. Luckily only D3262 was lost, and although several

others were damaged, 98 Squadron still managed to claim four of the attacking enemy scouts. The increasing availability of the D.H.9A meant that the D.H.9s were then allocated less distant targets – although this strategy did not always have the desired effect. For example, on 30 October, 49, 98, 103 and 107 Squadrons set out to bomb Mariembourg, Mons, St Denis and Tournai – but seven D.H.9s were lost and others were severely damaged, and only 107 Squadron reached its target.

Raids and losses continued until the Armistice. The D.H.9 crews had fought hard, but there is little evidence to suggest that their daylight bombing had achieved much in the way of success. Sadly, the lesson of the day bomber's vulnerability was one that was not learned, and a similar situation occurred twenty-two years later when the underpowered Battles and Blenheims of the RAF fought over the same territory.

Service On the Channel Coast

Squadrons of 1, 4 and 5 Wings of the RNAS had operated from bases around Dunkerque, with scout units detached to serve with the RFC for varying periods as needs arose. However, the discussions that led up to the formation of the RAF envisaged major changes, among them the decision that only one of the three Wings (1 Wing, later 61 Wing RAF) would be permanently attached to the Dover Dunkerque Command, to continue the bombing and anti-submarine operations against the German-occupied Channel ports. Thus on 1 April, 61 Wing became part of 5 (Operations) Group RAF. The others – 4 and 5 Wings, later 64 and 65 Wings RAF – would remain stationed in the Dunkerque area, but would be available for operations, when and where the GHQ BEF required their services. In other words, they could be transferred to bolster air strength anywhere on the front. In reciprocation, it was accepted that the naval wing would be temporarily reinforced by GHQ as operational needs dictated. In the longer term it was intended to create a bombing force on the Channel coast that would mirror operations of the Independent Force and be complemented by units of the US Air Services as they became operational.

When the German breakthrough began on 21 March, these plans were abandoned, as most available units were hastily transferred south. As related, 6N (later 206) Squadron was one of those transferred. 11N (later 211) Squadron remained at Petite Synthe, but under Army control. 11N Squadron gave up most of its new D.H.9s in order that 6N Squadron would be fully equipped for its work against the German advance.

211 Squadron, after being resupplied with machines, achieved operational status in April and became involved in the continuing bombing campaign against Zeebrugge, Ostende and Bruges, a campaign aimed at the naval bases that the German Navy had established at those locations. The targets were heavily defended by AA guns and scouts of the Marine-Feldstaffeln. The inland port of Bruges was an important submarine and torpedo-boat base and was connected to the sea at Ostende and Zeebrugge by canals. Closing the two coastal ports was seen as a way of preventing enemy vessels being harboured at Bruges. The operation that was put into action involved the sinking of block-ships at the entrances to Ostende and Zeebrugge. Trapped German vessels would then be targeted, while concurrent bombing operations attempted to clear the block-ships.

The daring naval raid on Zeebrugge on the night of 22/23 April succeeded in blocking the entrance to that harbour. A concurrent raid on Ostende had failed, with the block-ships grounded outside the harbour. Bruges was crowded with enemy vessels, and so a further attempt was scheduled, in order to close the trap. Ostende harbour was virtually blocked by grounding the *Vindictive* on 10 May, and the Admiralty wanted to inflict the most possible damage on vessels then penned in Bruges. A request to GHQ BEF for extra bombing units was made on 23 May, and two days later 98 Squadron was detached to work with 5 Group, moving to Coudekerque.

After relatively few losses in the land campaign, 98 Squadron suffered more heavily working with the navy. B7694 went down in flames over Zeebrugge on 28 May, and B7657 three days later, having been hit by AA. Both crews died. A further D.H.9 (C6271) was lost on 1 June, another (C6274) the following day, and then on the 5th, five were severely damaged during the enemy's bombing of Coudekerque aerodrome. It was probably with some relief that the unit flew south to Ruisseauville and a return to BEF duties the following day.

On 25 May, 218 Squadron had arrived at Petite Synthe with its D.H.9s, coming from Dover; the end of its familiarization period co-incided with the departure of 98 Squadron. For most of the remainder of the war, the squadron was to operate alongside the two D.H.4 units of 5 Group in attempts to deny the enemy use of the Channel ports by continuing the bombing offensive already in operation. 211 Squadron, although attached to the army, was often employed in support. The D.H.9 crews were faced by enemy opposition from German naval squadrons, but had a useful alternative to captivity should aeroplanes be damaged and unable to make it home: neutral Holland was just to the north of the main targets, and bringing a machine down in that country or within its coastal waters resulted in a reasonably comfortable internment.

The continual bombing of Bruges, Ostende and Zeebrugge brought inevitable casualties, and for 211 Squadron during June, these were running at a rate of about one per week. 218 Squadron did not suffer until 27 June, when D5687 was brought down and its crew killed, although a pair of D.H.9s had been damaged in combat on the 12th. The squadron lost C1211 two days later, after being hit by AA over Zeebrugge, but its crew managed to reach Holland. July continued in much the same vein, with D2781 of 211 Squadron being interned on the 25th, and D5717 of 218 Squadron joining it on the last day of the month. Then on 22 July, 211 Squadron was joined in 65 Wing by 108 Squadron – and this was the last D.H.9 unit to join the BEF. From its base at Cappelle, 108 Squadron was also tasked with the bombing of the German-held ports.

The bombing campaign continued to produce casualties; neither squadron had escaped in July, and that persisted into August. Thus, B7624 of 211 Squadron was interned on the 8th, and B7614 was lost on the 14th. The squadron lost two machines two days later, the crews of B7623 and C6348 being interned, and that of D7204 joined them on the 24th. 218 Squadron was less fortunate: the crew of C1207 was killed by AA over Zeebrugge on the 11th, while that of D1708 was interned along with the two 211 Squadron machines five days later. 108 Squadron had its first operational loss on 17

Representative D.H.9s Operating on the Channel Coast

6N Squadron Dover, Petite Synthe – B7583, B7586, B7587, B7589, B7590, B7591, B7592, B7594, B7595, B7596, B7597, B7598, B7599, B7600, B7602, B7603, B7604, B7605.

108 Squadron Capelle-la-Grande, Bisseghem, Gondecourt, Ronchin – B9417, C1158, C1342, C2205, C2216, C6220, C6314, C6342, C6345, D468, D499, D511, D601, D613, D1080, D1110, D1733, D2680, D2682, D3029, D3055, D3092, D3107, D3113, D3116, D5615, D5790, D5835, D5845, D7208, D7320, D7336, D7342, D7357, E605, E668, E669, E676, E5435, E8871, E8934, E8980, E9015, E9026, E9028, E9030, F5047.

202 Squadron Bergues – B7584, B7593, B7627, B7630.

211 Squadron Petite Synthe, Clary, Thuillies – B7581, B7588, B7604, B7614, B7615, B7616, B7617, B7618, B7619, B7620, B7621, B7622, B7623, B7624, B7625, B7626, B7629, B7632, B7637, B7638, B7643, B7661, B7675, B9346, B9348, C1168, C2180, C2210,

C6167, C6270, C6282, C6287, C6348, D482, D517, D551, D565, D568, D1021, D1025, D1693, D1701, D2781, D2782, D2784, D2918, D3093, D3210, D3241, D3251, D3252, D5624, D7204, E8880, E8936, E8937, E8954, E8962, F1159.

217 Squadron Bergues, Crochte, Varssenaere, Dover – B5785, B7669.

218 Squadron Dover, Petite Synthe, Reumont, Vert Galant – B7601, B7635, B7656, B7660, B7667, B7673, B7676, B7677, C1206, C1207, C1210, C1211, C1294, C1327, C2186, C2187, C2188, C6250, C6274, C6279, C6289, C6321, D1017, D1028, D1052, D1082, D1083, D1085, D1088, D1089, D1671, D1708, D1750, D2921, D3094, D3095, D3099, D3234, D3253, D3271, D3272, D5712, D7239, D7240, D7241, D7242, D7245, D7248, E8881, E8883, E8959, E8960.

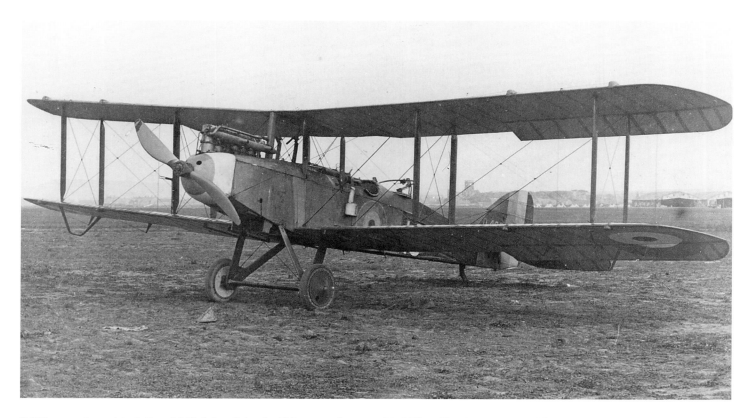

D.H.9s were issued to 1, 2 and 3 Fighting Schools. This example was with 2 FS at Marske in 1918 and featured a coloured (blue and white?) nose and a collector for spent ammunition belt links from its Vickers gun. JMB/GSL

August, when D7302 was hit by AA over Ostende, and from then on its losses reflected those of the other two units. German scouts caused sufficient damage to C1218 of 218 Squadron on 5 September to cause its crew to make for Holland, while 211 Squadron lost D2918 and C1258 on the 7th and 15th respectively: the first crew was killed, the second taken prisoner. 108 Squadron had a bad day on the 15th, when D1733, D3107 and D7336 landed in Dutch territory; and it had another on the 22nd, when the crews of D3092 and D5759 were killed. 211 Squadron also had D3251 land in Holland on the 24th; and two days later it was joined by D3271 of 218 Squadron, Captain J.F. Chisholm and Sergeant H.J. Williams being lucky to stay alive; their fellow crew of D5742 was killed.

An offensive opened in Flanders on 28 September, with the aim of preventing German forces from reinforcing their troops engaged further south. The thrust of the new attack was towards Ghent, and 218 Squadron, along with other 5 Group units, was placed under Belgian control, while 108 and 211 Squadrons operated with the British Second Army. For the time being, targets were no longer to be the ports, but inland rail centres and ammunition dumps.

Casualties continued, with 108 Squadron losing E669 on the 27th, while the following day 211 Squadron lost E8936 on a mission to Staden, and 218 Squadron lost D5654 while bombing Thourout. Another 218 Squadron crew was wounded, and D5712 damaged.

The pattern of occasional casualties was changing: thus 211 Squadron lost another two crews the following day, with a further three D.H.9s wrecked; and 218 Squadron suffered two losses, with one crew killed and the other made POW. The pattern of increased losses continued into October, when American D.H.9As were attached to 218 Squadron and flew missions alongside the D.H.9s. Both 211 and 218 Squadrons moved south during the last week of October in order to reinforce the main push against the retreating German armies. 108 Squadron moved eastwards to Bisseghem for the same reason. That made no difference to the type of operation flown, however, and the squadrons were in action until the end of the war. 108 Squadron lost E8980 on 9 November, and 211 Squadron suffered its final operational loss on the penultimate day of the conflict: D7362, with its pilot made POW and its observer killed.

Home-Based Service

The summer of 1918 saw a major rationalization of the UK-based training programme. The initial experiment with training depot stations had proved more efficient in providing trained pilots than the existing system of elementary and higher training squadrons supplemented by service squadrons. Consequently, from mid-July there was an almost wholesale move to the TDS system. Existing training squadrons and many of the service squadrons used in the training role were disbanded into the new units. Several of those units had numbers of D.H.9s on strength, usually flown as part of mixed equipment that also comprised D.H.4s, R.E.8s, B.E.2es and D.H.6s. Most of the service squadrons that were numbered between 120 and 137 were initially intended to mobilize with D.H.9s for service in France.

There were fifty-nine UK-based training depot stations, although one was soon disbanded. Eighteen of them were dedicated to providing day-bomber pilots, and by the autumn of 1918, these had a notional establishment of D.H.9s and Avro 504s.

Representative D.H.9s with Training Units

5 TS Wyton – C2165, D1011, D5562.

9 TS* Norwich (Mousehold Heath)/Sedgeford – B9359, B9360, D5556.

25 TS* Thetford – C1157, C1159, C1171, C6187, D1671, D1703, D2821.

26 TS Narborough – C6082, D5556.

29 TS Stag Lane/Croydon – B8864.

31 TS* Wyton – C2166, C2228, C6111, C6117, C6206, D2780, D2809, D5562.

44 TS* Waddington – C1160, C1161, C1163, C1169, C1196, C1197, C1198, C1199, C1200, C1201, C1256, C1260, C1379.

46 TS* Catterick – C1164, D1164, D1741, D1742, D1743, D2870.

47 TS Waddington – C1201, C1256.

48 TS Waddington – D5555.

51 TS Waddington – C1249, C7864.

52 TS* Catterick – C1164, C1325, C1365, D2864, D5621.

69 TS Narborough – D1706, D5556.

75 TS* Cramlington – C1203, C1209, C1224, C1225, C1263, C2169, C6259, C6261.

1 TDS Stamford (Wittering) – B9378, B9381, B9383, D1125, D1126, D3181.

5 TDS Easton-on-the-Hill – D527, D1132, D1154, D1242, D1703, D2779, D2987, D3072, D3159.

6 TDS* Boscombe Down – C1157, C6061, C6089, D491, D1094, D1315, D2903, D2982, D2997, D3001, D3077, D3109.

7 TDS* Feltwell – B9361, C1155, D1160, D5610.

8 TDS Netheravon – C1320, D7238, H4278.

9 TDS* Shawbury – B9351, C1321, C6255, C6258, D451, D455, D1014, D1041, D1202, D2815, D2817, D2818, D2828.

10 TDS* Harling Road – B9362, B9363, B9371, B9382, B9385, B9402, B9403, B9404, C6088, C6291, D579, D1672, D1696.

11 TDS* Old Sarum – B7912, B9367, C6059, C6068, C6072, C6097, D456, D458, D2899, D2901, D2902, D3030, D3104.

14 TDS* Lake Down – C1336, C6064, C6156, C6317, C6325, D1065, D1068, D2777, D3090, D3102, D3105, D7308.

15 TDS* Hucknall – B9420, D1292, D5618, E614, E9043, E9044, E9045, E9053, F1255, F1292.

16 TDS Heliopolis – D2926.

17 TDS El Firdan – C6290, D3144.

18 TDS Ismailia – D2926.

22 TDS* Gormanston – C1337, C1339, C1340, C1355, C1447, D1360, D1445, D1446, D9844, D9856, D9867, D9882, D9883.

23 TDS* Baldonnel -

24 TDS* Collinstown -

25 TDS* Tallaght – D9822.

31 TDS* Fowlmere (det Wyton) – C1154, C2228, C2229, D453, D1703, D3031, D3032, D3034, D3181, D5611, D5725.

35 TDS* Duxford – C2226, C2227, C6226, D1039, D1117, D1172, D1215, D1672, D1736, D1737, D5619, D5735.

48 TDS* Waddington – D595.

49 TDS* Catterick – C1164, C1227, C1236, C1237, C1319, C1364, C1365, C2169, D1742, D1743, D1744, D1745, D2864.

52 TDS* Cramlington – C1223, C1224, C1239, C2169, D1131, D1746, D2808, D5644, D5670, D5673.

55 TDS* (ex-203 TDS) Manston/Narborough – D472, D473, D495, D529, D1057, D1058, D1059, D2830, D3019, D3020.

57 TDS* (ex-202 TDS) Cranwell – C1240, C1244, C1245, C1270, C1290, C1293, C1372, C1373, C1374, C1390, D2831.

1 FS* Turnberry – C1189, C1190, C1192, C1215, C1216, C1219, C1220, C1230, C1231, C1264, C1265, C1268, C1323.

2 FS* Marske (ex-4 [Aux] SAG and 2 SAFG) – B9341, C1183, C1184, C1185, C1273, C1274, D493, E610.

3 FS* Bircham Newton/Sedgeford – D1030, D1033, D1039, D1735, D1738, D3217, D7309, D7310, D7311, D7332.

5 FS Heliopolis – D2927, D2928, D2929, D3144.

1 SNBD* Stonehenge – C1320, C6057, C6065, C6074, C6123, C6124, C6125, D471, D1101, D1677, D3246, D5681, D5738.

2 SNBD* Andover – B9425, D540, D3037, D3049, D5759.

3 SNBD Helwan – D2928, D2929, D2933.

4 SNBD* Thetford – C1162, D525, D579, D1182, D7364, D7367, E9019, E9024, H5599, H7180.

MOS Leysdown – C1385, C6280, C6286, D5638, D5686, D5713, D5728, D5731.

1 Observers School/2MOS Eastchurch – B9418, C6280.

2 Observers School Manston – D476, D479, D3028, D5672.

SASIPO/1 MOS Aldeburgh – C1380, C1381, D1096, D1098, D1747, D1749.

SMOP Dover (Guston Road) – C9021.

NEAFIS – D1129.

MAFIS – B9359, D453, D604, D1037, D1154, D1176, D1179, D2987, D9808.

Pool of Pilots Manston – D479, D3028.

AICS Worthy Down – E608, E609, H4237.

WT School Winton (Bournemouth) – D588.

OSRAP Shrewsbury (Monkmoor) – C1179, D1211.

*units with D.H.9 as major equipment

The TDS were of varying sizes. Most were the equivalent of three training squadrons and had intended establishments of thirty-six machines of each type. 31 TDS at Fowlmere, 52 TDS at Cramlington and 57 TDS at Cranwell were each the equivalent of two training squadrons and had proportionally fewer machines, as did 48 TDS at Waddington, which was simply 48 TS renumbered and was intended to have only twelve of each type. TDS training included an introduction to the use of armament, and most made use of nearby gunnery ranges and bombing grounds, on which targets such as railway junctions and aerodromes were laid out in chalk. 52 TDS at Cramlington, for example, utilized Wingates Moor on the bleak Northumberland moors as its bombing range, and Newbiggin as a coastal gunnery range.

The rationalization of the training programme also saw the introduction of specialist schools, to which aircrew were posted to learn operational tactics, hitherto untaught, before posting to operational units. For D.H.9 crews, the three UK-based Schools of Navigation and Bomb Dropping (No 1 at Stonehenge, No 2 at Andover and No 4 at Thetford) were one such destination; another was one of the Fighting Schools that taught gunnery techniques (No 1 at Turnberry, No 2 at Marske and No 3 at Bircham Newton, later Sedgeford). Each of these six units operated a number of D.H.9s as well as some D.H.4s and, later, D.H.9As.

Other D.H.9s served, in limited numbers, with a variety of home-based units that included the Wireless Experimental Station at Biggin Hill, the Observers' Schools at Eastchurch and Manston, and the Marine Observers' Schools at Leysdown, Aldeburgh and Eastchurch.

C1182 was aircraft 6 of 2 Fighting School; it was wrecked in this crash. JMB/GSL

It was not unusual for scout machines on training duties to be marked in decorative schemes, based on the existing dope stocks of the national colours plus black; however, distinctively marked two-seaters were a rarity. Training D.H.9s were almost invariably marked in either overall PC10 brown on the fuselage and upper surfaces of wings and tailplane, or in PC10 on all such fabric areas with ply and metal panels in battleship grey. There were, probably, two exceptions to this rule, both associated with D.H.9s of 49 TDS at Catterick: one of these was named The Lobster and featured white zigzags on what appears to have been an otherwise red fuselage; the second was named The Coffin, and featured a black fuselage with white trim and an American star insignia marked on its nose.

A fuller understanding of the D.H.9's role in the training unit can be gained by looking at the logbook entries of pilots who flew the type. A typical example was 2nd Lt G. Dixon, who trained with 127 Sqn and 49 TDS. His flying experience with 127 Sqn, from May 1918, was solely on D.H.6s and an A.W. F.K3; however, that squadron's

machines and personnel were subsumed into 49 TDS when it disbanded on 4 July 1918. Dixon's preliminary training continued on D.H.6s, an Avro 504J and R.E.8s until 3 September, when he moved to the Specialist Flight of 49 TDS and was introduced to the D.H.9, on a dual flight practising 'turns and straights'. He continued to fly Avros for general practice, R.E.8s for proficiency tests, and D.H.6s for fighting practice, but flights in D.H.9s became more frequent.

After a series of basic exercises to prove his ability to handle the type, he soloed on E618 on 23 September. Thereafter, the majority of his training was on the bomber. Exercises were undertaken in photography and dual firing (pilot and observer), followed by a simulated forced landing on the South Otterington landing ground. A series of sorties was made in late October, to test his bombing ability via the use of a camera obscurer. Formation flying at both low and high levels culminated in a height test that reached 16,000ft (5,000m).

Dixon's final flight at Catterick was in D.H.9 D2904, mentioned earlier for its

colour scheme. What was not mentioned earlier is the fact that D2904 was fully fitted for dual flying, with its Scarff ring deleted and its rear cockpit furnished with a proper pilot's seat; it also had a blind flying hood that could be extended over that rear cockpit. On 5 November Dixon occupied the rear seat, with a Lt Pike in the front cockpit, for his 'hood test' that simulated cloud flying. After a short period of leave, Dixon was posted to 2 Fighting School at Marske. A check flight in Avro 504K D6322 on 16 November was followed by a series of gunnery exercises, with a selection of observers occupying the rear seat of such D.H.9s as C1189, D1138 and D1140. These exercises included training in fighting against both single and two-seaters. Dixon finally passed Category C of his flying training on 9 December and was considered fit for posting to an active squadron. But by then the war was over, and his lengthy training had served no operational purpose.

Not all home-based D.H.9 service was with training units. The RNAS viewed the type as suitable for marine operations, to replace the Sopwith 1½ Strutters that

THE D.H.9 – THAT MACHINE OR NOTHING

had operated in the anti-submarine role from bases in the South West. B7613 was delivered to Mullion for such duty on 18 March 1918, and was followed by B7611 and B7612. Others were delivered to flights Padstow and Prawle Point. Those coastal flights were numbered during May, becoming 492 Flt (Prawle Point), 493 Flt (Mullion) and 494 Flt (Padstow). The 490-series of numbers was reserved for D.H.9s on coastal work, and others were 490 Flt at Yarmouth and 491 Flt at Dover. Later in 1918, further flights were added in the 550-series and, by then, the scattered coastal flights had been grouped into squadrons. 212 Squadron at Yarmouth had 490, 557 and 558 Flts; 219

Squadron at Manston had 555 and 556 Flts; and 233 Squadron at Dover had 550 and 551 Flts. 236, 250 and 254 Squadrons, at Mullion, Padstow and Prawle respectively, absorbed the existing D.H.9 flights at those stations. The coastal units undertook much monotonous patrol work, that was enlivened by occasional contact with the enemy.

An example of this was on 9 May when B7642 from Yarmouth bombed a submarine near the Shipwash light vessel. Another involved B7613 that had transferred from Mullion to Padstow and was used by Lt H.W. Whale and Lt T. Terrell to attack a U-boat on 18 September 1918. An expansion of the

coastal D.H.9 force was envisaged for late 1918, with the type being an intended addition to units of 18 Group, operating in the North East. 506 Flt (251 Squadron) at Owthorne, 507 Flt (252 Squadron) at Tynemouth and 527 Flt (256 Squadron) at Seahouses were all scheduled to re-equip from D.H.6s – but the scheme was abandoned with the signing of the Armistice.

Some other home-based squadrons still operated the type in late 1918. These were those intended bomber squadrons that had either survived being subsumed into the training depot system, or had been reformed when the extent of earlier disbandment was reviewed against BEF

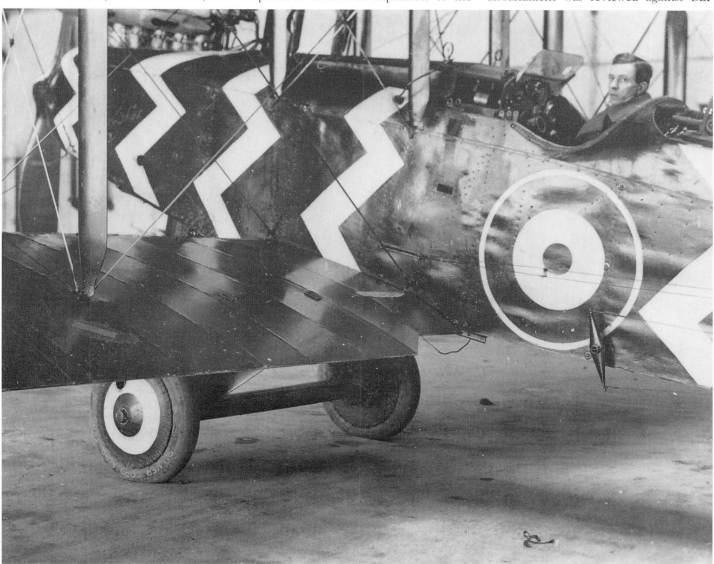

Colourful D.H.9s were few, but this machine, named 'Lobster', with 49 TDS at Catterick, was probably red with white zig-zags.
N. Forder via JMB/GSL

demands. The latter included 117 and 122 Squadrons, at Wyton and Upper Heyford. Units that had survived intact by the time of the Armistice were 119 and 120 Squadrons at Wyton and Bracebridge Heath. 119 and 122 Squadrons were disbanded before the year was out, but 120 Squadron moved to Hawkinge and operated as a postal squadron for the Army of Occupation before transferring to Lympne and disbanding on 21 October 1919. 117 Squadron had disbanded fifteen days earlier, having served in Ireland for more than five months. Its crews were absorbed into 141 Squadron, that operated Bristol F.2Bs.

Service With the Independent Force

Azelot and Tantonville were aerodromes to the immediate south of Nancy in north-eastern France, and away from the main centre of operations. Upon arrival at

these stations, 99 and 104 Squadrons joined the 41st Wing, a parent formation that had been created to conduct a bombing offensive against industrial targets in southern Germany. The two new units joined the D.H.4s of 55 Squadron to provide the day-bombing element of the wing. Its other units were 100 Sqn (F.E.2bs, later H.P. 0/400s) and 216 Sqn (formerly A Sqn RNAS with H.P. 0/400s) that conducted the night offensive against the same targets.

There is no doubting the bravery of all D.H.9 crews, but those that flew with 99 and 104 Squadrons faced a greater threat than most. The unreliability of the D.H.9's engine, combined with the distance of the raids undertaken, a lack of fighter escort and the progressively increasing German opposition to them, meant that losses were almost intolerably high.

The Independent Force was created on 6 June 1918, under the command of Major General H.M. Trenchard. The day-bomber units – 55, 99 and 104 Squadrons – remained as the 41st Wing, while the night-bomber units were grouped into the 83rd Wing; they were later joined by further night-bombing squadrons and 110 Sqn with D.H.9As. In a belated attempt to provide fighter escort, 45 Sqn's Sopwith Camels were transferred from Italy and were scheduled to be replaced by long-range Snipes. However, there was never a likelihood of the Independent Force reaching its initial planned optimum strength of nineteen day-bombing and eleven night-bombing squadrons.

Upon their arrival in north-eastern France, both D.H.9 units began by familiarizing crews with the territory, and practising formation flying. However, each was short of machines from the very start: 99 Sqn had lost C6133 and C6195, wrecked in forced landings on 16 May while on delivery flights from England, although the crews (2nd Lt R.F. Freeland/1st AM C.W. Mills and Lt H.D. West/1st AM L. Speed) were uninjured; and 104 Sqn lost C6268 on 20 May (Lt E. Cartwright/2nd AM J. Lornie) and C6263 on 29 May (2nd Lt W.G. Rivett-Carnac/2nd AM W.H. Escott). It will be noted that air mechanics and not observers were the passengers on these delivery flights: this was, of course, to enable minor repairs to be made should machines have successful forced landings. Only 99 Sqn was able to commence operations before the

formation of the Independent Force, and the first two missions seemed to promise a bright future. Thus on 21 May, six D.H.9s were sent to bomb the Metz-Sablon railway station, and all completed the task, and all returned safely. A follow-up raid was made the next day by a similar number of machines, with direct hits being observed on railway stores; again, all made the targets and returned without damage. A further raid was made on the same target on the 23rd, although this one gave an indication of what was to come: thus twelve D.H.9s were despatched, but one was forced to return early with engine trouble.

The choice of railway targets was not a random one, but part of Trenchard's overall strategy. He realized that his force was unlikely to reach its promised strength, and that his resources could best be used in a threefold campaign. The region's railways were obvious and very important targets, in that not only did they transport Lorraine iron and steel to Germany, but they were also the principal line of supply to German forces on the Western Front.

Blast furnaces were the second prime targets, their output being of major importance to the German war effort. They were located in the industrial towns of southern Germany, and it was considered that raiding them would also have a demoralizing effect on the civilian population. Aerodromes were the third targets: the neutralization of these in view of the mainly night attacks would ease the job of the day-bombing crews.

Trenchard had the option of ordering the attacks to concentrate on one target at a time, until each was destroyed, or allowing his force to spread the campaign over the whole region. He chose the latter, reasoning that his resources were too limited to complete the destruction of large industrial areas, and that the demoralization of the civilian population would be more widespread.

99 Squadron's targets for 24 May were the Thyssen blast furnaces and ironworks at Hagendingen – but only eight of the twelve D.H.9s that had set out managed to reach the target. Three had failed to join the squadron formation, and a fourth suffered engine trouble. Formation flying was the name of the game, being the only method of ensuring anything like an adequate defence against attacking enemy aeroplanes. The basic formation was a 'V' of six machines that enabled each to

provide defensive covering fire for the others. Two such formations were employed in a twelve-machine 'show'. Attempting individual raids was an invitation for trouble, and presumably, pilots were ordered to return if the main formation could not be joined. On this occasion enemy scouts intercepted the attacking machines as the target was reached and D5570 was hit, with 2nd Lt O. Jones and Lt M.R. Skinner being wounded, to become the squadron's first combat casualties. However, 2nd Lt E.L. Doidge and Lt W. Walter in D5568 managed to send one of the attacking Albatros scouts down out of control.

The first combat losses for 99 Sqn occurred three days later in a twelve-machine raid against railway targets around Bensdorf. Two D.H.9s had dropped out with engine trouble, and the remainder were attacked by EA when over the objective. C6137 went down in a spin near Dieuze, with Lt D.A. MacDonald and 2nd Lt F.H. Blaxill being made POW. As was to become a usual occurrence, the same target was revisited on the following day – but again, engine trouble caused two D.H.9s to leave formation, although there was no enemy interference with the attack.

The Metz-Sablon station was again the target for 99 Sqn on the 29th; it had also been attacked the previous night by F.E.2bs of 100 Sqn. However, half of the twelve D.H.9s that took off were obliged to return early. EA were encountered, with one driven down OOC. The same number of the squadron's machines set out for Thionville on the following day but visibility was poor and six aeroplanes turned back. A further two had engine problems, and so the remaining four diverted to attack the previous day's target. A second raid on Thionville was ordered later that day, but the weather conditions had deteriorated to such an extent that all eleven attackers turned back. The same number of D.H.9s was detailed to raid the Metz-Sablon railway station on the 31st, and ten of these reached that objective.

During its first eleven days of operations, 99 Sqn had detailed 106 sorties, although only seventy-one managed to bomb their targets (67 per cent). The persistent engine problems associated with the Puma engine had been the prime reason for missions being aborted – and those problems did not go away.

Once detailed to active service, 104 Squadron had incurred its first casualties

as it was travelling from England to its designated operational base at Tantonville on 25 May: C6266 suffered an engine failure and crashed in the ensuing forced landing, and Lt W. Bruce and Sergeant Major D.G. Smith were killed. Once established in France, 104 Sqn began a series of familiarization flights that incorporated formation practice; these lasted for two weeks. The unit then joined 99 Sqn on operations. The wastage of D.H.9s was high, and the *Official History* recorded that in just over five months of operations, the two squadrons reported fifty-four machines missing, twenty-one by 99 Sqn and thirty-three by 104 Sqn. Wastage through crashes was even greater: no fewer than a further ninety-four were reported wrecked, most during forced landings that followed engine failure after take-off. It must be noted that several of these damaged machines were repaired and reissued, only to be wrecked again.

99 Sqn mounted five raids during the first seven days of June, and the railway stations at Thionville and Metz-Sablon were the subjects of further visitations in these attacks. The success rate for machines actually reaching their targets was still only 68 per cent, which compared unfavourably with the 80 per cent

D2904, also of 49 TDS, was named 'The Coffin' and had a black fuselage with white trim. It had full dual control and a folding blind-flying hood for the rear cockpit. JMB/GSL

achieved by 55 Sqn, whose Eagle-engined D.H.4s proved much more reliable. That reliability probably accounted for the fact that the D.H.4s were usually used on more distant raids, with the D.H.9s concentrating mainly on rail targets nearer the lines.

99 Sqn had moved base to Azelot on 5 June, joining the recently arrived 104 Sqn. The new unit undertook its first operation on 8 June. Eleven of the twelve D.H.9s despatched reached the Metz-Sablon station. Heavy AA was

damaging the factory and cement works targets in the latter town.

After a ten-day interlude, raids were mounted by both squadrons against railways in the Metz area. Iron foundries in Dillingen were targeted on the 24th, but cloud conditions led to most of the attackers turning south-east and dropping their bombs on railways and factories in Saarbrücken. That raid was begun in the morning by 104 Sqn, but its D.H.9s were intercepted over Saarbrucken by four enemy scouts. One of the attackers was hit

operational status. After a familiarization period, relatively close targets were designated: those mentioned were only some 40 to 50 miles (60 to 80km) to the north of the units' bases, and once crews had become accustomed to the nature of formation flying and bombing, further targets were selected, at progressively greater ranges. The selection of Dillingen was part of this process, increasing the target range to 60 miles (100km).

That range was increased still further on the 25th, to allow the D.H.9s to attack,

Another 49 TDS machine: E619, and like D2904, it carried an American star on the side of its cowling. This may have been a connection with the 166th US Aero Squadron, whose ground personnel trained at Catterick prior to moving to France. R.C.B. Ashworth via JMB/GSL

encountered, and the bombing formation was also attacked by three EA. No D.H.9s were lost, and one of the enemy scouts was shot down out of control. On the 9th, 104 Sqn raided Hagendingen, following up a raid on the previous day by its sister squadron: but only six of the intended twelve bombers met their objective. 99 Sqn was more fortunate, and all twelve of its D.H.9s that set out bombed Dillingen. The twin targets of Dillingen and Hagendingen were the subjects of repeat attacks on the 12th and 13th, and the series of raids succeeded in severely

by defensive fire and fell in flames through the British formation. D7229 was also hit by enemy fire, but its crew, Lt O.J. Lange and Sgt G.T. Smith, managed to coax it home, putting down just short of Azelot. 99 Sqn attempted a follow-up raid later that morning, but also had to divert to the secondary target.

Important as Metz, Thionville and Hagendingen were as targets, their selection as the initial objectives for 99 and 104 Squadrons was also part of a carefully worked-out plan of Trenchard's that was intended to work his units up to full

for the first time, targets to the east of the River Rhine; unfortunately, two machines were lost in the process. 99 Sqn sent twelve crews to Offenburg, but one turned back with its pilot sick. The remaining eleven reached their destination, only to be attacked by enemy machines. Two of these were claimed as shot down, but D5570 (previously damaged on 24 May) was seen to go down with Lt N.S. Harper and 2nd Lt D.G. Benson reported as KIA. Observer 2nd Lt W.W.L. Jenkins was also fatally injured, although his pilot, Lt H. Sanders, was unhurt and brought his machine back to base. 104 Squadron made for Karlsruhe with only eight of the twelve machines that had set out: four had turned back with engine problems, another was hit by AA and forced to abandon its mission, and the seven remaining were attacked by EA as the target was reached. Two of the enemy were sent down out of control, but two of the D.H.9s were seriously hit. Lt E. W. Mundy was wounded, but managed to regain Allied territory before landing C6260. His observer, 2nd Lt H.A.B. Jackson had also been wounded, and died later that day. C2170 was also hit, and was seen going down over the Vosges mountains with its engine off. Lt S.C.M. Pontin and 2nd Lt J. Arnold were made POW.

Both squadrons attacked Karlsruhe on the following day, although only nine machines made it to the objective, fifteen having had to turn back for various reasons – with engine trouble, failure to gain formation and a sick pilot. The 104 Sqn pilot of one D.H.9 became lost after flying south-eastwards and passing over Switzerland; Swiss AA then damaged the aircraft, which crashed. 104 Squadron also had C6256 missing: it is reported to have come down in enemy territory, its pilot 2nd Lt C.G. Jenyns wounded and made POW. His observer, 2nd Lt H.C. Davis, was killed.

Railway installations at Thionville were the targets for the fourth raid in four days. 99 Squadron put up twelve D.H.9s and 104 Squadron six, but each had one machine drop out. Once again, enemy scouts intercepted the bombers, and D1669 of 99 Sqn went down in flames, with its crew of Lt E.A. Chapin and 2nd Lt T.H. Wiggins being reported as KIA. On the credit side, three of the attackers were claimed as destroyed, one of these in flames by Lt H. Sanders and 2nd Lt W. Walker in D1670, and a fourth as being brought down OOC, the latter by Lt C.A. Vick and 2nd Lt E. Beale in D1668.

After a two-day rest, 104 Squadron were detailed to attack the railway sidings and army barracks at Landau, some 95 miles (150km) distant. Nine of the eleven D.H.9s that took off made formation, the others suffering with their engines. By then, enemy scouts were becoming increasingly numerous, and the formation was attacked on both legs of its journey. Two of the enemy were claimed as destroyed, and a further pair as being sent

down OOC, but D5720 was seen going down in flames during the running fight with a reported twenty EA; its crew, Lt W.L. Deetjen and 2nd Lt M.H. Cole were killed. D1008 was so badly shot up that it was returned to 3AD for major repairs. Its pilot, 2nd Lt F.H. Beaufort, was an American, as were Deetjen and Chapin: these officers were learning their trade with the Independent Force while American units were mobilizing.

The greater operational experience that had been developed during June had led to an increasing number of the machines that took off actually reaching their targets, and sortie success rate had increased to 74 per cent. Machines were still turning back with the endemic engine problems, but fewer of those that carried on had failed to make formation. Only six machines had been lost to enemy action, from 274 sorties (2.2 per cent), and a further thirteen had been wrecked in accidents since the formation of the Independent Force. Twenty-two tons of bombs had been dropped, comprising 230lb (104kg), 112lb (50kg) and 25lb 11kg) types.

July began for 104 Squadron with an early morning raid, with Karthaus as the proposed target. However, only six of the intended ten D.H.9s made formation, one crashing on take-off, and a further three having to turn back with engine trouble; one of these failed to make it back to Azelot and was damaged in a forced landing. Furthermore, enemy machines intercepted the D.H.9s on their outward journey, and two were lost: C6262 (Lt G.C. Body and 2nd Lt W.G. Nordenand) and C6307 (Lt T.L. McConchie and 2nd Lt K.C.B. Woodman) both landed without injury to their crew, but neither escaped capture. The leader recognized

the futility of attempting to reach either the primary target or the secondary one, Thionville, and so made for Metz, with the intention of bombing the rail system. After attacking that target, the remaining four machines managed to return safely to Azelot. As a bonus, 2nd Lt R.J. Gammon and 2nd Lt P.E. Appleby in C6263 had, to their credit, sent one of the attackers down to crash.

99 Squadron set out for the same target, though its force of ten D.H.9s was soon reduced to six, two of the four aborting the mission because of a sick pilot. The objective was reached without incident, and the railway and workshop targets attacked. The squadron returned the following day, again with only six machines (three had dropped out) and, although attacked by enemy scouts, managed to more than hold its own. C6278 was damaged, but no D.H.9 was lost. One EA was shot down out of control by Captain W.D. Thom and Lt C.G. Claye in C6210. Kaiserlautern was some 95 miles (150km) from Azelot, and on 5 July its factories and railways were selected as the targets of a joint raid by 99 and 104 Squadrons. 99 Squadron's six machines were again led by Thom and Claye, this time in C6202, and a running fight developed with eight enemy scouts. One of the enemy was brought down by the combined fire from C6278 and D7232, the latter being flown by an NCO crew, Sgts H.H. Wilson and F.L. Lee. Unable to reach the target, the formation bombed Saarbrucken. C6202 was hit and Claye was killed; Thom was wounded, but managed to bring his machine home. Thom had been the leader on these last three raids and was awarded the DFC as a result. His machine was one of those modified, at the instigation of 99

Squadron's CO, to have larger carburettor intakes to allow the Puma engine to breathe more easily, and this was reported to bestow a further 5mph (8km/h) to the speed at altitude. 104 Squadron fared little better: reduced to a four-machine formation, it missed the target; moreover the flight leader's D.H.9 was suffering from engine trouble, and so he released his bombs before turning for home. His followers did likewise, considering it unrealistic to continue.

The enemy machines that were being encountered in increasing numbers were elements of the German home defence system. Just as the RNAS and RFC had responded to airship and, later, aeroplane raids, so too did the enemy's air service. Units were initially formed to counter the threat of French raids and were maintained in response to the operations of 3 Wing RNAS; in fact the development of the German HD system had many similarities with that of Britain. By mid-1918, the basic HD unit was the Kampfeinsitzerstaffel (Kest). There were eight of these in operation, two being sub-divided into half units. Just as with the British HD organization, units initially suffered from a lack of up-to-date equipment and often operated a miscellany of types. A further similarity was the use of WT-equipped 'tracker' machines (usually D.F.W. C.V.s) to trail and report the positions and/or courses of enemy formations.

Both 99 and 104 Squadrons managed to achieve full formations of six machines each for an intended raid on Duren on 6 July. But weather conditions that month were often unfavourable, and consequently it was impossible to proceed far into enemy territory; the usual standby target of the Metz-Sablon railway facility was therefore selected and bombed without incident. On the following day, both squadrons targeted railway installations and factories at Kaiser-lautern: 99 Squadron bombed without incident, but German fighters caught 104 Squadron's five aeroplane formation en route and a running fight developed, which continued after the targets were bombed. Although an enemy machine was claimed as driven down, two D.H.9s were lost: Lt M.J. Ducray and 2nd Lt N.H. Wildig were killed in D2878, as was the observer of D2868, Lt F.P. Cobden; Lt A. Moore, Cobden's pilot, was lucky to survive and be made POW. Over the next

two nights the Germans retaliated in bombing raids on Azelot that produced many casualties, though luckily none fatal; however, as a result of this offensive, 104 Squadron was rendered operationally inactive for three and a half weeks.

On 16 July, 99 Squadron was scheduled to undertake its most ambitious raid to date. The Bosch and Daimler factories in Stuttgart were the intended targets of a joint attack with 55 Squadron's D.H.4s; a secondary target was the Mauser factory at Oberndorf. This plan was again foiled by the weather, however, as unstable atmospheric conditions were throwing up cumulo-nimbus cloud, making an attack impossible. The railway complex at Thionville was therefore bombed instead, and this produced some of the best results

99 Squadron Casualties on the Abortive Mainz Raid, 31 July 1918		
Machine	**Pilot**	**Observer**
C6145	Lt E.L. Doidge (KIA)	Lt H.T. Melville (KIA)
C6149	2Lt T.M. Richie (POW)	2Lt L.W.T. Stagg (POW) (died)
C6196	Lt W.J. Garrity (POW)	2Lt G.H. Stephenson (POW)
C6278	Lt S.McB. Black (POW)	2Lt E. Singleton (POW)
D1029	2Lt F. Smith (POW)	2Lt K.H. Ashton (POW)
D1032	2Lt L.R. Dennis (KIA)	2Lt F.W. Woolley (KIA)
D3039	Lt M.T.S. Papenfus (POW)	Lt A.L. Benjamin (POW)

for the Independent Force: a direct hit on a munitions train caused secondary explosions among stored ammunition, and most of the station's key buildings were destroyed, as were five locomotives and fifty trucks. More than eighty military personnel were killed. The same squadrons returned the following day after a second planned raid on Stuttgart was aborted; on this occasion only half of 99 Squadron's twelve D.H.9s had managed to make formation.

On 20 July D1679 was lost as ten machines from 99 Squadron bombed railway targets at Offenburg; its crew, Lt F.G. Thompson and 2nd Lt S.C. Thornley, were made POWs. It seems likely that a Jasta 4 pilot was responsible. Front-line units of the German air service, as well as Kests, were also operating in that sector. Two days later the squadron managed to achieve a full twelve-machine formation for a raid on Stuttgart; however, that target was 135 miles (217km) distant from Azelot and it was abandoned in favour of Offenburg due to a combination of strong headwinds and engine trouble with the leader's D.H.9.

The next raid was not until the 30th, but as had become customary, the interlude was not spent idly. Major L.S. Pattinson, 99 Squadron's CO, understood well the necessity of accurate formation-keeping, and practice for this was detailed whenever possible. Until then, July had not been such a bad month for the squadron: 82 per cent of sorties had reached targets, and only one machine had been lost in action; moreover three EA had been claimed as destroyed, and the same number sent down out of control. It was beginning to look as if progress was at last being made. However, all that was to change.

Once again, Stuttgart was the intended target for the penultimate day of July – but yet again, only eight 99 Squadron D.H.9s managed to make formation, and then they encountered low cloud towards the objective, making bombing impossible. No secondary target had been designated, and so the leader decided to bomb Lahr. But large numbers of enemy scouts attacked the intruders: D7223 broke up during an attack by five of the enemy, and its crew was killed. 2nd Lt G. Martin was wounded, but managed to bring C6210 back to Azelot, but his observer, 2nd Lt S.G. Burton, was fatally wounded.

All operational squadrons had days that saw major reversals, and 31 July was just that for 99 Squadron. The unit had been detailed for an early morning raid on Mainz, and put twelve machines into the air. But the raid seemed doomed from the start: three aircraft dropped out as a result of the perennial engine problem, and the others were attacked en route by large numbers of EA, estimated at forty scouts; one D.H.9 went down in the first attack, and three more shortly afterwards. The leader, Captain A.D. Taylor, abandoned any attempt to reach Mainz and made for Saarbrücken, where all five remaining

104 Squadron Casualties on the Mannheim Raid, 22 August 1918

Machine	Pilot	Observer
C2179	Lt G.H.B. Smith (POW)	Sgt W. Harrop MM (POW)
C6202	2Lt J. Valentine (POW)	2Lt C.G. Hitchcock (POW)
D1048	2Lt R. Searle (POW)	2Lt C.G. Pickard, (KIA)
D1729	Capt J.B. Home-Hay MC DFC (POW)	Sgt W.T. Smith DCM MM (POW)
D2812	Capt E.A. McKay MC DFC (POW)	Lt R.A.C. Brie (POW)
D2917	Lt H.P. Wells (POW)	Lt J.J. Redfield (POW)
D5729	Lt E. Cartwright (KIA)	Lt A.G.L. Mullen (KIA)

D.H.9s dropped their bombs. But the formation then had to fight its way homewards, and lost a further three of its number. Only the D.H.9s of Taylor and Sgt H.H. Wilson made it back to Azelot. Of the fourteen men lost, four had been killed and the others were made POW, though one of these died of his wounds. It was impossible for the squadron to continue operations until new machines and crews had been drafted in, and this was not until 9 August; seventeen new aircrew members arrived on that date – but there was further delay because they had to be trained in formation flying.

104 Squadron had returned to operational status on the day of its sister unit's reversal, and had also bombed Saarbrücken, without incident. On the following day it made for Karthaus, but mist over the target necessitated a diversion to Treves, where railway installations were bombed. An estimated two dozen EA attacked, and although one was claimed as destroyed and another as driven down, D2960 was lost, and both its occupants killed.

Ten days later, 104 Squadron was detailed to attack the Benz works at Mannheim, in a combined raid with 55 Squadron's D.H.4s. Eleven of its twelve D.H.9s made formation, but once again thick cloud and persistent enemy attacks made that objective impossible and Karlsruhe was selected as an alternative. On the 12th, D2931 and D3084 were lost in a running battle with an estimated twenty-three EA, both crews being made POWs.

Mannheim was again the target on the next day, but neither it, nor the alternative target of Speyerdorf aerodrome was reached, and Thionville was bombed instead. Enemy scouts and heavy AA were encountered on the return journey, and D2881 was hit by flak and broke up; Lt F.H. Beaufort and 2nd Lt S.O. Bryant were killed instantly. Tragically the wreckage of their machine fell on D7229, killing 2nd Lt H.P.G. Leyden and Sgt A.L. Windridge. D3088 fell to enemy scouts – its pilot was killed, and its observer was lucky to survive as a POW. F5844 was damaged by enemy fire and its crew wounded, but 2nd Lt J.C. Uhlman managed to coax it over the lines before force-landing.

It was another nine days before the squadron was back to strength; it then launched a twelve-machine attack on chemical works at Mannheim. The objective was reached, but enemy scouts were active from the time the formation crossed the lines, and seven D.H.9s were lost, two before the target was reached, with three crew members killed and the remainder made POWs. The losses included two flight commanders. This reversal put the unit out of action for more than a fortnight.

99 Squadron had been building up for a return to operations. It had attempted to bomb Boulay aerodrome on the 15th, but only three of its novice crews managed to follow Major Pattinson to the target; ten had fallen behind. Then on 20 August Pattinson made a solo sortie – unusual for a squadron commander – against Dillingen, flying by compass through cloud to bomb successfully. On the 23rd the aerodrome at Buhl was attacked by eleven of the squadron's D.H.9s: losses were incurred, but no material damage was inflicted. Two days later, however, the unit was able to mount a full squadron raid on railway installations at Bettembourg, when all twelve of its D.H.9s accomplished the mission and returned safely. A return to Buhl was made on the 27th, but on this occasion six EA intervened: C6342 was hit, but was brought back over the lines for a successful forced landing.

The final D.H.9 raid in August, on the 30th, was intended to be against Bettembourg again, but cloud prevented it. Thionville was the nominated secondary target, but in fact the D.H.9s of 99 Squadron attacked Doncourt aerodrome and the railway at Conflans instead. Enemy scouts attempted to intervene, and 2nd Lt C.G. Russell, the observer in D3215, was killed. All machines, however, managed to re-cross the lines without further loss.

In addition to the fourteen D.H.9s lost to enemy action during August, a further twenty-two had been wrecked, and Trenchard was unwilling to continue with such losses. He had been pressing for the type's replacement by D.H.9As; 110 Squadron, equipped with the new type, joined the Independent Force on 31 August, but 99 and 104 Squadrons had to soldier on with their outclassed machines. It was planned to re-equip 99 Squadron with D.H.9As, and 104 Squadron with D.H.10s, and the former unit had indeed taken delivery of its first example of the new type on 28 August; but priority was given to ensuring the operational footing of 110 Squadron. 99 Squadron did receive further examples of the new type – four in September and three in October – but it was not until after the Armistice that its D.H.9s were at last fully replaced. 104 Squadron had to wait until the last weeks of the war before it received examples of the D.H.10, and by then it was too late; the unit therefore never re-equipped.

Trenchard's reluctance to sustain such heavy D.H.9 losses, combined with tactical necessity, meant that the two squadrons mounted only one long-distance raid during September. Most of their offensives were, therefore, against aerodrome and railway targets near the front line – although that did nothing to reduce casualties.

On 2 September 99 Squadron mounted two further raids on Buhl aerodrome, destroying three EA on the ground and wrecking at least two hangars and other ground installations. Morhange aerodrome was subjected to a similar attack the following day. Both D.H.9 squadrons returned to that target on the 4th, though on this occasion B9355 of 104 Squadron was damaged and its observer wounded. Such raids were part of a scheme to reduce enemy attacks against formations penetrating deeper into German airspace by destroying its machines on the ground.

They also served to counter the threat of enemy bombers attacking the Independent Force's own aerodromes.

The only strategic raid by D.H.9s in September was on Ludwigshaven, on the 7th. Both squadrons put up twelve machines, although two from 104 Squadron suffered engine trouble and dropped out. The raid was led by Major Pattinson. Enemy scouts were active from the start, and although the target was bombed, four D.H.9s were lost: Lt G. Broadbent and 2nd Lt M.A. Dunn, in D2916 of 99 Squadron, were attacked by six EA and went down to become POWs. A similar fate befell the 104 Squadron crews of B7653 and D7210. Sergeant E. Mellor and Private J. Brydon went down in D3268 and were reported killed. A fourth 104 Squadron machine, D7318, was hit and its observer fatally wounded; its pilot, Lt J.W. Richards, had been unable to maintain formation due to poor engine performance, but had pressed on at an altitude some 2,000ft (600m) lower than the main force.

The Independent Force's area of operations adjoined the American-held southern sector of the Allied front line.

The joint American-French advance to retake the St Mihiel salient was scheduled to begin on 12 September, and Trenchard was called upon to use his bombers in tactical support of this. Railway targets were a priority, in order to disrupt enemy reinforcements of men and material. The range of targets was so great that smaller formations were often to be used.

The weather conditions on the opening day of the offensive were atrocious, with severe thunderstorms and thick cloud making most bombing attempts impossible. Sorties were made against Courcelles by 99 Squadron, but its bombs had to be dropped on alternative targets. 104 Squadron sent twelve machines against the Metz-Sablon railway, but it could not be reached. The unit sent out fourteen individual sorties the following afternoon, formation-keeping being considered impossible; one observer, 2nd Lt T.J. Bond was wounded when D1050 was hit. 99 Squadron attempted an early morning squadron 'show' against Courcelles, but also could not reach its target. Smaller formations were sent out, and a variety of railway and MT targets were bombed; but two D.H.9s – D1670

and D3218 – failed to return, and it is reported that both crews were killed. Also 2nd Lt J.L. Hunter, the pilot of B9347, was wounded.

Metz-Sablon station was an important centre for German train movements, and on the 14th it was raided twice by each squadron. None of the four attacks was made at full strength, and 99 Squadron lost D3064, with 2nd Lts W.F. Ogilvie and G.A. Shipton being made POWs. Both units were at full strength for another attack on the same target the following day, however, when 99 Squadron fielded thirteen D.H.9s and 104 twelve. But enemy opposition was stiff, and intercepting Fokker D.VIIs broke 104 Squadron's formations and proceeded to pick out individual machines for attack. Three D.H.9s (D3245, D3263 and D7205) were shot down, with one crew killed and another made POW. D532 and D3211 regained the lines, but each carried wounded crew members. Both D.H.9 units were then withheld from operations for eleven days.

Massive losses suffered by 55 and 110 Squadrons on 25 September may have been the reason for the D.H.9 units being

Both 17 and 47 Squadrons had D.H.9s in Macedonia, where this machine is possibly located. It had a twin-Lewis gun armament for its observer. JMB/GSL

detailed to bomb Thionville on the next day. 104 Squadron had made good its losses and put twelve machines into the air, only to have two turn back; 99 Squadron sent out ten, but only seven made formation. Heavy enemy attacks began on the outbound journey, and 99 bore the brunt of these: only one of its machines (D544) returned to base; the other six were shot down, five in enemy territory with three crews killed and two made POWs. 2nd Lt S. McKeever, although wounded, managed to cross the lines before crash-landing; his observer was unhurt. 104 Squadron did not escape unscathed: D7232 was caught by enemy scouts and sent down to crash out of control, and Lt O.L. Malcolm and 2nd Lt G.V. Harper were killed.

Both squadrons were again withheld from raids, this time for a fortnight, but they were sent back to Metz on 9 October, and again the following day. Both missions were unhindered, and all attacking machines returned safely. After a spell of unsettled weather, 99 Squadron attacked that same target with eight D.H.9s on the 18th, and both units went back three days later; again these raids were relatively uneventful. Another was mounted on the 23rd, and although it caused considerably more damage than previous ones, 104 Squadron lost D2932, its crew – 2nd Lts B.N. Case and H. Bridger – wounded and made POWs.

On the 29th, the attacks against railways were switched to Longuyon, and in the course of a raid against this target 104 Squadron lost E8978, its crew killed in an attack by enemy scouts. A single machine of 99 Squadron attacked Avricourt station on 2 November, and on the following day 104 Squadron mounted a raid on Lorquin station, cloud having obscured its primary target of Buhl aerodrome. Both units returned to Buhl on 6 November, when 104 Squadron lost D1050 – 2nd Lts H.L. Wren and W.H. Tresham were taken POW. However, they gave a good account of themselves against stiff enemy opposition, and seven enemy scouts were claimed as being either destroyed or sent down out of control, four by 99 Squadron and three by 104 Squadron. Finally on the 9th, two machines from the latter unit made the last D.H.9 raid of the war for the Independent Force when they bombed Lorquin and Rachicourt stations.

During its operational life with the Independent Force the D.H.9 had proved

to be of limited value. Trenchard had realized this early on, but 99 and 104 Squadrons had had to continue flying the type as no alternative equipment was available. The value of their strategic raids is difficult to assess. It can be argued that the diversion of enemy resources away from the front line in order to counter the threat that they presented was justification enough. Add to that the demoralization of the civilian population, and its concomitant effect on the output of war material, and a case can be made in favour of the strategy. Actual damage caused by the bombing was, however, extremely limited, and so the switch to using the units in a more tactical role was possibly of greater value. Nevertheless losses were intolerably high, in both types of operation. Although claims were accepted for forty-one enemy aeroplanes destroyed or sent OOC (twenty-one by 99 Squadron and twenty by 104 Squadron), very few of these resulted in the actual loss of enemy machines or pilots. Against that (and the limited results of the bombing) must be weighed the definite loss of fifty-six D.H.9s and their crews (killed or made POW), thirty-one machines severely damaged in action (often with at least one crew member wounded or killed) and damage to numerous others as the result of forced landings or crashes. The two units had released 106 tons of bombs, giving a rate of one machine lost for approximately every 2 tons dropped. But if that tonnage is compared with the total wastage of machines, the figure is reduced to 0.7 tons per machine, and compares very unfavourably with the overall figure of 1.54 tons for the whole of the Independent Force, as quoted in the *Official History*. Thus the use of unescorted, light day-bombers of inadequate performance against well defended enemy targets was never worth it – but sadly this lesson was not heeded, and in 1940 Blenheim and Battle crews were sacrificed in exactly the same way as those who had served on D.H.9s with the Independent Force. It says much for the D.H.9 crews that they fought on so bravely.

On 31 October 1918, the Independent Force held seventy-one D.H.9s and seventy-six Puma engines. This was virtually sufficient to equip both squadrons and maintain reserves to re-equip both. The reserves were not needed, however, and within nine days of the Armistice, both squadrons had vacated Azelot for aerodromes in Flanders. 99 Squadron, re-

equipped with D.H.9As, was destined to remain, temporarily, on the continent, while its sister unit returned to the UK on 1 February 1919, as a cadre unit; it was disbanded five months later.

Post-War Run-Down of the BEF

Most of the D.H.9 squadrons with the BEF did not remain much longer than their IF counterparts. 49 Squadron re-equipped with D.H.9As during December 1918, but 98 Squadron was designated a Demobilization Squadron. Except for 206 Squadron, all other D.H.9 units had handed their machines over to 98 Squadron by March 1919 before the remaining personnel were shipped home. A cadre of each unit was transferred to a UK station, but disbandment soon followed. 206 Squadron went to Bickendorf to join the Army of Occupation and undertook policing duties until posted to the Middle East in May 1919.

Service in Italy, Macedonia, the Aegean and Russia

A considerable number of D.H.9s was shipped to Eastern stations during the late spring and early summer of 1918, destined for aircraft parks and depots at Salonika, Mudros, Taranto and Alexandria, for erection and testing prior to issue to squadrons.

The Aegean

Mudros, in the Aegean, was the base for 62 and 63 Wings that already operated some BHP-engined D.H.4s. The aircraft park there received D.H.9s from early May, and issued them to the squadrons of the Aegean Group that still retained their former RNAS letter designations: thus C Squadron on Imbros was an early recipient, and flew as the reconnaissance unit for the group; D Squadron at Stavros had an anti-submarine role, and it, too, received the type; and so did A and B Squadrons, which were technically fighter squadrons. The Aegean-based D.H.9s operated alongside and on similar mission

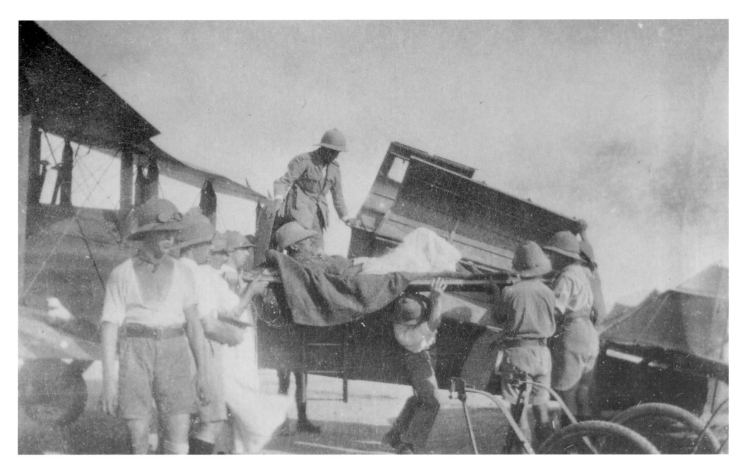

Z Unit operated independently of ground forces in the Sudan during 1919 and 1920. Among its D.H.9s was D3117, specially converted as an ambulance aeroplane. JMB/GSL

to the D.H.4s already received, conducting reconnaissances and bombing targets on the mainland, particularly railways and Turkish aerodromes.

The four squadrons assumed their intended numbers during September, A-D Squadrons becoming 222, 223, 220 and 221 Squadrons respectively. They experienced mixed fortunes: a raid on railways conducted on 22 September had the fortune effect of destroying a bridge at Buk – but a raid two days earlier had resulted in the only operational D.H.9 loss in that theatre of operations when D2889 failed to return; its crew was made POW. 223 Squadron was re-designated as a mobile bombing squadron during that month, and received extra D.H.9s for that purpose; but 221 Squadron disbanded on 15 October. 220 Squadron went to Italy at the cessation of hostilities, but returned to the Aegean before the end of the year. It disbanded at Mudros on 21 May 1919, five days after 223 Squadron had done likewise. 222 Squadron had gone by then,

disbanding on 27 February. On 20 December 1918, 221 Squadron had reformed at Lemnos as a mobile bomber squadron, and embarked for service in Russia on the 29th of that month.

Macedonia

The bombing campaign conducted from Macedonia against the Bulgarians and Albanians was the responsibility of 17 and 47 Squadrons. Those units had operated mixed equipment that included B.E.2cs, B.E.12s, A.W. F.K.3s and A.W. F.K.8s in corps, reconnaissance and bombing duties. Sufficient D.H.9s were received from the summer of 1918 to equip one flight in each squadron. Those initial deliveries were Vulcan-built machines, and they were issued from the 16th Wing Aircraft Park, Salonika, from August. Their arrival allowed the two squadrons to dedicate their F.K.8s to corps work. Both units operated their D.H.9s in the regular bombing campaign against enemy crops as

well as military targets. 17 Squadron moved to San Stephano, in Turkey, on 23 January 1919, where it operated in a policing role until it was disbanded on 14 November. 47 Squadron was selected to operate with the White Russian forces in South Russia, and moved to its initial base there, Novorossisk, on 24 April 1919.

Italy

D.H.9s despatched to South Italy were for use by units of the Adriatic Group that included 66 and 67 Wings; these operated three squadrons, 224-226, from bases at Alimini (Otranto) and Pizzone (Taranto). The squadrons had received some BHP-engined D.H.4s, but from May 1918 these were supplemented by the delivery of twelve D.H.9s to each. 227 Squadron at Pizzone also operated some of the type. The D.H.9s operated in the same roles as the wings' D.H.4s, maintaining the Otranto Barrage and bombing Albanian ports across the Adriatic; they also acted

Representative D.H.9s Based at Eastern Stations and in Russia

14 Squadron Ramleh –

17 Squadron Stojakovo, San Stephano – C6219, C6229, C6233, C6293, C6294, C6299, C6303, C6304, C6309, C6312, C6336, C6338, C6339, D554, D2839, D2845, D3151.

47 Squadron Yanesh, Amberkoj, Novorossisk, Ekaterinodar, Beketovka – C6214, C6215, C6216, C6217, C6218, C6234, C6235, C6236, C6367, D1142, D2840, D2841, D2843, D2844, D2846, D2940, D2942, D2943, D2944, D2953, D3141, D3147, D3149, D3150, F1187, F1193, F1196, F1202.

47 Squadron Helwan – H5551, H5682.

55 Squadron Suez – B7670.

142 Squadron Qantara, Suez – B7645, C6290, C6295, C6302, D573, D1143, D2930, D2935, D2937, D2938.

144 Squadron Port Said, Junction Station, Mikra Bay – B7644, B7645, B7646, C6227, C6228, C6230, C6231, C6232, C6281, C6293, C6295, C6296, C6297, C6298, C6299, C6300, C6301, C6302, C6303, C6304, C6305, C6309, C6310, C6311, C6312, C6313, D3146, D3143, E620.

206 Squadron Alexandria, Heliopolis, Helwan – C6224, C6236, D606, D636, D1086, D1141, D1149, D2927, D2928, D2954, D3144, D7376, D7377, D9835, F1180, F1213, H5551, H5628, H5701.

220 Squadron Imbros, Pizzone, Mudros, Imbros – C6221, C6222, D2842, D2843, D2797.

221 Squadron Stavros -

221 Squadron Lemnos, Mudros, Batum, Baku, Petrovsk – D2803, D2842, D2854.

Squadron Mudros, San Stephano, Mudros – D2844, D2848, D2851, D2853, D2854, D2887, D2951, D3003.

223 Squadron Mitylene, Lemnos – D3007.

224 Squadron Alimini, Andrano, Pizzone – C2161, D1760, D1761, D2794, D2795, D2796, D3002, D3005, D3008, D3062.

225 Squadron Alimini, Andrano, Pizzone -

226 Squadron Pizzone, Andrano, Lemnos, Pizzone – B7670, B9386, B9387, B9388, B9389, B9390, B9391, B9392, C2160, C2162, C6220, C6221, D1657, D1658, D1659, D1762, D2793, D2798, D2802, D2804, D2906, D2907, D3005, D3007, D3010.

227 Squadron Pizzone -

269 Squadron Port Said, Alexandria – D562, D573, E8996, E8997, E8998, E8999.

562 Flt Malta – D2801.

RAF North Russia Expedition Murmansk – D1409, D1412, F1126, F1133, F1142, F1143, F1168, F1209, F1210, F1247.

5 FS Heliopolis – D2927, D2928, D2929, D3144, H5551.

3 SANBD Helwan – D2928, D2929, D2933.

16 TDS Heliopolis – D2926.

17 TDS El Firdan – C6290, D3144.

18 TDS Ismailia – D2926.
    Special Instructors Flight Almaza – D3179, F1180, H5628, H5629, H5682, H5701.

4 FTS Abu Sueir -

H Unit Sudan – B9392, D9387, H5686.

Z Squadron Heliopolis – C6290, D2927, D2929.

Z Unit Berbera, El Dar Elan, Berbera – D649, D669, D679, D700, D2798, D2951, D3002, D3117, H5548, H5561, H5595, H5612, H5674

The Middle East

X Aircraft Depot at Alexandria handled equipment for the Middle East and Palestine Brigades, and began receiving crated D.H.9s from England in June 1918; others followed in July and August, and more arrived later. Those initial deliveries were used to equip a new unit, 144 Squadron, that had formed at Port Said during March and which had initially been given a mixed bag of B.E.2es, B.E.12as, Martinsyde Elephants and R.E.8s. The D.H.9s were issued to the unit around the time of its move to its operational base at Junction Station, Palestine, on 14 August. The squadron was designated to operate in support of General Allenby's final offensive against the Turks that began on 19 September.

On that date 144 Squadron had thirteen D.H.9s on charge, and raids were made as a prelude to the main offensive. On the 16th and 17th, formations of six D.H.9s bombed Der'a Junction in conjunction with an attack by the Arab irregular forces under Colonel T.E. Lawrence. On the opening morning of the offensive, five D.H.9s bombed Turkish telephone and telegraph installations, followed with similar raids by eight others; Turkish army headquarters at Nablus were also attacked. All these raids were planned to disrupt Turkish communications. The Turks were soon in retreat, but this, too, had been prepared for, early reconnaissance of valleys having revealed the locations where bombing of the fleeing enemy would have most effect. By noon the enemy was passing through a defile on the Tul Karm-Nablus road, and all available machines bombed and machine-gunned the enemy column that could not leave the road. C6305 was lost on the 20th, but by the following day the Turks were attempting to reach crossings of the River Jordan and a large column of troops was passing through the Wadi el Far'a. Bombing formations were to attack the column every half-hour, and massive damage was again inflicted.

144 Squadron followed the advance by Allenby's troops with detachments using Haifa and then Damascus, after its capture. C6231 was forced down in enemy territory on 29 September and its crew made POWs. Raids were carried out until the armistice with Turkey was signed on 31 October. Within six days the squadron was transferred to Macedonia; however, its existence was short-lived. Its D.H.9s

in support of the Italian advance into Albania that started in July 1918.

On 6 and 7 August, D.H.9s attempted to bomb the Kuchi bridge, that bridge being the weak link in the enemy line of communication between front-line forces and their base areas. Their attacks were made from high altitude and had no effect, but on the 8th, a pair of D.H.9s bombed from 800ft (250m) and caused sufficient damage to prevent enemy reinforcements passing, thus making it easier for the Italians to gain their objective.

On 30 August Cattaro, with its seaplane base and submarine facilities,

was attacked; however, 226 Squadron lost two D.H.9s (D2793 and D2802), with both crews killed. D2795 from 224 Squadron was badly damaged in a similar raid seven days later. Another major operation was the bombing of Durazzo on 2 October by successive waves of D.H.9s and D.H.4s, in conjunction with a naval bombardment.

The squadrons of the Adriatic Group did not last long after the end of hostilities. 227, 226 and 225 Squadrons were disbanded on 9, 18 and 19 December respectively, and 224 Squadron on 15 April 1919.

D.H.9s came onto the British Civil Register after the war. G-EBDE was converted to three-seater configuration and was used in 1922 for an aborted attempt at a round-the-world flight. JMB/GSL

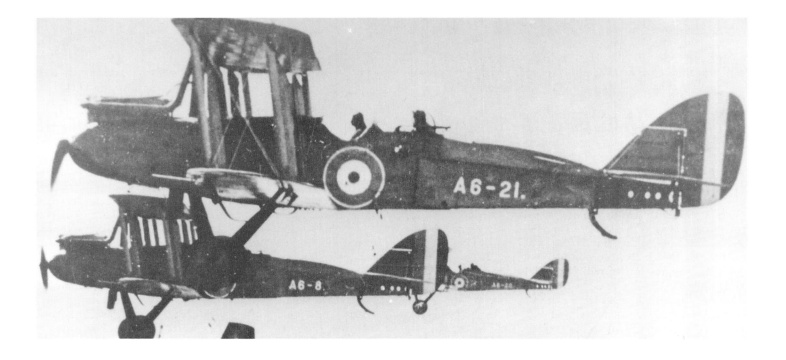

D.H.9s were a part of the post-war imperial gift to Australia, including the three pictured here: A6-21, A6-8 and A6-24; they had been H3462, E904 and H3465 respectively. C. Owers via JMB/GSL

were handed to 17 and 47 Squadrons, and its personnel sailed for England on 4 December. It was intended to create a further two D.H.9 bombing squadrons in Egypt, and 146 and 147 Squadrons were scheduled to form in July and August 1918, respectively; however, this plan never materialized.

Austrian and Turkish submarines were a threat to British shipping in the Mediterranean, that sea providing a major route, via the Suez Canal, for vessels journeying between India and Britain. 562 Flight had formed at the Marsa Racecourse, Malta, in June 1918 and was equipped with D.H.9s as a counter to the submarine threat. 269 Squadron was formed at Port Said on 6 October 1918, with a flight of Short Seaplanes and two of landplanes, for the same purpose. D.H.9s were issued as the main equipment, although a few B.E.2es were used until all operational equipment had arrived. The squadron saw no operational contact and moved to Alexandria during 1919, disbanding that November.

In Egypt, D.H.9s also served with training units, the main recipients being 3 SNBD at Helwan, and 5 Fighting School at Heliopolis. A significant unit had also been formed during early 1919: that was Z Unit, and it was specifically tasked with the control of Somaliland, independent of army control. Its equipment of twelve D.H.9s included two that had been specially converted as air ambulances by the RAF at Farnborough.

The chief threat to peace came from the followers of the 'Mad Mullah', but aerial reconnaissance had enabled ground troops to intercept and capture his caravan by 11 February 1920. It had operated temporarily alongside a similar outfit, H Unit, which also operated D.H.9s. After that the pressure was relieved, and on 20 April Z Unit was disbanded. Over the next twelve years D.H.9 and D.H.9A crews were charged with the suppression of tribal conflicts and insurrections in the Upper Nile.

Other available D.H.9s were issued to B Flight of 142 Squadron at Suez from January 1919, gradually replacing the R.E.8s and F.K.8s in that unit until re-equipment was complete by April. 142 Squadron was joined in Egypt by 206 Squadron on 19 June 1919, the new unit operating from Heliopolis and then Helwan. The two units continued the duty that Z Squadron had fulfilled. On 1 February 1920, 206 Squadron was renumbered as 47 Squadron, and 142 as 55 Squadron; the change was in name only, however, the crews and machines staying the same. The days of the D.H.9 were then numbered. D.H.9As began to arrive, and re-equipment was complete by September. Those were among the last D.H.9s with operational units of the RAF.

Russia

47 and 221 Squadrons were sent to South Russia after the end of the European war to give aerial support to White Russian forces that were fighting the new Bolshevik government's armies. The campaign was conducted across a large area and the fighting was fluid. 221 Squadron had set up base at Petrovsk by 12 January 1919, and 47 Squadron was at Novorossisk by 24 April and later moved to Ekaterinodar. Both squadrons continued to operate D.H.9s and used them in raids against concentrations of enemy troops and vessels patrolling the River Volga. Personnel were initially the original squadron members, but many were replaced by volunteers from Britain, who did not want to return to civilian life. There was some enemy aerial opposition, but the majority of sorties were unmolested, and the main dangers were from groundfire or engine failure.

There were some successes: 47 Squadron destroyed a large number of vessels that were bombarding Czaritzsin, and several cavalry formations were dispersed. On 17 September Captain W.F. Anderson and Lt R. Addison, in E8994, bombed a barge carrying enemy flying boats, and several were destroyed or damaged. However, internecine strife among the various White Russian leaders caused their cause to collapse.

221 Squadron disbanded on 1 September, and 47 Squadron on 20 October. Most squadron members returned home, although a few stayed on temporarily to staff the RAF Instructional Mission that trained its allies in the use of the D.H.9s that, along with D.H.9As, R.E.8s and some Camels, were handed over to the White Russians. Several of those machines ended up in Bolshevik hands.

The RAF also operated an Expeditionary Force in North Russia, the main base being established at Murmansk. There, DH9s were also used by the Slavo-British Aviation Corps but the worsening political situation saw the RAF pull out in the Autumn of 1919, again leaving its machines.

Post-War Use at Home and Abroad

Vast numbers of D.H.9s had been ordered, and although several contracts were terminated after the Armistice, vast numbers were in storage by 1919. The RAF had no use for those airframes, preferring the D.H.9A as its standard day bomber. However, civilian operators, Dominion countries and the emerging air services of numerous countries formed a ready market, one that was exploited fully.

A feature of post-war D.H.9s was the range of different engines installed. The deficiencies of the Puma were well established, and alternative, often more powerful engines were used in a large number of machines. A particular example was the 450hp Napier Lion fitted to C6078 from an early date, probably February 1918; that machine underwent performance trials at Martlesham that October, and on 2 January 1919 it established a new world height record of 30,500ft (9,300m); it was crewed on that occasion by Captain A. Land and Lt E.W. Blower. That height was remarkable, and took the D.H.9 to approximately double that of the operational limit of the Puma-engined version.

Some D.H.9s still served at home during 1919 and 1920, with squadrons mentioned earlier, and in the School for Co-Operation with Coastal Batteries at Cowes. 186 (Development) Squadron had a few of the type, and 1 FTS used some after its formation at Netheravon. However, by 1920 the D.H.9 had disappeared from the RAF's inventory. A few remained with experimental establishments, and the last in such service was, undoubtedly, D2825, used as a 'hack' by the RAE at Farnborough and still flying in 1930, when it was used in flight refuelling trials.

120 Squadron had been joined on its mail runs by civilian-operated D.H.9s of Holt Thomas' Air Travel & Transport Ltd.

The Australian D.H.9s were delivered in war-time camouflage schemes, but were re-doped in service. A6-23 had been H3464 and saw no service use. JMB/GSL

The Bolshevik Russians copied the D.H.9 under their designation R2. One hundred and thirty were built, and fitted with copies of the German Hazet lateral radiators.
H. Woodman via JMB/GSL

Those machines were loaned by the RAF, and others were bought, to bring the fleet to the substantial number of twenty-three. Initially they flew in RAF markings, until civilian registrations were allocated during July 1919. The company's C6054 had the distinction of making the first post-war commercial flight in Britain, on 1 May 1919, while its stable-mate, H9277, made the first cross-Channel charter flight on 15 July. Air Transport & Travel ceased its operations during December 1920, by which time the D.H.9s on loan had been returned to the RAF.

Thirty DH9s were supplied to Poland, and thirteen were operated by Estonia, the forces of those countries being engaged against the Bolshevik Russians in 1920. Their opponents also had the type. The RAF Missions had supplied large numbers of D.H.9s to White Russian forces, and many of those fell into Bolshevik hands. After the interventionist wars had ended, the USSR bought a further sixty D.H.9s from British stocks, and some were fitted with Mercedes engines. The Soviets went further, and in what was becoming a

D.H.9 Variants on the British Civil Register		
D.H.9B		
K109	G-EAAA	G-EAAC
G-EAAD	G-EALJ	G-EAMX
G-EAQM	G-EAQP	G-EAVM
G-EATW	G-EAYY	G-EAYZ
G-EAZA	G-EAZB	G-EAZC
G-EAZD	G-EAZE	G-EAZH
G-EAZI	G-EAZJ	G-EAZM
G-EAZN	G-EAZO	G-EAZP
G-EAZY	G-EAZZ	G-EBAA
G-EBAB	G-EBAD	G-EBAE
G-EBAI	G-EBAN	G-EBAO
G-EBAP	G-EBAQ	G-EBAR
G-EBAS	G-EBBA	G-EBBB
G-EBBJ	G-EBBK	G-EBCH
G-EBCI	G-EBCJ	G-EBDE
G-EBDF	G-EBDG	G-EBDL
G-EBEF	G-EBEG	G-EBEH
G-EBEI	G-EBEJ	G-EBEN
G-EBEP	G-EBEZ	G-EBFQ
G-EBGQ	G-EBGT	G-EBGU
G-EBHP	G-EBHV	G-EBIG
G-EBJR	G-EBJW	G-EBJX
G-EBKO	G-EBKV	G-EBLH
G-EBPE	G-EBPF	G-EBQD
G-EBTR	G-EBUM	G-EBUN
G-EBXR	G-AACP	G-AACR
G-AACS	G-AADU	
D.H.9B		
G-EAGX	G-EAGY	G-EAOZ
G-EAPL	G-EAPO	G-EAPU
G-EAQA	G-EAQL	G-EAQN
G-EATA	G-EAUC	G-EAUH
G-EAUI	G-EAUN	G-EAUO
G-EAUP	G-EAUQ	G-EAVK
G-EBAW		
D.H.9C		
G-EAXG	G-EAYT	G-EAYU
G-EBAX	G-EBCZ	G-EBDD
D.H.9J		
G-EBOQ	G-EBOR	G-EBTN
G-AARR	G-AARS	G-AART
G-AASC	G-ABPG	
D.H.9R		
K172	(G-EAHT)	

used first by Air Travel and Transport, and initially retained their military serial numbers until registrations were allocated. The type was converted to two types of three-seater: the D.H.9B had a third cockpit added in place of the internal bomb compartment ahead of the pilot, while the D.H.9C had an enlarged rear cockpit that was covered by a cabin, essentially similar to that of the D.H.4A. There were numerous other conversions. The D.H.9J had the Puma engine replaced by a Jaguar radial, while the D.H.9R was a 'one-off' racing machine with sesqui-plane wings and a Napier Lion engine. The ABC Nimbus was another engine that was fitted to several examples.

G-EAQM had been F1278, and it was registered to R. J.P. Parer on 2 January 1920. Six days later, Parer, accompanied by J.C. McIntosh, set out from Hounslow on a flight to Australia, a flight that took almost seven months to accomplish. They finally arrived at Darwin on 2 August, the flight being the first by a single-engined machine between Britain and that Dominion. The historic D.H.9 is preserved today at Canberra, in the Australian War Memorial.

Apart from Air Transport and Travel, the other major users were the flying schools operated by de Havilland at Stag Lane, Armstrong-Whitworth at Whitley Abbey, and Beardmore at Renfrew. Civilian D.H.9 variants were flying in Britain until the 1930s; the last was probably G-AACP, which was not withdrawn from use until 1938.

D.H.9s formed a part of the Imperial Gifts of aeroplanes made to Dominion countries, Australia receiving twenty-eight and New Zealand nine. Those sent to the latter were used for civilian purposes, but the Australian ones served in the new Royal Australian Air Force. They initially carried their RAF serials, but were renumbered in the range A6-1 to A6-28 during 1922 and 1923. The main operational base was Point Cook, Victoria, the home of the Australian CFS, 1 FTS and 1 Squadron. Others were used by 3 Squadron at Richmond, NSW. The survivors were struck off charge as obsolete during 1929.

Another Imperial Gift of forty-eight D.H.9s was made to the Union of South Africa. Those machines were delivered during 1919-20, serving with 1 Squadron and the Flying Training School of the South African Air Force. Some were

later re-engined with the radial Jupiter VI and Jupiter VIII, and were then known as Mpalas; others received Wolseley Vipers and were named Mantis. The SAAF D.H.9s continued in service until 1937. Some were then sold to civilian operators, and at least two were taken back onto SAAF charge during 1940, possibly for use as instructional airframes.

Large numbers were bought for use in Belgium, by both civilian operators and the Aviation Militaire Belge. More than one hundred were supplied for stocks held in storage, most by the Aircraft Disposal Company at Waddon. The Belgian authorities must have been suitably impressed, because further D.H.9s were built by SABCA for the AMB. Most AMB D.H.9s were used in the reconnaissance role and were flown by the 1ere, 2eme, 3eme, 4eme, 5eme, 6eme, 9eme, 10eme and 12eme Escadrilles. It was a Belgian D.H.9, crewed by Adjutant L. Crooy and Sergeant V. Groenen, that established a new endurance record of 2 days, 12hr and 7min after taking off on 2 June 1928, it was refuelled by others of the same type. That feat was achieved in the D.H.9's last year of service with the AMB.

The neighbouring Netherlands also operated and built D.H.9s. Seventeen of the type had been acquired during the war, when machines force-landed in the country after being damaged attacking German-held Channel ports. Several of these had been restored to airworthiness and were flown by the Netherlands air service, the Luchtvaartafdeeling (LVA). Ten others, followed apparently by another twenty-six, were bought, post-war, for use by the air service of the Dutch East Indies, the Vliegaftdeeling (VA). They were stationed in Java as part of its defence force, but also operated mail and casualty evacuation services. Two were converted to ambulance versions for the latter role. Thirteen new machines, with fuselages completely plywood-skinned, were constructed in the East Indies and known as HLs. Some were re-engined with Pratt & Whitney Wasp radial engines from 1934, and survived until they were replaced during 1938.

Other European air arms to operate the D.H.9 post-war included the Royal Hellenic Naval Air Service, which

tradition, began producing the type at the GAZ factory during 1923. About 130 were made, powered by Puma engines, and were designated R.2; they served in a range of roles. Some were apparently supplied to Mongolia and China, although those may have been R.1s, the Russian-built version of the D.H.9A.

Its ready availability meant that large numbers of D.H.9s came onto the British Civil Register after the war. Several were

D.H.9s were delivered to the Aviation Militaire Belge. This example has the number '12' on the yellow portion of its rudder stripes.
M. Willot via JMB/GSL

A Belgian D.H.9 fitted with a blind-flying hood over the pilot's cockpit. JMB/GSL

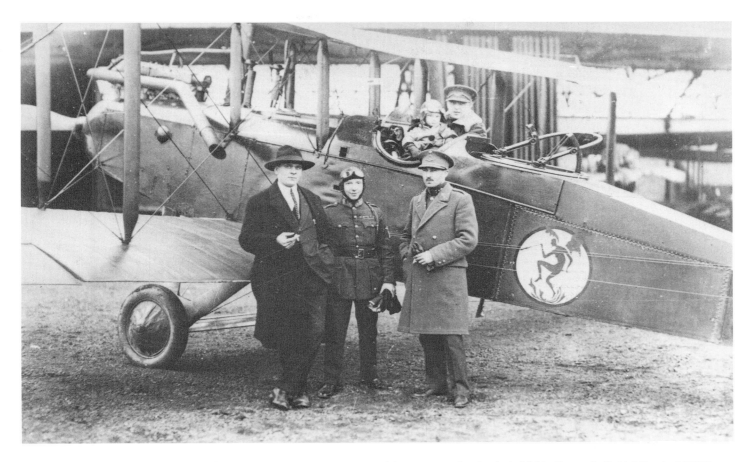

A D.H.9 of the 1ere Escadrilles of the AMB at Evere in the mid-1920s, with an appropriately clad child in the cockpit. M. Willot via JMB/GSL

D.H.9 G-IAAS had been D5686. It was converted to floatplane configuration for surveys of the Irrawaddy river in 1925. It later became a three-seater landplane, and was re-registered VT-AAS. A. Thomas via JMB/GSL

D.H.9s were built post-war in the Netherlands East Indies. At least one was converted to ambulance configuration. JMB/GSL

received forty-three; Romania, which ordered forty; and Spain, which received at least sixteen. More than 100 D.H.9s were built under licence by Hispano-Suiza during the 1920s. Spanish D.H.9s, alongside D.H.4s and D.H.9As, saw operational use in North Africa up until 1927, flying against uprisings in Morocco by Riff tribesmen. The type was still operational at the start of the Spanish Civil War in 1936, and was operated by the Republican air force. Some survived the Nationalist take-over and were still in use during 1940.

Eight D.H.9s were supplied to the Irish Air Corps, six being delivered to its main base at Baldonnel during early 1923, and two others following as replacements during 1929. They were used for a variety of roles that included training and aerial survey work. They were eventually declared obsolete in 1934.

Some D.H.9s even reached South America: Chile received twenty as part of a compensation package for the requisition of its ships under construction in Britain during the war, and the navy of neighbouring Peru also operated the type. Others served in locations that ranged from Denmark to Egypt, Persia, Afghanistan and India.

Apart from the F1287/G-EAQM mentioned earlier, two others survive today. The South African War Museum in Johannesburg holds one, marked with its instructional airframe number IS8. It had formerly been 2005 and ZS-AOI, although its previous RAF number is not known. F1258 is displayed, suspended in flying attitude, in the Musée de l'Air et de l'Espace at Le Bourget, Paris, where the thoughtful layout of that museum allows visitors to closely appreciate that and other exhibits.

CHAPTER NINE

The D.H.9A

From Bomber to Empire Policeman

The indifferent Martlesham Heath reports on the 230hp D.H.9 caused consternation for both the RFC and RNAS, since it was obvious that the latest de Havilland design offered no improvement in performance over the existing Eagle-powered D.H.4s already in service. It was the RNAS that conceived the seemingly obvious solution to the performance problem: the installation of a 375hp Rolls-Royce Eagle VIII in a D.H.9 airframe. Such an idea was mooted, and an engine requested – and the response was the almost instantaneous allocation of an Eagle VIII to AMC for fitting to a D.H.9.

The Initial Design

The installation was made to C6350, and the redesign of that airframe was intended to increase the range and bomb-carrying capacity of the type. The engine was carried in a cowling resembling that of D.H.4s with such a powerplant, but the nose was elongated to compensate for its effect on the machine's centre of gravity, as the Eagle was a much lighter engine. The increased bomb- and fuel-loads of the D.H.9A necessitated a greater wing area in order to reduce the wing loading. New mainplanes were fitted, each having a 3in (76mm) increase in chord, and a 2ft (60cm) increase in span; the effect was to increase area by more than 50sq ft (4.6sq m). The rear fuselage and tail-unit were standard D.H.4/D.H.9 components.

The conversion was ready in February 1918, and C6350 went to Martlesham Heath for performance tests on the 23rd. Those tests were carried out over the next three weeks, and returned figures for speed and climb that were superior to those of the D.H.9. It was at Martlesham that the new design was first recorded as the D.H.9A, the suffix referring to the redesigned mainplanes. It had been realized, almost from the outset, that there was little possibility of the Eagle VIII being available in the quantities needed for its use in the D.H.9A, in addition to use already agreed in Handley-Page 0/400s, Felixstowe flying-boats and Vickers Vimys. That was where the bold decision, taken during the summer of 1917, to buy large quantities of the American 400hp Liberty engine, on the basis of test-bench results, came to fruition.

An initial order for 1,000 Liberty engines was placed in 1917, with deliveries expected from June 1918 onwards, and others for a further 2,000. The first ten reached Britain in March 1918, ahead of schedule. The Liberty was of different size (being slightly shorter) and weight (101lb/47kg lighter) than the Eagle VIII, and the D.H.9A airframe needed modification to allow its installation.

At the time, AMC was in the process of developing the D.H.10, and did not have the drawing office capacity to work on both projects simultaneously. As a consequence, the design modification of the D.H.9A was entrusted to the Westland Aircraft Works at Yeovil, a company that had experience of manufacturing Short seaplanes and Sopwith Types 9400 and 9700. An AMC draughtsman, Mr J. Johnson, was seconded to Westland to assist in the Liberty D.H.9A development.

Production Standard

The first Liberty D.H.9A was C6122, which featured strengthened engine bearers, increased fuel load and a revised nose profile that had the top of the engine cowling slope upwards from the cockpit to an enlarged frontal radiator. It first flew from Yeovil on 19 April, in the hands of

C6350, the prototype D.H.9A, was created by mating a D.H.9 rear fuselage with a Rolls-Royce Eagle VIII and new mainplanes of increased span and chord. It is seen here at Martlesham Heath, where it went for performance tests on 23 February 1918. Its propeller was a pair of two-bladed units bolted together. JMB/GSL

The Liberty Engine

The Liberty was a classic example of American application of technology and mass-production. The USA entered the war with its air services equipped with aircraft of limited operational value. It was in a position to learn from mistakes made by its allies and, with the realization that any lasting expansion of its air services had to be met from indigenous production, was able to select the more successful Allied aeroplane designs for manufacture. It also took on board a lesson regarding engine production: Britain and France relied on the delivery of a wide range of engines from a large number of manufacturers; that was, rightly, recognized as being inefficient.

The Aircraft Production Board decided to have a standard engine design, that could be built in 4-, 6-, 8- or 12-cylinder form and deliver outputs ranging from 100–400hp. The board was fortunate that it received almost simultaneous representation from Elbert J. Hall and Jesse G. Vincent, each attempting to sell his own engine design. The ideas of both had merit, and they were persuaded to combine their talents. The two engineers took up residence in the Willard Hotel, Washington, on 29 May 1917 and, with input from various government departments, had finalized their ideas within two days. Drawings were prepared by 4 June and financial backing received from the Packard Company the following day.

The first, 8-cylinder, engine was ready for testing by 3 July and, by 25 August, a 12-cylinder plant had amassed fifty hours' bench running. Only the 12-cylinder, 400hp, version entered production and contracts were given to major American motor manufacturers, Packard, Lincoln, Ford and General Motors among others. In all, 20,478 were built.

The engine was a V12, with cylinders set at 45 degrees. A split crankcase made for easy assembly and aluminium was used for the pistons. It incorporated design features from a whole range of manufacturers: the use of cylinder linings from Rolls-Royce and Mercedes; water jackets from Packard; cylinder hold-down flanges from Ford; valve operation from Packard; and camshaft drive from Hispano-Suiza being some examples. Delco battery ignition replaced the conventional magnetos and allowed easy starting.

There were some initial problems with lubrication, but these were resolved, along with other problems that were revealed in operational use. Although production ended in March 1919, the vast stock of engines saw the Liberty used in new designs until officially forbidden in 1929. Even then the engine continued to be used, not just as an aero engine, but also in tanks and fast boats.

The stripped-down fuselage of a D.H.9A under reconstruction shows the large amount of plywood skinning over the wooden box-girder of the fuselage framework. via the author

To show the great depth of the fuselage and the size of the Scarff ring. This and the previous photograph were taken at Drigh Road, Karachi, in December 1925 via the author

Captain A.R. Boeree. That initial flight revealed the machine to be too nose-heavy, and lead ballast had to be added to the rudder-post as compensation. The upper wings were also given a further 2in (50mm) of stagger. C6122 went to Martlesham for its performance tests on 15 May, and the results were given in Reports M213/213A/213B. Its performance was comparable with that of the Eagle VIII-powered machine. The machine was subsequently used to produce reports on the engine – for example, E85 – and the armament. It crashed on 15 August, but had been joined a fortnight earlier by F966.

The D.H.9A had been ordered for large-scale production even before C6122 had flown. The Whitehead Aircraft Co. Ltd had received a contract for 400 as early as 26 January, and Mann Egerton & Co. a contract for 100 on 20 March. Further contracts were awarded on 21 March, with the Vulcan Motor & Engineering Co. Ltd, AMC and Westland, and others followed.

The fulfilment of those contracts was jeopardized during mid-1918 when the

A further view of C6350. The new designation D.H.9A was not allocated until March 1918.
JMB/GSL

A typical, early production D.H.9A showing the shape of the radiator on the type. That of the prototype had resembled that of the D.H.4. JMB/GSL

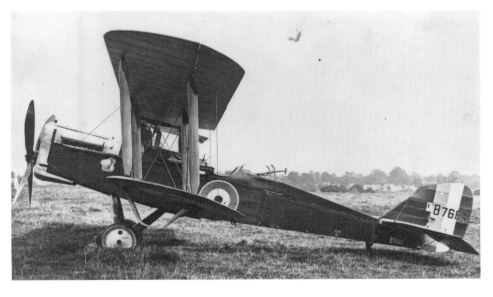

B7664 was a production D.H.9A fitted by Westland with an Eagle VIII to test the engine's compatibility with the airframe; this was by way of insurance against supplies of Liberty engines drying up. JMB/GSL

The instrument board of a D.H.9A taken in 1923. The oil and water temperature gauges, to the left, appear to be later additions, as does instrument lighting. JMB/GSL

further delivery of Liberty engines was stopped by the Americans. Great as the American manufacturing base was, it could not meet the demand of both the British and the American governments, the latter needing the Liberty to power aeroplanes being produced for its own air services. Westland had been asked, as a form of insurance, to fit a Rolls-Royce Eagle VIII into a D.H.9A airframe. Supplies of the Liberty 12 ceased in July 1918, but it may have been the case that this was expected, because components of D.H.9 B7664, on the assembly line at Yeovil during May, were utilized; the machine, outwardly a D.H.9A, was delivered to Martlesham on 17 August.

The short time-lag between the cessation of Liberty supply and the delivery of B7664 suggests that foreknowledge. At Martlesham, it was used in comparison tests with a standard Liberty D.H.9A, and its speed, service ceiling and climb rate were all inferior to the Liberty version. The version was not adopted, however, probably due to a combination of the fact that Eagle VIIIs were a scarce commodity, and the more powerful Galloway engines were in the pipeline.

Into Service

Westland aircraft were the first to leave the production lines, and its machines were reaching 5 AAP at Filton during the last week of June. Just as the first D.H.9s had been delivered to naval units, so too were the earliest D.H.9As: F955 and F956 were delivered to Yarmouth and Manston respectively during July, for use by the Marine Operations flights at those stations.

Specification – Airco D.H.9A	
Powerplant:	400hp Liberty 12A; fuel capacity 25 gallons
Weights:	Empty 2,656lb (1,205kg); loaded 4,815lb (2,184kg); wing loading 9.89lb per sq ft (48.29kg per sq m)
Dimensions:	Mainplane span 45ft 11in (14m); mainplane gap 5ft 6in (1.68m); chord 5ft 9in (1.75m); length 30ft 3in (9.23m); height 11ft 4in (3.46m); tailplane span 14ft (4.27m); wing area 486.73sq ft (45.23sq m)
Performance:	Maximum speed 110mph (177km/h); landing speed 59mph (95km/h); climb to 6,500ft (2,000m) 11 minutes

An early D.H.9A in flight. The number appears to be F5878, which would make it a reconstructed machine. JMB/GSL

F1000 was aeroplane B of 110 Squadron, the first operational unit to be fully equipped with the type. Like other machines that formed 110 Squadron's initial equipment, F1000 was presented by the Nizam of Hyderabad. The machine suffered combat damage during a raid on Frankfurt on 29 September 1918 and after repair was issued to 99 Squadron. JMB/GSL

F977 was another of 110 Squadron's presentation machines, in this case Hyderabad No.18. It was wrecked on 25 September 1918. Although from the same batch as F1000, it had a different style of handling markings on its rear fuselage. W.R. Evans via K. Kelly

The pressing need was to use the D.H.9A in its bombing role on the Western Front, and the first unit that was scheduled to receive a full complement of the type was 110 Squadron, mobilizing at Kenley. That squadron was scheduled to join the Independent Force, and its initial eighteen D.H.9A machines were all provided under the Presentation Aircraft Scheme by the Nizam of Hyderabad and marked accordingly with presentation lettering on the port engine cowling. Three of its machines were wrecked during this mobilization period. 110 Squadron, under the command of Major H.R. Nicholl, joined the Independent Force on 31 August when it set up base at Bettoncourt. Its machines were not the first of the type with the IF: 99 Squadron had received F967 three days earlier. Although scheduled to have its D.H.9s replaced with the new type, the process for 99 Squadron was a long one, and it was not until November that re-equipment was completed. Consequently, the vast majority of D.H.9A operations with the Independent Force was carried out by 110 Squadron.

Operations With the Independent Force

110 Squadron spent a fortnight familiarizing its crews with its area of operations, and then twelve machines took part in an uneventful mission to bomb Boulay aerodrome. It undertook its first strategic raid on 16 September, when twelve D.H.9As set out for Mannheim in conjunction with D.H.4s from 55 Squadron. It was not an auspicious start. One D.H.9A returned with engine trouble, and the remainder were intercepted by enemy scouts as they approached the target. The bombing caused some damage, but two D.H.9As (E8410 and F997) were shot down, and the observer of another (E8434) was wounded. The crew of E8410 was made POW, but that of F997 was killed. It was nine days before another raid was mounted, with a twelve-machine sortie to Frankfurt. Again, one machine turned back, but the rest were attacked from early in the raid. Four D.H.9As were brought

down in Germany, and the crews of E9660, F992 and F1030 were made POWs. Sergeants H.W. Tozer and W. Platt were killed in E8420. Three more D.H.9As suffered damage, F1000 coming down in allied territory, and E8420 returning with a dead observer. The observer in F993, Lt R.F. Casey, was wounded, but he had shot down two of the attacking enemy, while Captains A.C.H. Groom and G.E. Lange in F1005 claimed another out of control.

Frankfurt was targeted for another twelve-machine show on 1 October, but again, two returned early with engine trouble. Unfavourable weather en route caused a further four to return, and the remaining six diverted to bomb Treves and Luxembourg, before returning safely. The recurring engine trouble was probably due to lubrication problems that were encountered in early-production Liberty engines. The squadron sent the same number of machines to bomb Cologne four days later. Intense enemy opposition and deteriorating weather led to the primary target being abandoned, and bombs being dropped on Kaiserlautern and Pirmasens.

110 Squadron Losses 31 August to 11 November 1918

Date	Machine	Remarks
13 September	F1004	Wrecked, crew OK
16 September	E8434	Combat damage, Lt J.B. Wilkinson OK/2Lt H.M Kettener WIA
16 September	F996	Wrecked, crew OK
16 September	F997	LIA, Lt H.V. Brisbin & 2Lt R.S. Lipsett POW
16 September	E8410	LIA, Sgts A. Haigh & J. West KIA
21 September	E8420	Combat damage, 2Lt N.N. Wardlaw OK/Sgt W.H. Neighbour KIA
25 September	E9660	LIA, Lt C.B.E. Lloyd & 2Lt H.J.C. Elwig POW
25 September	E8422	LIA, Sgts H.W. Tozer & W. Platt KIA
25 September	F977	Wrecked, crew OK
25 September	F992	LIA, Lt L.S. Brooke & 2Lt A. Provan KIA
25 September	F993	Combat damage, Lt R.P. Brail li OK/Lt R.F. Casey WIA
25 September	F1000	Wrecked in forced-landing after combat, Lt H.J. Cockman WIA
25 September	F1030	LIA, Captain A. Lindley & Lt C.R. Gross POW
5 October	E8421	LIA, Lt R.C.P. Ripley & 2Lt F.S. Towler KIA
5 October	E8439	LIA, 2Lts D.P. Davies & H.M.D. Speagell POW
5 October	F980	LIA, 2Lt A. Brandrick POW/2Lt H.C. Eyre KIA
5 October	F1010	LIA, Captain A.G. Inglis & 2Lt W.G.L. Bodley POW
5 October	F1036	Combat damage, 2Lt N.N. Wardlaw OK, 2Lt C.J. May WIA
5 October	F1041	Damaged ? To ASD 6 October
21 October	E8484	LIA, 2Lt A.R.W. Evans & Lt R.W.L. Thompson POW
21 October	F984	LIA, Lt S.L. Mucklow & 2Lt R. Riffkin POW
21 October	F985	LIA, Major L.G.S. Reynolds & 2Lt M.W. Dunn POW
21 October	F986	LIA, 2Lts J.O.R.S. Saunders & W.J. Brain KIA
21 October	F995	Damaged in forced landing, crew OK
21 October	F1005	LIA, Captain W.E. Windover & 2Lt J.A. Simpson POW
21 October	F1021	LIA, 2Lts P. King & R.P. Vernon POW
21 October	F1029	LIA, Lt J. McLaren-Pearson & Sgt T.W. Harman POW
23 October	E702	Wrecked, crew OK
23 October	E705	Wrecked, crew OK

Representative D.H.9As with RAF Squadrons in France and with the Army of Occupation

18 Squadron Maisoncelle, Le Hameau, La Brayelle, Maubeuge, Bickendorf, Merheim – E707, E708, E709, E717, E8415, E8426, E8428, E8447, E8479, E8521, E8533, E8552, E8577, E8578, E9727, E9730, E9735, E9742, F1042, F1046, F1047, F1051, F1058, F1067, F1070, F1072, F1080, F2734, F2744.

25 Squadron La Brayelle, Maubeuge, Bickendorf, Merheim – E8458, E8509, E8557, F957, F993, F1045, F1068.

49 Squadron Bavai, Bickendorf – E8427, E8486, E8528, E8559, E8564, E9720, E9858, F1033, F1035, F1039, F2738, H3467.

57 Squadron Morville, Maisoncelle, Sart, Nivelles, Marquise – E729, E8448, E8525, E8572, F1048, H3446, H3466, H3468, H3470, H3477.

205 Squadron Bovelles, Proyart, Moislains, Maubeuge, La Louveterie – E7016, E8411, E8418, E8419, E8437, E8438, E8508, E9662, E9707, E9713, E9716, E9721, E9731, F990, F996, F1001, F1007, F1008, F1009, F1013, F1014, F1015, F1016, F1017, F1019, F1022, F1024, F1025, F1040, F1043, F1044, F1048, F1049.

Four D.H.9As failed to return. Lt R.C.P. Ripley and 2nd Lt F.S. Towler were killed in E8421, and the crews of E8439, F980 and F1010 were made POWs.

The D.H.9A was therefore proving to be as vulnerable as other day bombers on the Independent Force, and that was confirmed on the next raid that took place on 21 October: thirteen machines left Bettoncourt, with Cologne once more as the target – but again a machine suffered engine trouble and returned early. The weather was still unfavourable, and the formations became broken up. Enemy scouts attacked on the outward journey, and just five D.H.9As managed to hold together and bomb Frankfurt. Altogether, seven of the twelve failed to return. Six crews, those of E8484, F984, F985, F1005, F1021 and F1029 survived, but were shot down to become POWs. 2nd Lts J.O.R.S. Saunders and W.J. Brain were shot down and killed in F986. The squadron did not participate in any further strategic raids; along with other IF units, it undertook tactical raiding, but was only detailed for two such missions in November. The

The size of the Okapi can be judged from this view of the D.H.14A G-EAPY. Its great height has led to the Hucks starter being placed on a flatbed truck in order to reach the propeller. *Benwell via JMB/GSL*

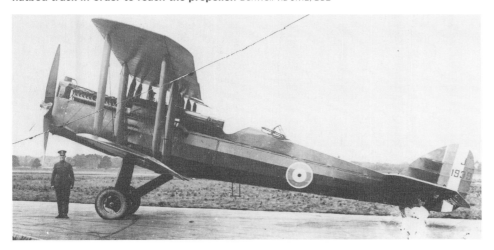

The D.H.14 Okapi with its Rolls-Royce Condor engine was a much-enlarged version of the D.H.9A. The airman lends scale to this massive – for a single-engined – machine. *JMB/GSL*

The D.H.15 Gazelle was essentially a D.H.9A with a Galloway Atlantic engine, and differed little from the earlier type in appearance. *JMB/GSL*

British-Built D.H.9As with the Day Wing, US Northern Bombing Group

Known transfers from British stocks were as follows :
E736-E741, E8450-E8455, E8463, E8465-E8467, E8469, E8470, E8472, E8475-E8478, E8480, E8501-E8507, E8538-E8545, E8565-E8568, E8570-E8571, E8583, E8632-E8635, E9868-E9873, E9874-E9876.

squadron had lost seventeen machines in enemy territory during the course of four raids, with many others damaged.

After the Armistice, 110 Squadron was employed on mail flights to Cologne, losing some machines in forced landings, such as E704, which went down in a snowstorm on 29 March 1919. By 6 May 1919 the squadron was at Marquise, where some D.H.9s were received to supplement the D.H.9As. It lasted a little longer, but was disbanded on 27 August.

Since late August, 99 Squadron had operated with a mixed complement of D.H.9s and D.H.9As. Early deliveries were F1018, F1031, F1033, F1035 and F1039, all of which were on strength by early October. Its D.H.9As were never numerous, and the operation of two types must have made life complicated for the squadron engine fitters. The squadron only began to seriously re-equip during the closing weeks of the war. Contrary to popular belief, some operations were flown, and these included an attack by a single D.H.9A on Avricourt on 2 November, and another by two machines on Chateau Salins two days before the Armistice. It may have been that the need to replace losses suffered by 110 Squadron had some influence on the lengthy re-equipment for 99 Squadron, but it was not until November that a full complement of D.H.9As was on charge. The last D.H.9 left on the 16th of that month, and the squadron was moved westwards that day, to Auxi-le-Chateau and St Andre-aux-Bois before settling at Aulnoy, on the Franco-Belgian border, and undertaking mail duties.

Tactical Bombing on the Western Front

The second operational unit to be fully equipped with the D.H.9A was 205 Squadron – in fact it was the first operational unit to receive the type in France. The decision had been taken to replace its Eagle-engined D.H.4s with the latest type, and E9662 was delivered to the unit as early as 12 August 1918. The priority, however, was to get 110 Squadron to the Independent Force, and it was early September before 205 Squadron began to re-equip in earnest.

The squadron was still operating in the tactical bombing role with the 22nd Wing in V Brigade, and re-equipment did not involve its being taken out of the front line.

Thus it was flying its first D.H.9As on operations by 15 September – on which date 2nd Lt J.B. Leach, the observer in F1009, sent an enemy two-seater down in flames. The crew of F1016 did even better on the following day, being credited with two enemy machines brought down. But the squadron, busily engaged on its bombing duties, lost several of its D.H.4s that month, although the only D.H.9A casualties were the crew of E8419, wounded on the 29th.

18 Squadron, flying RAF-engined D.H.4s from Maisoncelle and a component of the 10th Wing in I Brigade, also began to re-equip during late September. It, too, was continuing the regular combination of tactical bombing and reconnaissance work, but it suffered no casualties on the new type until 27 October, when the observer of E8415 was killed in an attack by enemy scouts.

The third D.H.9A unit with the BEF was 25 Squadron, with the 9th Wing in IX Brigade; it was re-equipped during October, and had the dubious distinction of suffering the first BEF combat loss with the type. That was E9705, lost on a photo-graphic reconnaissance on 3 November. F1022 of 205 Squadron failed to return from a bombing sortie six days later, and was the second and last RAF operational loss; its crew, like that of E9705, was killed.

The RAF, unlike the Independent Force, had a relatively happy introduction to the

D.H.9A. The provision of fighter cover and the closer nature of targets has to be taken into account, however. Post-war 49 and 57 Squadrons also received the type, as replacements for D.H.9s and D.H.4s respectively.

18, 25 and 49 Squadrons joined the Army of Occupation in the Rhineland, all being based at Bickendorf, near Cologne. 205 Squadron relinquished its machines during March 1919 and the unit returned to the UK as a cadre prior to disbandment; 57 Squadron did likewise during August. The remaining three units had all followed by the following month.

The Northern Bombing Group

Despite its losses, the Independent Force was considered successful, partly from the damage it inflicted but also because of its effect in diverting German military effort away from the front. With the build-up of American forces in 1918, it was decided to organize a similar formation on the Channel coast: this was the Northern Bombing Group, intended to target German-held Channel ports. It was anticipated that the group would be equipped with American-built D.H.4s in its Day Wing, and Handley-Page 0/400s in its Night Wing, but the delivery of the D.H.4s was delayed and so

A1-17 had been F2779 and was one of the D.H.9As given as a post-war imperial gift to Australia. It was in service by 1920 and served at the CFS and 1 FTS at Point Cook. It was withdrawn from use in 1930. C. Owers via JMB/GSL

the American government bought D.H.9As from the British as a stop-gap measure. Those machines were delivered for use by Squadrons A, B and C of that group, based at Oye and La Fresne, near Calais; at least sixty were bought. D.H.9As were delivered from September 1918, and missions flown from 14 October, usually in mixed formations with D.H.4s.

Wartime Training and Other Home Use

The D.H.9A never reached home-based training units in large enough numbers for it to replace the D.H.9. The training depot station system had dedicated units for the training of day-bomber pilots, which utilized D.H.4s and D.H.9s, and very few of these received D.H.9As – and those that did had only very small numbers on charge. The two Schools of Navigation and Bomb Dropping at Stonehenge and Andover received slightly more, and others were issued to the Fighting Schools at Turnberry, Marske and Bircham Newton. The priority was to equip squadrons mobilizing for service with the BEF.

The provision of extra bombing squadrons was a priority of RAF planning, and during the latter half of 1918 it was intended that the following squadrons be equipped with the D.H.9A: Nos. 109, 123, 134, 135, 136, 137, 155, 156, 160, 161, 162, 163 and 164. Those from 160 Squadron onwards never formed, however, the signing of the Armistice precluding their need. 109 Squadron and those in the 130-series disappeared in the rationalization of units that took place from July 1918; 155 and 156 Squadrons did actually form, and 155 was equipped at Chingford and planned to join the BEF on 21 November – but again, that move came to nought after the Armistice. 156 Squadron also received D.H.9As at Wyton, and when its planned transfer to the BEF was cancelled, its aeroplanes were transferred to 123 Squadron. That unit reformed at Upper Heyford on 20 November and was manned by Canadian personnel, having the alternative title of 2 Squadron Canadian Air Force. The squadron moved to Shoreham on 31 March 1919 and flew its D.H.9As until it was reduced to a cadre in June; it stayed there for another eight months, until it was disbanded on 5 February 1920.

Final Wartime Variants, the Okapi and Gazelle

The Liberty D.H.9A was still capable of development, and the promise of more powerful engines during 1918 pointed the way forwards. On 7 September AMC received an order for a D.H.9A to be fitted with a 500hp Galloway Atlantic engine; it was given the new type number D.H.15, and had already been allocated the name 'Gazelle'. The conversion of the D.H.9A to accommodate the Adriatic was relatively straightforward, and the aeroplane – J1937 – was completed by the following July. But by then the need for it had gone, though the engine had indeed

A D.H.9A fitted with a modified undercarriage to permit the fitting of Grain flotation gear for Marine Operations. JMB/GSL

given a massive increase in performance. Figures from its testing at Martlesham during May 1920 showed a speed some 11mph (17km/h) greater and a rate of climb almost double that of a Liberty D.H.9A. RAF planning, had the war continued into 1919, included the replacement of 55 Squadron's D.H.4s with the Gazelle, and the provision of the type for further units of the Independent Force.

The Rolls-Royce Condor was capable of developing 520hp, and orders were placed with AMC for three prototypes of a machine with that engine on 28 October 1918. It was designated D.H.14 and was,

essentially, an elongated D.H.9A with a widened centre-section and mainplanes that gave an extra 130ft (40m) of wing area. That extra area was necessary to compensate for the 150lb (68kg) extra weight of the Condor and the proposed bomb-load of 672lb (305kg). The serial numbers J1938-1940 were allocated, and the name 'Okapi' bestowed on the design. However, delays with the Condor engine caused the Galloway Atlantic to be considered as an alternative. The somewhat leisurely progress in the construction of the first airframe meant that completion was not until the spring of 1919, by which time the need for the type had disappeared.

J1940 was completed with a 450hp Napier Lion engine, and was flying by 4 December 1919. It did not at first carry its military number, but was registered as G-EAPY by AMC. Its Certificate of Airworthiness was issued to F.S. Cotton, and it left Hendon on 2 February 1920 for an attempted flight to the Cape. However, it crashed at Messina, in South Italy, two days later; it was subsequently returned to its makers, and was repaired by May. It left the civilian register in February 1921 and assumed its military number before going to Martlesham on 16 April. It crashed there that August and was not rebuilt.

A Condor engine was fitted to J1938 by

An unidentified D.H.9A being used for catapult trials from HMS *Ark Royal* in the Solent during November 1930. JMB/GSL

September 1920: it was completed by the 29th, and flew before the end of that month. J1938 went to Farnborough for testing during October, and to Martlesham in December, and it spent its career alternating between those two experimental establishments. It lasted until 10 February 1922, when it was burned out after a forced landing at Dropmore Park, near Burnham Beeches in Buckinghamshire.

J1939 was completed by December 1920, and it had more than forty-one hours of flying time when it arrived at Martlesham on 17 March 1921. It was re-engined with a more powerful Condor Ia that December, but was damaged during April 1921 and subsequently scrapped.

Post-War Gifts to the Dominions

Britain had vast stocks of unused airframes in storage during 1919, and it was decided that some of these should be presented as

Imperial Gifts to Australia and Canada, Dominions with their own emerging air services and the source of many distinguished RFC/RNAS/RAF airmen. D.H.9As were among the types selected for these gifts, thirty going to Australia and eleven to Canada.

The Canadian examples were delivered from June 1920, and were given civilian registrations. Two of these made an east-west crossing of the country that September, though the majority were used at the main Canadian Air Force station at Camp Borden, three (E993/G-CYBN, E994/G-CYAK and E995/G-CYBF) lasting until 1929 before being scrapped. The Australian machines were received at the same time as those in Canada, the vast majority being sent to serve at the premier Australian station at Point Cook, Victoria, home to the Australian CFS and, later, 1 Squadron and 1 Flying Training School. Most D.H.9A service was with the latter two units. E8616 was lost at sea on 23 September 1920 and an unnumbered replacement was bought from Britain. All Australian machines had

originally carried their RAF numbers, but those were replaced from 1921 with Australian Air Force numbers that ran from A1-1 to A1-30. Some of those machines lasted until 1930, when the D.H.9A was withdrawn from use, as an obsolete type.

Marine Operations

Initial D.H.9A deliveries had been to Marine Operations stations at Manston and Yarmouth. 219 Squadron (555 and 556 Flights) at Manston and 212 Squadron (490, 557 and 558 Flights) at Yarmouth continued to receive further examples as replacements for D.H.9s. They were employed on anti-submarine work, and F956, from Yarmouth, attacked a U-boat near Smith's Buoy on 12 August 1918; however, it was forced to come down in the North Sea. It would appear that flotation bags were fitted to F956, because after its crew was rescued, the aeroplane was taken in tow back to the coast. Others were issued to 273

The same machine being lowered onto its S.1.L catapult. JMB/GSL

A frontal view of the same scene. JMB/GSL

A Russian-built R1, a direct copy of the D.H.9A. Alexandrov/Woodman via JMB/GSL

An unarmed D.H.9A being refuelled at a home station in the early post-war period. JMB/GSL

**Representative Home-Based
D.H.9As with Bomber Squadrons**

11 Squadron Andover, Bircham
Newton, Netheravon – H3550, J7043,
J7044.

12 Squadron Northolt, Andover – J6963,
J6964, J6967, J7039, J8140.

15 Squadron Martlesham Heath (in
A&AEE) – E8696, J7038, J7057,
J7605, J7607, J7805, J7864.

24 Squadron Kenley, Northolt – E883,
F1611, F1621, F1646, H3559, J7079,
J7089, J7094, J7310, J7315.

33 Squadron Netheravon – J8471.

35 Squadron Bircham Newton – J8127,
J8143, J8213, J8482.

39 Squadron Spittlegate, Bircham
Newton – J7073, J7074, J7613,
J7614, J7615, J7816, J7817, J7818,
J7819, J8096, J8104, J8105, J8123,
J8127, J8133, J8136, J8137, J8143,
J8144, J8147, J8151, J8152, J8159,
J8169, J8170, J8173, J8471.

99 Squadron Bircham Newton – J8480.

100 Squadron Baldonnel, Spittlegate
– E827, H3586, H3588, H3590, H3659,
J7066, J7074, J7081.

207 Squadron Bircham Newton, San
Stephano, Eastchurch – F1616,
F2819, F2820, F2854, H19, H22,
H3501, H3635, J557, J559, J560,
J561, J566, J6964, J6967, J7034,
J7041, J7062, J7352, J7354, J7610,
J7611, J7612, J7859, J8144, J8145,
J8471, J8472.

**H3478 at Netheravon after the end of the war. This aeroplane was later used by the
Armament and Gunnery School at Eastchurch.** via F. A. Yeoman

**A view of a D.H.9A taxiing out through long grass at Netheravon exaggerates the size of
the frontal radiator.** via F. A. Yeoman

Squadron at Covehithe until that unit
was reduced to a cadre in March 1919.
219 Squadron also gave up its D.H.9As in
1919; but 212 Squadron continued to
operate the type until it was disbanded on
9 February 1920.

After the war a new coastal patrol
machine was needed to replace the
miscellany of types that had operated in
the role (the D.H.6, D.H.4, D.H.9 and the
Blackburn Kangaroo, as well as Short and
Sopwith floatplanes) and the Sopwith
Ships Strutters that could operate from
the new generation of
'flat-top' aircraft carriers. An advantage of
the Kangaroo was its ability to carry a crew
of three. In the immediate post-war years
of tight budgets there was little chance of
a new type being ordered, and so use was
made of the vast stock of D.H.9As in
storage and on order. Some D.H.9As on
the production line at Yeovil in early 1919
(H3512, H3515, H3518 and H3533-
H3545) were converted to three-seat

**A rear view of the same machine shows the watch office at Netheravon that must have
been one of the first to resemble a modern control tower.** via F. A. Yeoman

A D.H.9A coming into land against a dramatic sunset in Mesopotamia. via the author

E9939 of 8 Squadron with under-wing panniers and a spare wheel bolted to the fuselage between the undercarriage legs. JMB/GSL

J7027 of 55 Squadron was marked with a small swastika on its cowling; it was also fitted with most of the extra equipment that was customarily given to D.H.9As in Mesopotamia: underwing gravity tank, spare wheel under the fuselage, and picketing screws fastened to the wing-tip skids. via the author

FORCED LANDING CODE.

Meaning.

No. of Signal.

1. Send out new propellor.

2. Forced landing due to ignition trouble. Send out necessary spares.

3. Send out new tail skid.

4. Forced landing due to carburation trouble. Send out necessary spares.

5. Send out new wheels.

6. Can carry out repairs and take off without further aid.

7. Send out dismantling party. I cannot repair machine or take off.

8. Send out new undercarriage complete.

9. Doctor required urgently.

10. Bring spares by air or) I will lay out T into wind, where
    Land & give assistance)   you should touch, and / or
                              I will stand facing the wind, land
                              on side of my extended arm.

11. Require water for radiator.

12. Require ration, and / or money to last until dismantling party arrives.

13. Forced landing due to shortage of petrol and oil. Send fuel.

14. Tribesmen hostile.

No. 10 displayed by itself would mean "Land and give assistance".

Preceded by a Group would mean "Bring spares by air".

The emergency forced-landing signals used by crews in Mesopotamia. via the author

configuration, with an enlarged communal rear cockpit. Some of these were issued to the Fleet School of Aerial Gunnery & Fighting at Leuchars during 1919, and others to 205 Squadron at that station and 210 Squadron at Gosport when those units reformed during 1920. 205 Squadron operated a Mobile Flight that worked with the fleet at Cromarty and used landing grounds at Denly and Novar during exercises. When 3 Squadron reformed at Leuchars on 1 October 1921, it inherited the D.H.9A three-seaters from 205 Squadron. H3506 and H3508 were delivered to the Eagle Flight at Gosport on 14 April 1920 and carried out trial landings on the aircraft carrier of that name until November. H3451 is known to have been with HMS Argus in November 1919, but it is not known whether that was for the same purpose.

The value of the D.H.9A three-seater was diminished by the lack of provision for a bomb-aimer. That was the reason for the creation of the Armstrong-Whitworth

A pair of D.H.9As, still in war-time camouflage, in the air over Mesopotamia. JMB/GSL

E8804 of 84 Squadron flying flight leader's streamers from its elevators. JMB/GSL

'Tadpole', a further D.H.9A conversion. Work by representatives of that company was undertaken at Farnborough, using the airframe of E8522. The raised rear decking was extended further than on the three-seater, although it, too, accommodated two of the crew, and a ventral fairing was added to allow a prone bomb-aiming position. The Liberty engine was retained, but the alterations to the fuselage necessitated a marked reduction in wing stagger. The Tadpole may not have flown until 1923, and it was wrecked on 11 July 1924 when its undercarriage collapsed on landing. By that time a production version was in service, its development having been entrusted to Westland: it was called the 'Walrus', and it was a Tadpole fitted with the reliable twelve-cylinder, 450hp

moving to Gosport on 8 November and disbanding on 1 April 1923. The disbandment was due to the formation of the Fleet Air Arm, and the unit's men and machines formed 420, 421 and 422 (Fleet-Spotting) Flights of that new service. The Walrus of those flights were joined at Gosport by five of six D.H.9As (J6957-J6962) that had been rebuilt by Westland and also given the Lion engine. J6957 was used for tests at Martlesham and Farnborough, but the others were issued to the RAF Base, Gosport, from June 1924. They were withdrawn a year later, and most were re-engined with the Liberty and reissued to other units as standard D.H.9As.

D.H.9As were also tried out at sea. Several, including E752, E753 and F979

Other Foreign Service

47 and 221 Squadrons had flown some D.H.9As, alongside D.H.9s, during service in the Ukraine with the White Russian forces in 1919. E764 and F1626 served with the latter unit, while more are known to have served with 47 Squadron, for example F1084, F1086-89, F1091 and F1094. Others, such as E968-972 and E8765, served with the RAF Expeditionary Force in North Russia; when the RAF left, some of these D.H.9As inevitably fell into Bolshevik hands. Some were restored to airworthiness and were flown by the Soviet Russian Air Force. Just as with the D.H.9, the Soviet Russians built their own version of the D.H.9A at the GAZ No.1 Factory. They were powered by a copied version of

J8102 in service with 55 Squadron towards the end of the D.H.9A's operational life.

Napier Lion engine that was of 'broad arrow' configuration with three cylinder banks. The fitting of the new engine in a closed cowling meant that the radiator was transferred to a position under the forward fuselage. A new undercarriage incorporated sprung shock absorbers and a hydrovane. New mainplanes were fitted, those having square-cut tips and carrying balanced ailerons.

Thirty-six Walrus were built (N9500-N9535), and initial deliveries were to 3 Squadron in January 1922, that unit

flying from Gosport, had been used during June and July 1920 for landing trials on HMS *Eagle*, the first 'flat-top' aircraft carrier to be fitted with an island-type control and steering tower. E775 was used in further experiments from that vessel during April 1924. E748 had been used in experiments on HMS *Argus*, a true 'flat-top' in August 1921. In November 1930, a well-worn machine was used for catapult trials from HMS *Ark Royal* while that vessel was moored in the Solent.

the Liberty engine and designated R1. Almost 3,000 were produced, and they served in a miscellany of roles; for instance, some were converted to seaplane configuration, and from 1922 they were joined by others, purchased from British stocks held at Waddon. It would appear that about nineteen were delivered, but they were soon phased out in favour of the locally built D.H.9 with the Liberty engine, the R1.

Further D.H.9As were bought by Latvia: at least seven were acquired by that state

Representative D.H.9As with Units Based in the Middle East

8 Squadron Helwan, Suez, Basrah, Baghdad West, Hinaidi, Khormaksar – E8474, E8499, E8514, E8622, E8639, E8642, E8643, E8650, E8657, E8666, E8669, E8680, E8684, E8688, E8692, E8734, E8753, E8754, E8764, E8794, E8806, E9913, E9921, E9939, F1631, F1640, F2771, F2836, F2843, F2844, F2856, H24, H47, H54, H102, H108, H110, H116, H120, H141, H145, H147, H162, H163, H175, H3451, H3483, H3510, H3515, H3523, H3525, H3526, H3529, H3570, H3628, H3630, H3639, J552, J554, J7017, J7100, J7102, J7111, J7113, J7302, J7303, J7307, J7321, J7332, J7344, J7849, J7872, J8118, J8192, J8193, J8194, J8195, J8196, J8197, J8198, J8199, J8200, J8201, J8202, J8203, J8204, J8205.

14 Squadron Ramleh, Amman – E8688, E8744, E9922, E9937, H85, H144, H151, H3453, H3519, H3542, H3570, J7012, J7022, JR7024, J7035, J7067, J7068, J7084, J7086, J7104, J7108, J7115, J7116, J7251, J7253, J7257, J7303, J7327, J7337, J7615, J7823, J7825, J7827, J7829, J7831, J7833, J7834, J7839, J7840, J7841, J7844, JR7873, J7874, J7889, J8099, J8101, J8112, J8141, J8203.

30 Squadron Baghdad West, Hinaidi, Kirkuk, Hinaidi – E8497, E8498, E8513, E8514, E8580, E8602, E8643, E8651, E8658, E8668, E8684, E8711, E8713, E8755, E8758, E8805, E9690, E9691, E9894, E9908, E9918, E9922, E9930, E9938, F1614, F1615, F2771, F2785, F2810, F2815, F2817, F2838, F2840, F2846, F2853, F2855, H1, H40, H43, H44, H45, H53, H68, H71, H78, H80, H81, H86, H90, H101, H104, H105, H107, H108, H109, H114, H119, H120, H121, H122, H145, H150, H155, H161, H3424, H3433, H3451, H3481, H3500, H3504, H3512, H3523, H3524, H3525, H3632, H3633, H3634, J560, J6961, J7015, J7054, J7099, J7104, J7111, J7113, J7114, J7115, J7124, J7302, J7307, J7309, J7346, J7607, J7847, J7854, J7870, J7877, J7880, J7881, J8102, J8151, J8192.

45 Squadron Heliopolis, Helwan – E8642, H3501, JR7093, J7339, J7823, J7829, J7831, J7832, J7840, J7841, J7860, J7874, J8098, J8118, J8178, J8188, J8189, J8198, J8202.

47 Squadron Helwan, Khartoum – ER8599, E8615, ER8615, E8637, E8646, E8662, E8727, E8733, E8744, E8760, E9693, E9894, E9900, E9937, F969, F1641, F2762, F2784, F2794, F2857, HR82, H83, H85, H107, H174, H3500, H3519, H3520, H3522, H3535, H3634, H3635, H3639, H3640, H3641, J553, J7010, J7028, J7049, J7063, JR7070, J7071, J7086, J7093, J7094, J7095, J7096, J7101, J7104, J7106, J7107, J7108, J7119, J7257, J7331, J7337, J7338, J7339, J7605, J7796, JR7796, J7806, J7827, J7828, J7842, J7847, J8117, J8122, J8142, J8172, J8174, J8191.

55 Squadron Suez, Maltepe, Basrah, Baghdad West, Mosul, Hinaidi – E8493, E8512, E8580, E8622, E8625, E8631, E8640, E8643,

E8651, E8652, E8657, E8658, E8668, E8680, E8692, E8720, E8743, E8756, E8757, E8764, E8796, E8798, E8805, E8806, E9688, E9690, E9885, E9909, E9911, E9912, E9918, E9939, F1093, F1642, F2042, F2770, F2775, F2778, F2813, F2819, F2833, F2842, F2845, F2850, H10, H23, H26, H46, H53, H55, H57, H62, H67, H77, H79, H81, H88, H91, H92, H96, H97, H102, H106, H116, H118, H140, H142, H145, H150, H153, H154, H164, H173, H3430, H3480, H3481, H3483, H3510, H3513, H3523, H3524, H3525, H3526, H3545, HR3551, H3563, H3566, H3627, H3638, J554, J560, J565, J6958, J7013, J7014, J7017, J7018, J7031, J7036, J7042, J7043, J7044, J7045, J7050, J7052, J7056, J7101, J7102, J7104, J7110, J7113, J7119, J7123, J7127, J7249, J7252, J7255, J7256, J7305, J7306, J7307, J7320, J7330, J7344, J7608, J7700, J7807, J7818, J7819, J7838, J7847, J7848, J7850, J7851, J7853, J7865, J7867, J7870, J7887, J7888, J8102, J8152, J8154, J8155, J8176, J8177.

70 Squadron Hinaidi – E8639, E8744.

84 Squadron Baghdad West, Shaibah – E8493, E8514, E8589, E8593, E8601, E8622, E8625, E8650, E8655, E8658, E8663, E8666, E8669, E8694, E8711, E8728, E8730, E8741, E8763, E8801, E8804, E8806, E9688, E9857, E9891, E9909, E9918, E9919, F970, F1093, F1644, F2839, F2846, F2848, F2856, H22, H56, H58, H59, H60, H66, H91, H96, H108, H117, H122, H138, H141, H143, H147, H155, H165, H169, H3432, H3483, H3505, H3510, H3524, H3535, H3622, H3623, H3628, H3633, H3643, J552, J7021, J7026, J7027, J7054, J7056, J7099, J7100, J7101, J7109, J7120, J7121, J7127, J7254, J7307, J7309, J7311, J7348, J7352, J7608, J7797, J7798, J7799, J7826, J7832, J7847, J7852, J7854, J7866, J7872, J7876, J7879, J7882, J7887, J7890, J8149.

208 Squadron Ismailia – H93.

4 FTS Abu Sueir – E8592, ER8615, E8637, ER8637, ER8642, ER8649, E8661, E8675, ER8733, E8736, E8751, E8760, E8798, E9685, E9703, E9887, E9895, E9910, ER9956, F969, F2743, F2757, FR2763, F2796, F2806, F2807, F2813, F2816, F2847, FR2857, H26, HR82, F2847, FR2857, HR82, H84, H156, H3453, H3486, H3525, H3545, HR3551, H3636, J575, J6963, J6965, J6966, J6967, J7012, J7019, J7022, J7024, JR7024, J7029, J7040, J7046, J7049, J7060, JR7063, J7067, J7069, J7071, J7084, J7095, J7096, J7105, J7106, J7116, J7117, J7249, J7251, J7255, J7257, J7304, J7308, J7331, J7335, J7349, J7604, J7614, J7788, J7806, J7815, J7818, J7839, J7843, J7861, J7868, J7871, J8097, J8098, J8100, J8115, J8122, J8126, J8128, J8135, J8138, J8139, J8142, J8146, J8174, J8175, J8179, J8182, J8183, J8186, JR8186, J8187, JR8188, JR8189, JR8206.

Central Air Communications Section Shaibah E8498, E9915, H105, H3483.

Post-War Use at Home

during 1926 and they served for eleven years. The other European country to operate the type was Spain, where limited production by Hispano-Suiza took place.

Vast numbers of D.H.9As had been ordered during the war, and in 1919 many of those airframes were still in storage. The RAF was reduced in size, as many of its units both on the continent and others at home were disbanded. The strict budgetary controls of the post-war years meant that existing designs would equip the service, and the D.H.9A was retained in service as a bomber and trainer until 1930; it also served in the communications role with 24 Squadron at Kenley. That unit had been reformed from the Air Council Inspection Squadron and was designated as the RAF's

communication unit, ferrying senior officers, politicians, diplomats and occasional royalty to destinations both at home and in the near continent. 24 Squadron received its D.H.9As in July 1920, and operated them alongside Bristol F.2Bs for almost seven years.

A cadre of 100 Squadron had moved from the continent to Baldonnel in September 1919, and the unit was re-established on 1 February 1920 by the

JR7107 of 47 Squadron over the Nile Valley. It has an unidentified canister attached to its lower starboard mainplane. JMB/GSL

subsuming 141 Squadron. It inherited this squadron's task of policing duties against Sinn Fein activity, receiving D.H.9As to do so, and operating these alongside the Bristol Fighters that it had inherited. Detachments of its machines operated from a variety of landing grounds, such as Oranmore and Castlebar, where the hangars and living quarters were protected by armed guards, patrolling barbed-wire enclosures. The D.H.9As were withdrawn in the summer of 1921, though some were re-issued in February 1922 when the unit had returned to the mainland and established itself at Spittlegate. It flew D.H.9As there, alongside Vimys and Avro 504Ks, until re-equipped with the Fairey Fawn in 1924.

The main light bomber element of the peace-time RAF comprised just two squadrons, 39 and 207. The former had been re-established from its cadre at Spittlegate on 12 March 1921, and the latter reformed at Bircham Newton on 1 February 1920. Both were issued with D.H.9As during April 1921; initially these were finished in the war-time colours for the type: PC10 brown on fabric and battleship grey on plywood.

Half of the light bomber force left Britain in September 1922. 207 Squadron was despatched to San Stephano in Turkey, as part of an RAF force to intervene in trouble that had broken out between Greece and Turkey. The unit arrived in Turkey during October and

spent an uneventful eleven months, seeing no action, but losing some aeroplanes (eg H19, J557 and J566) in the inevitable forced landings and crashes that all units suffered. After returning home in September 1923, 207 Squadron was resettled at Eastchurch; from here it continued to operate D.H.9As for more than three years, until Fairey Gordon replacements arrived in January 1928.

A gradual expansion of the RAF had begun during 207 Squadron's absence, and a manifestation of this was the reformation, with D.H.9As, of 11 Squadron at Andover and 12 Squadron at Northolt, on 15 January and 1 April 1923 respectively. 15 Squadron reformed the following year, on 20 March: its D.H.9As were affiliated to the

Representative D.H.9As with Squadrons in India

27 Squadron (ex-99 Squadron)
Mianwali, Risalpur, Dardoni,
Peshawar, Risalpur, Kohat – E728,
E785, E828, E844, E845, E846, E877,
E880, E884, E887, E911, E935, E937,
E942, E953, E973, E977, E979, E8500,
E8573, E8584, E8589, E8595, E8619,
E8629, E8632, E8637, E8641, E8646,
E8655, E8656, E8660, E8665, E8673,
E8674, E8687, E8722, E8723, E8725,
E8729, E8742, E8754, E8761, E8769,
E8799, E9683, E9687, E9924, E9925,
E9948, F979, F1098, F1623, F2772,
F2774, F2782, F2787, F2788, F2812,
H23, H28, H29, H41, H48, H51, H52,
H70, H72, H89, H95, H3450, H3487,
H3528, H3534, H3550, H3555, H3632,
J567, J7030, J7039, J7055, J7057,
J7085, J7091, J7098, J7103, J7125,
J7158, J7340, J7342, J7343, J7345,
J7347, J7353.

31 Squadron Quetta – E8678, H3487.
60 Squadron Risalpur, Peshawar, Kohat
– E728, E774, E785, E812, E875, E876,
E877, E878, E880, E887, E911, E951,
E973, E977, E979, E8473, E8584,
E8611, E8623, E8632, E8636, E8637,
E8641, E8646, E8648, E8655, E8659,
E8660, E8665, E8671, E8672, E8673,
E8674, E8685, E8687, E8717, E8721,
E8722, E8726, E8727, E8729, E8731,
E8745, E8746, E8750, E8751, E8754,
E8755, E8758, E8761, E8792, E8796,
E8799, E8803, E9683, E9888, E9925,
E9948, E9949, F979, F1098, F1623,
F2774, F2812, H4, H52, H72, H74,
H89, H3396, H3450, H3528, H3534,
H3550, H3620, H3626, H3643, J566,
J599, J7030, J7039, J7055, J7057,
J7085, J7091, J7098, J7109, J7125,
J7340, J7341, J7342, J7343, J7345,
J7347.

A&AEE at its Martlesham Heath base and used for a variety of experimental work. The squadron's reformation preceded the re-equipment of 12 Squadron, which moved to Andover to receive its Fairey Fawns, by three days, and on 31 May 11 Squadron followed suit, having moved to Bircham Newton the previous September. That again left 39 and 207 Squadrons as the RAF's home-based dedicated D.H.9A light bomber squadrons.

Those two units became very proficient with the type, and were regular participants in the Annual Hendon Pageants that allowed the RAF to demonstrate its skills to the public. An overall finish of aluminium doped fabric and ply had been standardized to replace the drab camouflage finishes of war-time machines, and on the D.H.9A, the metal panels of the radiator shell and top

fuselage were painted with black enamel to give the venerable type a very smart appearance. 39 Squadron became something of a specialist in display flying, putting up some notable displays in line-abreast formation. The unit moved to Bircham Newton in January 1928, but only kept its D.H.9As until the end of the year, when it left for duty in India, operating Wapitis. 15 Squadron had, by that time, received Hawker Horsley replacements for its D.H.9As.

Its aeroplanes were handed over, prior to departure, to 101 Squadron, which had reformed at Bircham Newton on 21 March 1928. Those hand-me-downs were interim equipment only; 101 Squadron began to receive Boulton Paul Sidestrands the following March, and the last of its D.H.9As had gone by June 1929. The last D.H.9A unit to operate the type in front-line service at home had reformed, also at Bircham Newton, on 1 March 1929. That was 35 Squadron, and it continued to fly the type until July 1932, by which date the D.H.9A was an anachronism among the Harts and Gordons then in service, and no match for the contemporary generation of fighters.

Many of the D.H.9As used by home-based units during the 1920s were reconditioned machines in the J-serial range that was predominant in that decade. That is not to say that the airframes were new. Firms such as de Havilland, Westland,

A 27 Squadron machine armed for a raid on Dhetta Khal on 12 January 1922. It has a 230lb (100kg) bomb under its fuselage, and a 112lb (50kg) weapon under each lower mainplane. Its serial number is not known, but the machine behind it is H72. JMB/GSL

Hawker and Short Bros received contracts to provide reconditioned machines. Old airframes taken out of storage were used, with components being stripped, refurbished or replaced and then reassembled. Upon completion, a new serial number was issued. Most were rebuilt as standard D.H.9As, but the batches J8460-J8482 and J8483-J8494, from Westland and Parnall & Co respectively, were ordered in 1926 as dual-control versions for issue to training units. Many of the later reconditioned D.H.9As were fitted with leading-edge slats on their upper mainplanes in an attempt to improve take-off and low speed manoeuvring. The serials J8148-J8153 were from a batch of reconditioned machines ordered from de Havilland in that same year, but the six differed in that they had wings of metal construction.

The dual-control D.H.9As were not the first to be used as trainers. Large numbers had already been issued to 1, 2 and 5 Flying Training Schools, at Netheravon, Duxford (later Scopwick) and Sealand respectively, where they served as advanced trainers. 3 FTS at Spittlegate and 6 FTS at Manston also had some. Another major user was the RAF (Cadet) College at Cranwell, where pilots intended for permanent commissions were trained. As well as being home to bomber squadrons, Eastchurch was also the base for the Armament and Gunnery School, which trained air-gunners and operated D.H.9As amongst a miscellany of types.

Service In the Middle East

The D.H.9A is best remembered as a 'maid of all work' in operations policing the Empire and territories mandated to British control by the League of Nations. In the majority of instances the RAF worked in conjunction with the army, but occasionally it had sole control. The operation of D.H.9As in far-flung locations, where units quite often had to conduct their affairs in primitive living and servicing conditions, stretched the endurance of personnel; but their presence maintained stability in regions of tribal conflict and anti-British uprisings. In the Middle East, D.H.9A service can be separated into three geographical areas, namely Egypt/Sudan, Palestine and Mesopotamia. By the time

This D.H.9A at Drigh Road may have passed parade muster, but the 'erk' in front would not! via the author

E8799 as aircraft 2 of 60 Squadron with its spare wheel under the rear fuselage. via the author

of the type's introduction to Middle Eastern service it had become known as the 'Ninak'.

The greatest danger facing an aircrew on Middle Eastern duty was having to make a forced landing in a remote desert area when they risked death from heat exhaustion or thirst, or at the hand of native tribesmen. In order to minimize such risks it was reasonably commonplace for the wing-tips of D.H.9As to be painted in distinctive colours so they were more easily recognized from the air in the event of a crash or a forced landing. Also, a spare wheel was often bolted under the fuselage, and picketing screws strapped to under-wing skids. Panniers for carrying supplies were often mounted on the under-wing bomb ribs. Engine failure was the usual cause of such an emergency, but it could also be shortage of fuel, and many Middle Eastern-based D.H.9As were therefore fitted with enlarged gravity tanks, mounted under the upper starboard mainplane. Later, wireless was adopted, and machines carried telescopic masts for aerials. A pre-arranged series of signals, using the code numbers 1-10, was used to notify the cause of a mishap and the needs of the survivors; these are given in the accompanying illustration.

The mandate to police Mesopotamia led to the re-formation, at Baghdad West, of 84 Squadron with D.H.9As on 13 August 1920, and it was joined in the following month by 55 Squadron's D.H.9As from Turkey. These units were reinforcement for 30 Squadron that had operated R.E.8s in the region from 1917 to 1919, and had been re-established with D.H.9As from a nucleus at Baghdad West on 2 April of that year. The three squadrons operated detachments at remote stations further north in order to maintain control over the volatile Kurdish regions. The Arab population of the entire region was involved in a revolt against the British mandate, and the Ninak units were almost immediately involved in operations aimed at subduing the uprising. Bombing and strafing missions were conducted on a regular basis, and return fire was far from ineffective – 84 Squadron lost F3828 in this way on 22 September when it was hit by groundfire and forced to land in a river near Samarra; its crew made it to the river banks, only to be killed by hostile Arabs. The pilot was Flying Officer I.D.R. McDonald MC DFC, who had opened his list of combat successes during the Great War while flying D.H.5s, and who went on to become a noted exponent of the S.E.5a. Such groundfire was mainly from rifles, and the accuracy of it also accounted for F2785, H71 and H3482 of 30 Squadron and H58 of 84 Squadron.

Complete aerial coverage of Mesopotamia was impossible with the squadrons centralized around Baghdad, and so in September 1920, 84 Squadron was moved to the new station at Shaibah, near Basrah at the head of the Persian Gulf. That station became the unit's home for the next twenty years, and was later regarded with some affection. During the 1920s, however, it was very remote and very inhospitable: at the time it was said that the Gulf was 'the arse-hole of the Empire, and Shaibah three hundred miles up it'.

8 Squadron arrived at Baghdad West with D.H.9As on 4 March 1921, in which month 55 Squadron moved north to

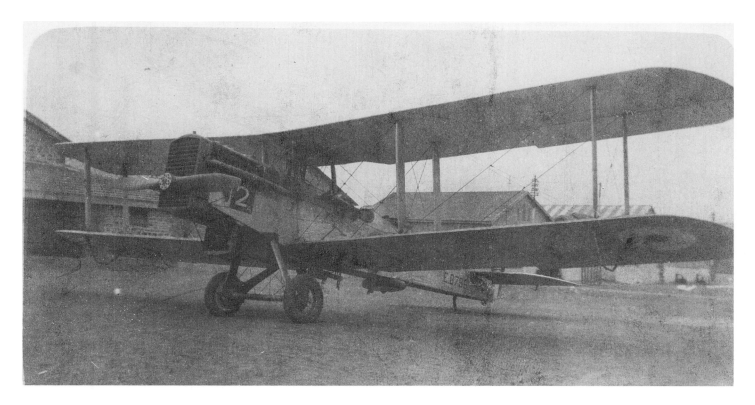

A further view of E8799. This D.H.9A also served with 27 Squadron and was in use in India between 1923 and 1928. via the author

Mosul. The new unit moved to the new and purpose-built aerodrome at Hinaidi on 29 December of that year.

The personnel of the Mesopotamia-based squadrons included many with distinguished war-time careers, and the commanding officers included G.H. Bowman, A.W. McClaughrey, R. Collishaw, J.M. Robb, T.F. Hazell, H.A. Whistler and B.L. Huskisson, all of whom had distinguished fighting careers during the Great War. All of these commanded D.H.9A units in the area. Their experience and decoration was matched at pilot level, the RAF of the period being manned by those whose records had entitled them to permanent commissions at a time when the majority of wartime personnel were being demobilized; S.M. Kinkead and J.I.T. Jones are two such pilots.

30 Squadron operated detachments at Mosul and Kirkuk in order to maintain the peace, but there were still losses: for instance E822 was shot down on 7 July; it was repaired, but was shot down again, when it was abandoned. During 1920, 30 Squadron's machines were also used to harass Bolshevik activities around the Caspian Sea. E780 was lost on such an operation on 8 December 1920, being

forced to land in Northern Persia with its pilot, Pilot Officer W. Sidebottom, shot by ground troops when trying to make a getaway.

Although the Arab revolt was technically over by the end of 1920, the Ninak units spent many hours of patrolling, and in the uneasy 'peace' continued to lose the occasional machine to groundfire: E918 and H153 of 55 Squadron were examples of such casualties. The overall effectiveness of the RAF was not in question, however, and from October 1921 the service assumed responsibility for control of the region.

Unrest was stirred up in Kurdistan during 1922 by Sheikh Mahmoud, and another anti-British uprising began. Hostile tribesmen cut Sulaimania off from outside assistance by ground forces, and so D.H.9As were used to supply the outpost. Several were crashed in the attempt and later abandoned. The hopeless position of the defenders resulted in the first major evacuation by air, when Ninaks and other machines of the RAF in Iraq flew out all British residents and any material of military value.

The Mesopotamian-based squadrons settled into a routine that would continue for the rest of the D.H.9A's service and

beyond. Punitive raids against any insurgence were only part of the work, and much effort was put into photographing and mapping the region; in the course of this task, many sites of archaeological significance were revealed. In fact more casualties were caused by engine failures, accidents and sandstorms than by enemy action.

30 Squadron moved into Hinaidi during December 1922, and was joined there by 55 Squadron in May 1924. Hinaidi was the major base in the region, and the home of the aircraft depot that repaired used machines and assembled deliveries from the UK. That depot was vital to the continuance of RAF operations. The average life of a D.H.9A in a squadron was about two years, and the inevitable damage that it would incur through accident and combat called for regular reconditioning. Repaired machines were often reissued to other units, and there were many examples of machines spending time with all four squadrons. Hinaidi was to be the home for those two units for the rest of their time with the Ninak, except for a brief period in 1927 when 30 Squadron operated from Kirkuk. 70 Squadron, the bomber/transport unit in Iraq, was also based at Hinaidi, and had operated a few D.H.9As alongside its

H89 after coming to grief at Drigh Road on 3 February 1926. via the author

Vernons; and further south, at Shaibah, the Central Air Communication Section flew the type. Here, D.H.9As were provided as 'personal' machines for the various AOCs in the region, and these had the distinction of being finished in an overall red colour scheme; E8754, J6959 and its replacement J8177 were all so finished.

8 Squadron left Hinaidi on 27 February 1927 and transferred south to Aden, where it operated from Khormaskar aerodrome as part of the protectorate's defence against Yemeni incursions. The unit virtually re-equipped with reconditioned machines delivered from the UK, receiving the majority of the batch J8190-J8207 in May 1927. It operated its D.H.9As for a further sixteen months. The first of its replacement Fairey IIIFs arrived in January 1928, and re-equipment was completed by June.

The three D.H.9A squadrons in Mesopotamia soon followed suit. All received Wapitis as replacement equipment. The last Ninak left 84 Squadron in January 1929, 30 Squadron was re-equipped by that October, and 55 Squadron by the following February.

To the west, in Jordan, 14 Squadron also operated the type. The squadron had reformed with Bristol F.2Bs from 111 Squadron in 1920, at Ramleh in Palestine,

---

Representative D.H.9A with AAF and Special Reserve Squadrons

500 (County of Kent) Squadron, Manston -

501 (City of Bristol) Squadron, Filton – J8491.

600 (City of London) Squadron, Northolt & Hendon – J7083, J7837, J8116, J8154, J8164, J8165, J8171, J8184, J8223, J8472, J8491.

601 (County of London) Squadron, Northolt & Hendon – E8605, J7319, J7835, J8108, J8114, J8121, J8130, J8161, J8212, J8221, J8224, J8478, J8482.

602 (City of Glasgow) Squadron, Renfrew – H144, J7863.

603 (City of Edinburgh) Squadron, Turnhouse – J8129, J8136, J8145, J8211.

604 (County of Middlesex) Squadron, Hendon – J7319, J8472.

605 (County of Warwick) Squadron, Castle Bromwich – E8711, J7319, J7613, J7836, J8105, J8107, J8109, J8125, J8162, J8163, J8480.

608 (North Riding) Squadron, Thornaby – J7856.

---

and received D.H.9As from June 1924. It moved to Amman in February 1926, that station becoming its home until the outbreak of World War Two. Its Ninaks operated on similar duties to those in Mesopotamia until replaced by Fairey IIIFs from November 1929.

The strategic importance of Egypt and the Suez Canal also necessitated an RAF presence, and D.H.9As served in that country with 45 and 47 Squadrons, as well as 4 FTS. 45 Squadron was a bomber/transport squadron flying Vernons, but it had been issued with a few Ninaks upon its formation at Helwan and pending deliveries of its twin-engined equipment. Also at Helwan, from June 1920, 47 Squadron quickly replaced its D.H.9s with the Ninak; then in October 1927 it moved south to Khartoum, and two months later began to re-equip with Fairey IIIFs. 45 Squadron had disposed of its Vernons in January 1927 and had been reduced to a cadre. It was intended that the squadron would also re-equip with Fairey IIIFs, but when the unit was re-established at Heliopolis, four months later, it received D.H.9As as interim equipment. That interim in fact lasted two years, during which time the squadron replaced 47 Squadron at Helwan. Aboukir was the home of the aircraft depot in Egypt, and received machines from the UK for assembly. It also reconstructed damaged aeroplanes, and these were unique in the RAF by the manner in which their serial numbers were reapplied: the letter R (for reconstructed) was inserted after the prefix letter so that, for example, J8186 re-emerged as JR8186.

The RAF and its predecessor, the RFC, had a training organization in Egypt during the Great War, but its training depot stations had all disbanded during 1919. A source of pilots was needed for Middle East-based squadrons, and this led to the opening of 4 FTS at Abu Sueir on 1 April 1921; D.H.9As formed a major part of that unit's equipment during the rest of the decade. Thus after initial training on Avro 504Ks, trainees graduated to the Ninak if they were destined for squadrons operating

a pattern for D.H.9A aircrews for more than a decade, namely reconnaissance work interspersed with the dangerous task of bombing settlements associated with hostile tribesmen. Such work was dangerous for two reasons: the Pathan rifle fire was accurate against the relatively slow machines, and the operation of the type in the rarefied atmosphere of the North-West Frontier reduced the D.H.9A's performance dramatically. Engine overheating was a persistent problem, only partially overcome, as in the Middle East, by the fitting of auxiliary radiators under the nose of the aeroplanes; this may have aided cooling, but it induced a lot of extra drag. Engine failure was a potentially fatal occurrence, as the terrain did not favour forced landings; and even if a machine could be landed safely, there was then the high risk of falling into

D.H.9As occasionally flew on such raids in company with the available D.H.10s of 60 Squadron, such as those on Dhatta Khal in January 1922. The squadron's D.H.9As at that time still included some of those originally delivered with 99 Squadron, and replacement machines were of similar wartime vintage. Those involved in anything more than minor accidents were passed to the aircraft depot at Drigh Road, Karachi, for reconstruction. Serviceability was always a problem, and the number of D.H.9As on charge seldom matched the 'official' squadron establishment. The D.H.10s of 60 Squadron were becoming regarded as obsolete by 1923, and their serviceability rate was, if anything, worse than that of the D.H.9A. Its twin Liberty engines were an unnecessary expense, given the duration of raids undertaken, and so 60

E880 of 27 Squadron in similar circumstances on 25 October 1927. P. Baillie via JMB/GSL

the type. A large number of the Ninaks used at Abu Sueir were converted to full dual control by the depot at Aboukir.

Service In India

The first D.H.9A unit to operate in India on such policing duty was 99 Squadron, hastily despatched to India from Aulnoy in May 1919. It went with eighteen crated D.H.9As and was part of an RAF contingent that also included 48 and 97 Squadrons (Bristol Fighters and D.H.10s) to reinforce the existing 31 and 114 Squadrons in operations that followed the outbreak of the Third Afghan War. The personnel arrived ahead of the aeroplanes, and it was September before the unit was established at Mianwali. Its operations set

Pathan hands and being killed. 99 Squadron existed, in that incarnation, only until 1 April 1920. The overall run-down in RAF strength led to the adoption of a policy whereby units with longer histories and more distinguished service were retained; thus 99 Squadron was renumbered as 27 Squadron – although that had little impact on the personnel, and caused no change in equipment. Concurrently 48 and 97 Squadrons became 5 and 60 Squadrons.

27 Squadron continued flying operations in support of the army during the next thirty-seven days, until the official ending of the Afghan War. The uneasy truce that followed meant that the unit was seldom inactive. Tribal uprisings and opportunist attacks on isolated garrisons demanded retaliation, and the

Squadron was re-equipped with the D.H.9A during March of that year. The relatively short duration of missions is indicated by the fact that D.H.9s in India were seldom fitted with the under-wing gravity tank that was commonplace on similar machines in the Middle East. In addition to those with 27 and 60 Squadrons, at least two D.H.9As were issued to 31 Squadron, nominally a Bristol F.2B unit. Those remaining were withdrawn to Drigh Road where the airframes were cannibalized for any useful components, particularly engines.

Further D.H.9As had been received to support the re-equipment of 60 Squadron, but those aeroplanes were from ex-wartime stocks that had been taken out of storage. They did, however, look new in their aluminium-doped finish that had

An immaculate D.H.9A of 600 (City of London) Squadron, displaying the unit badge on its cowling. JMB/GSL

begun to replace the wartime battleship grey and PC10 khaki of earlier deliveries. For whatever reason, the two D.H.9A squadrons in India received very few of the well reconditioned J-serial machines that were delivered during the 1920s, most of these going to units at home and in the Middle East. Attrition rate was high, and each of the two squadrons was issued with almost 100 machines during their period of using the type. In fact this can be explained by the harsh operating conditions: landing grounds were primitive and rocky, the nature of the terrain in the event of a forced landing was uncompromising, and planes had to fly in a rarefied atmosphere, which meant they were pushed to the limits of their performance. The accompanying table shows that many machines operated with both units, often being withdrawn from one for repair, and then re-issued to the other.

The two squadrons operated together in many minor operations. Many of these involved giving advance notice of intent to bomb by the dropping of leaflets, and then conducting operations with the hope that the material damage caused to tribal settlements would force a call for a truce. Operations were interspersed with proving flights, and the attempted development of an aerial mail service.

One of the rarest bars to the India General Service medal is that for Waziristan 1925. That clasp was only awarded to RAF personnel who took part in a campaign against Waziri tribesmen who were waging yet another uprising on the North-West Frontier. For the first time the RAF in India was permitted to conduct an action independently of the army, and to bomb the opposition into submission. 27 and 60 Squadron D.H.9As and the Bristol F.2Bs of 5 Squadron were given the task, and operated out of Miranshah. The campaign opened on 9 March 1925 and lasted less than two months. Despite losses in accidents and

one to enemy rifle fire, the bombing had the desired effect and the Waziris sued for an end to hostilities. The single operational loss was E8792, and its crew of F/Os E.J. Dashwood and N.C. Hayter-Hames was killed when the machine's bomb-load exploded as it crashed.

The other major operation that involved 27 and 60 Squadrons was the evacuation of British residents from Kabul. Anti-British sentiments had come to a head in Afghanistan's civil war, and Britons had taken refuge in their country's Legation building. The request for evacuation was made during December 1928, by which time of year the passes through to Kabul were snowed in, precluding the use of ground forces. All available machines of the India wings were therefore mobilized, and spent two months in accomplishing that evacuation, despite the extreme winter weather.

1928 was the beginning of the end for the D.H.9A in India. The first Westland

Wapitis arrived for 11 Squadron, and others were scheduled to follow – though it was not until March 1930 that 60 Squadron received its first of the new type, and 27 Squadron the following month. Nevertheless, all D.H.9As had been withdrawn by May, and so the type's eleven years of service in India came to an end.

The Auxiliary Air Force and Special Reserve

One of Trenchard's great post-war moves was the creation of the RAF equivalent to the Territorial Army, the Auxiliary Air Force. Its squadrons were formed with regional or urban affiliations, providing weekday lectures and weekend flying to create a reserve of all RAF trades. Treasury parsimony in the 1920s ensured that equipment was drawn from available stocks, and so the D.H.9A, as well as the Avro 504K, was standardized as the type issued to the new force. The first such unit was 602 (City of Glasgow) Squadron, which formed at Renfrew on 12 September 1925 and received its first machine, D.H.9A (Dual Control) H144 on 7 October. Three further AAF units formed a

week later, 600 (City of London) and 601 (County of London) Squadrons at Northolt, and 603 (City of Edinburgh) Squadron at Turnhouse. These too were issued with D.H.9As, as was 605 (County of Warwick) Squadron, formed at Castle Bromwich on 5 October 1926.

The Special Reserve differed from the AAF in that its members were, initially, serving RAF personnel. 501 Squadron was formed at Filton, with at least one D.H.9A, on 14 June 1929, and received the title City of Bristol Squadron the following May. 600 and 601 Squadrons had moved to Hendon on 18 January 1927, and were joined there by 604 (County of Middlesex) Squadron, which formed on 17 March 1930; however, it received only two D.H.9As.

A feature of D.H.9As in service with the AAF was the immaculate condition of their finish. With flying restricted mainly to weekends, much time was spent cleaning and polishing the machines, and few photographs show anything other than gleaming airframes. AAF D.H.9As usually carried their unit numbers on the rear fuselage, and unit badges were displayed, often on the engine cowlings. The last D.H.9As did not leave AAF service until November 1930, later than the withdrawal of the type from regular squadrons. J7856 is recorded as being with 608 Squadron at

Thornaby during 1934, although by that date it must have been for ground instructional duties only. Replacement was with the Westland Wapiti and Wallace, types that, ironically, utilized the mainplane layout of the D.H.9A.

The Survivor

It is still possible to appreciate the lines of the D.H.9A today, because by a quirk of fate, F1010 survives in the RAF Museum at Hendon. That D.H.9A was one of the five machines of 110 Squadron that were lost to enemy action on 5 October 1918. It came down intact, with its crew made POW, and became part of the German exhibition of aircraft at the Deutsche Luftfahrt Sammlung in Berlin. Damage to the exhibition by Allied bombing during World War Two caused the exhibits to be transferred to occupied Poland for safety, and F1010 survived there in a dilapidated condition until 1977, when it was exchanged for a Spitfire and brought to Britain. Restored by the craftsmen of the RAF Museum's facility at Cardington, it was then placed in the Bomber Command section at Hendon. It is conjectural as to how much of the airframe is now original, but it is the sole example of its kind in existence.

CHAPTER TEN

The American Connection

The Liberty Plane and the USD-9A

Few British designs were built outside this country during the Great War, and only two achieved large-scale production abroad: the Sopwith 1½ Strutter and the D.H.4. The Sopwiths built in France and the D.H.4s built in the USA were both delivered in greater quantities than those built in Britain. The American association with the D.H.4 stemmed from the parlous state of that nation's air services when it entered the war on 6 April 1917. Equipment comprised mainly Curtiss and Wright types that were unsuited to combat, and the allocation by Congress of more than $24 million for aviation between August 1916 and May 1917 was something of a paradox because

there were no indigenous up-to-date designs on which to spend it.

That sad state of affairs was addressed by the Aircraft Production Board, set up on 16 May 1917, its brief to co-ordinate the selection and production of aircraft for both the military and the navy. The choice of chairman for that board was fortuitous: the position was given to Howard Coffin, a man with experience of the motor industry who understood the need for standardized production. The French government had requested that the USA contribute a force of 4,500 aeroplanes for the war in 1918, and America was only too willing to comply – but what it needed was the selection of

designs for those aeroplanes. With the American aviation industry unable to supply the necessary types, the manufacture of French, British or Italian types was the logical answer. A technical commission was sent to Europe under the leadership of Colonel R.C. Bolling and ordered to examine Allied designs, to report on those most suitable, and to secure manufacturing rights. Negotiating with French and Italian manufacturers was difficult, though the Bolling Commission had a warmer welcome in Britain. Although subject to later changes, plans were made for the manufacture of Bristol F.2Bs, Handley Page 0/400s, Caproni bombers, SPAD

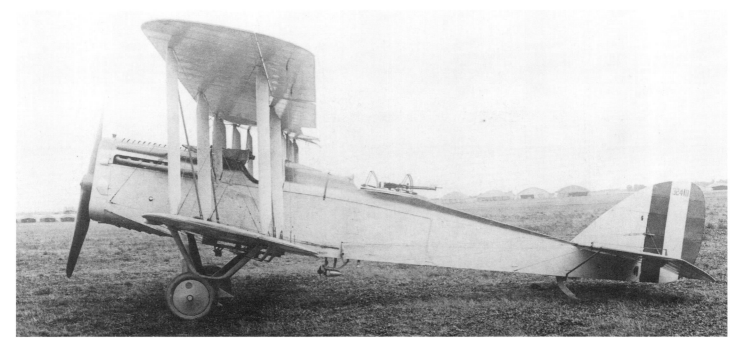

32410 is representative of the first D.H.4s delivered to the US Army Air Service. Its twin 0.3in Marlin machine-guns have a protective covering, and there is a single Lewis gun on the observer's Scarff ring. A double Lewis armament was common on active service. The machine is fitted with bomb ribs under the wings, and a generator is mounted under the fuselage. Like other early deliveries, the fuselage sides and fin were finished in cream, and the fuselage decking and mainplane/tailplane upper surfaces in khaki brown. Operational experience soon led to the whole fuselage being doped in khaki. JMB/GSL

Specification – American-Built DH-4	
Powerplant:	400hp Liberty 12; fuel capacity 88 gallons
Weights:	Empty 2,337lb (1,060kg); loaded 3,439lb (1,560kg) (observation), 3,693lb (1,675kg) (bombing); wing loading 7.9lb per sq ft (38.64kg per sq m) (observation), 8.5lb per sq ft (41.49kg per sq m) (bombing)
Dimensions:	Mainplane span 42ft 5in (12.94m); mainplane gap 5ft 6in (1.68m); chord 5ft 6in (1.68m); length 30ft 6in (9.3m); height 10ft 3in (3.13m); tailplane span 10ft 1¾in (3.09m); wing area 434sq ft (40.37sq m)
Performance:	Maximum speed 118mph (190km/h); climb to 10,000ft (3,000m) 14 minutes

XIIIs and D.H.4s. The American decision to standardize on the Liberty engine led to only the D.H.4 being produced in volume. A7531, an AMC-built specimen, was sold to the American government and was probably the engine-less D.H.4 that arrived in the USA during July 1917. It was accompanied by George Hancock from AMC and two other British technicians. Drawings had been provided, but the specimen D.H.4 was stripped down in the Dayton-Wright factory, that firm having been contracted to build the type, and new ones prepared to American measurements. They were used to create the first US D.H.4 that received the fourth Liberty engine and first flew on 29 October.

By then the Bolling Commission had heard of the D.H.9, still on the drawing board, and reported it as an improvement on the D.H.4. The Aircraft Production Board naturally wanted the best for its air services, and so opted for the new design but with the Liberty engine.

Once it had been decided to standardize on the D.H.9 as a day bomber, and with the Liberty as its powerplant, American production was ordered and the mass-production techniques pioneered by its automotive industry were brought into play. Thus 4,000 D.H.9s, plus spares, were ordered from Dayton-Wright, 3,750 D.H.9s and 250 D.H.4s from the Fisher Body Division of General Motors, and 500 D.H.9s from the Standard Aircraft Corporation. Those orders were in place by late October 1917, when the D.H.9 prototype was just finishing its assessment at Martlesham Heath. The D.H.4s ordered from Fisher were intended to be used as trainers for the D.H.9s, which would be the operational day bombers. After the reports of the D.H.9's

shortcomings were received, the decision was made by 12 February 1918 to amend all existing D.H.9 contracts to orders for the same number of D.H.4s.

It would seem, however, that the D.H.4 had not been altogether abandoned, as Dayton Wright had continued development work on its first machine. Cooling problems had arisen, due to the use of the larger Liberty, and a new, taller radiator was designed. The internal fittings in the front fuselage had had to be modified to accommodate the twin Marlin machine-gun armament specified by the US Army Air Service, and other minor problems had been sorted. It would appear that an engine was delivered for A7531, because the Dayton Wright machine was flown in comparative tests with a British-built D.H.4 powered by a Rolls-Royce Eagle VIII. Although the airframe of the American machine was some 55lb (25kg) lighter, its loaded weight was 156lb (70kg) heavier. It may have been that first machine that was 'delivered' for service on 31 December 1917, in an attempt to have an American aeroplane en route for France before the New Year. In fact, it was 11 May before an American-built D.H.4 actually reached that destination.

D.H.4 production must have been re-ordered before all D.H.9 contracts had been amended because deliveries of production machines began in February 1918, when nine were handed over from Dayton Wright. Only four followed in March and fifteen in April, but production was by then getting into its stride, and 153 were delivered in May. The company had its 1,000th machine on the production line by July, and had delivered 3,101 when contracts were terminated in April 1919. By that latter date, Fisher had delivered 1,600 and

Standard 140. That would give a total of 4,801 machines – but there are many variations given in assorted reports; one source, for example, states that 4,587 had been delivered by the end of 1918. The American publicity machine expected great things of the D.H.4, and the name 'Liberty Plane' achieved widespread currency.

It is fairly certain that only 1,213 had reached France by the time of the Armistice, with 155 of those being transferred to the US Navy. Only 499 had been issued to operational units of the US Army Air Service, and only 196 of those were still in use.

American personnel had been training in Britain since the beginning of 1918, and members of many units that were intended to receive American-built D.H.4s trained mainly at RFC/RAF stations that housed D.H.4 training units. Many of those personnel were ground staff, aircrews being attached to operational units of the RFC, RNAS, RAF and Independent Force to gain operational experience. Home-based RAF stations that gave instruction to American personnel included Waddington, Catterick, Wyton, Wye, Narborough, London Colney and Stamford/Wittering. Some of those aircrew that served with operational RAF units did not live to join their intended USAAS squadrons.

On 24 June 1918 the first D.H.4 squadrons were activated. The 22nd Aero Squadron was already in France, its flights being attached to 49, 205 and 211 Squadrons RAF; it was brought together and received D.H.4s at the Issoudun depot before moving to Orly. The 135th Aero Squadron began its move from England that same day, and was at Issoudun to receive its operational equipment by 2 July. It then moved to Amanty, and then Ourches on the 30th of that month. On 2 August, the unit's eighteen machines made their first crossing of the lines. Brigadier General B.D. Foulois, Commander of the Air Service, was in the observer's cockpit of the lead aeroplane but the formation was broken up by poor weather and failed to reach its target. Operational D.H.4s were fitted with twin Lewis guns on the observer's Scarff ring, and provision was made for a vertically mounted camera to be carried in the rear fuselage of those machines with observation squadrons.

This US.D.9A was AS40060, the second such machine built by the Factory Department at McCook Field. It was completed by August 1918 and used for performance tests that October. It carried the station number P43. After the war it was used in experiments with a 37mm cannon mounted in the rear cockpit. It survived until 1922. JMB/GSL

Other units from England joined the existing D.H.4 squadrons: thus the 8th, 24th, 50th and 104th Aero Squadrons arrived during July, followed by the 9th, 11th, 20th and 166th the following month. Other units followed, including the 85th, 100th, 163rd, 168th, 278th and 354th Squadrons.

The D.H.4 was used in American service in much the same way as it was in the RFC, RNAS and RAF. The US Army Air Service did, however, give specialist roles to its squadrons, and so some operating the D.H.4 were observation squadrons, charged with reconnaissance and contact patrolling, while others were bombardment squadrons. The D.H.4 acquired an evil reputation in American service, becoming known as the 'Flaming Coffin' due to an alleged propensity to catch fire. In reality, however, only thirty-seven were lost, and less than one quarter of those went down in flames. More than seven times that number of American

D.H.4s were lost in France due to accidents.

The first American operational casualties on the type were from the 135th Observation Squadron, 2nd Lt D.B. Cole and 1st Lt L.A. Smith being wounded on 16 and 25 August respectively. The first combat fatalities were not incurred until the following month when, on the day before the opening of the St Mihiel offensive, the crew of a 50th Observation Squadron D.H.4 was killed. The 8th Observation and 20th Bombardment Squadrons each lost a D.H.4 that day, with both crews taken prisoner. Losses were to be expected, but the 11th Bombardment Squadron took a severe hammering on 18 September, when five out of six D.H.4s that had set out to bomb La Chaussee were shot down by ten Fokker D.VIIs. The sixth was badly damaged, but its crew managed to regain the lines before making an emergency landing. Eight days later the 20th

Bombardment Squadron suffered in an almost identical manner, losing a complete flight of five, from a force of ten that had set out to bomb Dun-sur-Meuse.

During the fighting at the start of October, the 308th Regiment of the 77th Division was cut off in the Argonne Forest: it became known as the 'Lost Battalion'. The 50th Observation Squadron was involved in attempts to locate and resupply that regiment, and on 5 October lost a pair of D.H.4s in the process. And on the following day, post-humous Congressional Medals of Honor were awarded to a crew of the squadron, 1st Lt Harold E. Goettler and 2nd Lt Erwin R. Bleckley, for their bravery: they had already flown one mission that day in the face of intense groundfire, and were killed in a repeat attempt.

Army D.H.4s continued operations until the Armistice, sustaining further losses that were, however, no greater than those suffered by units operating Breguet

Wartime United States Army Air Service Units Operating the D.H.4 in France

8th Observation Squadron* –
Amanty, Ourches, Toulon,
Saizerais, Colombey-les-Belles, Far-
gues-Ste-Hilaire.

9th Observation Squadron* –
Colombey-les-Belles, Amanty,
Vavincourt, Preutin, Trier
(Germany), Colombey-les-Belles.

11th Bombardment Squadron* –
Delouze, Amanty, Maulan,
Colombey-les-Belles, Guitres,
St Denis de Pile, Sablons.

20th Bombardment Squadron* –
Delouze, Amanty, Maulan,
Colombey-les-Belles, Guitres,
St Denis de Pile.

22nd Observation Squadron* – Guines,
Issoudun, Orly, Toul,
Belrain, Colombey-les-Belles,
Le Mans.

24th Observation Squadron* – St Max-
ent, Ourches, Gondreville-sur-
Moselle, Vavincourt,
Weissenthurm (Germany).

37th Aero Squadron – Issoudun,
Bordeaux.

50th Observation Squadron* –
Amanty, Behonne, Bicqueley,
Remicourt, Clermont-en-Argonne,
Langres, Clamency.

91st Observation Squadron – Amanty,
Gondreville-sur-Moselle,
Vavincourt, Preutin, Trier
(Germany), Koblenz (Germany),

Colombey-les-Belles, Le Mans.

96th Bombardment Squadron –
Clermont-Ferrand, Amanty,
Maulan. Colombey-les-Belles,
St Denis de Pile.

100th Bombardment Squadron* –
St Maxient.

104th Observation Squadron* – St
Maxient, Epiez, Luxeuil-les-Bains,
Soilly, Foucaucourt, Parois,
Belrain, Colombey-les-Belles, St
Denis de Pile, Bordeaux.

135th Observation Squadron * –
Issoudun, Amanty, Ourches, Toul,
Colombey-les-Belles,
Tresses, Bordeaux.

166th Bombardment Squadron* –
Delouze, Vinets-sur-Aube,
Delouze, Amanty, Maulan,
Joppecourt, Trier (Germany),
Colombey-les-Belles, Le Mans,
Brest.

168th Observation Squadron* – bases
not known

800th Bombardment Squadron* – St
Maxient, Champ de Tir de Souge.
* Squadrons wholly equipped
with D.H.4
Issoudun, Clermont-Ferrand and
Tours were the main American
Instruction Centres (training
schools) in France and also
operated small numbers of
the type.

14s or Salmson 2A.2s. Operational experience had pointed units towards adopting close defensive formations, a squadron strength for bombing, and in units of three or more for reconnaissance. E.S. Gorrell, in his *History of the Air Service AEF*, made a critical appraisal of the D.H.4 in comparison with the Breguet 14, much of it apparently based on apocryphal evidence, and that seems to have influenced many later 'historians'.

American-built D.H.4s were the intended equipment of the elements of the US Marine Aviation Force that were to operate as the Day Wing of the Northern Bombing Group. Seventy-two were due to operate with Squadrons A-D of that wing, but deliveries were delayed and, as related earlier, British D.H.9As were supplied as interim equipment. Only fourteen D.H.4s had been delivered by the time of the Armistice, and small numbers served in each of the four squadrons; these had been re-designated 7-10 on 5 October. The D.H.4s were given the local numbers D1-D14, and on 1 October 1918, D1 made the first raid by a USMC crew flying an American-built machine. Thirteen days later that D.H.4 was the vehicle for an operation that resulted in two more Congressional Medals of Honor being awarded to a crew of the type. 2nd Lt Ralph Talbot and Gunnery Sergeant

D.H.4s continued in service post-war, some 3,000 being available in the USA during 1919. This unidentified machine is typical of those used in the immediate post-war period, and is seen here probably unarmed, with a training unit. In common with many D.H.4s, it was flown without the top cowling above its Liberty engine, probably as an aid to cooling. JMB/GSL

In the D.H.4B, the positions of the pilot's cockpit and the main fuel tank were reversed, an arrangement which certainly improved communication between the crew. The complete fuselage was skinned in birch plywood to improve its structural integrity. via the author

Robert Guy Robinson had already been credited with a Fokker D.VII out of control on the 8th, but during a bombing raid to Thielt on the 14th, their formation was attacked by fourteen of the enemy scouts. Robinson sent one down before being wounded, but he continued his firing until he was hit again, twice; he then collapsed. Talbot sent another enemy scout down using the front guns, and then made for safety so that Robinson's wounds could be treated. D3 was damaged on that same raid, and D4 was shot down on 22 October, its crew killed. The only other loss was one to which the RAF had become accustomed: five days later D11 failed to return, but in fact it had managed to reach neutral Holland, where its crew was interned.

Post-war deliveries brought the total of D.H.4s sent to France to 1,440 – but there was little use for them. With more than 3,000 available in the USA, the majority of those in Europe were stripped of valuable components and then burnt, an action referred to in the contemporary American press as the 'Billion Dollar Bonfire'.

The USD-9

As we have seen, even before the American-built D.H.4 entered service, plans were in hand to replace it with the D.H.9A, the American authorities seeing greater value in its use of the Liberty engine. A sample was requested, but it was

Specification – USD-9A	
Powerplant:	400hp Liberty; fuel capacity 25 gallons
Weights:	Empty 2,815lb (1,277kg); loaded 4,872lb (2,210kg); wing loading 9.94lb per sq ft (48.49kg per sq m)
Dimensions:	Mainplane span 46ft 1/2in (14m); mainplane gap 6ft 1¹/₂in (1.87m); chord 5ft 9in (1.75m); length 30ft 2in (9.2m); height 10ft 6in (3.2m); tailplane span 13ft 11¹/₂in (4.26m); wing area 490sq ft (45.58sq m)
Performance:	Maximum speed 118mph (190km/h); climb to 6,500ft (2,000m) 11 minutes 40seconds

a D.H.9, C6058, that actually went to the USA. That machine went to the experimental station at McCook field, where the first USD-9 prototype was constructed. D.H.9A drawings must have been available, because the first prototype had the enlarged wings. The USD-9 was fractionally longer than its British equivalent.

That first prototype first flew during July 1918 and was followed by twelve others, six at McCook Field and six by Dayton Wright. Two of the latter were completed as USD-9s, the remainder as USD-9As; the latter incorporated modifications to allow greater quantities of fuel to be carried. Five of the others built at McCook Field were also USD-9As, and a pair of those went to France for evaluation by the AEF on 4 November 1918 but arrived after hostilities had ceased. At least one of the five was fitted with a new, more rounded rudder that was intended as standard on production machines. The

sixth was designated USD-9AB and had an increased wing area. It was intended for night-bombing, but was surplus to requirements by the time it flew in March 1919. Orders for 4,000 production USD-9As had been given to Curtiss on 1 November 1918, but these were cancelled after the Armistice.

D.H.4 Post-War Service

Squadrons of the AEF returned to the USA, minus their aeroplanes, from April 1919; however, unlike their British equivalents, most were not disbanded. The vast stocks of D.H.4s allowed easy re-equipment, but the combat lessons learned in France led to further modifications of the original design. A rolling programme was instituted to convert at least 1,500 existing machines to D.H.4B standard. The conversion entailed the transposition of the pilot's cockpit and main tank to the

This frontal view of an unidentified D.H.4B shows the shape of the enlarged radiator that was fitted to cool the Liberty engine. The aeroplane is also fitted with larger tyres that became standard on the later D.H.4M. via the author

AS.23-162 was fitted with Loening COA-1 wings that featured N struts and upper ailerons operated by connecting struts. It served at McCook Field, where it was given the local number P369. It lasted until 1930. via the author

This D.H.4B carries the serial number AS.23-669, and was an example of the revived serial system introduced in 1922, showing that it was the 669th machine delivered for the Air Service in the 1923 financial year. It was fitted with wings from a Loening COA-1 amphibian and delivered to McCook Field, where it acquired the station number P329. 23-669 was destroyed in a crash on 1 January 1925. JMB/GSL

DH-4 Sub-Types

Sub Type	Description	Sub Type	Description
DH-4	Initial US production D.H.4 with Liberty engine	DH-4BP-3	Fitted for photographic duties (longer range)
DH-4B	Re-positioned pilot's seat, all plywood fuselage, undercarriage moved forward	DH-4BT	Dual control trainer
		DH-4BW	Fitted with 300hp Wright-Hispano engine
DH-4B-1	DH-4B with total 118 gallon fuel capacity	DH-4M-1	Boeing-built with metal fuselage frame and revised undercarriage
DH-4B-2	DH-4B with total 83 gallon fuel capacity and self-sealing main tank	DH-4M-1K	Fitted for target towing duties
DH-4B-3	DH-4B with total 143 gallon fuel capacity	DH-4M-1T	Fitted with dual control for training
DH-4B-4	Airways version	DH-4M-2	Atlantic-built DH-4M
DH-4B-5	Fitted with rear cabin as on British D.H.4A	DH-4M-2A	Airways version
DH-4BD	Fitted for crop-dusting for Department of Agriculture	DH-4M-2K	Fitted for target towing
		DH-4M-2P	For photographic duties
DH-4BG	Fitted to lay smoke-screens and gas barrages	DH-4M-2S	DH-4M-2 fitted with supercharger
DH-4BK	Fitted for night-flying		
DH-4BM	Fitted for transport duties, DH-4BM1 (dual control) and DH-4BM2 (longer range)	DH-4M-2T	Fitted with dual controls for training
		O2B-1	DH-4M for US Marine Corps
DH-4BP-1	Fitted for photographic duties	O2B-2	O2B-1 fitted for transport duties

Post-War American Squadrons Operating the DH-4

Army Air Service Squadrons in Continental USA:

2nd Aero Squadron, 3rs Aero Squadron, 4th Aero Squadron, 5th Aero/ Observation Squadron, 6th Aero Squadron, 7th Aero/Observation Squadron, 8th Aero/Attack Squadron, 9th Aero Squadron, 11th Aero/ Bombardment Squadron, 12th Aero/Observation Squadron, 13th Attack Squadron, 15th Aero/ Observation Squadron, 16th Observation Squadron, 17th Pursuit Squadron, 18th Observation Squadron, 20th Bombardment Squadron, 22nd Observation Squadron, 23rd Bombardment Squadron, 24th Pursuit Squadron, 28th Aero Squadron, 41st Aero Squadron, 42nd Aero Squadron, 43rd Aero Squadron, 44th Aero/ Observation Squadron, 49th Aero/ Bombardment Squadron, 50th Aero/ Observation Squadron, 54th School Squadron, 55th Pursuit Squadron, 72nd Bombardment Squadron, 74th Aero Squadron, 77th Pursuit Squadron, 88th Aero/Observation Squadron, 90th Aero/Attack Squadron, 91st Aero/ Observation Squadron, 94th Aero/ Pursuit Squadron, 95th Aero/Pursuit Squadron, 96th Aero/Bombardment Squadron, 99th Aero/Observation Squadron, 104th Aero Squadron, 106th Observation Squadron, 114th Observation Squadron, 115th Observation Squadron, 118th Observation Squadron, 135th Aero/Observation Squadron, 147th Aero Squadron, 154th Observation Squadron, 166th Aero Squadron.

Army Air Service Squadrons in Hawaii:

4th Observation Squadron, 6th Pursuit Squadron, 19th Pursuit Squadron.

Army Air Service Squadrons in the Philippines:

2nd Observation Squadron, 3rd Pursuit Squadron, 28th Bombardment Squadron.

D.H.9/9A positions, and the skinning of the complete fuselage in plywood. Less noticeable was the moving forward of the undercarriage legs by 2in (5cm) or so. Contracts for such conversions were given to a variety of American manufacturers, including Boeing, Fisher, the Atlantic Aircraft Corporation, Thomas-Morse and Witteman-Lewis. Such contracts helped to keep those firms going during the lean times of the early 1920s, in much the same way that reconditioning contracts for D.H.9As helped British firms.

The D.H.4B was intended as the standard observation machine for the American services, the US Navy acquiring 177 from the War Department. Some of those were examples of the first sub-variant, the D.H.4B-1, which had an enlarged main fuel tank of 110gal (500l) capacity, supplemented by an 8gal (36l) gravity tank. The main tank capacity was increased to 135gal (614l) in the D.H.4B-3, while the D.H.4B-2 had a self-sealing tank that held 76gal (345l). Numerous other variants were produced, those other than 'one-off' experimental types being listed in the accompanying table.

Two machines were delivered as X.D.H.4B-5 and were given the nickname 'Honeymoon Express'. They had a sleeping cabin in place of the observer's position. This machine, AS.23-432, was tested at McCook Field, where it acquired the local number P76. It was entered for the New York-Toronto Air Race. JMB/GSL

Ski-undercarriages were fitted to several D.H.4Bs. This is AS.22-1128 – it was P292 at McCook Field – and was finished in the overall aluminium doping scheme that became common in the mid-1920s. The machine was withdrawn from use in 1927. JMB/GSL

Many attempts were made to modify D.H.4s for civilian use, and most resulted in an ugly-looking machine. This is the Dayton Wright Cruiser – note the position of its glazed canopy, which must have made for a limited field of vision for the pilot. It had a radiator let into its centre section; it appears that the louvres positioned at the front and top of its nose were only to allow air to reach the engine. JMB/GSL

This machine looks similar, but it had the benefit of a slightly better field of vision for the pilot. Such conversions attracted little interest among prospective civilian buyers. JMB/GSL

A more significant development appeared in 1923: the D.H.4M, the new suffix letter meaning 'modernized', indicating the switch to a metal fuselage structure. American manufacturers had been greatly impressed with the metal-framed fuselages used by some of their German counterparts during the war, and this was developed for the D.H.4 by Boeing, which was awarded a contract for 180 fuselages. The Atlantic Aircraft Corporation was a branch of the Dutch firm of Fokker, a pioneer of mass-produced metal fuselage structures, and that firm also received orders for 100 D.H.4Ms. Boeing machines were designated D.H.4M-1, and those from Atlantic D.H.4M-2. Suffix letters were added to these designations to indicated specific roles, and these are also shown in the accompanying table. Later Atlantic-built D.H.4M-2s had the undercarriage moved 7$\frac{1}{2}$in (19cm) further forwards and had larger tyres, of 30in (76cm) diameter. The US Navy received thirty Boeing-built D.H.4M-1s for the Marine Corps, and those were designated O2B-1. Four were converted for passenger work and were re-designated O2B-2.

D.H.4Bs and Ms served with the American air services throughout the world. Units in the Philippines, Hawaii and Haiti were equipped, as were a full range of units at home. O2B-1s of the Marine Corps saw active service in Nicaragua and China during anti-American uprisings during 1927. By then,

however, the design was becoming very outdated and the type was withdrawn within two years.

American D.H.4s were used in several significant flights in the years immediately following the war. During 1919, certain of these participated in and successfully completed staged flights across the continent and between New York and Alaska. The time record for a trans-continental flight was broken on 4-5 September 1922 by 1st Lt J. Doolittle, whose modified D.H.4B took only 21hr 20min to complete the journey. Modifications to his machine included the provision of a 240gal (1,090l) main tank and the fitting of an axle-wing to increase lift. D.H.4Bs were also used in early in-flight refuelling experiments and Lts L. Smith and P. Richter used that technique in October 1923 to make a non-stop flight from the US/Canadian border to Mexico.

About forty D.H.4s entered the American Civil Register, and others were used by the US Postal Service. Postal D.H.4s were converted to single-seat configuration, the pilot's cockpit being moved aft to allow room for a compartment for mail to a weight of 500lb (227kg). Some were modified especially for overnight deliveries, with lengthened exhaust pipes to prevent pilots being blinded, and landing lights fitted to the upper mainplanes. A more extreme conversion was made by LWF for both the military and the Postal Service: this was a twin-engined machine powered by a pair of

200hp Hall-Scott engines, mounted at the extremities of a widened centre-section, and a cockpit ahead of the wings. The twenty that were built were not used. When the Postal Service relinquished its D.H.4s during 1927 several were taken over by the Forestry Service for observation work, while the remainder were returned to the military. Civilian D.H.4s displayed a wide range of modifications from cabin conversions to the installation of radial engines. Several participated in the spectacular flying sequences that appeared in many 1930s movies.

A few American D.H.4s were exported. Mexico received possibly twenty ex-service D.H.4Bs during 1924, and its air force operated them for at least four years. Two others went to Nicaragua but were apparently not used. Cuba acquired six D.H.4M-1s that flew until the late 1920s.

Several D.H.4s are in existence today. Pride of place must go to the example marked as 29159, carefully restored and on display in the National Air and Space Museum, Washington DC. That machine is thought to have been the original Dayton Wright-built machine, given its number when it was presented to the Smithsonian Institute in March 1919 and brought up to operational standard. The US Air Force Museum at Dayton, Ohio has a D.H.4M-1 on display, and another is held by the National Postal Museum. There are others, but some may be replicas or re-builds that incorporate very few original parts.

CHAPTER ELEVEN

The D.H.3, D.H.10 and D.H.11

Twin-Engined Bombers

The D.H.3 and D.H.3A are brought in at this point because they were the forerunners of the only twin-engined de Havilland design to see operational service. Even while the D.H.2 was still in prototype form, de Havilland was engaged in finalizing his ideas for what was a massive machine for its day. It may have been that he had heard of the HP 0/100, requested by the Admiralty, and that he had also decided to design a twin-engined machine for bombing purposes. Many of its features were to re-emerge in the D.H.10.

The D.H.3 and D.H.3A

The novel feature of de Havilland's design was the positioning of the fuselage relative to the wings. Perhaps internal bomb stowage was needed, but the fuselage was set to hang below the wings with the lower centre-section spars passing through that component, just below the level of the upper longerons. The fuselage was made in two parts that mated just aft of the wings. The forward fuselage, as was to become standard on de Havilland's other wartime designs, was plywood skinned, while the

rear fuselage was a typical, fabric-covered wooden box girder structure. The vertical tailplane unit comprised a fin, with balanced rudder, whose profile was to become a de Havilland trademark. A large horizontal tail surface was also fitted with balanced control surfaces. The wide upper wing centre-section, under which was a gravity tank, was supported by struts from the fuselage and joined to the lower equivalent by struts that incorporated the engine mountings.

The engines were 120hp Beardmores, the logical replacements for the Austro-

The first twin-engined de Havilland design to be built was the D.H.3 numbered 7744. Initially it had twin 120hp Beardmore engines, but later it was given twin 160hp units from the same manufacturer. Fitted with these, it was known as the D.H.3A, and it is seen here in that guise. The trailing edge of the centre-section and upper mainplanes was cut away to accommodate the new four-bladed propellers: these were not fitted to crankshaft extension tubes. JMB/GSL

Specification – Airco D.H.3 AND D.H.3A

Powerplant:	Two 120hp Beardmore (D.H.3) or two 160hp Beardmore (D.H.3A); fuel capacity 140 gallons
Weights:	Empty 3,982lb (1,806kg); loaded 5,776lb (2,620kg); wing loading 7.31lb per sq ft (35.65kg per sq m)
Dimensions:	Mainplane span 60ft 10in (18.55m); mainplane gap 7ft (2.14m); chord 6ft 9in (2.06m); length 36ft 10in (11.23m); height 14ft 6in (4.42m); tailplane span 23ft 2in (7.07m); wing area 790sq ft (73.5m)
Performance:	Maximum speed 95mph (153km/h); landing speed 53mph (85km/h); climb to 6,500ft (2,000m) 24 minutes

Daimlers originally proposed. The engines were in pusher configuration, and crankshaft extensions brought the two-bladed propellers clear of the wing trailing edge. Those engines each had a frontal radiator and aluminium shields, fixed to the interplane struts, to protect the cylinder blocks. The necessarily wide mainplanes brought the span to 60ft 10in (20m). Those mainplanes were unstaggered, and each carried a long aileron along two-thirds of its span. As with the HP 0/100, these were designed to fold rearwards to ease hangarage. The main undercarriage struts were mounted under the outer centre-section struts and were supported by auxiliary struts that connected to the lower fuselage longerons.

The ground clearance was minimal, and may have accounted for the mounting of twin nose-wheels. There was to be a crew of three, the pilot sitting under the upper wing leading edge, a bomb-aimer/observer in the nose, while a gunner had a position aft of the wing training edges.

The first D.H.3 emerged during early 1916, and the serial numbers 7744 and 7745 were allocated for it and for another prototype that never reached completion.

7744 went to the testing squadron at the CFS, Upavon, during May 1916 and underwent trials at the beginning of July. By that time its engines had acquired cowlings to enclose its engines. The ensuing report, No. 36, was not unfavourable about 7744's flying characteristics, but it was apparent that the machine, as it stood, was underpowered. Nevertheless, a contract for fifty production machines was awarded to AMC that September.

By then, 7744 had been fitted with a pair of 160hp Beardmore engines that drove four-bladed propellers, in an attempt to improve performance. Some airframe modifications had also been made. The crankshaft extensions were dispensed with, necessitating the cutting away of the wing and centre-section trailing edges. No performance figures are available for this version.

The first prototype D.H.10, C8658, was also a pusher, and this frontal view shows great similarity to that of the D.H.3/D.H.3A. It retained the nose-wheel undercarriage of its predecessor. This shot shows the position of the engines, fixed to the outboard faces of the outer centre-section struts and the wide track of the undercarriage. JMB/GSL

C8658 showing the trailing edges cut out to clear the propeller arc, and the small portion of the centre-section trailing edge that was left to provide as much lifting surface as possible. JMB/GSL

C8658 showing the clean lines of the engine cowlings, the Puma engines identified by their characteristic cylinder-head castings, and the small gravity tank. The fin and rudder were of more typical de Havilland shape than those on the D.H.3A. JMB/GSL

E9057, the firm's first machine, factory-fresh outside the Daimler works, is representative of D.H.10s in war-time finish. The ply area of the forward fuselage and the metal panelling of the engine cowlings were doped in 'battleship grey'; the rest of the camouflaged areas were in PC10. JMB/GSL

The contract with AMC for fifty of the type was cancelled as production was getting under way; it has been suggested that this was the result of the D.H.4, with its superior performance, emerging shortly before. That would be a logical explanation – but another might be that the demand for Beardmore engines for the F.E.2b, and the Martinsyde G.102 programmes, were seen as having greater priority. Whatever the reason, 7744 was dismantled at Farnborough and its engines removed for use elsewhere. Despite its apparent failure, the design work undertaken was to be of value when the idea of a twin-engined bomber was revived during 1917.

Air Board Specification A.2b called for a bombing machine for the RFC that could fly at 110mph (177km/h) at 15,000ft (4,500m) and have a 500-mile (800km) range. The D.H.3 design was revived with the idea that it could be modified to take a pair of 200bhp engines. That extra power, combined with an increased wingspan, was considered

sufficient to allow the D.H.3 to achieve the ambitious performance targets set. An order for three such D.H.3s was placed with AMC during August 1917, and de Havilland set about redesigning the type. The order was revised during October, to four machines; the serial numbers C8658-C8660 and C4283 were allocated, the last to the extra, fourth, machine.

The D.H.10

The revised design was designated the D.H.10, and obviously owed much to the earlier machine. It was, however, a bit longer and of slightly greater span. The pusher configuration was retained for twin engines of the first prototype: those were 230hp Siddeley Pumas, developments of the 200hp BHP originally called for, that drove two-bladed propellers. The engines were mounted with the inner bearers carried on the centre-section struts and the outer ones overhanging the lower mainplanes; they were partly enclosed by

neat cowlings that left the cylinder blocks exposed, and again were fitted with frontal radiators. The centre-section was of greater span, and clearance for the propellers was made by cutouts in that and the upper mainplanes that left a central portion at full chord. The mainplanes and ailerons were of slightly smaller span than on the D.H.3. Twin nose-wheels were again fitted, and the rudder had the enlarged balance area of the 160hp D.H.3; the first of the four prototypes, C8658, emerged in that configuration – like the D.H.3, it had a crew of three. By this time the RFC had begun bestowing names on its machines, and the D.H.10 became the 'Amiens'.

C8658 first flew on 4 March 1918; on 7 April it went to Martlesham Heath for testing. It was under consideration as a contender for both the original bomber specification and as a Home Defence fighter, but it transpired that in its 460hp form, the D.H.10 did not meet the bomber specification, which had subsequently been upgraded; however, it did show promise for Home Defence duty. To further assess its suitability for the latter role, C8658 went from Martlesham to Marham, which housed the headquarters and C Flight of 51 Squadron, on 4 May. VI Brigade thinking, at that time, expressed a preference for the pusher configuration (for its field of vision) and a desire to equip its fighters with a cannon capable of firing a 1lb shell. No record has survived of the VI Brigade assessment of the D.H.10, but it can hardly have been favourable. The brigade wanted a machine that could reach 20,000ft (6,000m) in 45min. C8658 had a ceiling of only 18,000ft (5,500m), although it could reach 15,000ft (4,000m) in less than half an hour. Even before C8658 had been delivered to Martlesham, the contract for four prototypes had been amended to sixteen production machines, to be numbered F1867-F1882.

The second prototype, C8659, was designated 'Amiens II' – C8658 was Amiens I – and introduced design changes that were developed through to the production stage. The lack of performance in C8658 was addressed by fitting a pair of Rolls-Royce Eagle VIIIs that almost doubled the power, to 720hp. Those engines were mounted as tractors, they were completely enclosed by cowlings, and were fitted with frontal radiators that had obviously come from Eagle VIII D.H.4 stocks. The consequent change to the centre of gravity was countered by giving the mainplanes a sweepback of 2½ deg. Those mainplanes had a generous 7 deg of incidence and 4½ deg of dihedral. The twin nose-wheels were retained and clear glazed panels were set in the nose, to give vision to the observer/bomb-aimer in the prone position. That crew member was provided with a Scarff ring-mounted Lewis gun, as was the gunner in the rear position. The rear gunner's cockpit had, in de Havilland tradition, duplicated controls. C8659 did not undergo official trials at Martlesham, and in fact it may only have been completed to test the possibility of fitting the Eagle to the D.H.10 airframe; however, the scarcity of Eagle engines, and the existing demand for those available, made the possibility of a production machine so powered fairly unlikely.

More likely was a version fitted with the American Liberty engine, examples of which had reached Britain, with many others on order. The third prototype,

C8660 – 'Amiens III' – was so fitted, again with the engines as tractors and installed in large, almost box-like cowlings. The fuselage of C8660 was extended, probably as another adjustment to the centre of gravity, and it dispensed with the cumbersome-looking nose-wheels. The tip shape of its mainplanes was altered to allow the introduction of balanced ailerons. It did go to Martlesham and was used for tests that generated reports on both its handling and its engines, which by then were Liberty HC (high compression). C8660 was joined at Martlesham on 28 July by the fourth and final prototype, C4283, also powered by Liberty HCs but which introduced further modifications.

C4283, an Amiens III, was essentially the pre-production machine, though it had another slight alteration to the fuselage length and an increased span to its mainplanes; this retained the balanced ailerons, but gave it more raked tips. C8660 crashed shortly after C4283's arrival, but the fourth prototype was used to continue tests of the type, being joined for these by F1869 on 17 August. That was the third production machine, and it was completed with the engines mounted on the lower mainplane. During its stay that machine, too, underwent performance, engine and other tests, that lasted until 15 September. Even with a full military load, its performance exceeded that of the previous machines tested – it could reach 15,000ft (5,500m) in 24½ minutes, and had a speed at that height of 112mph (180km). T

he bomb-load was intended to be carried internally, with a case for six 112lb (50kg) bombs carried between the twin fuel tanks in the fuselage aft of the pilot's cockpit. Each of those fuel tanks had a propeller-driven fuel pump mounted on a pillar above the fuselage; the forward pump was offset to starboard, and the rear one to port, each feeding one engine. There were fuel feed problems at low speeds, however, when the pumps did not work efficiently, and the failure of one could lead to problems. This was compounded by the engine rev counters being placed on the inner faces of the cowlings and not on the instrument board, thus located behind the pilot and out of his immediate vision. There must have been absolute faith in the type, however, because even before those tests, orders had been placed with four other

contractors, as well as AMC, for 1,265 further examples.

Into Service

By the autumn of 1918, the RAF had plans for utilizing the D.H.10. 104 Squadron of the Independent Force would be the first to re-equip, and would be joined during 1919 by a further seven squadrons. Two squadrons with the BEF would equip with the type, and three Marine Operations squadrons, beginning with 252 Squadron in the North East, would have their D.H.6s replaced with the new type. But these plans came to almost nothing, the signing of the Armistice negating the need for their implementation.

C4283 was scheduled to go from Martlesham to join the Independent Force, so that that organization could make its own assessment. It left on 29 August, but did not reach the VIII Brigade's 3 AD at Courban until 18 September – three days after the first production D.H.10, F1867, had arrived at that depot. Both went to 104 Squadron at its Azelot base, and F1867 actually gained operational status, being flown on a raid against Saarebourg on the penultimate day of the war by Captain E. Garland. On that same day, F1868 was delivered to the BEF for evaluation.

In service, the Amiens sub types were distinguished by the addition of a suffix letter. The D.H.10 was the basic production variant, the Amiens III, with a pair of Liberty engines mounted at mid-gap position. Those completed as D.H.10As were Amiens IIIAs and also had the Liberty engines, but they were carried on the lower centre-section. The D.H.10C was essentially a D.H.10A in which a pair of Roll-Royce Eagle VIIIs replaced the Liberty engines. No photograph of the D.H.10B is known, and it is doubtful whether any were completed, but it was intended to have Eagles, and logic suggests that it bore the same resemblance to the D.H.10 as the D.H.10C did to the D.H.10A. Only D.H.10s and D.H.10As entered service, and the latter was withdrawn as obsolete in September 1921. The D.H.10 was similarly withdrawn in April 1923. Initial production machines were fitted with 900 × 200mm tyres, but 1100 × 220mm ones were soon substituted.

F1868 was also built by AMC, and was one of only three D.H.10s to reach France before the Armistice was signed: it went to the Expeditionary Force on 10 November 1918. Post war it saw service with 216 Squadron in Egypt. T. Foreman via JMB/GSL

E5557 was a D.H.10C, in which Rolls-Royce Eagle VIIIs replaced Liberty engines. The engines of this sub-variant and the D.H.10A were mounted on the inboard upper surfaces of the lower mainplanes, rather than at mid-gap position. This machine was operated by Air Travel and Transport Ltd during 1919, flying mail runs to Scotland during the railway strike of that year. JMB/GSL

A close-up of E5557's nose, with Captain G. Gathergood in the pilot's cockpit. The propellers were not 'handed'. JMB/GSL

Mail-runs were also on the agenda for the only D.H.10 to enter the British Civil Register. E5488 became G-EAJO and was part of the Air Travel and Transport fleet, in which it flew alongside E5557 (that did not acquire civilian registration). During the railway strike in the autumn of 1918, these two machines delivered mail to Scotland and the north of England. E5557 was also used as a demonstrator, in an attempt to develop the interest of foreign operators in the type; however, its exhibitions brought no orders. A solitary D.H.10 went to the USA in the 1920s and was used alongside American-built D.H.4s in the developing air-mail service.

Experimental Work

The original Home Defence scheme for mounting a cannon in aircraft was revived after the war, though the reasoning for this was uncertain. D.H.10 was delivered to the Armament Experimental Station at Orfordness and had its nose extended to accommodate a 1½lb Coventry Ordnance Works (COW) gun. That nasal extension increased the chance of the machine nosing over, and so the twin nose-wheels were revived. E5458 was joined by a similarly modified D.H.10C, E5550. That machine

Whatever the D.H.10's merits, the Armistice put an effective end to plans for its large-scale introduction. Orders were immediately cancelled, and at the end of the day, only 264 production machines were completed. The post-war run-down of the RAF saw little immediate use for the type. 120 Squadron, at Hawkinge, received some for its mail-service role, those operating alongside the unit's D.H.9s. It flew mail deliveries on the first stage of the route that connected the UK with British garrisons and bases in the Rhineland, flying to Maisoncelle in France, from where D.H.9As of 110 Squadron took over. That squadron did not last long, however, being disbanded on 21 October 1919.

A production D.H.10A with the 'battleship grey' of the forward fuselage appearing very light in the sunshine. JMB/GSL

The one and only D.H.11, H5891, is seen making one of its rare flights. Delays caused by the selection of ABC Dragonfly engines meant that it did not fly until 1920, by which time there was no demand for a new type. JMB/GSL

was delivered during April 1920, and went to Martlesham three months later. From there it went to the Marine Aircraft Experimental Establishment at Grain, still fitted with its COW gun but also used for parachute trials. For the latter purpose it was fitted with an under-fuselage housing for a Calthrop parachute. The RAE at Farnborough received D.H.10 E6042 on 25 October 1919, and used that machine in a variety of experiments that culminated in assessments of various tailplane layouts to ascertain the most suitable for twin-engined machines. The original fin and rudder were replaced by a twin unit that was fitted at various angles to the thrust line.

By 1922 the twin unit had been replaced by a single fin with a large and balanced rudder. E6042 appeared at that year's Hendon Pageant in that guise, and still in its original camouflage finish. By the same time of the following year a different outline of twin fin and rudder had been added, and the machine had been re-doped in the aluminium finish then coming into use. E6042 was the last D.H.10 in military colours. It was not withdrawn until 1926, making its final flight on 8 July of that year.

Squadron Service Post-War

The British commitment to maintaining stability on the north-west frontier of India, and upholding its mandate from the League of Nations to police the Middle East, provided a niche for the D.H.10. The need to reinforce the RAF contingent in India led to 97 Squadron being one of three units despatched to augment the existing 31 and 114 Squadrons. 97 Squadron had flown HP 0/400s with the Independent Force and had returned to the UK and Ford Junction in March 1919. It was re-equipped with D.H.10s during the following month, all from the AMC-built batch E5437-E5558, and sailed for the sub-continent in July, arriving a month later. Its machines were reassembled at its first base, Allahabad (outside Delhi), and joined in the bombing campaign that was conducted during the Third Afghan War, its machines being detached, as needed, to bases nearer the north-west frontier. The unit moved up to Lahore that November, and thence to Risalpur on 28 March 1920. Three days later it was renumbered 60

Squadron, in keeping with the RAF policy of maintaining its more famous units. The change of titles did not affect the squadron personnel and their routine remained unchanged, with crews, mechanics and machines being detached to stations such as Tank and Dardoni to conduct operations as and when tribal uprisings demanded. 112lb (50kg) bombs were the usual ordnance for such missions, although photographs show that 230lb (100kg) weapons were also used. Lewis guns were fitted to the Scarff mountings in both front and rear positions, it being common practice to 'shoot up' any concentrations of enemy tribesmen.

The D.H.10s were briefly used in what was intended to become a regular mail-run between Bombay and Karachi, but that scheme was soon abandoned because the serviceability rate was too low – spares were lacking, and the aeroplanes' performance suffered in the thinner air of the Tropics and mountains. Engine-overheating was a persistent problem, and the D.H.10s were fitted with enlarged radiators to counter this. 60 Squadron had lost several, mainly in landing accidents (e.g. E5450, E5462 and E7839),

Specification – Airco D.H.10 and D.H.10A

Powerplant: Two 400hp Liberty 12HC (both); fuel capacity 215 gallons (both)
Dimensions: Mainplane span 65ft 6in (19.98m) (both); mainplane gap 7ft (2.14m) (both); chord 7ft (2.14m) (both); length 39ft 7in (12.07m) (both); height 14ft 6in (4.42m) (both); tailplane span 22ft (6.71m) (both); wing area 837.4sq ft (77.9sq m) (both)
Weights: Empty 5,355lb (2,429kg) (D.H.10), 5,488lb (2,489kg) (D.H.10A); loaded 8,500lb (3,855kg) (both); wing loading 6.39lb per sq ft (49.49 kg per sq m) (D.H.10), 6.55lb per sq ft (49.49kg per sq m) (D.H.10A)
Performance: Maximum speed 117½mph (189km/h) (D.H.10), 128mph (210km/h) (D.H.10A); landing speed 62mph (100km.h) (both); climb to 6,500ft (2,000m) 9 minutes (D.H.10), 7 minutes (D.H.10A)

and 97 Squadron had written off E5471 after it force-landed at Tank with its bomb-load still aboard. The D.H.10s were withdrawn in April 1923, and 60 Squadron re-equipped with the D.H.9A, a move that helped create some standardization in the bombing contingent of 1 (India) Wing.

The final RAF unit to receive the D.H.10 was 216 Squadron at Abu Sueir, in Egypt. That unit had taken its HP 0/400s to the Canal Zone in July 1919, and the withdrawal of that type led to D.H.10s being supplied as replacements from April 1920. As with D.H.10s operated in India, those of 216 Squadron were fitted with enlarged radiators to counter the heat of the climate. 216 Squadron's primary role was communications, and its D.H.10s were usually unarmed. The unit inaugurated the air-mail service between Cairo and Baghdad, the headquarters of the RAF in Egypt and Mesopotamia respectively. It lost at least nine D.H.10s in accidents, most of them due to an engine failing on take-off; E9060, E9063, E9066, E9075 and E9084 were all victims of that problem. 216 Squadron re-equipped with Vimys in June 1922.

Representative D.H.10s with RAF Units

24 (Communications) Squadron Kenley – E5459.
60 Squadron Risalpur – E5450, E5453, E5456, E5460, E5462, E5464, E5466, E5484, E5490, E5507, E5509, E6040, E6050, E6053, E7839, E9058, E9065, E9081, F8428, F8430, F8439.
97 Squadron Allahabad, Lahore, Risalpur – E5438, E5450, E5453, E5456, E5460, E5461, E5462, E5464, E5466, E5471, E5486, E5490, E5507, E6040.
104 Squadron Azelot – C4283, F1867.
120 Squadron Hawkinge.
216 Squadron Abu Sueir, Heliopolis – E5507, E7845, E7846, E7847, E7851, E7854, E9060, E9061, E9062, E9063, E9066, E9067, E9070, E9077, E9080, E9084, E9085, E9090, F1868, F1871, F1875, F1877.
6 FTS Manston – E5497.

THE D.H.11 OXFORD

The quest for standardization of engines in the RFC and, later, in the RAF resulted in the Air Board selecting the untried ABC Dragonfly. That was an air-cooled radial engine that promised to deliver 320hp. The idea was sound, but the Dragonfly never lived up to its promise, and it delayed the development of many aeroplane designs that it had been selected to power; amongst those were de Havilland's last twin-engined designs for AMC, the D.H.11, and its (unbuilt) development, the D.H.12.

The D.H.11 was intended to meet requirements for both short and long-range bombers, and also a long-range fighter reconnaissance machine (Types VI, VIII and IV respectively). In attempting to match the first two of those requirements, the D.H.11 was an alternative to the D.H.10. The design was formulated in June 1918, and on 24 July the serial numbers H5891-H5893 were allocated for three prototypes.

The biplane design, of approximately the same size as the D.H.10, employed an unusually deep fuselage and the mainplanes were attached to it at the upper and lower longerons, in the manner of the later and better known Dragon and Rapide. The engines were to be mounted in nacelles that were placed on a lower centre-section. Balanced ailerons were fitted to the two-bay mainplanes, and the tail unit was of typical de Havilland shape with a balanced rudder. The disposition of the cockpits was similar to that on the D.H.10, and those for the two observer/gunners were fitted with Scarff rings for Lewis guns.

The construction of the first prototype was delayed by the lack of Dragonfly engines, and it was intended to fit a pair of Pumas instead. That never came about, and further delays ensued. One result of those was the re-allocation, on 6 September 1918, of the serials for the second and third prototypes to the pair of Sopwith Buffalos. By that time the type had been given the official name 'Oxford'. Although the airframe of H5891 was completed by early 1919, there were still no sign of the engines, and work on the other two airframes was halted by June of that year. H5891 finally flew in January 1920, and its manufacturers trials lasted until late in that year. By this time AMC had ceased to exist, and the de Havilland Company had been formed.

Specification – Airco D.H.11

Powerplant: Two 320hp ABC Dragonfly
Weights: Empty 3,795lb (1,721kg); loaded 7,000lb (3,175kg)
Dimensions: Mainplane span 60ft 2in (18.35m); length 45ft 2¼in (13.78m); height 13ft 6in (4.12m); wing area 719sq ft (66.88sq m); wing loading 9.7lb per sq ft (47.47kg per sq m)
Maximum speed c.120mph (193km/h)

APPENDIX I

Manufacturers

Production of the vast number of de Havilland types ordered by the air services was beyond the capacity of the Aircraft Manufacturing Company. As a consequence, the RNAS, RFC and RAF relied on the contributions of a large number of other contractors, many of which were either engineering firms or coach-builders. The output of those contractors exceeded that of the parent company.

Manufacturer	Address	Remarks
The Aircraft Manufacturing Co Ltd	Hendon, London	Assembly and construction of Maurice and Henri Farman designs and production of all de Havilland designs except D.H.1/1A.
Airships Ltd	Merton, Surrey	Assembly of Maurice Farman designs and construction of Submarine Scout Class airships and kite balloons.
The Alliance Aeroplane Co Ltd	Hammersmith, London	Formerly Waring & Gillow. Contracted production of D.H.9 and intended production of D.H.10.
FW Berwick & Co Ltd	Park Royal, London	Contracted production of D.H.4, D.H.9 and D.H.9A.
The Birmingham Carriage Co Ltd	Birmingham, Warwickshire	Contracted production of D.H.10.
The Blackburn Motor & Engineering Co Ltd	Brough, Yorkshire	Contracted rebuild of D.H.9A
The British Caudron Co Ltd	Cricklewood, London	Contracted production of D.H.5
The Daimler Co Ltd	Coventry, Warwickshire	Contracted production of D.H.10
The Darracq Motor Engineering Co Ltd	Fulham, London	Contracted production of D.H.5
De Havilland Aircraft Co Ltd	Stag Lane, Hertfordshire	contracted rebuild of D.H.9A
The Glendower Aircraft Co Ltd	South Kensington	London contracted production of D.H.4
The Gloucestershire Aircraft Co Ltd	Cheltenham, Gloucestershire	contracted production of D.H.6
The Grahame-White Aviation Co Ltd	Hendon, London	contracted production of D.H.6.
Handley Page Ltd	Cricklewood, London	contracted rebuild of D.H.9A
Harland & Wolff Ltd	Belfast, Antrim	contracted production of D.H.6
H.G. Hawker Engineering Co Ltd	Kingston, Surrey	contracted rebuild of D.H.9A
The Kingsbury Aviation Co	Kingsbury, London	contracted production of D.H.6
Mann Egerton & Co Ltd	Norwich, Norfolk	contracted production of D.H.9, D.H.9A and D.H.10
March Jones & Cribb Ltd	Leeds, Yorkshire	WR contracted production of D.H.5
May Harden & May Ltd	Hythe, Hampshire	Sub-contracted production of F2A
Morgan & Co	Leighton Buzzard	contracted production of D.H.6
National Aircraft Factory No.1	Waddon, Surrey	Managed by Holland, Hannen & Cubitt Contracted production of D.H.9
National Aircraft Factory No.2	Heaton Chapel, Lancashire.	Managed by Crossley Motors Contracted production of D.H.9 and D.H.10
Palladium Autocars Ltd	Putney, London	Contracted production of D.H.4
Geo Parnall & Co Ltd	Bristol, Somerset	Contracted rebuild of D.H.9A
RAF Packing Depot	Ascot, Berkshire	Contracted rebuild of D.H.9A
Ransomes Simms & Jeffries	Ipswich, Suffolk	Contracted production of D.H.6
S.E. Saunders Ltd	East Cowes, Isle of Wight	Contracted rebuild of D.H.9A
Savages Ltd	Kings Lynn, Norfolk	Contracted production of D.H.1, D.H.1A and D.H.6
Short Bros	Rochester, Kent	Contracted production of D.H.9 and rebuild of D.H.9A
Siddeley Deasey Motor Car Co Ltd	Coventry, Warwickshire	Contracted production of D.H.10
The Vulcan Motor & Engineering Co Ltd	Southport, Lancashire	Contracted production of Dh4, D.H.9 and D.H.9A
Waring & Gillow Ltd (became Alliance Aeroplane Co Ltd)	Hammersmith, London	Contracted production of D.H.4 and D.H.9
G & J Weir Ltd	Cathcart, Glasgow	Contracted production of D.H.9
Wells Aviation Co Ltd	Chelsea, London	50 D.H.9 sub-contracted from Waring & Gillow
Westland Aircraft Works	Yeovil, Somerset	Contracted production of D.H.4, D.H.9 and D.H.9A
Whitehead Aircraft Ltd	Richmond, Surrey	Contracted production of D.H.9 and D.H.9A

Serial List – Contracted Airframes

Serial numbers are given for airframes of de Havilland and Farman design ordered under contract from the Aircraft Manufacturing Company and others. Some machines switched identities, Farmans on transfer between the Military Wing and CFS, and de Havillands on transfer between the RFC and RNAS. New identities are noted in the addendum. D.H.9As 'built' in the 1920s were airframes taken out of storage, stripped down and reconditioned. They are included in this section because they were new machines when given their J-serial numbers.

Serial block	Type	Mfr	Ordered	Delivered	Remarks
23	MF 7	AMC	1	1	For RFC Naval Wing
67	MF 7	AMC	1	1	For RFC Naval Wing
69–70	MF 7	AMC	2	2	For RFC Naval Wing
71–73	MF7	AMC	3	3	Floatplanes
91–92	MF 7	AMC	2	0	Order cancelled
139–144	F.22	AMC	6	6	For RFC Naval Wing
188	MF 7	AMC	1	1	For RFC Naval Wing
207	MF	AMC (assembled?)	1	1	Possibly French origin
403	MF	AMC	1	1	Possibly French origin
214–216	MF 7	AMC	3	3	For RFC Military Wing (MW)
223–224	MF 7	AMC	2	2	For RFC MW
246	MF 7	AMC	1	1	For RFC MW
266	MF 7	AMC	1	1	For RFC MW. To CFS as 472
269–270	MF 7	AMC	2	2	For RFC MW
274	F.20	AMC	1	1	For RFC MW
302	MF 7	AMC	1	1	For RFC MW
305–307	MF 7	AMC	3	3	For RFC MW
322	MF 7	AMC	1	1	For RFC MW
337–338	MF 7	AMC	2	2	For RFC MW
342–345	MF 11	AMC	4	4	For RFC MW
350–352	F.20	AMC	3	3	For RFC MW
355–360	MF 7	AMC	6	6	For RFC MW
363	F.20	AMC	1	1	For RFC MW
369–371	MF 11	AMC	3	3	For RFC MW
376	MF 7	AMC	1	1	Foe RFC MW
379	MF 11	AMC	1	1	For RFC MW
410–411	MF 7	AMC	2	2	For CFS
415	MF 7	AMC	1	1	For CFS
418	MF 7	AMC	1	1	For CFS
425–429	MF 7	AMC	5	5	For CFS
431	MF 7	AMC	1	1	For CFS
434–435	F.20	AMC	2	2	For CFS
440	F.20	AMC	1	1	For CFS
444–445	F.20	AMC	2	2	For CFS
450–451	MF 7	AMC	2	2	For CFS
455–456	F.20	AMC	1	1	For CFS
458–459	MF 7	AMC	2	2	For CFS
461	F.20	AMC	1	1	For CFS. To RFC MW as 328
463–464	MF 7	AMC	2	2	For CFS
467	F.20	AMC	1	1	For CFS

Serial block	Type	Mfr	Ordered	Delivered	Remarks
476–478	MF 7	AMC	3	3	For CFS
480–481	MF 11	AMC	2	2	For CFS
490	MF 7	AMC	1	1	For CFS
494–496	MF S7	AMC	3	3	For CFS
498–501	MF S7	AMC	4	4	For RFC
502–513	F.20	AMC	12	12	For RFC
514–518	MF S11	AMC	5	5	For RFC
519–539	MF 7	AMC	21	21	For RFC
540–545	MF 11	AMC	6	6	For RFC
546–557	MF 7	AMC	12	12	For RFC
558–566	F.20	AMC	9	9	For RFC
610	MF 7	AMC	1	1	For RFC
633	MF 11	AMC	1	1	For RFC
653	F.20	AMC	1	1	For RFC
661	MF 7	AMC	1	1	For RFC
669	F.20	AMC	1	1	For RFC
679	MF 7	AMC	1	1	For RFC
680	F.20	AMC	1	1	For RFC
707	MF 11	AMC	1	1	For RFC
708	F.20	AMC	1	1	For RFC
712–713	MF 7	AMC	2	2	For RFC
720	F.20	AMC	1	1	For RFC
735	MF 7	AMC	1	1	For RFC
739	MF 7	AMC	1	1	For Remarks
742	MF 11	AMC	1	1	For RFC
744	MF	AMC	1	1	For RFC
909–914	MF 7	AMC	6	6	For RNAS, last 5 to RFC
2460	MF	AMC	1	1	For Indian Government
2832	F.20	AMC	1	1	For RFC
2838	F.20	AMC	1	1	For RFC
2844	F.20	AMC	1	1	For RFC
2851	F.20	AMC	1	1	For RFC
2940–2959	MF 11	AMC	20	20	For RFC
2960–3000	MF 7	AMC	41	41	For RFC as trainers
3696–3697	D.H.4	AMC	2	2	For RFC
4001–4019	MF 7	AMC	19	19	For RFC as trainers
4220	D.H.1	AMC	1	1	Prototype
4600–4648	D.H.1/1A	Savage Ltd	49	49	Initial deliveries as D.H.1a
4732	D.H.2	AMC	1	1	Prototype
5335–5383	D.H.2	AMC	49	0	Not taken up
5880–5909	MF 11	AMC	30	30	For RFC as trainers
5916–6015	D.H.2	AMC	100	100	Initial production
6678–6727	MF 7	AMC	50	50	For RFC as trainers
7346–7395	MF 11	AMC	50	50	For RFC as trainers
7396–7445	F.20	AMC	50	50	For RFC as trainers
7744–7745	D.H.3	AMC	2	1	7744 only delivered
7746–7749	F.20	AMC	4	4	Assembled from French parts
7752–7755	F.20	AMC	4	4	Assembled fro French parts
7842–7941	D.H.2	AMC	100	100	Second production batch
A324–A373	MF 11	AMC	50	50	For RFC as trainers
A728	MF 11	AMC?	1	1	For RFC as trainer
A904–A953	MF 11	AMC	50	50	For RFC as trainers
A1611–A1660	D.H.1	Savage Ltd	50	50	Not all issued
A1712–A1741	F.20	AMC	30	30	For RFC as trainers

Serial block	Type	Mfr	Ordered	Delivered	Remarks
A2125–A2174	D.H.4	AMC	50	50	Initial production
A2433–A2532	MF 11	AMC	100	100	For RFC as trainers
A3295–A3302	MF 11	AMC	8	8	Floatplanes for SAG Loch Doon
A4061–A4160	MF 11	AMC	100	100	For RFC as trainers
A5088–A5137	D.H.3A	AMC	50	0	Cancelled
A5172	D.H.5	AMC	1	1	Prototype
A5175–A5176	D.H.6	AMC	2	1?	Prototypes
A6801–A6900	MF 11	AMC 100	100	100	For RFC as trainers
A7001–A7100	MF 7	AMC	100	100	For RFC as trainers
A7401–A8090	D.H.4	AMC	690	690	A7559 to D.H.9 prototype
A9163–A9362	D.H.5	AMC	200	199	A9362 cancelled
A9363–A9562	D.H.5	Darracq	200	200	
A9563–A9762	D.H.6	Grahame–White	200	200	Initial production
B331–B380	D.H.5	British Caudron	50	50	
B1389	D.H.2	AMC	1	1	
B1401–B1500	F.20	AMC	100	80	Last 20 cancelled
B1482	D.H.4	AMC	1	1	Replacement machine
B1951–B2050	MF 11	AMC	100	100	For RFC as trainers
B2051–B2150	D.H.4	Berwick & Co	100	100	
B2601–B3100	D.H.6	AMC	500	500	
B3955–B3967	D.H.4	Westland	0	13	Ex-RNAS (see addendum)
B3987	D.H.4	Westland	0	1	Ex-RNAS
B4651–B4850	MF 11	AMC	200	200	For RFC as trainers
B4901–B5000	D.H.5	March Jones & Cribb	100	100	
B5451–B5550	D.H.4	Vulcan	100	100	
B7581–B7680	D.H.9	Westland Aircraft	100	100	B7664 converted to D.H.9A
B9031–B9130	D.H.6	AMC	100	4	Balance cancelled
B9331–B9430	D.H.9	Vulcan	100	100	
B9434–B9439	D.H.4	Westand	0	6	Ex-RNAS (see addendum)
B9456	D.H.4	Westland	0	1	Ex-RNAS
B9458	D.H.4	Westland	0	1	Ex-RNAS (see addendum)
B9460–B9461	D.H.4	Westland	0	2	Ex-RNAS (see addendum)
B9470	D.H.4	Westland	0	1	Ex-RNAS (see addendum)
B9476–B9500	D.H.4	Westland	25	25	
C1051–C1150	D.H.4	Vulcan	100	0	Contract cancelled
C1151–C1450	D.H.9	Weir Ltd	300	300	
C1951–C2150	D.H.6	Grahame–White	200	200	
C2151–C2230	D.H.9	Berwick & Co	80	80	
C4283	D.H.10	AMC	1	1	Fourth prototype
C4501–C4550	D.H.4	AMC	50	50	10 delivered as spares
C5126–C5275	D.H.6	Kingsbury Aviation	150	150	
C5451–C5750	D.H.6	Harland & Wolff	300	100	Balance cancelled
C6050–C6350	D.H.9	AMC	300	298	C6122 & 6350 D.H.9A prototype
C6501–C6700	D.H.6	Morgan & Co	200	200	
C6801–C6900	D.H.6	Savages Ltd	100	100	
C7201–C7600	D.H.6	Ransomes Simms etc	400	250	Balance cancelled
C7601–C7900	D.H.6	Grahame–White	300	300	
C8658–C8660	D.H.10	AMC	3	3	First 3 prototypes

Serial block	Type	Mfr	Ordered	Delivered	Remarks
C9336–C9485	D.H.6	Gloucestershire	150	150	
D451–D950	D.H.9	NAF No.1 (Cubitt)	500	246	Balance cancelled
D951–D1000	D.H.6	Grahame–White	50	50	Spares to assemble Egypt
D1001–D1500	D.H.9	NAF No.2 (Crossley)	500	444	Balance cancelled
D1651–D1750	D.H.9	Mann Egerton & Co	100	100	
D1751–D1775	D.H.4	Westland	25	25	
D2776–D2875	D.H.9	Short Bros	100	100	
D2876–D3275	D.H.9	AMC	400	400	
D4011–D4210	D.H.9	Weir Ltd	200	0	Cancelled
D5551–D5850	D.H.9	Waring & Gillow	300	300	50 built by Wells Aviation
D5951–D6050	D.H.9	Westland	100	0	Cancelled
D7201–D7300	D.H.9	Westland	100	48	Balance cancelled
D7301–D7400	D.H.9	Berwick & Co	100	80	30 as spares
D8351–D8430	D.H.4	AMC	80	80	
D8581–D8780	D.H.6	AMC	200	0	Cancelled
D9231–D9280	D.H.4	AMC	50	50	
D9800–D9899	D.H.9	Weir Ltd	100	85	Balance cancelled
E701–E1100	D.H.9A	Whitehead Aircraft	400	340	Balance cancelled
E4624–E4628	D.H.4	AMC	5	5	
E5437–E5636	D.H.10	AMC	200	122	Balance cancelled
E6037–E6136	D.H.10	Birmingham Carriage	100	19	Balance cancelled
E7837–E7986	D.H.10	Siddeley Deasey	150	28	Balance cancelled
E8407–E8806	D.H.9A	AMC	400	400	
E9057–E9206	D.H.10	Daimler Co	150	40	Balance cancelled
E9657–E9756	D.H.9A	Mann Egerton & Co	100	100	
E9857–E9956	D.H.9A	Vulcan	100	100	
F1–F300	D.H.9A	NAF No.1 (Cubitt)	300	0	Cancelled
F351–F550	D.H.10	NAF No2 (Crossley)	200	12	Balance cancelled
F951–F1100	D.H.9A	Westland	150	150	
F1551–F1552	D.H.4	AMC	2	2	
F1603–F1652	D.H.9A	Westland	50	50	
F1867–F1882	D.H.10	AMC	16	16	
F2633–F2732	D.H.4	Glendower	100	100	
F2733–F2902	D.H.9A	Berwick & Co	170	140	Balance cancelled
F3346–F3441	D.H.6	AMC	96	96	
F5699–F5798	D.H.4	Palladium	100	100	
F7147–F7346	D.H.10	Alliance Aeroplane Co	200	0	Presumed all cancelled
F7597–F7598	D.H.4	AMC	2	2	
F8421–F8495	D.H.10	Mann Egerton & Co	75	32	Balance cancelled
H1–H200	D.H.9A	AMC	200	169	Balance cancelled
H2746–H2945	D.H.10	AMC	200	0	Presumed all cancelled
H3196–H3395	Dh9	Naf No1 (Cubitt)	200	0	Cancelled
H3396–H3545	D.H.9A	Westland	150	150	
H3546–H3795	D.H.9A	Vulcan	250	120	Balance cancelled
H4316	D.H.9	AMC	1	0	Cancelled
H4320–H4369	D.H.9	Berwick & Co	50	50	Cancelled
H5290	D.H.4	AMC	1	1	
H5891–H5893	D.H.11	AMC	1	1	Prototype, others cancelled
H5894–H5939	D.H.4	Palladium	46	46	
H7563–H7612	D.H.9	Weir	50	0	Cancelled
H8263	D.H.4	Palladium	1	1	
H7913–H8112	D.H.9	NAF No2 (Crossley)	200	0	Cancelled
J401–J450	D.H.9A	Westland	50	0	Cancelled

Serial block	Type	Mfr	Ordered	Delivered	Remarks
J551–J600	D.H.9A	Mann Egerton & Co	50	50	
J1937	D.H.15	AMC	1	1	Prototype
J1938–J1939	D.H.14	AMC	2	2	Prototypes
J1940	D.H.14A	AMC	1	1	Prototype to civil register
J5192–J5491	D.H.9A	AMC	300	0	Cancelled
J6585	Tadpole	Armstrong Whitworth	1	1	Ex-D.H.9A E8522
J6957–J6962	D.H.9A	Westland	6	6	Rebuilds with Lion engines
J6963–J6968	D.H.9A	Handley–Page	6	6	Rebuilds
J7008–J7017	D.H.9A	De Havilland	10	10	Rebuilds
J7018–J7032	D.H.9A	Handley–Page	15	15	Rebuilds
J7033–J7072	D.H.9A	Westland	40	40	Rebuilds
J7073–J7087	D.H.9A	Gloucestershire	15	15	Rebuilds
J7088–J7102	D.H.9A	HG Hawker	15	15	Rebuilds
J7103–J7127	D.H.9A	RAF Packing Depot	25	25	Rebuilds
J7249–J7258	D.H.9A	Gloucestershire	10	10	Rebuilds
J7302–J7309	D.H.9A	De Havilland	8	8	Rebuilds
J7310–J7321	D.H.9A	HG Hawker	12	12	Rebuilds
J7327–J7346	D.H.9A	Westland	20	20	Rebuilds
J7347–J7356	D.H.9A	Gloucestershire	10	10	Rebuilds
J7604–J7615	D.H.9A	HG Hawker	12	12	Rebuilds
J7700	D.H.9A	De Havilland	1	1	Rebuild
J7787–J7798	D.H.9A	De Havilland	12	12	Rebuilds
J7799–J7819	D.H.9A	Westland	21	21	Rebuilds
J7823–J7834	D.H.9A	Short Bros	12	12	Rebuilds
J7835–J7854	D.H.9A	HG Hawker	20	20	Rebuilds
J7855–J7866	D.H.9A	Westland	12	12	Rebuilds
J7867–J7876	D.H.9A	HG Hawker	10	10	Rebuilds
J7877–J7883	D.H.9A	De Havilland	7	7	Rebuilds
J7884–J7890	D.H.9A	Short Bros	7	7	Rebuilds
J8096–J8128	D.H.9A	Westland	33	33	Rebuilds
J8129–J8153	D.H.9A	De Havilland	25	25	Rebuilds, 6 with metal wings
J8154–J8171	D.H.9A	Short Bros	18	18	Rebuilds
J8172–J8189	D.H.9A	Parnall	18	18	Rebuilds
J8190–J8207	D.H.9A	S.E. Saunders	18	18	Rebuilds
J8208–J8225	D.H.9A	Blackburn	18	18	Rebuilds
J8460–J8482	D.H.9A	Westland	23	23	Rebuilds
J8483–J8494	D.H.9A	Parnall	12	12	Rebuilds
N2530–N2554 N4530–N4554	F2A	AMC	25	0	Replaced by
N4530–N4554	F2A	May Harden & May	25	25	Under sub–contract from AMC
N5960–N6009	D.H.4	Westland	50	50	See addendum for transfers
N6380–N6429	D.H.4	Westland	50	50	See addendum for transfers
N9500–N9535	Walrus	Westland	36	36	Only production batch

ADDENDUM

Re-serialled MF Se.7 Longhorns
266 was transferred from the Military Wing to the CFS and renumbered 472.

Re-serialled MF Se.11 Shorthorns
343 was transferred from the Military Wing to the CFS and re-numbered 464.

Re-serialled HF F.20s
461 was transferred to the Military Wing from the CFS and re-numbered 328.

Re-serialled D.H.2s
6014 was given the RNAS number 8725 during its evaluation by that service, but resumed its original identity on return o the RFC.

The un-numbered D.H.2 (and possibly non-contracted) with a 110hp Le Rhone was numbered A305 at 1 AD St Omer.

Re-serialled D.H.4s
3696 assumed the RFC identity B394.
N5970, N5980, N5986–87, NN990–91, N5994–95, N5998–99, N6002–03 and N6006 assumed the RFC identities B3955–B3967 on transfer. N6007 was intended to assume the RFC identity B3968 but was destroyed before transfer.

N6380, N6382–87, N6393, N6397, N6401, N6405 and N6409 assumed to RFC identities B3987, B9434–39, B9456, B9458 and B9460–61 on transfer.

RECONSTRUCTED AIRFRAMES

The increased wastage rate of machines, through operational damage or training accidents, led to the practice, from mid-1917, of reconstruction wherever possible. Minor damage could often be repaired at unit level, but more serious damage required repair at an Aircraft Depot in France or an Aircraft Repair Depot at home: in this case it became standard practice to issue a new serial from blocks of numbers reserved for that purpose. Some reconstructions at home were carried out at unit level or at the relevant Wing Aircraft Repair Section. Post-war, reconstructions of D.H.9As were made on a contractual basis and blocks of new J-serials allocated. These are noted in Appendix II. Post-war, reconstructions made by the Aircraft Depot at Aboukir, in Egypt, were distinguished by the insertion of the letter R (for reconstruction) after prefix letter of the serial. Known reconstructed and re-serialled machines are as follows:

MF Se.7 Longhorn
5617, B3982.

MF Se.11 Shorthorn
5718, A1711, A2175, A9162, A9921, B1483, B3981, B3988, B8788, B8793, B8815, B9433, B9441, B9442, B9443, B9466, B9475, B9956, B9991, B9996, B9999, C3499, C4278, E9986, E9987, E9988, E9998, F2183, F2184, F2185, F2186, F2187, F2230.

HF F.20
A3022.

Airco D.H.1
A5211, A9919, B1389 and B3969.

Airco D.H.2
B8824.

Airco D.H.4
B774, B775, B776, B882, B884, B7747, B7764, B7768, B7812, B7818, B7819, B7826, B7854, B7857, B7865, B7866, B7871, B7878, B7885, B7891, B7895, B7910, B7911, B7925, B7933, B7937, B7938, B7939, B7940, B7941, B7942, B7950, B7951, B7962, B7964, B7966, B7967, B7969, B7976, B7977, B7982, B7985, B7986, B7987, B7991, B7992, B7993, B7996, B8005, B8013, B8016, B8091, B8125, B9471, B9951, B9994, F5825, F5826, F5827, F5828, F5829, F5930, F5831, F5832, F5833, F5834, F5835, F5836, F5837, F5838, F5839, F5840, F6000, F6001, F6002, F6003, F6004, F6059, F6070, F6075, F6076, F6077, F6078, F6096, F6099, F6103, F6104, F6114, F6119, F6120, F6133, F6136, F6139, F6164, F6165, F6166, F6167, F6168, F6169, F6186, F6187, F6207, F6209, F6212, F6214, F6215, F6222, F6232, F6234, F6236, F6511, F6512, F6513, H6858, H6859, H6873, H6881, H6882, H6885, H6887, H7118, H7119, H7120, H7121, H7122, H7123, H7124, H7125, H7147, H7148.

Airco D.H.5
B897, B7750, B7753, B7762, B7775, B9468, B9942.

Airco D.H.6
B8789, B8790, B8799, B8800, B9472, B9992, C3506, C4281, C9994.

Airco D.H.9
B7749, B7886, B7912, B7945, B8854, F5841, F5842, Ff5843, Ff5844, Ff5845, F5846, F5847, F5848, F5849, F5850, F6054, F6055, F6057, F6065, F6066, F6072, F6073, F6074, F6095, F6098, F6112, F6113, F6125, F6141, F6170, F6171, F6172, F6183, F6196, F6205, F6213, F6231, F6237, F6239, F6450, F6451, F6452, F6453, H7075, H7076, H7180, H7201, H7202, H7203

Airco D.H.9A
F9515, H7107, H7204, ER731, ER792, ER850, ER928, ER959, ER968, ER8599, ER8615, ER8637, ER8642, ER8649, ER8733, ER8736, ER8744, ER9887, ER9956, FR2763, FR2857, HR82, HR85, HR93, HR3501, HR3545, HR3551, JR7024, JR7063, JR7070, JR7084, JR7093, JR7106, JR7107, JR7249, JR7339, JR7796, JR7825, JR7873, JR8186, JR8189, JR8206.

Index

Addison, Lt R 126
Adun-le Roman 65
Aeronautical Inspection Directorate 13
Aeronautical Syndicate 9
Aeroplane Supply Company 9
Aeroplanes
Airco DH1/1A 12–13, 27–33, 48
Airco DH2 12–13, 22, 29, 32–47, 74–5, 77, 169
Airco DH3 13, 48–9, 74, 169–70, 172
Airco DH3A 169
Airco DH4 13, 26, 45, 48, 73, 74–5, 85, 99–102, 104, 111, 114, 122, 132, 139, 141, 159–60
Airco DH5 13, 45–6, 74–85
Airco DH6 13, 85–98, 111, 113–4, 141
Airco DH9 14, 26, 64–6, 97, 99–132, 141, 163
Airco DH9A 14, 99, 120–1, 124, 132–57, 178
Airco DH10 13, 48, 97, 120, 132, 156, 169–178
Airco DH11 176, 178
Airco DH14 14, 138, 140
Airco DH15 14, 66, 138, 140
Albatros D.1 32, 42–5
Albatros D.II 44
Albatros D.III 44, 47, 77
Albatros D.V 78
Armstrong Whitworth FK3 46, 113, 122
Armstrong Whitworth FK8 122
Armstrong Whitworth Tadpole 146
Avro 504A/J/K 46, 66, 83, 85, 88–9, 113, 150
B.S.1 12, 32
Blackburn Kangaroo 141–2
Bleriot 50–hp 13
Boulton Paul Sidestrand 151
Breguet 14 162
Bristol Boxkite 8
Bristol F2A/F2B 45, 47, 53, 77, 114, 149, 156, 159
Cody V Biplane 11
Curtiss JN3 90
Curtiss JN4 (Can) 90, 92
Dayton Wright Cruiser 167
DFW C.V 81, 118
DH4 (American-built) 159–68
DH Comet 14
DH Dragon 14
DH Hornet 14
DH Mosquito 14 , 63
DH Moth 14
DH Rapide 14
DH Sea Vixen 14
DH Vampire 14

DH Venom 14
DH108 14
Fairey IIIF 155
Fairey Fawn 150
Fairey Gordon 150–1
F.E.1 12
FE2 12, 27
Felixstowe F2A 13, 25–6, 68, 102, 132
Fokker D.III 42
Fokker E.I 13, 32
Fokker E.III 42
Grahame-White GW 15
Halberstadt D.1 32
Halberstadt D.II 47
Handley-Page 58, 62, 92, 169–70
Handley-Page 114, 132, 139, 159, 178
Hawker Hart 151
Henri Farman F.20 10, 18–20, 29
Loening COA-1 164
Martinsyde G.100/102 55, 66, 123, 172
Maurice Farman 70-hp Biplane 9, 10
Maurice Farman Se. 11 'Shorthorn' 19–25, 85
Maurice Farman Se.7 'Longhorn' 15–18, 22, 85
Nieuport 17 44–5
Pfalz D.III 77
RAF BE1 11, 12
RAF BE2 10, 11, 18, 20
RAF BE2c 12, 30, 37, 46, 71, 122
RAF BE2d 12
RAF BE2e 12, 66, 111, 123–4
RAF BE12 46, 122–23
RAF FE2a 27
RAF FE2b 28–9, 41, 43, 45–6, 48, 53, 62, 66, 114–5, 172
RAF FE2d 29, 53, 102
RAF FE8 22, 29, 44, 46, 77
RAF RE7 66
RAF RE8 66, 71, 111, 113, 123
RAF SE5/5a 47, 76–7, 80, 83
Roland C.II 44
Salmson 2A–2 162
S.E.1 12
S.E.2 12, 13
Sopwith Types 9400 & 9700 (1_ Strutter) 70, 113, 141, 159
Sopwith Pup 44–6, 77, 83
Sopwith Camel 76–7, 83
Sopwith Triplane 45
Sopwith Buffalo 178
SPAD S.VII 53, 71
SPAD XIII 160
USD-9A 161, 163
Vickers ES.1 39
Vickers FB.5 32, 35, 39, 46
Vickers Vernon 155

Vickers Vimy 97, 132, 150, 178
Westland Walrus 148
Westland Wapiti 151, 157–58
Aeroplanes Henri et Maurice Farman 9
Agnew, 2Lt CF 78
Air Battalion, Royal Engineers 9
Aircraft Disposal Company 128
Aircraft Production Board 133, 159–60
Air Park 21
Air Transport & Travel 14, 73, 126, 174
Aircraft Manufacturing Company (AMC/Airco) 7, 9, 13–15, 17–18
Airships Ltd 9, 13, 24
Aizelwood, Capt LP 42, 44
Albert 60
Allenby, General 123–4
Amiens 60–1
Anderson, Capt GB 46
Anderson, Capt WF 126
Andrews, lt/Capt JO 37, 39, 41–3
Appleby, 2Lt PE 118
Archer, Lt EAC 36
Armstrong Whitworth 7, 11
Army Aircraft Factory 12
Army Balloon Factory 8, 12
Arnold, 2Lt J 117
Arnot, 2Lt TC 46
Ashby, Sgt S 46
Ashton, 2Lt KH 119
Astra Torres 9, 24
Atlantic Aircraft Corporation 166, 168
Aulnoy 109
Australian War Memorial 126
Auxiliary Air Force 158
Aviation Militaire Belge 128–130
Avricourt 138
Avro 7
Bainbridge, 2Lt EF 42
Bapaume 109
Barber, Horation 9
Barclay, Capt WEB 55
Barney, Lt LW 46
Barrett, Capt EW 39
Bartlett, Flt Comm CPO 57
Beale, 2Lt E 117
Bean, Lt WS 71
Beanlands, Capt BPG 77, 83
Beaufort, 2Lt FH 117, 119
Begbie, Lt 44
Begg, 2Lt HB 43
Bell, Capt J 80
Benge, 2Lt AN 44
Benjamin, Lt AL 119
Bensdorf 66, 115Benson, 2Lt DG 117

Bertry 109
Berwick, FW & Co 102
Bettembourg 65, 120
Bevillers 109
Bewick, FW 51
Billancourt 9
Binning, Captain 24
Birmingham Small Arms Company (BSA) 14
Bir Salmana 31
Black, Lt SMcB 119
Blackburn Aeroplane & Motor Co Ltd 98
Blaxill, 2Lt FH 115
Bleckley, 2Lt ER 161
Bleriot, Louis 7
Blower, Lt EW 126
Blythe, 2Lt H 4
Board, Major AG 34
Body, Lt GC 118
Boddy, Lt JAV 81
Bodley, 2Lt WGL 137
Boeing 166, 168
Boelcke, Ltn O 42–3
Bolling Commission 159–60
Bolling, Col RC 159
Bolton, Capt AC 43
Bond, 2Lt TJ 120
Bonn 66
Boeree, Capt AR 132
Boulay 119, 136
Bourlon Wood 80–1
Bouvincourt 61
Bowling, Lt VM 45
Bowman, 2Lt/Sqn Ldr GH 42, 153
Bowring, 2Lt JV 42
Bragg, Lt EC 71
Brain, 2Lt WJ 137
Brandrick, 2Lt A 137
Brearley, 2Lt N 43
Breslau 70
Bridger, 2Lt H 121
Brie 61
Brie, Lt RAC 120
Briggs, Lt LR 42
Brisbin, Lt HV 137
British & Colonial Aeroplane Co 8
Britton, 2Lt WKM 44
Broadbent, Lt G 120
Brooke, Lt LS 137
Brown, Lt 30
Bruce, Lt W 115
Bruges 58, 70, 110
Brush Electrical Engineering Co Ltd 18
Bryant, 2Lt SO 119
Brydon, Pte J 120
Buhl 120
Bullock, 2Lt RN 54
Burbach 63, 66

Burroughes, Hugh 13
Burton, Lt LM 95
Burton, 2Lt SG 119
Bush, Capt JS de I 78
Busigny 109
Busk, ET 11
Byrne, Lt PAL 42
Byron, Lt 54
Cadbury, Major E 69
Caldicott, 2Lt R 63
Cambrai 56, 79, 83
Campbell, 2Lt ID 83
Campbell, 2Lt J 65
Canadian Air Force 141
Canberra 126
Capon, Lt RS 41
Cardington 158
Carr, Sergeant 13
Carroll, Lt JM 63
Carter, 2Lt LL 44
Cartwright, Lt E 114, 120
Case, 2Lt BN 121
Casey, Lt RF 136
Castle, 2Lt GF 63
Castor, AM3 RG 71
Cattaro 123
Cave, 2Lt EA 36
Central Flying School, AFC 92
Chapin, Lt EA 117
Charleroi 64
Chateau Salins 138
Chaulnes 61, 107
Chisolm, Capt JF 111
Chivers, 2Lt W 78
Clappen, Lt DW 67
Clark, 2Lt DG 80
Clark, 2Lt FS 79
Clark, 2Lt WB 44
Clarke, Capt AC 40
Clarke, Capt EE 47
Claye, Lt CG 118
Clery 109
Cobden, Lt FP 118
Cockerell, Sgt/2Lt S 42, 44, 46, 77
Cockman, Lt HJ 137
Coffin, Howard 159
Cole, 2Lt DB 161
Cole, 2Lt MH 117
Collishaw, Sqn Ldr R 153
Cologne 65–6, 136–7
Conflans 120
Coningham, Capt A 77
Conneau, Lieutenant 8
Connolly, Sgt Mechanic M 70
Cooch, Lt TA 45–6
Cook, 2Lt AB 54
Cook, 2Lt HC 97
Coombs, Lt VC 54
Corbett, Lt R 43
Corkery, 2Lt JP 71
Cornell, 2Lt HC 81
Cornish, 2Lt WO 78
Cotton, FS 140
Courcelles 120
Coutrai 108
Coventry Ordnance Works 11
Cowan, 2Lt/Lt SE 39–43
Coward, 2Lt GB 70
Crawford, Lt WC 43
Crawford, Lt K 43, 46
Cremetti, 2Lt MAE 67
Crooy, Adjutant L 128
Cross, 2Lt JH 45

Crossley Motors 102
Cruikshank, 2Lt KG 77
Crystal Palace Engineering School 10
Cunningham Captain JA 35
Cunningham, 2Lt PJ 65
Curlewis, 2Lt I 42–3
Curphey, 2Lt/Capt WGS 41, 44, 46
Curtiss Aeroplanes Ltd 90
Cutler, Lt HC 46
Daily Graphic (newspaper) 7
Daily Mail (newspaper) 7, 8
Daimler Company 12
Daly, Capt APV 44
Damascus 124
Dance, 2Lt CC 107
Darmstadt 65
Darracq Motor Engineering Co Ltd 75
Darwin 126
Dashwood, FO EJ 157
Davies, 2Lt DP 137
Davis, 2Lt HC 117
Davis, 2Lt HD 44
Dawes, Major L 37
Dayton-Wright 160
Deetjen, Lt WL 117
De Havilland Aircraft Company 14
De Havilland, Charles 10
De Havilland, Geoffrey 14
De Havilland, Geoffrey 8, 11–13, 27, 32
De Havilland, Hereward 12, 14
De Havilland, John 14
De Havilland, Louie 12
De Havilland, Peter 14
Dennis, 2Lt LR 119
Der'a Junction 123
Deutsche Luftahrt Sammlung 158
Dhatta Khal 156
Dieuze 115
Dillinghem 64, 116, 120
Dixon, Captain Bertram 8
Dixon, 2Lt G 89, 113
Dobson, Sgt EH 41
Doige, 2Lt EL 115, 119
Doolittle, 1Lt J 168
Douai 61
Dougall, Lt NS 70
Douglas, Flt Sgt 97
Dray, AC1 WH 106
Driver, 2Lt PS 56
Ducray, Lt MJ 118
Dunkerque 70
Dunn, 2Lt MA 120
Dunn, 2Lt MW 137
Durazzo 123
Duren 65
Eccles, Lt CG 46
Edwards, 2Lt HJ 78
Edwards L Mech WJ 58
Ehrang 65–6
Elwig, 2Lt HJC 137
Engines
    100–hp Gnome 13, 32–3, 35, 37, 42–3, 83
    100–hp Green 27
    160–hp Gnome 20
    60–hp Renault 11
    60–hp Wolseley 11
    70–hp Renault 16, 17, 21–2, 25, 27, 29
    80–hp Gnome 18

80–hp Le Rhone 18, 22
80–hp Renault 16, 21–2, 28–9, 88, 94
90–hp RAF 1a 85, 88, 94
90–hp Curtiss OX-2 94
90–hp Curtiss OX-5 88, 92, 94
110–hp Berliet 26
110–hp Le Rhone 43, 74, 76, 83–4
120–hp Austro-Daimler 171
120–hp Beardmore 28, 31, 169–70
130–hp Clerget 84
140–hp Hispano-Suiza 25
160–hp Beardmore 169–70
200–hp BHP 48–9, 55, 58, 68, 70, 100, 122, 172
200–hp RAF 3a 51–2, 54–5
230–hp Siddeley Puma 51–2, 102, 172
230–hp Galloway Adriatic 51, 102, 104
250–375–hp Rolls Royce Eagle 49–52, 54, 58, 61, 63, 68, 70, 72, 132, 134, 160, 173–74, 176
260–hp Fiat A-12 51, 56, 102, 104
320–hp ABC Dragonfly 178
400–hp Liberty 61, 132–34, 160, 163, 173, 176–7
450–hp Napier Lion 126, 140
500–hp Galloway Atlantic 140
520–hp Rolls-Royce Condor 140
ENV 12
Ermerchicourt 109
Escott, AM2 WH 115
Etreux 109
Evans, 2Lt ARW 137
Evans 2Lt HC 41–2, 44
Exley, 2Lt GA 44
Eyre, 2Lt HC 137
Farman Maurice 7
Farman, Henri 7, 9
Faure, Lt D 44
Fawcett Captain 17
Fish, 2Lt WR 78
Fisher Body Division, General Motors 160, 166
Fitzgerald, 2Lt WW 54
Flavy-le-Martel 107
Flesquieres 79
Flights
    404 Flt 93
    420 Flt 148
    421 Flt 148
    422 Flt 148
    490 Flt 69, 114–15, 141
    491 Flt 114–5
    492 Flt 114–5
    493 Flt 114–5
    494 Flt 114–5
    496 Flt 71
    497 Flt 71
    498 Flt 71
    500 Flt 93–4
    501 Flt 93–4
    502 Flt 93–4
    504 Flt 93–5
    505 Flt 93–4
    506 Flt 93–4, 97, 114
    507 Flt 93–4, 97, 114
    508 Flt 93–4
    509 Flt 93–4

510 Flt 93–5, 97
512 Flt 93–4
513 Flt 93–4
514 Flt 93–4
515 Flt 93–4
515 Flt 94–5
516 Flt 93–4
517 Flt 93–4
518 Flt 93–4
519 Flt 93–4
520 Flt 93–4
521 Flt 93–4
522 Flt 93–4
523 Flt 93–4
524 Flt 93–4
525 Flt 93–4
526 Flt 93–4, 97
527 Flt 93–4, 97, 114
528 Flt 93–4
529 Flt 93–4
530 Flt 93–4
531 Flt 93–4
532 Flt 93–4
533 Flt 93–4
534 Flt 69, 115
555 Flt 114–5, 141
556 Flt 114–5, 141
557 Flt 114–5, 141
558 Flt 114–5, 141
562 Flt 124
Foord, Lt 54
Foster, AM2 A 59
Foulois, Brig General BD 160
Fox, Capt JB 63
Fox, 2Lt JR 65
Frankfurt 136–37
Freeland, 2Lt RF 114
Freeman, 2Lt JEH 37
Freiburg 64
Fry, 2Lt JL 38
Galloway Engineering Co 102
Gammon, 2Lt RJ 118
Gamon, Capt J 61
Gardiner, Lt GC 47
Garland, Capt E 176
Garrity, Lt WJ 119
Gathergood, Capt G 175
Ghent 111
Ghistelles 58
Gibson, Lt CB 97
Gibson, 2Lt HJ 47
Gilmour, Capt SG 40–1
Giradot, Lt FR 95
Glaisby FSL LN 57
Glendower Aircraft Co 51
Glew, Lt EA 41–2
Gloucester Aviation Co Ltd 88
Goble, Major SJ 61
Godlee, 2Lt J 40
Goeben 70–1
Goetham, Capt HE van 88
Goffe, Sgt CR 54
Gompertz, 2Lt AVH 45
Gontrode 35, 58
Goodall, Lt JHH 77
Goodfellow, Capt H 95
Gough-Calthorpe, Vice-Admiral, the Hon SA 70
Graham, Lt 73
Grahame-White Aviation Co Ltd 22, 88, 94
Grahame-White, Claude 8, 19
Graphic (newspaper) 7

Grattan-Bellew, Major AW 44–5
Gray, Lt DH 40
Green, Frederick 12
Greenwood, OSL V 57
Greg, Capt AT 54
Gregory, Lt GE 70
Grey, Charles C 22
Groenen, Sgt V 128
Goettler, 1Lt HE 161
Groom, Capt ACH 136
Gross, Lt CR 137
Grove Park 14
Hacklett, Lt LA 73
Hagendingen 115–6
Haifa 124
Haigh, Sgt A 137
Haines, Lt CL 57
Halford, Frank 13
Hall, Capt DS 55
Hall, EJ 133
Hall, Capt WT 77
Hallam, 2Lt HA 43
Ham 107
Hambley, FSL DM 89
Hambly, Lt FL 67
Hancock, George 160
Handley-Page 7
Handley-Page Transport 73
Harker, Lt B 63
Harker, Capt HR 55
Harland & Wolff 88
Harman, AM1 AT 68–9
Harman, Sgt TW 137
Harper, 2Lt GV 121
Harper, Lt NS 117
Harrop, Sgt W 120
Hartigan, 2Lt EP 55
Hawker, Captain/Major LG 35, 40, 43
Hawker Siddeley Group 14
Hater-Hames, FO NC 157
Hazell, Flt Lt TF 153
Hearle, Frank 10, 12, 14
Henney, 2Lt WJ 56
Heyworth, Lt EL 46
Hill, 2Lt GTR 42
Hirson 09
Hitchcock, 2Lt CG 120
Hobart, Major PCS 71
Holden, Lt LH 81
Holder, Lt FD 46
Holiday, Lt RA 107
Holle AA 98
Holman, Lt GC 78
Holthom, 2Lt JN 3
Home Defence Brigade 29
Home-Hay, Capt JB 120
Houston-Stewart, FSL W 57
Howard, Lt RW 81
Howe, 2Lt G 45
Howsam, 2Lt CJ 3
Hucks, BC 13
Hughes-Chamberlain, Capt REAW 41
Hunnisett, Sgt Mechanic 70
Hunt, Lt PBG 43
Hunter, 2Lt JL 120
Hurst, 2Lt HB 44
Huskisson, Sqn Ldr BL 153
Huxley, Lt FG 80
Immelmann, Ltn M 39
Imperial Russian Air Service 56
Independent Force 109, 114–22,

136–8, 160, 176
Inglis, Capt AG 137
Instone Airlines 73
Integral Propeller Company 13
Iris Car Company 10
Irish Air Corps 131
Jackson, 2Lt HAB 117
James, AM F 67
James, Lt WFT 44
Jeffries, AM1 AL 59
Jenkins, 2Lt WWL 117
Jenyns, 2Lt CG 117
Jessop, AM1 JO 67
Johannesburg 131
Johnson, J 132
Jones, Capt HWG 41–5
Jones, Flt Lt JIT 154
Jones, 2Lt O 115
Jones, Lt SS 63
Kabul 157
Kaiserlautern 63–5, 118, 137
Kampfeinsitzerstaffeln 118
Karlsruhe 64–5, 117
Karthaus 64–5, 118–9
Keep, Lt AD 65
Kennedey, 2Lt WU 97
Kent, 2Lt E 46
Kerr, 2Lt C 40
Kerry, Lt CR 46
Kettener, 2Lt HM 137
Keys, Lt RE 68–9
Khan Baghdadi 71
Kifri 71
King, Locke 7
King, 2Lt P 137
Kingsbury Aviation Co Ltd 88
Kinkead, Flt Lt SM 154
Kirkness, 2Lt TR 78
Koblenz 63, 65
Knight, Lt AG 42–4
Knott, Capt EM 73
Kuchi 123
La Fresne 139
Lahr 119
Land, Capt A 126
Landau 117
Lange, Capt GE 136
Lange, Lt OJ 116
Latham, Hubert 7
Latta, Lt JD 37
Leach, AM1 GP 51
Leach, 2Lt JB 139
Le Bourget 19, 99, 131
Leckie, Capt R 69
Lee, Sgt FL 118
Legge, 2Lt W 64
Legge, Lt WH 51
Lerwill, 2Lt O 37
Lewis, 2Lt EL 41, 44
Lewis, Lt GH 40
Leyden, 2Lt HPG 119
Liege 64
Lille 107
Lindley, capt A 137
Lipsett, 2Lt RS 137
Lloyd, Lt CBE 137
Lloyd, Major Lindsay 7
Lomie, AM2 J
Long, Capt SG 43–4
Longcroft, Captain CAH 11
Longuyon 65, 121
Lorquin 121
Lorraine, Captain R 35

Loughborough 18
Lovell, 2Lt WL 54
Luchtvaartafdeeling 128
Ludwigshaven 120
Lund, 2Lt RJS 44
Luxembourg 65, 136
MacDonald, Lt DA 115
MacLaren, Lt ASC 31
Mahmoud, Sheik 154
Main, Lt R 51
Mainz 63, 119
Malcolm, Lt OL 121
Manfield, Lt NP 37, 39–40, 42
Mann Egerton & Co 102, 133
Mannheim 63–5, 119, 136
March, 2Lt CH 44
March, Jones & Cribb 75
Mare-Montembault, 2Lt 42–3, 45
Mariembourg 109
Markussen, Lt S 95
Martin, Capt B 95
Martin, 2Lt F 55
Martin, Lt FJ 46
Martin, Lt G 119
Martin-Bell, 2Lt E 70
Matz, Battle of 107
May Harden & May 13, 25–6
Maxwell Pike, Captain R 34
May, 2Lt CJ 137
McBlain, Lt 30
McClaughrey, Sqn Ldr AW 153
McConchie, Lt TL 118
McCudden, Sgt/2Lt JTB 42, 44
McDonald, 2Lt/FO IDR 79, 153
McDougall, 2Lt PA 79
McIntosh, JC 126
McKay, Lt AE 43–4
McKay, Capt EA 120
McKeever, 2Lt S 121
McKenzie, 2Lt A 64
McKie, Lt 43
McLaren-Pearson, Lt J 137
Mellor, Sgt E 120
Melville, Lt HT 119
Merton 9, 26
Messina 140
Metz 64–5, 115–16, 118, 120–1
Middelkerque 58, 70
Middlebrook, 2Lt N 42
Military Trials 9, 11
Military Wing 16, 19
Mills, AM1 CW 114
Miscellaneous RFC/RNAS/RAF
Units
    Artillery Observation School 91
    AICS 112
    Air Council Inspection Sqn 149
    X Aircraft Depot 47, 90, 123
    X Flt 36, 47
    1 Aircraft Depot 35–6, 42–3, 51,
        75, 78
    2 Aircraft Depot 40, 45, 51, 62
        75, 78
    3 Aircraft Depot 176
    2 Aeroplane Supply Depot 56
    1 SAF/SAFG/FS 36, 39, 47
    DH4 School 67
    2 (Aux) SAG 36, 39
    SAG Aboukir 90
    SAG Heliopolis 90
    1 FTS 126
    1 SANBD 66, 68, 91, 112
    2 SANBD 91, 112

3 SANBD 91, 112
4 SANBD 91, 112
Marine Observers School 91, 112
Observers School 112
    1 Observers School 112
    2 Observers School 112
School for Marine Operational
    Pilots 91, 112
Observers School/2 Marine
    Observers School 112
SASIPO/1 Marine Observers
    School 112
SCCB 126
OSRAP 112
Medical Flight 68
The Communications Sqn 72
    1 Communications Sqn 72
    2 Communications Sqn 72
Central Flying School 16, 19–20,
    22–4, 28, 31, 35–6, 53, 88, 170
Testing Squadron 50, 75, 79
2 Wireless School 90
Pool of Pilots 68, 112
Eagle Flight 146
MAFIS 68, 112
NEAFIS 112
Special Instructors Flight 124
2 AAP 50, 53, 67, 72, 105
5 AAP 134
8 AAP 67
RNAS CTE 67
1 Fighting School 111–2
2 Fighting School 68, 111–2
3 Fighting School 68, 111–2
5 Fighting School 112, 124
Fleet SAF & G 144
1 FTS 152
2 FTS 152
3 FTS 152
4 FTS 124, 149, 156
5 FTS 152, 178
6 FTS 152
Wireless Experimental
    Establishment 68
WT School 112
H Zquadron 124
H Unit 124
Z Unit 124
Mobile Flight 144
Central Air Communications Section
    149, 154
Mitchell, Capt EH 39
Moir, Lt CJ 70
Moislains 61
Mons 109
Mont d'Origny 109
Montigny 109
Morgan & Co Ltd 88, 94
Moore, Lt A 118
Moore-Brabazon, JTC 10
Moreman, AM2 S 55
Morhange 120
Morrison, Lt DG 79
Mucklow, Lt SL 137
Mullen, Lt AGL 120
Mundy, Lt EW 117
Musee de l'Air et l'Espace 19, 131
Nablus 123
Namur 64
National Air and Space Museum 168
National Postal Museum 168
Naval Wing 17
Naylor, AGLW 57

Neighbour, Sgt WH 137
Newbiggin 112
Newcastle-upon-Tyne 7
Nichol, Major HR 136
Nicholson, Lt R 97
Nieuport 58
Night Training Squadrons (ex Depot Squadrons)
  186 NTS 91
  187 NTS 91
  188 NTS 91
  189 NTS 91
  190 NTS 90–1
  191 NTS 91
  199 DS/NTS 90
  200 DS/NTS 19, 30
Nixon Wilfred 13–4
Nixon, 2Lt WE 40, 42
Nizam of Hyderabad 135–6
Noakes, Sgt J 39
Nordenand, 2Lt WG 118
Northcliffe, Lord 7
Nuttall, Capt F 71
Oakeshott, FSL LE 106
Oberndorf 65, 118
Offenberg 63, 65, 116, 119
Ogilvie, 2Lt WF 120
O'Gorman, Mervyn 12
O'Lieff, Sgt P 55
Omerod, Flt Comm LW 60
O'Neill, 2Lt J 55
Osborne, Gunner WG 55
Ostende 57–8, 70, 110
Otranto 122–3
Owen, Capt D 55, 63
Oye 139
Padmore, Lt AR 70
Palethorpe, Capt J 67
Palladium Autocars 51
Papenfus, Lt MTS 119
Parer, RJP 126
Parkhouse, 2Lt WR 89
Parnall & Co 151
Pashley, 2Lt EC 43–4
Pattinson, Major LS 119–20
Pattison, OSL WH 60
Paulhan, Louis 7, 8
Payne, 2Lt A 104
Pearson, Lt AJ 44–5
Peebles, Lt AJD 95, 97
Peter Hooker Ltd 13
Phillipps, Capt RC 78
Pickard, 2Lt CG 120
Pickthorne, Lt CEM 44–5
Pirmasens 137
Pither, Lt 40
Platt, Sgt W 136–7
Poellnitz, Capt HW von 44
Point Cook 92, 127
Pontin, Lt SCM 117
Provan, 2Lt A 137
Pyott, Lt IV 54
RAF Museum 86, 158
RAF Special Reserve 158
Rachicourt 21
Randall, 2Lt AC 45
Ransome, Sims & Jeffries 88
Read, Lt JF 70
Redfield, Lt JJ 120
Rees, Major/Colonel LWB 39–40
Reserve Aeroplane Squadrons (see Training Squadrons)
Reserve Squadrons (see Training

Squadrons)
Reynolds, Major LGS 137
RFC Military Wing 11
RFC/RAF Stations
  Abbassia 91
  Abeele 36–7, 79
  Aboukir 36, 91, 155
  Abscon 108
  Abu Sueir 17, 23, 124, 149, 156, 178
  Aldeburgh 91, 112
  Alexandria 47, 124
  Alimini 71, 122, 124
  Allahabad 177–8
  Almaza 91, 124
  Alquines 108
  Amderkoj 124
  Amman 149, 155
  Amria 91
  Andover 23–4, 68, 91, 105–6, 112, 140, 144, 150
  Andrano 124
  Anglesey 93
  Aniche 79
  Aqaba 36, 47
  Ashington 93–4
  Atwick 93–5
  Auchel 36, 39, 59
  Aulnoy 138, 156
  Avricourt 138
  Ayr 46
  Azelot 105, 114, 116, 118–9, 121, 176, 178
  Baghdad 149, 153
  Baizieux 78–80
  Baku 124
  Baldonnel 112, 144, 149
  Bangor 93–4
  Basra 23, 149
  Batum 124
  Bavai 108, 137
  Beaulieu 88, 91
  Beauvois 59, 108
  Beketovka 124
  Berbera 124
  Bergues 59, 110
  Bertangles 36, 60
  Bettoncourt 136–7
  Bickendorf 59, 104, 108, 137, 139
  Bierne 59
  Biggin Hill 68
  Bircham Newton 67–8, 112, 140, 144, 150–1
  Bisseghem 110–11
  Blangemont 108
  Bois de Roche 59
  Boisdinghem 54, 59, 108
  Boscombe Down 68, 91, 106, 112
  Bovelles 59
  Bracebridge Heath 114
  Brading 93–4
  Bramham Moor 17, 23, 31, 66, 91
  Brooklands 7–8, 17, 19, 23
  Bruay 36
  Buc 72–3
  Cairncross 93–4
  Candas 76
  Capelle-la-Grande 110
  Castlebar 149
  Castle Bromwich 17–9, 21, 23, 51, 79, 155, 158
  Catterick 18–9, 23, 31, 36, 46, 66, 68, 90–1, 112–13, 160

  Chailly 59, 108
  Champien 59–60
  Chickerall 93–4
  Chingford 90–1, 140
  Chipilly 36
  Clairmarais 105–6, 108
  Clary 110
  Collinstown 112
  Conteville 60–1, 108
  Copmanthorpe 91
  Coudekerque 107–8, 110
  Courban 176
  Covehithe 115
  Cowes 126
  Cramlington 36, 68, 91–5, 111–12
  Cranwell 68, 91, 111–12, 152
  Crochte 59, 110
  Croydon 79, 82–3, 112
  Dardoni 151, 178
  Deir-el-Belah 36, 47
  Delny 144
  Doncaster 17, 23, 36, 46
  Dover 17, 19, 23, 36–7, 46, 56, 59, 68, 83, 91, 110, 112, 114–15
  Drigh Road (Karachi) 152, 156
  Drionville 108
  Droglandt 59, 79
  Duxford 68, 91, 112
  Eastbourne 90–1
  Eastburn/Driffield 91
  Eastchurch 68, 90–1, 112, 144
  Easton-on-the-Hill 68, 90–1, 112
  East Retford 19, 30–1, 91
  Ekaterinodar 124, 126
  El Dar Elan 124
  El Firdan 112, 124
  Farnborough 10, 15, 17–9, 23, 27, 88, 91, 126, 172
  Felixstowe 67
  Feltwell 112
  Fienvillers 51, 54, 59
  Filton 31, 134, 155, 158
  Flez 36, 79
  Floringhem 108
  Ford Farm 105
  Ford Junction 177
  Fourneuil 59, 108
  Fowlmere 68, 91, 111–12
  Francwaret 108
  Gormanston 112
  Gosport 17, 19, 23, 31, 36–7, 84, 144
  Goudecourt 110
  Grain 177
  Greenland Top 93–4
  Gullane 91
  Harlaxton 68, 78–9, 91, 105
  Harling Road 68, 79, 89, 91, 112
  Hawkinge 114, 178
  Heliopolis 31, 112, 124, 149, 155, 178
  Helperby 91
  Helwan 91, 112, 124, 149, 155
  Hendon 8–9, 13–4, 17, 19, 27, 68, 72–3, 104–5, 155, 158, 177
  Hinaidi 149, 153-154
  Hornsea 93
  Hounslow 19, 23, 31, 36, 66, 68, 91, 126
  Hucknall 91, 112
  Imbros 122, 124

  Ismailia 23, 31, 91, 112, 124, 149
  Joyce Green 17, 19, 23, 31, 36, 46, 68, 79, 83, 93
  Junction Station 124
  Kenley 72–3, 106, 136, 149
  Khartoum 149
  Khormaksar 149, 155
  Killingholme 94
  Kirkuk 149, 154
  Kohat 151
  La Bellevue 54, 56, 59
  La Brayelle 59, 137
  Lahore 177–8
  Lake Down 66, 68, 89, 91, 106, 112
  La Louvveterie 137
  Larkhill 17, 19
  Lealvillers 36, 79
  Le Casteau 59
  Le Hameau 36, 59, 79, 137
  Leighterton 91–2
  Lemnos 122, 124
  Le Quesnoy 59, 108
  Le Planty Farm 66
  Les Eauvis 59
  Leuchars 144
  Leysdown 112
  Lilbourne 51, 59, 68
  Linselles 108
  Loch Doon 23–4, 46
  London Colney 91, 160
  Lopcombe Corner 79, 81, 91
  Lozinghem 54, 59
  Luce Bay 93–4
  Lympne 105
  Machrihanish 93–4
  Maisoncelle 59, 108, 137, 139
  Maltepe 149
  Manston 68, 90–1, 112, 114–5, 134, 152, 155, 178
  Marham 91, 173
  Marieux 79
  Marquain 108
  Marquise 108, 137–8
  Marsa Racecourse 124
  Marske 67–8, 73, 111–3, 140
  Martlesham Heath 53, 55, 79, 83, 99, 104, 126, 132, 134, 140, 150, 160, 172–3, 177
  Maubeurge 59, 108, 137
  Merheim 59, 137
  Mianwali 151, 156
  Mikra Bay 31, 124
  Minchinhampton 17, 23, 91–2
  Miranshah 157
  Mitylene 124
  Moislains 108, 137
  Mons-en-Chaussée 59
  Montrose 13, 17, 23, 68
  Morville 59, 61, 137
  Mory 59
  Mosul 149, 153–4
  Mudros 122, 124
  Mullion 93–4, 113–5
  Murmansk 124, 126
  Narborough 23, 31, 68, 86, 91, 112, 160
  Netheravon 11, 17, 23, 31, 39, 91, 101, 112, 126, 144, 152
  New Haggerston 93–4
  Newmarket 91
  New Romney 67
  Nivelles 108, 137

North Coates Fitties 93
Northolt 17–9, 23, 91, 144, 150, 155, 158
North Shotwick 91
Norwich 17–9, 23, 31, 66, 68, 112
Novar 144
Novorossisk 122, 124, 126
Ochey 55, 62
Old Sarum 68, 91, 105, 112
Oranmore 149
Orfordness 23, 31, 46, 79, 83, 177
Owthorne 93–4, 114
Padstow 93–5, 113–5
Pembroke 93–5
Penshurst 91
Penston 9
Peshawar 151
Petite Synthe 59, 106, 108–10
Petrovsk 124, 126
Pizzone 71, 122, 124
Portmeadow 31, 91
Port Said 124
Prawle Point 93–4, 113–5
Proyart East 59, 137
Qantara 124
Ramleh 124, 149, 155
Redcar 93–5
Renfrew 155, 158
Rennington 93–5
Reumont 110
Risalpur 151, 177–8
Rochford 19, 68, 91
Ronchin 108, 110
Rozay-en-Brie 108
Ruisseauville 59, 106, 110
Salonika 122
San Stephano 122, 124, 144, 150
Sart 137
Scampton 91
Scopwick 152
Seahouses 93–4, 114
Sealand 152
Seaton Carew 93–4
Sedgeford 66, 68–9, 79, 106, 112
Serny 59, 105
Shaibah 149, 153
Shallufa 91
Shawbury 23, 91, 112
Shoreham 17–9, 23, 140
Shrewsbury 112
South Carlton 19, 20, 36, 46, 59, 68, 79, 91
South Otterington 113
South Shields 93
Spittlegate 17, 23, 91, 144, 150, 152
Spy 59
Stag Lane 91, 112
Stamford/Wittering 89–91, 112, 160
Stavros 122, 124
St Andre aux Bois 66, 138
Ste Marie Cappel 59, 106
Stirling 68
Stojakovo 124
St Omer 36–7, 39, 51, 75, 79, 105, 108
Stonehenge 23–4, 68, 91, 112, 140
Suez 17, 124, 149
Sutton's Farm 91
Tallaght 93–4, 112

Tank 177
Tantonville 63–4, 105, 114–15
Telscombe Cliffs 93–4
Ternhill 36, 79, 81, 91
Teteghem 79
The Curragh 68
Thetford 17, 19, 23, 31, 91, 107, 112
Thornaby 155, 158
Throwley 91
Thuillies 110
Treizennes 36, 39, 59
Turnberry 36, 46, 67, 112, 140
Turnhouse 17, 19, 23, 158
Tynemouth 94–5, 114
Upavon 17, 19, 31, 36, 38, 50, 53, 79, 170
Upper Heyford 114, 140
Varssenaere 59, 110
Vert Galant 36, 59, 110
Villers Bretonneux 59
Villers le Cagnicourt 108
Waddington 17, 22–3, 49, 66, 68, 90–1, 112, 160
West Ayton 93–4
Winton 112
Worthy Down 112
Wye 36, 66, 68, 79, 91, 160
Wyton 17, 23, 66, 68, 91, 112, 114, 160
Yanesh 124
Yarmouth 68–9, 114, 134
Yatesbury 31, 79, 90–1
Rheims 7
Richards, Lt JW 120
Richie, 2Lt TM 119
Richter, Lt P 168
Richthofen, Ltn/Ritt M von 43–5, 54, 82
Riffkin, 2Lt R 137
Ripley, Lt RCP 137
Rivett-Carnac, 2Lt WG 115
RNAS Stations
  Anglesey 26
  Bacton 68
  Bembridge 17
  Bergues 69
  Burgh Castle 68
  Bray Dunes 57
  Calshot 17, 21, 24, 26
  Capel 26
  Chingford 17, 23–4, 89–91
  Covehithe 68
  Cranwell 23–4, 26, 67, 91
  Dover/Guston Road 39, 105
  Dundee 17
  Dunkerque 50
  Eastbourne 17, 23–4, 90–1
  Eastchurch 17, 23, 90
  Felixstowe 17, 26
  Gliki 70
  Gosforth 21
  Grain 17, 54, 68
  Hendon 17, 39
  Imbros 122
  Kirkwall 21
  Kingsnorth 26
  Lee-on-Solent 24
  Leven 17
  Luce Bay 26
  Manston 23–4, 90
  Marquise 26
  Mudros 70, 122

Pembroke 26
Petite Synthe 105
Redcar 23, 91
Stavros 122
St Pol 57–8
Vendome 17–18
Wormwood Scrubbs 26
Yarmouth 17, 21, 23, 26, 54, 68
Robb, Sqn Ldr JM 153
Robinson, Gunnery Sgt RG 162
Roche, 2Lt CPV 42
Robb, Capt JM 45
Roe Green Garden Village 14
Roe, AV 7
Rose, Sgt AT 54
Rowley, Lt EG 54
Royal Aircraft Factory 12, 15, 27, 88
Royal Australian Air Force 127
Royal Australian Air Force Units
  1 Sqn 127, 141
  3 Sqn 127
  CFS 127, 139, 141
  1 FTS 139, 141
Royal Flying Corps (RFC) 9, 15
Royal Hellenic Naval Air Service 128
Royal Naval Air Service (RNAS) 18–19
Rutter, FSL JN 70
Ryder, Lt WH 54
Saarebourg 176
Saarbrucken 63–4, 116, 118–9
Salt, 2Lt TE 78
Sanders, Lt H 117
Sansom, Lt RC 64
Saundby, Lt/Capt RHMS 41, 43–4, 46
Saunders, 2Lt JORS 137
Saunders Jason 10
Savages Ltd 13, 28–9, 88
Seagrave, Lt HOD 39
Searle, 2Lt R 120
Sedgwick, 2Lt FR 44
Seth-Ward, 2Lt E 78
Seven Barrows 10, 12
Sherwood, 2Lt WV 41
Shipton, 2Lt GA 120
Shorter, Lt HH 95
Shufflebotham, Sgt Mechanic FW 70
Sibley, 2Lt SJ 37, 41
Siddeley-Deasey 102
Sievier, Lt RBB 71
Simpson, 2Lt JA 137
Simpson, Capt MA 93
Singleton, 2Lt E 119
Skinner, Lt MR 115
Slater, Capt JA 81
Slavo-British Aviation Corps 126
Smith Sgt Major DG 115
Smith, 2Lt F 119
Smith, AM2 GC 64
Smith, 2Lt GHB 120
Smith, Sgt GT 116
Smith, Lt L 168
Smith, 1Lt LA 161
Smith, Sgt WT 120
Smithsonian Institute 168
Sopwith Aviation Company Ltd 7
Sopwith, TOM 7, 14
South African Air Force 128
South African Air force Units
  1 Sqn 127

Flying Training School 127
South African Air Force Museum 131
Southon, Capt HG 45
Spa 64
Sparappelhoek 58
Speagell, 2Lt HMD 137
Speed, AM1 L 114
Squadrons
  A Sqn RNAS (5 Wing) 62, 114
  A Sqn RNAS (2 Wing) 122
  B Sqn RNAS 71, 122
  C Sqn RNAS 70–1, 122
  D Sqn RNAS 71, 122
  F Sqn RNAS 70
  G Sqn RNAS 70
  1 Sqn 17, 83
  1 Sqn AFC 30
  2 Sqn 17, 19
  2N Sqn 56–60
  3 Sqn 17, 19, 22–3, 144, 148
  4 Sqn 15, 17, 23–4
  5 Sqn 17, 19, 23, 33–6, 156–57
  5N Sqn 56–60
  6 Sqn 17, 22–4
  6N Sqn 59, 105–7, 109–10
  7 Sqn 17
  8 Sqn 145, 149, 153
  9 Sqn 17, 19
  11 Sqn 35–6, 45, 144, 150, 157
  11N Sqn 105, 109
  12 Sqn 144
  12N Sqn 59
  13 Sqn 23
  14 Sqn 23, 30-31, 36, 124, 149, 155
  15 Sqn 144, 150–1
  17 Sqn 30–1, 36, 69, 121, 124
  17N Sqn 59–60
  18 Sqn 17–19, 35–6, 53–4, 56, 59, 61, 137, 139
  20 Sqn 53
  22 Sqn 23, 53
  23 Sqn 23, 53
  24 Sqn 23, 35–46, 72, 76–9, 83, 144, 149, 178
  25 Sqn 51, 53–6, 59–61, 137, 139
  27 Sqn 54–6, 59–60, 106–9, 151, 156–7
  28 Sqn 19, 28, 31, 79, 84
  29 Sqn 36–45
  30 Sqn 23–4, 71, 149, 153–55
  31 Sqn 151, 156
  32 Sqn 36–45, 76–9, 83
  33 Sqn 144
  35 Sqn 19, 28, 31, 144, 151
  39 Sqn 19, 23, 144, 150–1
  40 Sqn 19, 36
  41 Sqn 17–19, 23, 28, 31, 36, 76, 78–9, 83
  45 Sqn 114, 149, 155
  47 Sqn 36, 121, 124, 126, 149–150, 155
  48 Sqn 156
  49 Sqn 56–7, 59–60, 68, 102, 106–9, 121, 137, 139, 149, 160
  51 Sqn 173
  55 Sqn 51, 54–6, 59, 62–6, 114, 124, 136, 140, 145, 149, 153–5
  57 Sqn 28, 31, 51, 53–6, 59–61, 137, 139
  59 Sqn 29, 31

60 Sqn 151, 153, 156–7, 177–8
61(HD) Sqn 91
63 Sqn 36, 71
64 Sqn 79, 81, 83
65 Sqn 79, 84
68 Sqn 78–9, 81, 83
70 Sqn 149, 154
72 Sqn 71
76(HD) Sqn 91
77(HD) Sqn 91
83 Sqn 68
84 Sqn 147, 149, 153, 155
88 Sqn 79
97 Sqn 156, 177–8
98 Sqn 68, 91, 105, 108–10, 122
99 Sqn 64–5, 67–8, 105, 107, 114–22, 136, 138, 144, 151, 156
100 Sqn 62, 114–5, 149
101 Sqn 151
103 Sqn 68, 105–8
104 Sqn 65, 68, 102, 105, 114–22, 176, 178
105 Sqn 67–8, 106
106 Sqn 67–8, 106
107 Sqn 105, 107–9
108 Sqn 68, 105, 110–11
109 Sqn 67–8, 89, 106, 140
110 Sqn 65, 68, 106, 114, 120, 135–8, 158, 177
114 Sqn 156, 177
111 Sqn 36, 155
117 Sqn 114
119 Sqn 90–1, 114
120 Sqn 106, 111, 114, 177–8
121 Sqn 68, 86, 90–1
122 Sqn 114
123 Sqn 90–1, 140
124 Sqn 90–1
125 Sqn 68, 90–1
126 Sqn 68, 90–1
127 Sqn 68, 90–1, 113
131 Sqn 90–1
134 Sqn 140
135 Sqn 140
136 Sqn 140
137 Sqn 111, 140
141 Sqn 114, 149
142 Sqn 124
144 Sqn 123–4
146 Sqn 124
147 Sqn 124
155 Sqn 140
156 Sqn 140
160 Sqn 140
161 Sqn 140
162 Sqn 140
163 Sqn 140
164 Sqn 140
186 (Development) Sqn 126
202 Sqn 56, 61, 110
205 Sqn 60–1, 137, 139, 144, 160
206 Sqn 104, 107–9, 122, 124
207 Sqn 144, 150
208 Sqn 149
210 Sqn 144
211 Sqn 102, 105, 109–11, 160
212 Sqn 69, 114–5, 141
214 Sqn 105
215 Sqn 105
216 Sqn 114, 174, 178
217 Sqn 61, 69–70, 110
218 Sqn 110–11
219 Sqn 114–5, 141

220 Sqn 71, 122, 124
221 Sqn 71, 122, 124, 126, 148
222 Sqn 122
223 Sqn 71, 122, 124
224 Sqn 71, 122–4
225 Sqn 122–4
226 Sqn 71, 122–4
227 Sqn 122–4
233 Sqn 114–5
236 Sqn 93–4, 114–5
241 Sqn 93–4
242 Sqn 93–4
244 Sqn 93–94
250 Sqn 93–4, 114–5
251 Sqn 93–4, 114
252 Sqn 93–5, 114, 176
253 Sqn 93–4
254 Sqn 93–4, 114–5
255 Sqn 93–4, 97
256 Sqn 93–4, 97, 114
258 Sqn 93–4
260 Sqn 93–4
269 Sqn 124
272 Sqn 93–4
273 Sqn 69, 115, 141
500 Sqn 155
501 Sqn 155
600 Sqn 155, 157–8
601 Sqn 155, 158
602 Sqn 155, 158
603 Sqn 155–8
604 Sqn 155, 158
605 Sqn 155, 158
608 Sqn 155, 158
Squire's Gate 7
Staden 111
Stagg, 2Lt LWT 119
St Barbe, Francis 13–14
St Clair, 2Lt 78
St Denis 109
St Denis Westrem 58
St Mihiel 120
Staden 70
Stag Lane 13–14
Standard Aircraft Corporation 160
Steele, 2Lt RC 47
Stephenson, 2Lt GH 119
Stubbs, Capt JS 107
Stubbs, 2Lt RA 40
Stuttgart 63, 65, 119Sulaimania 154
Sykes, FH 14, 73
Talbot, 2Lt R 162
Taranto 122
Tatham, 2Lt IM 88
Tayler Lt HM 54
Tayler, 2Lt St CC 46, 77–8
Taylor, 2Lt AD 54
Taylor, Capt AD 119
Taylor, 2Lt RE 78
Taylor, Capt 46
Tempest, Capt ER 81
Tennant, Lt Col JE 71
Thionville 63, 65, 116–7, 119–21
Thom, Capt WD 118
Thomas, AF 9
Thomas, 2Lt GPF 63
Thomas, George Holt 7–9, 13–14, 73, 126
Thomas, George Luson 7
Thomas, Gertrude 7
Thomas, Lt M 78
Thomas, 2Lt OV 40
Thompson, Lt FG 119

Thompson, Lt RWL 137
Thornley, 2Lt SC 119
Thourout 111
Tidmarsh, 2Lt DM 37, 39
Tong, 2Lt AF 70
Tonge, Lt UGA 70
Tournai 107, 109
Towler, 2Lt FS 137
Tozer, Sgt HW 136–7
Training Brigade 29
Training Depot Stations
 1 TDS 89–91, 112
 2 TDS 66, 68, 91
 3 TDS 79, 81, 84, 91
 5 TDS 68, 90–1, 112
 6 TDS 68, 91, 106, 112
 7 TDS 112
 8 TDS 91, 112
 9 TDS 91, 112
 10 TDS 53, 68, 89, 91, 112
 11 TDS 68, 91, 105, 112
 12 TDS 91
 13 TDS 91
 14 TDS 91, 105, 112
 15 TDS 91, 112
 16 TDS 91, 112, 124
 17 TDS 112, 124
 18 TDS 91, 112, 124
 20 TDS 91
 21 TDS 91
 22 TDS 112
 23 TDS 112
 24 TDS 112
 25 TDS 112
 31 TDS 68, 91, 111–12
 35 TDS 68, 91, 112
 36 TDS 91
 37 TDS 89, 91
 40 TDS 91
 41 TDS 91
 48 TDS 112
 49 TDS 52, 68, 89, 91, 112–13, 116–7
 51 TDS 91
 52 TDS 91, 111–12
 55 TDS 68, 67, 112
 57 TDS 68, 111–12
 202 TDS 67–8, 91
 203 TDS 67, 90–1
 204 TDS 68, 90–1
 205 TDS 17
 206 TDS 90–1
 207 TDS 90–1
 210 TDS 24
 213 TDS 91
Training Squadrons (formerly Reserve Aeroplane Squadrons and Reserve Squadrons)
RAS/1RAS/1RS/1TS 17–19
 2 RAS/RS/TS 15, 19
 3 RAS/RS/TS 17, 19
 4 RAS/RS/TS 17, 19, 91
 5 RAS/RS/TS 17, 21, 91, 112
 6 RAS 17, 19, 29, 31, 36
 7 RAS/RS 17
 8 RAS/RS 17, 19, 31
 9 RAS/RS/TS 17, 19, 29, 31, 68, 112
 10 RAS/RS 17, 19, 29, 31, 36
 11 RAS/RS 17, 19
 12 RAS/RS 17
 13 RS/TS 36, 91
 14 RAS/RS 17

15 RAS/RS 17, 19, 36
16 TS 88, 91
17 RS/TS 31, 91
19 RS/TS 19, 29, 31, 53, 66, 68
20 RS/TS 36, 91
21 RS/TS 17–18, 22, 91
22 RS 18, 36
23 RS/TS 18, 91
24 RS/TS 17, 19, 91
25 RS/TS 17, 91, 112
26 RS/TS 17, 19, 68, 91, 112
27 RS 19, 28
28 RS 19
29 TS 91, 112
30 (Australian) TS 79
31 RS/TS 17, 19, 66, 91, 112
34 RS 36
35 RS/TS 31, 91
37 TS 91
9 RS/TS 17, 91
40 TS 79, 82–3
41 RS/TS 17
42 TS 91
43 TS 79, 81, 83
44 TS 66–8, 90–1, 112
45 RS/TS 19, 36
46 RS/TS 29, 31, 66, 68, 79, 91, 112
47 RS/TS 17, 90–1, 112
48 RS/TS 17, 22 , 91, 112
49 TS 17
50 TS 91
51 TS 49, 66–8, 91, 112
52 TS 52, 66, 68, 91, 112
53 TS 91
54 TS 79, 91
55 TS 79, 83–4
56 TS 91
58 RS/TS 17
59 RS/TS 29, 31, 91
61 TS 68, 79, 91
62 TS 79, 83
63 TS 79–80, 83, 93
64 TS 91
66 TS 91
68 TS 31, 91
69 TS 68, 91, 112
75 TS 68, 91, 112
193 TS 91
194 TS 91
5 TS AFC 17, 91
7 TS AFC 91
Tremellen, Lt AC 95
Tresham, 2Lt WH 121
Treves 63, 119, 136
Trenchard, HM 14, 44, 50, 104, 114–5, 120–1
Tubbs, 2Lt HLV 24, 80
Tul Karm 123
Turner, 2Lt AF 63
Turner 2Lt KK 41
Uhlman, 2Lt JC 119
United States Air Services Stations
 Amanty 160, 162
 Behonne 162
 Belrain 162
 Bicqueley 162
 Bordeaux 162
 Brest 162
 Champ de Tir de Souge 162
 Clamency 162
 Clermont-en-Argonne 162
 Colombey-les-Belles 162

Delouze 162
Epiez 162
Fargues 162
Foucaucourt 162
Gondreville-sur-Moselle 162
Guines 162
Guitres 162
Issoudun 160, 162
Joppecourt 162
Koblenz 162
Langres 162
Le Mans 162
Luxeuil-les-Bains 162
Maulan 162
McCook Field 161, 163–6
Orly 160, 162
Ourches 160, 162
Parois 162
Preutin 162
Remicourt 162
Sablons 162
Saizerais 162
Soilly 162
St Denis de Pile 162
St Maxient 162
Ste Hilaire 162
Toul 162
Toulon 162
Tours 162
Tresses 162
Trier 162
Vavincourt 162
Vinets-sur-Aube 162
Weissenthurm 162
United States Air Force Museum 168
United States Air Services Units
    USMC Day Wing, Northern
        Bombing Group 138–9, 162
    2nd Observation Sqn 166
    3rd Pursuit Sqn 166
    4th – 9th Aero Sqns 166
    4th Observation Sqn 166
    6th Pursuit Sqn 166
    8th Aero/Observation Sqn 161–2
    9th Aero/Observation Sqn 161–2
    11th Aero/Bombardment Sqn
        161–2, 166
    12th–13th Aero Sqns 166
    15th–18th Aero Sqns 166

19th Pursuit Sqn 166
20th Aero/Bombardment Sqn
    161–2, 166
22nd Aero/Observation Sqn 160,
    162, 166
23rd Aer Sqn 166
24th Aero/Observation Sqn
    161–2, 166
28th Aero/Bombardment Sqn
    166
37th Aero Sqn 162
41st–44th Aero Sqns 166
49th Aero Sqn 166
50th Aero/Observation Sqn
    161–2, 166
54th–55th Aero Sqns 166
72nd Aero Sqn 166
74th Aero Sqn 166
77th Aero Sqn 166
85th Aero Sqn 161
88th Aero Sqn 166
90th Aero Sqn 166
91st Aero/Observation Sqn 162,
    166
94th–95th Aero Sqns 166
96th Aero/Bombardment Sqn
    162, 166
100th Aero/Bombardment Sqn
    161–2
104th Aero/Observation Sqn
    161–2, 166
106th Aero Sqn 166
114th–115th Aero Sqns 166
118th Aero Sqn 166
135th Aero/Observation Sqn
    160, 162, 166
147th Aero Sqn 166
154th Aero Sqn 166
163rd Aero Sqn 161
166th Aero/Bombardment Sqn
    117, 161–2, 166
168th Aero/Observation Sqn
    161–2
278th Aero Sqn 161
354th Aero Sqn 161
800th Aero/Bombardment Sqn 162
United States Postal Service 168
Valenciennes 108–9
Valentine, 2Lt J 120

Valentine, James 8
Varssenaere 58
Vernon, 2Lt RP 137
Verrier, Pierre 10
Vick, Lt CA 117
Vickers 7, 11Vidler, Gunlayer AW 70
Villacoublay 51
Vincent, JG 133
Vliegaftdeeling 28
Voss, Ltn W 44–5
Vulcan Motor & Engineering Co 51,
    133
Waddon 128
Wagner, 2Lt EGS 44
Walker, Charles 13–14
Walker, Capt FW 95
Walker, 2Lt W 117
Wallace, 2Lt RH 43
Wallingen 65
Walsh, Lt O
Walter, Lt SRP 7
Walter, Lt W 115
Walters, Cpl A 55
Ward, 2Lt LN 80
Wardlaw, 2Lt NN 137
Waring & Gillow 51
Watkins, 2Lt LP 46
Waziristan 157
Weare, Sgt MJC 55
Weir, C & J Ltd 102
Wells, 2Lt GA 78
Wells, Lt HP 120
West, Lt HD 114
West, Sgt J 137
West, Lt TJ 31
Westland Aircraft Works 51, 57, 102,
    104, 132–3
Whistler, Flt Lt HA 153
White, 2Lt JG 78
White, 2Lt MA 46
Whitehead Aircraft Co 133
Whitehead, 2Lt RM 79
Whitmore, Lt 5
Whyte, Lt CB 107
Wiggins, 2Lt TH 117
Wildig, 2Lt NH 118
Wildman-Lushington, Captain 17
Wilkinson, Lt/Capt AM 37, 39–41
Wilkinson, Lt JB 137

Williams, Sgt HJ 111
Williams, 2Lt LB 80
Williams, Capt RM 78
Willis, FSL H 59
Wills, AM 67
Wilson, Lt D 9
Wilson, Sgt HH 118–9
Wilson, Capt RE 42
Windover, Capt WE 137
Windridge, Sgt AL 119
Wingates Moor 112
Wings
    1 Wing RNAS 109
    2 Wing RNAS 70
    3 Wing RNAS 118
    4 Wing RNAS 109
    5 Wing RNAS 105, 109
    6 Wing RNAS 70
    9 Wing 139
    10 Wing 139
    16 Wing 122
    22 Wing 139
    31 Wing 71
    33 Wing 105
    41 Wing 62–4, 114
    61 Wing 109
    62 Wing 71, 122
    63 Wing 122
    64 Wing 109
    65 Wing 105, 109
    66 Wing 71
    67 Wing 71
Winnicott, Lt R 79
Wise, Lt FHV 104
Wolseley Tool and Motor Car
    Company 10
Wood, Lt/Capt HA 41, 44
Woodman, 2Lt KCB 118
Woollett, 2Lt HW 77
Woolley, 2Lt FW 119
Wormwood Scrubbs 8
Wyton 17
Yates, Lt 41
Yeovil 51, 132, 134, 144
Ypres 58, 79
Young, 2Lt WAG 45
Zeebrugge 57, 70, 110
Zeppelin , 46
Zweibrucken 63–4